IN TODAY'S DRUG WORLD, THERE IS ONLY
ONE JOB MORE DEADLY THAN DEALING—
MICHAEL LEVINE'S.

UNDERCOVER

"If Michael Levine didn't exist, some novelist would have
invented him. A fast, engaging read with action and tension
. . . an exciting book."

—*Booklist*

"An exciting account of one agent's obsessive war against
drug traffickers."

—*The New York Times Book Review*

"A detailed story of Levine's chilling work . . . it is
enough to give anybody the shivers. . . . The American
public and political structure can learn from Levine's story a
lot that it doesn't know—but surely ought to."

—*Associated Press*

"Exciting . . . this isn't a book for the queasy, as Goddard
vividly brings the dangerous job of drug agent to life."

—*Kirkus Reviews*

Also by the author

Blimey! *Another Book About London*
Joey
The Last Days of Dietrich Bonhoeffer
Easy Money
All Fall Down

UNDERCOVER
The Secret Lives of
a Federal Agent

DONALD GODDARD

A DELL BOOK

For Natalie

Published by
Dell Publishing
a division of
Bantam Doubleday Dell
Publishing Group, Inc.
666 Fifth Avenue
New York, New York 10103

For information address: Times Books, New York, New York.

The trademark Dell® is registered in the U.S. Patent and Trademark
Office.

ISBN: 0-440-20516-6

Reprinted by arrangement with Times Books, a division of Random
House, Inc.

Printed in the United States of America

Published simultaneously in Canada

January 1990

10 9 8 7 6 5 4 3 2 1
OPM

INTRODUCTION

At least 25 million Americans are afraid they may miss something in life unless they smoke, snort, swallow, inhale, shoot up or otherwise ingest one or more of the Controlled Substances listed under the Comprehensive Drug Abuse Prevention and Control Act of 1970.

Some can't help it. They are locked into their habits beyond redemption, and probably know it. The rest will say they can stop if they want to, and perhaps they can. But far too many have actually managed to persuade themselves that taking drugs is *part* of the good life, and willingly pay their shares of the $100-odd billion that Americans now spend every year on marijuana, hash, hallucinogens, pills, cocaine, heroin and a vast assortment of chemical junk. If they *have* a complaint, it's the usual consumerist beef about quality, availability and price.

The irony is that among these mostly affluent, mostly respectable citizens are those who bellyache loudest about the collapse of traditional values, about crime on the streets, corruption in high places, and the general decline of ethical standards. While patronizing the mightiest criminal enterprise in history, they refuse to see any connection between self-indulgence and social catastrophe—and not for the first time, of course. Self-denial has rarely ranked high among American virtues.

Until it does, with respect to drug abuse at least, the safety of the republic may come to depend more and more on a comparative handful of remarkable policemen using methods not commonly associated with federal law enforcement. As their job is to penetrate this subculture of "victimless" crime and gather evidence to unravel its tangles of mutually protective traffickers and users, they have necessarily had to learn how to pass themselves off as one or the other—and face-to-face with the most deadly audience ever to judge a public performance.

Today the basic tools of narcotics law enforcement are not just a badge and a gun, but lies and deception refined to the level of art.

This, then, is the true story of the man who wrote the book on working undercover, the Orson Welles of America's criminal theater.

New York
July 1988

AUTHOR'S NOTE

As a serving federal officer, Michael Levine is bound by oath, personal conviction and contract of employment not to divulge the contents of case files to unauthorized persons or pass on any confidential information acquired in the course of his duties that might endanger his fellow officers, jeopardize informants, compromise an investigation, infringe upon the rights of private citizens or in any way hamper the process of law enforcement.

Like the other serving officers who contributed massively to this book, Levine has drawn solely upon his diaries and personal papers to supplement his recollections, and, as in any work based essentially on interviews, he is responsible only for those passages which are directly quoted or directly attributed to him.

The responsibility for the rest, including whatever observations, opinions, comments or conclusions are expressed about the people, institutions and events described in the book, is entirely mine.

To make quite certain that the damage done is confined to the enemy, I have where necessary altered names and circumstantial details, to avoid the junk lawsuits that are threatening to emasculate the publishing business and to protect those who might otherwise find themselves exposed in the firing line. Apart from these trifling changes, Levine's story is as it happened, and I salute the wisdom of those in the Drug Enforcement Administration who advanced their cause, and ours, by permitting him to tell it.

—D.G.

ONE

"Oh boy, oh boy, am I in fucking trouble."

Things can go very quiet in St. Albans, Queens, at six o'clock in the morning. When José with the Cigarettes killed the motor of his old baby-blue Mustang, he could feel the silence of people watching.

Double-parked alongside one of the stripped-out wrecks that littered 107th Avenue, he had deliberately left himself half a block to walk to Archie Dent's place. Far enough to fine-tune his nerves and take in the scene before committing himself. In the dead light before sunrise, Dent's shabby old frame house looked as blank as a fortress.

He didn't linger. There was no one on the street, but they knew he was there. Preening himself in the mirror, he pulled the black beret down square on his head, smoothed his Fu Manchu mustache with a wet forefinger, adjusted the big black shades and stepped out on the garbage-strewn sidewalk, whistling softly between his teeth. With another precautionary glance up and down the block, he leaned into the back of the car, slipped his arms through the handles of the shopping bags stuffed with Kools and Marlboros and dragged them out, backheeling the door shut. Then, hands thrust into the pockets of his bulky white windbreaker and the bags jouncing on his forearms, he swaggered jauntily up to the door of the toughest after-hours joint in Queens, breaking into a little mambo step every now and then, as though oblivious to everything but the music in his head.

It *was* a fortress. The windows were barred and shuttered with steel. The front door was solid steel, anchored in steel and concrete. Fitted with dead-bolt locks, both electric and manual, it had a little spy window of bulletproof, one-way glass.

Still jiggling his feet and humming to himself, José with the Cigarettes flexed the fingers of his right hand and wrapped them tenderly around the butt of the .357 Magnum in his pocket. He then extended his left forefinger and, with a flourish, pressed the buzzer marked A. Dent.

Dent was a major crime figure in Queens, a big black entrepreneur into everything from gambling and policy to prostitution and drugs, and this was his home office. As an after-hours joint, it was famous for high-rolling card games, where $20,000 on the table was no more remarkable than a barmaid's tip, but where the only players to pull up a chair were known figures from the black underworld and the occasional black celebrity slumming for kicks. Two black guys brought down specially from Rhode Island to crack the place had hung around the neighborhood for weeks, spending thousands of dollars trying to get inside, and had never once made it past the door.

Hands still deep in his pockets, José with the Cigarettes trucked around the porch in his beige polyester flares and bright blue shirt with collar points down to the navel. Coco the Clown, just back from the bodega. To a black guy, only a Puerto Rican would dress like that.

After a long moment a voice from the other side of the door said, "Whatchoo wan'?"

"I got cigarettes, meng," replied José. "Ju wanna buy cigarettes?"

"Wha'?"

"Fockin' cigarettes," he said indignantly, a busy man with no time to waste on idle chitchat. "Modder-fockin' cigarettes." He held up the bags so the guy could see them. "Okay? Ju wanna buy?"

"You sellin' cigarettes?"

"Orright." José staggered back a little, shaking his head in admiration. "Ju gottit, meng."

"Well, how much you sellin' 'em fo'?"

"Fock. Gimme a dollar a carton and ju gotta deal, bro'."

Silence.

"Sheet, meng."

He turned away in disgust, but then, clanking and buzzing, the door opened, and José with the Cigarettes was *in*.

He sold most of the cartons to his new friend Champ, aka Cleveland Zanders, just out of Attica after seven years hard time for armed robbery. As José had known he would, Champ allowed him to stay until the house had won back its cigarette money at the bar and crap table.

A week later José with the Cigarettes showed up with another hundred cartons and the glimmer of an idea. As he cha-cha'ed up the steps, four men closed in around him on the porch, and his inner alarm screamed like a punctured nerve. Easing unhurriedly between them, he got his left thumb on the buzzer and kept it there until one of them turned him around.

"Whatchoo got?" They pulled gently at his shopping bags. "Whatchoo got in there, man?"

José smiled winningly, backed up against the door so that no one could get behind him. "I got cigarettes, meng. Cigarettes for Champ. Ju wan' some?"

Through the jacket and the shopping bags, the Magnum was pointing straight at the first guy's breastbone. The last thing he wanted was trouble, for that would blow the whole scam, but he was now focused exclusively on getting off all six rounds in about a second, give or take a blink. There was no other thought in his head. At the first suspicion of a move against him, they were gone. All four.

"Thassall you got? You sure?"

"I tellin' ju, meng. Jus' cigarettes. *Conjo!* Where *ees* da fockin' guy? What's he doin'?"

They looked at one another, making up their minds, and dead on cue, Champ called out from inside the house. "Who dat?"

"Ees José," he replied, not taking his eyes off them. "José weetha cigarettes."

"Who?"

"José," he said patiently, inviting their sympathy. "I got cigarettes."

"Oh, yeah. The mutha-fucka with the cigarettes, yeah. Wait a minute."

The door opened. José backed inside. And only then did he start to sweat.

This time he sold the cigarettes to Charlie Fats, a wobbly mountain of a man who twinkled with diamonds and, once squashed into his seat at the poker table, was effectively immobilized for the night.

"Got any more, José?" he asked, dealing a pair of fifties onto the table from a wad the size of a toilet roll, and all at once the original glimmer of an idea blossomed like a magnesium flare.

"Oh, meng," breathed José. "I got as much as ju wan'."

"Well, like how many you got?"

"How many?" Now Archie Dent was listening, which was what José wanted. "I got like ten tousan' cartons, okay? Ju take the whole theeng, I gonna make a price ju no gonna believe."

"Yeah?" Fats admired the diamonds on his left hand. The rings were so deeply embedded in his pudgy fingers that the stones seemed set in the flesh. "Try me."

"Fock, you ready?" José admired them, too. "Seventy-five cents a carton."

"Fifty."

"*Wha'?* Ju keelin' me, meng."

Fats replaced the cigar in his mouth.

"Okay." José sighed. "Pay me Sat'day. I gonto have my partner breeng the trock."

After that he was again allowed to stay until his money ran out. He bought a few drinks for himself and the barmaid, a spoon of cocaine from Ronnie Guy, the resident doper, verified the mental notes he had made on his first visit about the layout of the place, right down to the positions of the furniture, blew his last few bucks at the crap table, and on his way out stopped at Charlie Fats's elbow. Archie Dent, a muscular man with a cropped head and a powerfully unsympathetic disposition, was also watching the game.

"You always got cigarettes?" he asked.

"Eef I don' got, I get," said José. "Why? Ju wan' some?"

"You jus' fill yo' truck, man. Any Fats don' take, Ah will."

"Ju sure ju coul' handle it?"

"Ah can handle whatever the mutha-fuck you got," said Dent, annoyed.

"Yeah?" He laughed and slapped Dent's palm. "Then Sat-day, ju gonna gettit, meng."

The truck was José's Trojan horse. There was no way a raiding party of white faces could get within three blocks of Dent's place without tipping its hand—and no way of breaking in either, short of a Sherman tank. But all he had to do now was hide his men in a truck, drive up to the door, and Champ would let them in.

By the time the team had straggled in on Saturday morning, however, the earliest it could stage the hit was around 10:00 A.M. This was already several hours too late in José's opinion. Broad daylight and a street full of onlookers were less than ideal conditions for a frontal assault, and by then there was a danger that some, if not most, of the people he wanted would have gone home anyway.

Nor was he happy about the choice of driver for the truck. Sammy York was the only black guy they had, but he was also a sick man. Already nursing a suspected heart condition, he had fallen down with an attack of convulsions barely a week before, but it was too late to argue. As the job involved no more than finding the right house and then holding the door open so the guys could charge in, José allowed himself to be persuaded. They had wasted enough time already. At about 9:45 A.M. he trucked up the steps of Dent's place and was let in by the houseman.

Champ, he was told, had already left, which meant that one had gotten away before they had even started. And by the time he had eased his way through to the bar, he was pretty sure he had missed Charlie Haynes as well. That was a particular disappointment because Haynes had been the leader of the four men who had accosted him on the porch at the time of his second visit. He was now known to be wanted for bank robbery.

But Archie Dent was there, watching Charlie Fats in the middle of a game with more money in front of him than José had ever seen on a poker table before. And probably more than anybody else had seen either, for at least twenty people were clustered around the players. Another fifteen or so were crowded into what little space remained in the smoke-layered room, sitting on couches or standing at the bar, talking and drinking.

At the end of the hand José checked in with Fats, and when Dent heard that the truck was due anytime now, he told the houseman to let him know when somebody came asking for José with the Cigarettes. Declining the offer of a tube of coke from Ronnie Guy, José ordered a VO and water instead, and after paying his dollar, drifted into the position he had picked out for himself at the end of the semicircular bar.

From here, with his back to the wall, he had almost everybody in front of him, with just the barmaid to his left, and beyond her, two hookers with their johns on a couch. The group around the game was just to the right, growing bigger all the time as people drifted over to catch the action. They now blocked his view of the entrance to the room, but fortunately there was a window in the wall opposite, looking through to the hallway, so that he could still keep an eye on whoever came and went.

With two minutes to go, Guy sold the tube of cocaine to a customer who immediately left the premises. That was annoying, but it resolved any doubts about where to stand, for José watched him go by the window, making for the door. With a minute to go, he got off his stool and, leaning back against the wall, put his hand in the pocket of his baggy white windbreaker to ease the Magnum from catching in the cloth.

At two minutes after ten he checked his watch again, and in the same instant heard the faint rasp of the buzzer through the hubbub. An unexpected lift of adrenaline forced him to take a steadying breath as the houseman passed the window. Levering himself off the wall with his elbows, he distributed his weight in readiness, and strained to catch the rattle of locks and bolts. Instead, after a few seconds' delay, the houseman shuffled back down the hall, pushed through the crowd around the card table, and bent to whisper in Charlie Fats's ear.

Fats glanced up at Archie Dent, and then both looked around the room until they caught sight of José. With a nod, Dent sent the houseman back to the door, and José swallowed. It was eerie. Out of all the people in the place, he alone knew what was going to happen next. Head cocked to pick up the faintest sound from the hallway, he heard the door open, waited for the shouts and the pounding of feet before drawing his gun . . . *and heard the door close again.*

Sammy York had locked out the U.S. Cavalry!

Hollow with disbelief, José saw him pass by the window, following the houseman like a zombie. *What the fuck is he doing?* Taken by another surge of adrenaline, both terrible and elating, he watched, motionless, as the two shuffled to a stop under Dent's suddenly watchful eye.

York was putty-colored. Sweat ran down his face like soapy water. Trembling and speechless, he just stood there, shoulders slumped, meekly resigned to execution.

Dent looked him over, looked at Fats and then at José. Then he looked again at York and backed off a step. The room was going quiet, and José couldn't wait for a miracle.

"Federal agents," he yelled, gun extended at the full reach of both arms. "Nobody fucking move. Sammy, go open the fucking door."

Some hands had gone up, but now wavered.

"Hands, hands," screamed José, spittle flying. "Get 'em up or I'll fucking kill you."

He bounced forward, jerky as a marionette, and bounced back again, so keyed up that anyone who caught his eye instantly found himself looking down the barrel of his massive gun.

"The door, Sammy. GET THE FUCKING DOOR!"

Oh boy, oh boy, am I in fucking trouble, he kept silently crooning to himself. *What am I gonna do now?*

If they forced him to shoot, he was dead. So was York. Too many people. Too many guns. While the guys outside were trying to figure out how to break down the door, Dent and his people would have time enough to cut up their bodies and flush them down the toilet.

"I'll kill you. I'll fucking kill you," he screeched, deciding his only chance now lay in high-voltage hysteria. Wild-eyed, he danced a vicious, flat-footed war dance up and down the length of the bar, twitching galvanically, spewing out threats and abuse. Given the sheer speed of his reaction to the slightest lowering of hands, no one seemed eager to go first, but he couldn't even *see* everybody. The odds were so bad, it could only be a matter of seconds at most.

"Sammy, the *door*. The fucking *door* . . ."

To his unspeakable relief, he saw York turn and stumble slowly back the way he had come.

More hands started to edge down—without certainty or confidence, but he couldn't hold them any longer. Concentrating on Archie Dent, he only just caught sight of Ronnie Guy reaching for his pocket, and came within a flicker of squeezing off the first shot.

"Mother-fucker," he screamed. "You're *dead.*"

A metal spoon and a tube of powder tinkled at Guy's feet as he clawed at the air.

It was all slipping away. He tracked around deliberately to shoot Dent first, but then he heard the front door smash back against the wall, and the place rocked under the stomp and weight of armed men.

José lowered his gun with a windy sigh. Turning to Guy, he picked up the spoon and tube of white powder, and patted Guy's cheek with a gentle smile. Then he returned to his stool at the bar to finish the VO and water. And to sit down before his knees buckled.

"Any questions on that?" Michael Levine looked out across the rows of faces dutifully fixed on his. "Anybody?"

It was more like a congregation than an audience. Some of his best friends were FBI agents, but when gathered together in Quantico, at the shrine of their academy, they were unmistakably civil servants first and cops second. He also had the feeling they were not entirely comfortable with the idea of being lectured on the art of undercover by a narcotics agent.

"See, you gotta remember these guys are smart but not *that* smart, or we'd never catch 'em. The thing about undercover, especially in narcotics work, is that the moment they see you, before you even open your mouth, they're thinking, he could be the Man. That's *all* they think about when they meet somebody they don't know. Undercover agent. Cop. That's why the two black agents they brought down from Rhode Island crapped out. They looked right. They sounded right. They did the right things, but they could have been cops. So you got to push the right psychological buttons to get around that fear and suspicion and make 'em do what *you* want. And every case is different—that's the beauty of working undercover. José with the Cigarettes was born to press their greed button. 'Mutha-fuckin' cigarettes at fifty cents a carton? No way *he* can be the Man. No way, José.'"

Silence.

"Ah, what gave you the idea?" asked the studious little guy below him in the front row.

"For José? Well, first, I spoke real good street Spanish. I grew up with guys like José in the Bronx, in a neighborhood where you really didn't want to say your name was Michael Levine. So I used to lie. I'd say I was half Puerto Rican. And I lied so much that I started to believe it, because I loved the way they lived. I loved their music and the rhythms of their speech. I looked like one of them. I sounded like one of them. And at any given moment I could *become* one of them and find I *was* José." He smiled suddenly. "And that's really funny, because my father came from Russia and my mother from Poland."

Watching the little guy's expression change, it occurred to Levine that they were probably the only Jews in the room.

"Anyway, after the guys from Rhode Island flunked out, Dennis Dillon was ready to try anything. He's District Attorney in Nassau County now, but in those days he was an Assistant U.S. Attorney in the Eastern District of New York, and he wanted Dent badly. So he says to the case agent, 'Ask that crazy bastard Levine if he wants to give it a shot.' Now who could resist an invitation like that? Boom! José comes to life. And off he goes to the A&P to buy a hundred cartons of Kools and Marlboros. *'No mutha-fuckin' way José could be the Man, right? The dude don' even speak English. An' who ain't gonna buy cigarettes fo' fifty cents a carton?'* "

Most of them laughed, but there were still a few holdouts near the back.

"Sometimes I'm not even aware myself how real José can be," he went on, looking at them directly as they put their heads together in another muttered aside. "We picked up Champ later, and while I was fingerprinting him he says to me, 'It's a mutha-fuckin' shame, José, they gotta have a brother doin' a brother.'

And do you know, for a moment I actually felt guilty? He now knew my real name and who I was, but to him I was still José and Puerto Rican. The act was that complete." He grinned, seeking to disarm. "Not bad for a Jewish kid from the Bronx, right?"

That was usually good for a laugh—the incongruity of the Woody Allen image when applied to a six-feet-two, 220-pound street fighter who looked like Errol Flynn.

"Anybody else?"

"Well, yeah. Was it worth it?" asked the agent in the middle of the holdout group. "Now Ah'm not questioning your judgment, Mr. Levine"—he pronounced the name as though grapes grew on it—"but was it worth all that just to knock off an after-hours joint?"

"Dennis Dillon thought so," Levine said peaceably. "Dent's place was like the stock exchange for crime in that section of Queens, so we closed it down. But see, a good undercover doesn't ask himself questions like that. It'll drive him crazy. I've put all kinds of people in jail—thousands of 'em, from street-corner scumbags to government officials—and I still can't tell you that it's *worth* it. As a professional, you make the case and move on to the next one. Ask the people who pay us if it's *worth* it."

"Yeah, but you mind telling us how many warrants you executed that day?"

"Three, I think. That's all we needed."

"Not much of a body count, then."

"Well . . . Archie Dent and Champ were charged with felony liquor law violations. We got Ronnie Guy for drug sales and possession. And when I arrested Charlie Haynes at the airport, we found 120 decks of heroin in his bags and $1,500 in stolen bills. Turned out the crazy bastard robbed the same bank twice in one week." Levine chuckled at the memory.

"But see, you're missing the point. The reason I told you that story is, first, because it shows you the kind of imagination you got to use to get in undercover, and second, how easy the thing can fall apart on you after that. And not just because somebody fouls up, like Sammy York. Haynes told me afterwards he came within a hair of killing me that morning in front of Dent's place. So don't ever forget that. Every moment you spend undercover, you're just a hair from dead. The only reason I'm alive today is dumb luck, bad marksmanship and something I can tell you about but can't *teach* you."

"Yeah, but Mr. Le-vine," said another agent at the back, sitting next to the first. "Like you say, these guys are smart but not *that* smart. Seems to me that undercover's only going to get real dangerous when you work major cases against major violators. When you go up against some guy maybe smarter than you are."

Levine eyed him tolerantly. "Well, if I ever did that," he said, "neither of us knew it."

What he couldn't say, not in front of an audience as unimpressed by self-advertisement as a roomful of federal agents, was that he had an edge. Experience. After twenty-two years he was still here. He had worked the streets. He had worked overseas—in Europe, the Middle East, the Far East, the Caribbean and South America. He had served as country attaché for the Drug Enforcement Administration in Argentina. He had worked undercover and as a supervisor on the Vice President's Task Force in Florida. In the FBI/DEA Task Force. The New York Joint Task Force.

"You want to talk body counts?" In twenty-two years Levine had locked up around 3,000 violators, give or take a hundred or two—from South American cocaine barons and government officials to low-lifes on the corner of 93rd

and Amsterdam. "Anybody working narcotics,"
he said, "gets a shot at locking up as many
people as he wants to. That's the shame of
what's happened to our country. And let me
tell you, I've done a lot of undercover work
overseas, but what you guys face is a lot more
dangerous. You got a better chance of getting
blown away when you take off some freaked-out
Dominican in a Washington Heights crack house
than when locking up a Mexican general or a
Panamanian banker. The bigger the violator,
the less he *needs* a gun. He uses attorneys instead."

He paused invitingly, but there were no further contributions from the back.

"Okay. I can't teach you guys undercover. I
can't teach you how to be a José. Undercover is
the art of screwing people, and that's not a
game you can play by the numbers. All I can do
is tell you some rules to follow to stay alive,
save your jobs and *maybe* save your families."
He embraced them all with a movie-star smile.
"A lot of strange shit has happened to me in
twenty-two years, and it's an absolute fucking miracle I'm still alive. So maybe sometime, someplace, something you heard here today may keep you from dying. . . ."

TWO

"Is there someone up there controlling this shit?"

Nothing in Michael Levine's early years suggested a career in law enforcement. Quite the opposite.

He was born in Bronx Hospital, New York, on December 20, 1939, the first child of Henry and Caroline Levine. His father was a first-generation American whose Russian parents had settled originally on a few acres in Hurleyville, New York. When the farm failed the family moved to the Bronx, and it was there that Henry met Caroline Abramowitz, shortly after she arrived with her parents from Poland.

Growing up on the streets, Henry quit school at thirteen, much to the grief of his mother, who raised chickens in their house on Prospect Avenue and kept down the rats by drowning them in the toilet. At eighteen, after trying out unsuccessfully as a boxer, he married Caroline and went into the smoked fish and pickle business instead, opening a place on West 72nd Street called Oscar's Appetizing Store.

As Oscar prospered so the marriage went bankrupt. With money and success, Henry took up with gamblers and fast women. While supposedly out walking Michael in his baby carriage on Bathgate Avenue, Henry was picked up by the police for shooting craps on the corner, and people used to say that Mike was the youngest kid ever arrested in the 48th Precinct. Caroline was not amused. Soon after their second son, David, was born in 1943, Henry moved out, and a few years later Caroline sued for divorce.

She had taken the separation hard, so hard that her health broke down, and at the age of six Michael was packed off to boarding school upstate. His brother, now two, was shared between the grandmothers until Caroline eventually recovered and was reunited with her children in a small apartment on Honeywell Avenue.

After the divorce she married Ike Goldstein, formerly of the Detroit Tigers. He and Hank Greenberg were buddies, having come up together in the major leagues, but by the time he met Caroline Ike's arm had gone, and he was reduced to earning $60 a week as a men's clothing salesman, which just about paid the rent. Too easygoing to exert much authority over two growing boys, he soon gave up trying, which left Michael and David pretty much to their own devices, as their mother now had to go downtown every day to work in the garment center.

Michael, in any case, was still involved with his real father. Before his mother married again, he would go to Oscar's every week to collect her check from Henry and earn a little pocket money delivering groceries. As for David, he turned naturally to his older brother as champion and protector, embroiling Michael in even more street fights than he attracted on his own account.

The neighborhood had always been mixed—Irish, Italian and Jewish in about equal proportions—but by the time Michael was twelve, Puerto Ricans and blacks were moving in and the gringos were moving out. Within a year, his best friends were Jesús and Alberto, and his grades at P.S. 98, when he bothered to go there, were sinking fast. In retrospect, it's a mystery to him that he managed to avoid a police record or a drug habit that would have precluded a career in law enforcement.

"Some of my friends were thieves. Some were already into drugs. But my thing was street fighting. I remember when I was thirteen I found Alberto in an alley sniffing Carbona cleaning fluid. Now, if you're a kid you'll do anything to belong, so naturally I had to sniff the shit, too.

"Well, if that had been heroin I'd probably be dead by now, because I know I would have done it, even if Nancy Reagan had been there screaming, 'Just say no,' in my ear. But I was lucky. The Carbona made me sick for three days, and after that I wasn't even curious about drugs anymore. They were still something new then, anyway—not flooding into the country the way they are now. It's a miracle *any* kid stays off dope today, and God bless those who are strong enough to do it. They're the real heroes. . . ."

The fifties in New York spawned dozens of violent street gangs in all five boroughs, most of them recruited on racial lines to defend old neighborhoods or conquer new ones, but also because kids like Michael and David Levine needed to *belong.* As divorce became as commonplace as marriage and mothers either *had* to work or chose to, the collapse of traditional family life sent a generation of inner-city kids onto the streets to find families of a more reliable sort, some of them as rigidly disciplined as the Marine Corps.

The gangs that Levine ran with were more racially mixed than most—a few Jews mixed in with blacks and Puerto Ricans—and that suited him. "I looked like I had Spanish blood, and to me there was something inviting about Latin people. I liked the way they stuck together. No matter what anybody said about them, there was strength in their unity. I loved that and didn't have it with Jews." At thirteen he fell for Lydia Díaz, who lived up the block on the corner of Honeywell and 178th Street, and his Spanish improved dramatically.

By now, he was within an inch or two of his adult height and fast building a reputation as a warrior—not entirely from choice, because he was secretly terrified, but because the respect of his peers seemed to depend on it. Another reason was his brother David, who constantly needed his protection. Nearly every day kids would come running to find him—"Hey, Mike, they're beating up your brother"—then tag along, jumping with excitement, like pilot fish around a shark, as "Crazy Mike" went to the rescue. Crazy Mike would fight anybody.

He became so good at it that Henry Levine arranged for Lou Burstin, the fight manager, to take Michael downtown to try out at Cus D'Amato's Gym, near Gramercy Square. Impressed by the potential of this big Jewish kid with the fast feet and hands, they started training him in earnest, until his mother found out and put a stop to it.

That was the last Michael saw of his father for a while. Soon after, Henry fled to Florida to escape his second ex-wife, but she tracked him down and put him in jail for falling behind with his alimony payments. Years later, having survived the humiliation to marry three more times and become "The Pickle King of South

Florida," he explained to the local newspaper reviewing his career that he had settled in Miami on account of "family problems."

On moving up to Theodore Roosevelt High School in 1954, Crazy Mike became a charter member of the Lucky Lords, an elite fighting gang with an ideology: We don't give a fuck. At this point what probably saved him from going irreparably bad was first, his aversion to drugs, a lasting result of his experiment with cleaning fluid; and second, his natural athleticism. The former kept him out of the trouble his friends drifted into to support their habits, while the latter secured him the recognition he craved, not only from his peers as a fighter, but also from the adult world, as a swimmer. With no formal coaching, he made the high school swimming team in his first year, and rapidly proved himself to be among the best half-dozen swimmers of his age in the city. On the strength of this promise, he was allowed to cut classes at noon most days in order to train. But more often than not he went home and got smashed on Thunderbird wine.

The fighting was now a nightmare. He didn't know how to stop.

"I had a violent temper, but it came from being afraid. My whole childhood, when I look back on it, was always being afraid. Afraid of the gangs. Afraid of drugs. Afraid of losing. I was always living on borrowed time. I'd win a fight and right away start worrying about the next. Because the next one would be *it*. I was sure to lose next time. And the idea was so terrifying I'd fight like a wild animal. Hands. Bottles. Chains. Clubs. It's a miracle I never killed somebody.

"My hands soon got broken, but I didn't care. My reputation was getting around. 'Don't fuck with that kid.' My father grew up on the street with a lot of black guys, and he used to tell me, the one thing they always respect is, no matter what, you *fight*. 'If they're gonna get their dinner,' he'd say, 'you make sure you get your breakfast.' And I remembered that. If you hit me you were gonna have to kill me. But I was terrified the whole time. Terrified of losing my reputation because that was my protection. If I lost that I'd lose everything."

And yet, when his mother finally got enough money together to move the family out of the Bronx in December 1956, Crazy Mike actually *missed* it. Bayside, Queens, was still a respectable, middle-class white suburb, and on top of his other insecurities, he now felt like a kid who had grown up with the Indians, only to be reclaimed suddenly by civilization. Enrolled in Martin Van Buren High

School for the last half of his senior year, he hardly knew how to cope, although his marks were never worse than average. His response was to act crazier than ever.

"The Bronx was like being in jail. Somebody looks at you, Wahboom! You fight. 'Who the fuck you lookin' at?' Now I'm in Queens with all these nicely brought up white kids, and I'm beating the shit out of anybody that looks at me. I'm also drinking a lot, and getting into sex like I just invented it. But I can't make anybody care. I'm a dangerous, unhappy, fucked-up kid with no idea what I want to do. All I know is the streets of the Bronx, but here I am in *Queens*. I felt like a guy from another planet. I had this desperate, physical ache for somewhere to belong—so bad I didn't even see the hell my brother David was going through. Following in my footsteps, he also managed to find the worst elements in the neighborhood to run with."

After two miserable months Crazy Mike ran away. He returned to the Bronx to be with his friends, but the ranks had already closed behind him. It was also winter, and after two weeks of sleeping in cars he went home again—to find his mother half frantic with worry. Partly for her sake, but mostly because he could see no alternative, he then applied himself to his studies for the next several months, and after graduating from high school that summer, presented himself, in September 1957, to Sears Roebuck in Jamaica, Queens, which was sufficiently impressed by his demeanor and diploma to put him to work as an inventory clerk.

The pay was $40 a week, scarcely enough, as he soon discovered, to keep up the payments on the 1955 black Chevy convertible he bought for $1,400 on his eighteenth birthday. Once, to help make ends meet, he came to an arrangement with his friend Betty, an amiable black hooker who lived, and worked, at 111th Street and Lenox Avenue, in Harlem.

"I figured I ought to do my bit for the sex education of my brother and his friends before some fag got hold of 'em, so I made a deal with her. I said I'd bring over a carload of white kids, and she said, 'Sure, honey. I'll take care of 'em.' So now I go find David and some of his buddies, and I say to 'em, 'Listen. You kids wanna get laid?' 'Fuck, yeah.' 'Okay. If you guys can come up with seven bucks each, I'll get you laid.'

"So now off I go with six of 'em in the Chevy. We drive over to 111th and Lenox, and all these black pimps are out there, staring at us. I get out of the car, lock the kids in and tell 'em, 'Don't open this door for nobody.' Then I go upstairs and fix it with Betty. She'll take 'em all for eighteen dollars, which means about half a car payment left for me. So back I run downstairs again and quickly herd these six kids across 111th Street into the building. And let me tell you, anybody watching has got to remember it to this day.

"But now I gotta take 'em home again, and it's like three o'clock in the morning. As I'm driving down 73rd Avenue in Bayside, I see this crowd of parents around my house. Holy shit! I dropped the kids off a block away, hung a U-turn and didn't go home for four days."

It was a losing battle, against aimlessness, booze and repossession of the car. But then, one wet night in the spring of 1958, he went to the movies with one of his string of girlfriends and came out determined to be a pilot. If the film had been anything to go by, it looked like the job of his dreams: just flying around the world, getting laid. Next morning he rode downtown in the Chevy and enlisted in the Air Force. He told them he wanted to be a pilot, and they said, sure, why not? In those days recruiting offices were on a quota and would tell prospective recruits whatever they wanted to hear.

"So now I'm gonna be a pilot, and I'm out partying every night. All of a sudden I'm in a great fucking mood, like a guy who's made up his mind to commit suicide. To celebrate my last night as a civilian, I go out drinking with the guys and naturally get involved in a tremendous brawl up by a Carvel ice-cream stand. There I am, on top of some guy, punching the shit out of him, and the next thing I know, his friend kicks me in the face. For the first two weeks of my service career, I can't even chew my food. My jaw *still* clicks.

"Next morning, what with my banged-up face and the booze, I overslept, and they had to call up from Whitehall Street to get me out of bed. I'm a deserter already. I was supposed to check in at seven A.M., but by the time my mother and stepfather drive me over it's closer to eleven, and right away, everybody starts screaming at me, like they don't even *know* I'm going to be a pilot. So far, this is *not* like the movie.

"Then we get on a bus, me and five or six black guys and a couple of white kids who already *know* they made a mistake, and we drive out to what was then Idlewild Airport. And there, sitting in the middle of the field like ten tons of lead is this Eastern Airlines, four-engined propeller plane. I'd never seen one up close before, and the whole concept of how a plane flies suddenly became very important to me. Looking at that big heavy machine, I found out I didn't really believe in the scientific principles of flight and was suddenly stone-cold sober for the first time in a week."

Levine never did become a pilot. Nor did he become a radio operator, which seemed the likeliest assignment after his aptitude tests. His enlistment, in May 1958, coincided with the first Lebanese crisis, and the Air Force took everybody in basic training at its Lackland base in San Antonio, Texas, and put them into Air Police School.

"Wha'? I'm gonna be a radio operator."

"Fuck yo' ass you gonna be a radio operator. You're in Air Police School, and that's *it.*"

For the first time in his eighteen years, Levine had come up against an unyielding obstacle, and the impact turned him around. It was not so much a matter of life imitating the clichés of romantic fiction by having the military make a man of him, as of life in the military presenting an unrepentant survivor with a much more interesting challenge than anything he had met so far on the streets. With his wits and his fists, he now knew he could handle life there. But from the moment the Air Force shaved his hair off and put him in uniform for four years, he realized he had a serious decision to make. He could either rebel and spend four years in and out of the stockade, which was dumb, or he could surrender up front and do as he was told, which was unthinkable, or he could figure out how to make the system work for *him.* But as a *cop?*

His only experience of cops had been with those in the Youth Gang Squad, usually four plainclothes officers in an unmarked car whose job it was to dispense advice and counsel and keep the peace among teenagers on the street. In practice, this meant cutting the troublemakers out from the herd, shoving them into an alley and beating the shit out of them. This had happened several times to Crazy Mike, and it was only later that he was grateful, in a qualified way, that the squad never took him in, as is now standard procedure, because a police record would almost certainly have disqualified him from federal law enforcement.

Apart from that, his opinion of cops was the prevailing view among his social set: they were just a bunch of fucking bums with a license to kick ass and generally interfere with free spirits like himself. He accordingly approached the ten-week training course

with some reserve, and within days was ready to go AWOL—
except that they had thought of that, too.

"They were fucking maniacs, those people. The Air Police
thought that because the rest of the Air Force had the reputation of
being a country club, they had to out-macho the fucking Marine
Corps. For ten weeks we were beat, slapped, punched, kicked and
cursed without letup. Say one word back and you went to jail.
'This is Air Police, boy—the only real military the Air Force has
got. We wear *boots.*'

"Nowadays, they couldn't get away with the shit they pulled in
1958. Race, religion, nothing meant shit. Recruits were scum. Until you proved yourself, you were sub-fucking-human, and they
didn't let you forget it for a minute.

"In my seventh week I couldn't take it anymore, but there was
one sharp sergeant who knew the signs. 'Le-vine,' he says, 'you
almos' theah. Ain't too many guys can take this shit. Jus' think
how fuckin' proud you gonna feel in three weeks.' Well, I don't
even remember the guy's name, but I love the sonofabitch. Every
time I think of the saying, 'What does not destroy me makes me
stronger,' I think of those days. It was like Providence was preparing me for what was to come."

The seeds of esprit de corps were sown. Ten weeks later they
flowered at his graduation parade. Proud of his boots and distinc-
tive hat with the pinch-pointed crown, Levine was now authenti-
cally tough, in better charge of his temper, and equipped not only
with the comforting, off-the-peg identity of a military policeman,
but the position and authority that went with it. Though essentially
unchanged, the streetwise survivor now had better tools to work
with.

His first post of duty was the Strategic Air Command base at
Plattsburgh, New York, near the Canadian border. After a depress-
ing start, looking after prisoners in the stockade and going out on
town patrol to find more, he was transferred to the Security Division and assigned to guarding the B47s. That was better, but almost at once he was sent on thirty days' temporary duty to the
SAC base in Greenland. Deeply unimpressed by the climate and
Eskimo nightlife, he returned thankfully to Plattsburgh, only to
learn that the Air Force was about to send a detachment of Air
Police up to Greenland for a whole year. In the nick of time he
volunteered to be a sentry dog handler, and shipped out to San
Antonio instead.

Having been terrified of strange dogs as a kid, he was surprised to find he not only loved the work, but had a real aptitude for training ad handling them. After celebrating his nineteenth birthday with Silver, a 110-pound German shepherd, the two traveled back by train to Plattsburgh in January 1959, to look after B47s together. It was 80 degrees when they left Texas, and 17 degrees below zero on the Canadian border.

The dog didn't mind, but his handler hated it, and the next uncomfortable lesson in survival now began. Together, they spent their nights deep in the woods patrolling the perimeter, working either from sundown to midnight, or midnight to sunup, although working is probably too strong a term to describe their winter routine. Literally to survive in the crippling cold, Levine would usually have to build an igloo and take shelter inside, with Silver to keep him warm. But as spring came on, and the nights warmed and shortened into summer, he learned to love the starlit wilderness, and Silver learned to read his mind. The dog would now respond to over a hundred commands, by hand or voice, and the two began to spend as much time putting on demonstrations at dog shows as guarding the nuclear deterrent.

For almost the first time in his life, Levine was content. Fully grown into his physical powers, he not only began to enjoy fighting but even managed to confine most of it to the ring. Weighing in at 220 pounds, he battled his way into the heavyweight slot on the Plattsburgh base boxing team.

Then, early in December 1959, Airman Michael Levine should have died. On account of a $3 hat.

Outwardly, Plattsburgh had remained calm during the flare-up of racial hostility that almost crippled the military in the late fifties. By 1959, it was one of the few bases in the country to which black GIs returning home from overseas with white wives could be posted without provoking an immediate and often bloody racial incident. But the hatred was there just the same, festering below the surface, and always threatening to inflate some trivial difference into a full-scale confrontation.

Having hung out with blacks and Latins for most of his life, Levine saw no reason to change his habits in the service. He liked their music and their talk, liked to drink and play cards with them, and inevitably got drawn into occasional barroom brawls when those he counted as friends were set upon by larger numbers of whites. More than once he had been denounced on this account by the redneck element in camp as being "a fucking nigger" himself, or at least for having "nigra blood." If anything, therefore, he was prejudiced in *favor* of the blacks on the base, which made it all the more ironic when he suddenly found himself a standard-bearer for the wrong side.

It began on Veterans Day with a black air policeman named Heywood asking around the barracks if anybody had a spare parade hat. Heywood had just been transferred up from Georgia, and Levine knew nothing about him, other than that he was married and lived off the base.

"Sure," he said affably. "I got one. Here, take it."

"Ah don' want nothin' fo' nothin'," Heywood replied. "I'll pay you fo' the fuckin' thing."

Levine sighed. Slimly built and of medium height, Heywood was nothing out of the ordinary. He was just another surly GI, and there were plenty of those around.

"Okay." He shrugged. "Three dollars." That would buy enough Thunderbird wine for a lost weekend.

Heywood snatched the hat. "You'll git it payday."

Levine had no great hopes of that. Given the size of the base, and the fact that he worked the hours of darkness and slept the rest, it was more than likely he would never see Heywood again, and who cared? Payday came and went, with varying degrees of luck for Levine at the poker tables, but with no sign of Heywood or the $3.

Poker was a traditional feature of Air Force life at Plattsburgh. Around payday, four or five rooms in the barracks would turn into smoke-filled pressure cookers stuffed with sweating players, some of whom would stay at the tables until destitute. After the paychecks were gone, it was not unusual to see car registrations, jewelry, and even ownership papers for house trailers and property in Florida changing hands. One sergeant was known to have redeemed his markers after the game by having his wife meet two guys at a motel in town, and they even made him pay for the room.

Joining a game one day, late in November, Levine lost his entire paycheck of $47 in less than an hour. He was about to make way for another player when Heywood looked into the room to see who was there.

Levine hesitated, but he *was* flat broke. "Hey, there, Heywood," he called, waving him over to the table. "Howya doin', man?"

The other glanced at him without interest and turned to go out again. Levine straightened up in his chair.

"How about it, man?" His tone hardened. "You got the three bucks you owe me?"

Heywood jolted back, as though slapped in the face. "Whatchoo say?" His eyes bulged, and he lunged into the room. "What the fuck you talkin' about? Whatchoo on my fuckin' case fo'?"

The way to the table cleared before him, and the room went quiet. Too experienced in such matters to be caught sitting down, Levine met him head-to-head, instinctively matching the other's attitude.

"The mother-fuckin' hat," he hissed. "You bought a hat from me for three mother-fuckin' dollars. Now I want the mother-fuckin' money."

They were actually leaning on each other, face-to-face, although Levine was at least four inches taller and sixty pounds heavier.

"Mother-fuck yo' hat," Heywood screamed, spraying Levine with spit. His face was contorted with fury, and the cords in his neck stood out like cables. "An' fuck yo' mother-fuckin' money. All you mother-fuckers alike. Get off my mother-fuckin' ass."

Levine was now in a quandary. Heywood was clearly out of his mind, as well as out of his league, but there was no simple way for Levine to back off. Onlookers already filled the doorway, and others were hurrying down the hall. If he tried to stop now, everybody would simply write him off as just another punk-assed Jew.

He tried intimidation, hoping that Heywood would back off. He leaned into him physically, so Heywood could feel the weight of muscle he was up against.

"You think you some kinda mother-fuckin' bad man?" he asked, soft with menace, but Heywood was too far gone to get the message. He pushed back hard, almost pressing his forehead against Levine's nose.

"You think *you* a mother-fuckin' bad man?" Heywood demanded in turn, again spraying his face.

Levine felt his temper slip. It wasn't his fault. He had tried. He could have punched Heywood's lights out right there, in front of everybody, but instead he had given him a chance.

"Listen, Heywood," he said, beginning quietly, although loud enough for those in the hallway to hear. "You and me, we both know you ain't worth shit, but now I want the whole fuckin' base to know that. If you as bad as you think you are, you look for me tonight around twelve behind the barracks. You come and show me if you're more than just dogshit I stepped in."

By late evening, most of the rednecks on the base had stopped by his room to advise him to "kill that nigger," but when he arrived at the field behind the barracks soon after midnight, he knew at once they'd be disappointed. There were very few blacks in the waiting crowd. And after half an hour's fidgeting in the gloom, they *all* knew. Heywood wasn't coming.

"You gonna let that mother-fucker get away with this? He put you down, man. In front of everybody. You gonna let him *do* that?"

Left to himself, Levine might well have done so. Heywood was no sort of match for him, and they both knew it. But he had psyched himself up for a fight, and the rednecks were not to be denied. At the head of his supporters, he marched over to the all-night mess hall, where the Air Police who had just finished the swing shift were eating supper before turning in, the blacks sitting together as usual at a separate table. There were eight of them, and Levine knew them all—some of them well enough to call friends—but with a white mob at his back he was suddenly a stranger.

"Anybody seen Heywood?" he asked, his voice choked. Nothing would be the same after this.

Nobody answered. They just stared back at him, without expression. Then one of them started eating again, and Levine exploded with frustration.

"Well, I got a message for that . . . mother-fucker."

He had almost said *black* mother-fucker, and they knew it. He could hardly credit what was happening to him. Maddened by the knowing glances that passed between them, he reached back into the gutter and raked through the litanies of street abuse for the most degrading insults he could offer, arriving finally at Heywood's mother.

"You tell him I got his mother right here," he whispered, covering his crotch with a shaky hand. "And she's *enjoying* it. You tell him that."

Somebody behind him laughed nervously, but the blacks looked down at their plates.

"Sure," said the one getting on with his meal. "I'll tell him."

Levine returned to his room a hero.

A week later he had a date with a sophomore from Plattsburgh State, where he had enrolled in an English course that fall. Team-ing up for the evening with his roommate Richie O'Hara and his girl, they spent a couple of hours in the kennels, showing off with their dogs, and then piled into O'Hara's old Chevy for the ride into town. But as they reached the guard shack, a uniformed figure stepped out in the middle of the flight-line access road and waved them over to the side.

"Jesus," said O'Hara. "It's Heywood."

Some sort of premonition stabbed Levine so hard he winced. Disengaging his girl's arm as the car slowed down, he craned forward to look through the windshield.

O'Hara glanced over his shoulder. "You want I should stop?"

"Fuck, yes," he said, cramming down an unaccountable impulse to duck out of sight. "Let's get this over with."

As the car came to a halt, Heywood moved around to Levine's door like an alley cat stalking a pigeon.

"Get out," he said thickly. "We got something to settle."

"Yeah." Levine, too, could hardly speak above a whisper. "You got it, man."

He stepped out on the blacktop and felt the cold. The light had almost gone, and the sky was heavy with snow. This time there was no hesitancy in Heywood's face.

"I got your message," he said, and turned away to the guard shack, stripping off his gunbelt and parka. Dumping them on the ground, he came back slowly with his hands in the pockets of his jacket. They stared at each other in the silence, until Levine provoked him with a smile.

Withdrawing his left hand from his pocket, Heywood slapped him across the face, and Levine let it happen. Now he had a pretext. And witnesses. Shaking his shoulders loose, he shuffled forward to put him in the hospital, and saw the gun too late in Heywood's other hand.

He was on top of it already, the muzzle inches from his chest. For a fragment of eternity, he saw his own death in progress, the finger tightening on the trigger—and in the last extremity of protest, heard a dull metallic click . . .

The gun had been fully loaded, and it fired every time after that. It was tested over and over and over again by Sergeant James Smith of the Air Police, now a U.S. Deputy Marshall in the Southern District of New York.

"There goes the luckiest sonofabitch I know," he says, every time he sees Levine in the federal courthouse. And he shouts down the hallway after him, "It fired every time after that. . . ."

"Okay." Levine surveyed his FBI class as it reassembled after the break, remembering a time when most of the faces would have been white. "After that story I told you about José with the Cigarettes, somebody asked me out in the hallway if I ever had to shoot anybody, working undercover, so let's talk about death for a minute."

The fidgeting stopped at once, but he made them wait while he collected his thoughts.

"When you work undercover, death is part of the game. And not like in the movies or shit like *Miami Vice*—I mean death as slow as a thirty-year sentence or quick as a jailhouse suicide. I mean the murder of an informer's children. I mean waiting for that bullet behind the ear. All the time you're undercover, death'll be in the air, and you've got to be able to handle that. To be comfortable with it. . . ."

He shook his head, as he often did, over the sheer impossibility of transplanting his own experience. "Listen to this. 'The idea most vital to the warrior is that of death, which he ought to have before his mind day and night.' " Levine touched the air at a point about an inch and a half from his forehead—and smiled at their bewilderment. "That is from the teachings of Bushido. The way of the warrior.

"I've studied the martial arts for most of my adult life, and I see no difference between the way of the warrior and the way of the undercover. In feudal Japan a man *was* a warrior. It was not something he did. It was something he was, from the moment of his birth to his last breath. And it's the same for an undercover. An undercover is what you *are*. Not something you *do*. It's not acting a part, it's *being* the part. You understand the difference?

"If actors who flopped on Broadway were taken out and shot in Shubert Alley, they'd still have it easy compared with the undercover. Actors have the luxury of immersing themselves in their roles for audiences who pay to see their act—people who expect and *want* to be convinced. They're on the actor's side, rooting for him. But an undercover works with his audience a foot from his face. An audience looking for something wrong in his performance. For any hint that he's not the real thing. An audience that suspects he's a narc when they meet. One slip, one error of judgment, and *his* audience won't just take a walk at intermission. They'll probably blow his fucking brains out."

He lowered the tension with a sudden smile.

"So think of what a fragile thing life is, and how fine a thread it hangs on. Think about that *hard*. And if the realization of just how fragile a miracle life is helps you savor every moment then maybe you'll make it as an undercover. But if it frightens you, if the fear of death—the inevitable—is too strong, then walk away. Don't fight it. Because the fear will show through. They'll see it in your eyes. They'll smell it on you. . . ."

He strung out the silence, underlining the warning, but as soon as he looked down at his notes somebody said, "You didn't answer the question."

"What?"

"Did you ever have to shoot anybody, working undercover?"

Levine looked at him doubtfully. "If that's the main thing on your mind after listening to me," he said, "then maybe undercover's not for you. If you start out expecting to fail, you'll never get over with anybody. But if you're asking me, did I ever have to shoot my way out of trouble when something went wrong, then the short answer is no." He hesitated, unwilling to be drawn, and yet unwilling to let it go at that. "But it's also a misleading answer, so I better explain. I'm not going to get in too deep, though, because this whole subject is like a red-raw nerve to me. And anyway, we've got a lot more stuff to talk about."

He was quiet for a moment. "I've worked with guys who loved to kill. Maybe some of you have, too. Well, I don't. I will if I have to. If an armed suspect resists arrest or he's a public danger, I'll shoot him. But in a lot of cases I hear about it's just bad police work. Most of the time, if you do the job right, you don't give the guy a *chance* to resist. As an under-cover, it's a measure of your skill if you can survive as long as I have without having to use a gun.

"In twenty-two years I've only fired my gun twice that I can remember, and I've probably locked up more people than anybody else in government service. The first time it went off by accident. I won't go into the details now, but it was during a difficult and dangerous arrest, and no one got hurt. The second time I missed. And that was okay because I shot at a Doberman attack dog going for my throat, and he missed as well. So the short answer is no.

"But standing here now, I can think of at least twelve people I killed in my head. And by that I mean twelve people who lived only be-cause of some incredible split-second fluke. If Champ hadn't opened Archie Dent's door ex-actly when he did, Charlie Haynes and his friends would have died on the porch that morning. If Sammy York had been a fraction slower getting the door open to let the guys in, Archie Dent himself would have gone.

"No, it's a lot more than twelve. That's five

guys right there. I'll get to some of the other
cases as we go along, but when I think of all
the times I should have been cold meat myself,
and all the people I came within a hair of killing, you start to wonder. Is there someone up
there controlling this shit? This has all got
to be for *something*, right . . . ?"

After Heywood's gun misfired against his chest, Levine began to
wonder if Providence had spared him for some inscrutable purpose
of its own. Then, as he put this theory to the test, he also began to
wonder if perhaps he was indestructible until he had served that
purpose, whatever it was. At any rate, the immediate legacy of the
incident was a profound restlessness, a driving hunger for new
experience to measure himself against and to sift for some clue as
to why he had been saved.

The incident itself was quickly hushed up. "I can't *make* you
drop charges," the lieutenant had said, "but we're all Air Police.
And Air Police like to settle these things among themselves."

Still in shock, nineteen-year-old Air Policeman Levine duly
dropped charges and Heywood was shipped out to Greenland, but
life in the service had somehow lost its point. A few months later,
in March 1960, his right hand was severely bitten by somebody
else's sentry dog, and he wound up in the base hospital for two and
a half weeks with blood poisoning. Immediately after that, he began to wheeze.

As a child Levine had suffered from asthma, most of the attacks
coinciding with the breakup of his parent's marriage.

"My father had a violent temper," he recalls. "A couple of times
when he came to see us, he just punched her, and she fell down.
Now she says she doesn't remember that, but *I* do."

He remembered it when he started wheezing again at Plattsburgh. The symptoms were the same and soon grew worse. By
September he was so short of breath he was declared unfit for duty
and again admitted to the hospital. Two months later, his condition having failed to respond to medication, he was flown down to
the main USAF Hospital at Maxwell Air Force Base, Alabama, for
more specialized tests and treatment. But these, too, failed to establish the cause of the problem or alleviate his distress, and after
another four miserable bedridden months the Air Force finally
gave up and discharged him on medical grounds in April 1961.

Following six months' inaction in the hospital, Levine's condition began to improve as soon as he left it. Upon reaching Atlanta, he felt fit enough to get laid, and by the time he crawled back on a bus three days later, half his discharge pay had gone, and he was well on the way to recovery. North of Baltimore, when the bus became desegregated, he moved to the back to share a seat and a jug of moonshine with a man named Nelson Dixon, who not only became an undemanding friend, but also fixed him up with a job where he worked, at Amerbrit Kennels, in Hempstead, Long Island. (Though an act of kindness, this only delayed the discovery that Levine's medical problems were, in fact, due to an undetected allergy to dogs.)

That fall he enrolled at Hofstra University to study accounting, mainly because people said it would be a good foundation for a career in any business. He also met Liana Hochberger at his cousin Bobby's wedding. Levine was an usher and she a bridesmaid—platinum blonde, petite, beautiful and seventeen years old. The first time they dated, on the Fourth of July, he announced his intention to marry her, and she didn't say no, although she *did* make it plain she was not in the habit of marrying total strangers. There would have to be a courtship.

Born in an Italian monastery, Liana had been baptized as a Christian to protect her from the Nazis and their collaborators. Arriving as refugees after the war, the Hochbergers set up as importers of paintings and art works, and by the time Levine crossed their daughter's path, they had a prosperous business in Manhattan and a comfortable home in the Bronx.

"The neighborhood then was mainly Irish and Italian," Liana remembers. "I liked Italians, but my parents were very strict. I could date whoever I liked as long as he was Jewish. Now here I am at my girlfriend's wedding and in walks this—this *movie star*. This tall, dark, curly-haired *hunk*. He was stunning. I was really knocked out by the way he looked. 'Wow!' I said to my girlfriend, who had told me about him. 'Is he *Jewish?*' And then when he told me later he was going to be an accountant, I couldn't believe it. This was like every nice Jewish girl's dream."

But she was realistic enough to see that he might not meet her parents' specifications for an ideal son-in-law. He drank too much, certainly womanized too much, and was generally too wild in speech and behavior to fit the conventional mold. She knew she would have to play him in gradually, hoping to smooth off some of the rougher edges before presenting him as a serious candidate.

There were also certain things about him she didn't understand at all. One was that he seemed to have no friends. No *real* friends. There were guys he knew and hung out with, but she had the impression it would not have mattered to him much if they all dropped dead overnight. They were just guys. Like furniture in his life. The nearest he had to a friend was Nelson Dixon, who was little better than a derelict in her estimation. When Levine took her to visit him in his shack, they sat and philosophized for hours while killing a bottle of bourbon. But with the kind of people *she* was used to, he simply had nothing to say.

His attitude toward his family was also unsettling. On the surface it looked normal enough, but underneath she sensed a lack of real warmth. He seemed curiously detached, as though *acting* the part of son and brother. There were even times when she felt he was acting the part of the ardent lover. The physical ardor was real enough, but she still felt at arms' length. He just didn't seem to need *anybody*—and at seventeen she naturally chose to interpret this as the surest sign that he *did*.

Nor was she completely wrong. At twenty-two Levine was not comfortable with himself or with others. Coupled to the wariness and suspicion he had learned on the street was a restless intelligence that reminded him constantly of how far he was living below his potential. He had also discovered in the service a survivor's self-sufficiency that did away with any need of social contact for its own sake. On top of that, he had evidently been spared for something other than what he was doing, and the combined effect of all this had been to introduce a distance between himself and everybody else. Instead of being fully engaged in whatever was going on, he could not avoid observing others, and observing himself in relation to others, with a detachment he often regretted, particularly when it applied to Liana and his brother. In striving to be close to them, he found himself acting again. Sometimes overacting.

Now eighteen, David Levine had lived most of his life in his brother's shadow, generally looking to Michael for support and protection in the absence of their father. Few would have taken them for brothers. Michael was positive and charged with energy; David was not. Michael sought to overcome the insecurities of his childhood by seeking out situations in which to prove himself; David would evade them until forced to a confrontation, when he would turn and fight with the despairing ferocity of a cornered wildcat. Michael was a survivor; David was not.

That September, just before starting at Hofstra, Michael was riding around one evening with a girl named Joyce—Liana had stayed home to show him he was not completely irresistible—when some friends of his brother drove up alongside. One was barely conscious, and covered in blood. He had just been beaten severely by Tony and Bruno,* two ex-cons who worked as bodyguards for Howard,* a local mob-connected pimp and dope dealer.

"Look what they did to Johnny," said his friends. "We're taking him to the hospital."

"What happened? Why'd they do it?"

"He didn't know where your brother was, that's all."

"David? Why are they looking for him?"

"Who knows? But you better find him."

As a kid David had constantly involved Michael in fights, but this was serious. Tony and Bruno were contract muscle, each thirty or forty pounds heavier than he was, and known for gratuitous violence. Tony, particularly. Involved once in a minor traffic collision, he had laid into the other driver with a tire iron and inflicted permanent brain damage. Revving up his battered old Chevy, Levine anxiously quartered the neighborhood, hoping he would find David first.

Rounding a corner into Springfield Boulevard, he spotted his brother's car up ahead, just as it passed and cut in front of a white Corvette. Before Levine could reach them, David was out of his car and leaning over the other driver, stiff with tension. It was Howard.

"You lookin' for me?" David demanded, as Levine moved in to head off even worse trouble.

The other replied unintelligibly, and before Levine could stop him David punched Howard full in the face.

There was an audible tremor among the onlookers, who had gathered like flies as the cars stopped. Everybody in the neighborhood knew that Howard had just had the tapes taken off a brand-new nose job. Snuffling blood between his fingers, he straightened up in his seat, screaming and choking with anguish. "You fuckin' fag," he sobbed, trying to examine the damage in the mirror. "You're fuckin' *dead*. You know that?"

* Not their real names.

David reached in to pull him out of the car, but Levine dragged him away. "You *crazy?*" he demanded. "What the fuck's goin' on?"

He hustled David back to his car, only half-listening to a vague story about some broad that he would surely have questioned had he not been so preoccupied with the immediate problem of Tony and Bruno.

"Follow me home," he said, shoving him in behind the wheel. "And no fuckin' arguments."

Whatever the right and wrong of it, the dispute with Howard was beyond arbitration. Their best hope of surviving it was to settle the affair right away, and in public, rather than let Tony and Bruno settle it privately some night in an alley. By the time they reached home, Levine had worked out the tactics of what residents of Bayside would remember for years as the Battle of Alley Pond Park.

Every neighborhood kid who stopped by the house to warn them about Tony and Bruno or report on their movements was sent off with instructions to round up all the other Levine supporters and sympathizers they could find and have them assemble outside. He then sent Joyce home and, like a matador getting into his working clothes, changed out of his on-the-town finery into jeans, boots and a black T-shirt. Their mother could see that something was in the wind, but as usual, she was powerless to interfere.

When the brothers were ready they went out to await the enemy with their followers, now thirty or forty strong. As Levine had calculated, their friends might be few, but there were fewer still who could resist the prospect of a fight, or the possibility of the Levines getting their comeuppance. Whatever Howard and his heavies chose to do, it would now be a public event.

They were not kept waiting long. A car drove up with a deputation from a local gang of young winos who kept themselves amused, when reasonably sober, with rape, muggings and vandalism.

"They're waiting for you up in the park," said their spokesman, his eyes roving the crowd at Levine's back. "Tony and Bruno. But just you and your brother. Two on two, right?"

"Right," said Levine, stepping back from himself, and directing this now like a movie.

About twenty cars followed them down to Springfield Boulevard, skirting the edge of the park, while the rest of their supporters streamed behind on foot. Pulling up on the opposite side of the street, Levine exchanged a glance with his brother, and the two crossed over without a word to jump the fence. At the head of their straggling army, they advanced steadily up the rise toward the park's ballfields, where they stopped, for there was now too little light from the street to see where they were going. But there was enough to pick out the white shirts of Tony and Bruno as they came out of the darkness to meet them.

Levine set himself to take Tony, the bigger of the two. As they closed with each other, he saw Tony reach inside his shirt and come out with a blackjack. Cursing himself for not thinking of that, Levine stepped back a pace and bumped into his friend Jerry Gorsky, who pressed a wrench into his hand.

But Tony was already on him. Levine managed to throw up his left forearm to protect his head against the descending blackjack, and heard the bone snap like a branch. Flooded with outrage, he swung the wrench with such force that as it hit the side of Tony's head, it was jarred right out of his hand and was lost in the darkness somewhere.

In two minds whether to stop and look for it, he saw Tony stagger away with both hands pressed to his head, and stumbled after him. Picking his openings, Levine hit him methodically with a succession of 220-pound right-handers, but Tony wouldn't go down. Instead, he started to scream like a steer in an abattoir, and as much to shut him up as anything else, Levine kicked him as hard as he could in the side.

Tony fell away and went down like a tree, still screaming, and Levine kicked him again, to finish it. But Tony got up, screaming worse than before, and started to totter away toward the light. Levine couldn't believe it. His left arm hung down, frozen and huge. The breath rasped in and out of his throat too hard for him to protest, and Tony was getting away. Vaguely aware of people running alongside, shouting, "No, no, that's enough, that's enough," Levine lumbered after him, punched and kicked him again, and when nothing seemed to stop the awful screaming, jumped on his back. Flailing at each other, they rolled down onto a stretch of concrete, where Levine grabbed Tony by his blood-soaked hair and started to dash his head against it.

Knowing he was about to die, Tony frantically twisted around and bit his tormentor's hand to the bone. Levine dragged it free with a great sigh of pain, but people were taking hold of him from behind, and in a moment he stopped struggling and just watched with the others as Tony somehow made it to the fence, solemnly fought his way over it and fell facedown in the gutter. A passing car stopped alongside, someone dragged him into the back, and they drove away.

Levine shook himself free and looked around. His brother was squatting beside him on his haunches, unmarked and hardly out of breath. Bruno without Tony had presented few problems. Having knocked him down with his first punch, David had turned away to help his brother, encouraging Bruno to try again. Knocked down a second time, he had then decided to call it a day.

Horns honking in triumph, the motorcade now set off for Queens General Hospital, where Levine was patched up, and made a play for the nurse. Next morning he crawled out of bed, knowing his problems had just begun. Everybody in Queens seemed to be talking about the fight, and a rumor was going around about a contract on the brothers' lives. That was all their mother had to hear. She went to her friend, Mrs. Vincent Puccias,* wife of a much-respected local mafia capo who liked to live in a peaceful neighborhood.

"Please, Michael, talk to Vince," she pleaded on her return. "He wants to see you."

Skipping breakfast, Levine had his brother drive him over.

Vince shook his head when he heard what had happened. "You *sure* you're Jewish?" he said.

He left them to make a few calls, and came back looking serious.

"You got a little trouble," he said. "So do like I say. Take a vacation. I'll tell you when to come home."

David took a bus upstate to stay at a bungalow colony, and Levine took a cab to the Bronx to stay with Liana, whose parents were in Florida. When she heard what had happened, she agreed to hide him out, but refused to succumb to his other blandishments. Already frustrated by his inability to get her into bed, he found her continued resistance almost unendurable with the two of them sleeping under the same roof. Toward the end of the week, Liana recalls, he had to go to the doctor to have his injuries inspected. An hour or so later, he called her at home and sounded so gloomy that she asked if everything was okay.

"No," he said. "It's not okay. I'll be there in half an hour."

* Not her real name.

She awaited his return with some anxiety, and as soon as he rang the bell drew him inside and made him sit down.

"Now then," she said, steeling herself for the worst. "Tell me what's wrong."

He shook his head and protested, but at last she dragged it out. "Well," he sighed, "if you must know, the doctor says I got a case of sperm backup. Worst he's ever seen. Practically a blockage. Yeah. He says if it goes on, with all the pressure buildup, it's gonna do me a lot of harm. Could even stop us from having children." He hung his head sorrowfully.

"Oh," she said. "I see." And then, yielding to the weight of medical opinion, "Well, in that case . . ."

They were now officially engaged.

A few days later his mother called to say that Vince had told her it was okay for him to come back; Liana's parents returned home from Florida, and he embarked on his college career at Hofstra. Things were probably closer to normal in Michael Levine's life than they would ever be again.

In March 1962 he gave up the dog-training job (and with it, the last of his asthma) because the hours conflicted with school. He became a part-time ladies' shoe salesman instead, working on 8 percent commission at Baker's Shoe Store in Manhasset. Enjoying the social opportunities that went with the job, he lasted there for eighteen months—roughly as long as it took Liana to win her parents around to the idea of having him for a son-in-law. In September 1963 they were finally married at a splendid, catered affair, and Vince came to the wedding.

With his new responsibilities and two more years ahead of him at Hofstra, Levine switched from commission selling at Baker's to selling shoes at Gimbels, in Valley Stream, for $1.85 an hour. He also took up the tenor saxophone. Though he still dreamed of Heywood's gun misfiring against his chest, Providence had evidently decided he should finish his college education before it showed its hand, and in the meantime sent along Hy Hackman to help out financially. Hackman was a little accountant who made a business out of buying up moribund bars in black neighborhoods, putting them on their feet and then selling them off at a profit.

"People tell me you're good with your hands, kid," he said.

"Yeah," said Levine. "I also play tenor sax."

"Well, that's good, too. You ever tend bar?"

"No."

"You wanna learn?"

"Sure."

"Okay. Then listen to me. I'll tell you what the problem is. The problem is I got this schwartze bar in Great Neck, Long Island. It's called the Nite Cap, and the bartender's a big black guy. He used to be a 50–50 partner. Now he's 75–25, and I can't stand it anymore."

"So what do you want me to do?"

"I'll tell you what I *don't* want you should do. If I give you the bartender's job, I don't want you should steal from *me*, okay? You can steal from *them* all you want. Steal the gold from their teeth, I don't care. But from me you take nothing except a salary. I'll give you a good salary."

He gave him $65 for a sixty-hour week. And Levine enjoyed the work. He played the saxophone until all hours with a black piano player, bounced a few awkward customers out on their ear once in a while, and generally had a good time until one night about four months later when the son of a local mob-connected businessman came into the bar, drunk and spoiling for trouble. He was accompanied by two baby-sitters whom Levine already knew slightly. They would buy two or three beers, flex their muscles thoughtfully, as if inviting his black customers to make something of it, and then leave. But this time they were scarcely through the door before their charge was feeling up the barmaid.

"Hey, don' you touch me," she said. It was Saturday night, and the place was jumping.

"What?" he said. "Well, fuck you, nigger."

At that, the music fizzled out, and the whole place went quiet.

Levine groaned internally. "Come on, man," he said. "Do me a favor."

The other rounded on him. "Fuckin' nigger bar," he said savagely. "Run by mother-fuckin' Jews. Who the fuck does she think she is?"

Hy Hackman, a little man with glasses, was smiling at them painfully. "Get 'em outa here," he mumbled, trying not to move his lips.

Levine came around from behind the bar with his hands turned out peaceably. He was at the wrong end of the bar for this problem. All three could get to him at once, and even the kid was bigger than he was. Down the other end, near the door, there was just a narrow aisle between the bar and the wall. If he could get down there, they could only come at him one at a time.

"Come on, man," he said, still warm and friendly. "Why make trouble? You've had one too many, that's all. Why don't you take a walk around outside, come back, and the drinks are on me?"

He put a hand on junior's arm. As the kid knocked it away, Levine walked past him, shaking his head.

"Now what d'ya wanna do *that* for?" he complained. "Just wanna talk to you, okay?"

Turning then, at the narrowest point in the aisle, he now had them in single file, with junior first in line.

"Be a good kid," he said, still with a smile. He put his left hand on junior's shoulder. "What d'ya say?"

"Fuck you," is what he said.

Again he knocked Levine's hand aside, but failed to see the other one on the way. His face split open under the impact like an over-ripe watermelon, splattering Levine with blood. As he bounced off his friends behind him and toppled forward, Levine hooked him twice more, left and right. The kid's eyes rolled up in his head, and he was gone.

In an instant every man in the bar was up with his blade out, and far from having to deal next with the muscle men, Levine now had to go to their rescue.

"Get him outa here," he hissed through his teeth, trying to keep between them and his more energetic supporters. "Get him into the men's room. Clean him up."

Backing up behind them to cover their retreat, he did his best to pacify his customers, and as the knives and razors were put away Hy came out from behind the bar.

"Hey," he said admiringly. "You really *are* good."

"Aw, shit, Hy." Levine already knew that this had to be his last night on the job. As a bartender, he had been dead wrong to get involved in a brawl, and not only that, the guy was connected. "What am I gonna do now? I need the money. My wife just had a baby."

Twenty minutes later the two muscle men emerged from the men's room, half carrying their charge, who mumbled through split lips something about suing him, and after a staring match with Levine they dragged him out into the night to a chorus of jeers. As soon as he could, Levine detached himself from his admirers and sat down on the other side of the bar for a farewell drink with Hy. They were just discussing the best way of explaining to Liana all the blood on his clothes when two Nassau County patrolmen came in, and the bar went quiet again.

Suddenly self-conscious, they explained they had come to arrest Levine for assault, but in tones suggesting that such a laughable mistake was bound to be cleared up as soon as he discussed it with their sergeant.

"You can't arrest *Mike*," said Hy. "Unless he did what he did, you'd have a riot on your hands. Sit down. What d'ya want? A beer?"

"No, we gotta take him in," said the senior patrolman. "The guy's pressing charges. There's nothing we can do."

"Officer, that man mo-lest me," the barmaid interrupted angrily. "If you arres' Mike fo' 'sault, then you gotta arres' *that* muthafucka fo' mo-lest. And Ah got witnesses."

"That's *right,*" said about thirty-five voices as one.

The patrolmen looked at each other, shrugged, and went out to confer with the plaintiff. They returned, grinning, in under a minute.

"Go home, Mike," said the older one.

When Liana opened the door she screamed and fainted. In all the excitement, he'd forgotten the blood on his clothes.

Unemployed again, with a wife and their baby son Keith to support, and still with a year to go at Hofstra, Levine allowed Liana to fix him up with a job in her father's business. For ten unhappy months he trailed around the tristate area in a company car, trying to sell oil paintings and prints to galleries, decorators and furniture stores, knowing full well he was being paid $8,000 a year only because he was the boss's son-in-law.

Then, on the day he graduated with a bachelor's degree in business administration. Providence finally showed its hand. He was sitting by himself on campus, brooding on a future that seemed to hold nothing more exciting than coding entries in company ledgers, when a fellow graduate named Steve Crane came by and asked him what was wrong. Levine told him. He had even thought of rejoining the service, he said, but Liana wouldn't hear of it. He would have to choose, she told him, between her and Uncle Sam.

"Well, not necessarily," said Crane.

He pulled from his pocket a pamphlet with a picture on the cover of a James Bond look-alike getting off a plane carrying an attaché case. It was entitled, "A Career in U.S. Treasury Law Enforcement."

"Keep it," Crane said.

He got up and left, and Levine never saw him again.

The fuse had been lit.

THREE

"Only all of a sudden, it's not so routine anymore . . ."

The Treasury brochure had promised a life of travel, adventure and excitement as a Special Agent with the Internal Revenue Service, Intelligence Division, but after filling in the forms and taking the test Levine heard nothing more and assumed he had flunked. Depressed with visions of a life of travel on the subway, adventures in double-entry bookkeeping and the excitement of three-martini lunches, he took a junior accountant's job with the Enjay Chemical Company in Rockefeller Center. On his third miserable Monday morning in the office, the IRS called.

"Hey, Levine. What's going on? You were supposed to report here today."

His letter of appointment had got lost in the mail.

The next four months were taken up by a flurry of training programs in Washington. Treasury Law Enforcement School. IRS Special Agent School. Basic Tax Law School. He enjoyed the Treasury School best because there he was taught to handle weapons, make arrests, go on raids and subdue the bad guys in unarmed combat. His fellow students included agents from the Secret Service, the Federal Bureau of Narcotics, the Bureau of Customs, and Alcohol, Tobacco and Firearms—the enforcement agency which, in those days, was thought to handle the most hazardous work in government, and which therefore became his principal goal.

It was at Treasury School that he struck up a friendship with Sante Bario, a fellow agent of the IRS Intelligence Division, and one of the very few government investigators at that time with any experience in undercover work, a subject barely referred to in the training program. Bario's stories of how he had infiltrated a mafia family in New Orleans as a cook and eventually convicted a dozen or more of his people for income-tax evasion took root in Levine's imagination like a vision of the promised land.

This made it all the more galling when, in June 1965, he strapped on his brand-new, snub-nosed Smith & Wesson .38 and reported for duty with the IRS Intelligence Division at 120 Church Street, New York. He was assigned to "investigate" income-tax returns for possible criminal violations by reeling through miles of microfiche in the basements of city banks. In his first ten months as an IRS agent, he made one arrest, bringing in Francis Norelli, a sixty-four-year-old, part-time language teacher, accused of preparing "fraudulent" returns for non-English-speaking, minimum-wage workers on the Lower East Side.

Levine was almost as depressed as Norelli. Without telling anybody, he sat for the New York City Police Department examination—and passed—before finally bringing himself to ask his supervisor, Max Unger, for a transfer.

"Max," he said, "after ten months on the job, I still don't know how to *begin* an income-tax case. I'm gonna fuck up every allegation you give me."

"I know, I know." Unger held up a hand. "I'm convinced already. The job is not for you. So what now? You wanna be a door banger?"

"No, I just want to be in law enforcement."

Unger shook his head indulgently. "We hire a *Levine*. With a degree in accounting yet. And he wants to be a door banger? Ah, well. . . . Tell you what I'll do. We got prosecution cases growing whiskers. We got witnesses and subpoenas to serve. You clean up the fieldwork around here, and I'll see you make the gambling squad."

"It's a deal," Levine said fervently.

He had just begun to study the martial arts, and was fascinated by the code of Bushido, the way of the warrior, which seemed not only to distill the essence of his life so far but to rationalize his craving for danger and excitement.

"If you carry the code of Bushido to its most fanatical degree, it says that the true warrior, when confronted with a choice of life or death, will always choose the way of death. That doesn't mean he wants to kill or *be* killed. It simply means he won't choose the safe way *because* it's safe. And I've never done that. I've never played safe. Family and child, it didn't matter. I already knew you come in alone and go out alone. Nothing is permanent. I was, and I am, prepared to live my life the way the cards are dealt. I felt that as strongly then as I do now, only then I didn't think about it. Now I do. Now I understand it better. But then, it was just a hunger to be where the action was."

With that sort of outlook, putting Levine in the gambling squad was like pigeon-shooting with SAM missiles. On the day he reported for duty, he was taken out on a raid by Special Agent John Cotter, a veteran, cigar-chewing ex-vice cop, who believed that the offices of the City Line Taxi Service in Mount Vernon, New York, were a front for a bookie operation. Impressed by his bulk and enthusiasm, Cotter assigned Levine to hit the back door as he hit the front, whereupon the other agents in the party would move in to secure the prisoners and evidence.

"Nothing to it," said Cotter, as zero hour approached. "Walk up there, past those backyards, until you come to a concrete porch and a screen door. You'll see me out front on the street, walking up the same way. Keep pace with me so you get there the same time I do. Go up to the screen door, show your badge, say, 'Federal officer with a warrant,' and if they don't open up, break it in. I'll be coming in the front, so you got nothing to worry about."

But as he walked up the back alley, all by himself, on his very first raid, Levine found quite a lot to worry about. For one thing, he was anxious to make a good impression. Second, he had no idea how many people he would have to take on inside single-handed. Third, he had even less idea of how gamblers, horseplayers and bookies normally reacted to the prospect of arrest. Did they run? Shoot? Burst into tears, or what?

Arriving at the screen door, he could see nothing through it, although there was plenty of noise inside. Uncomfortably aware that there was little room for hesitation with Cotter in position out front, he held his badge against the screen and said, "Federal officer with a warrant," in what sounded to him a despicably weak and ineffectual tone.

No one answered, and if it had not gone suddenly quiet inside, he would have assumed that no one had heard him. Even more painfully aware that while he could see nothing, they could see him very clearly against the light, he cleared his throat and said, in a much louder but still embarrassingly high-pitched voice, "Open up. Federal officer."

Again, nothing.

A full charge of adrenaline pushed the throttle wide open, and the screen door exploded into fragments under the impact of his shoulder.

Recovering his balance, he found himself in the middle of what could easily have passed for an afternoon session of the Mount Vernon Senior Citizens Club, except for the betting slips on the table. Frozen for a moment in varying attitudes of dismay, some fifteen elderly sportsmen gently subsided into shock as they realized the intervention was mortal, not divine. One sank to his knees, clutching at his chest. Another stood and stared, a puddle forming at his feet. Several more moaned piteously. Some just closed their eyes and fought for breath.

As Cotter came through from the front, raising an eyebrow at the splinters of door still hanging from the hinges, Levine shook his head. This wasn't what he'd meant at all.

His next excursion promised better. He was again chosen to accompany John Cotter and Special Agent Marvin Sontag, organized crime expert, in the lead car of an IRS motorcade sent to bring in Johnny "Peanuts" Manfredonia, a big-time gambler who lived in Yonkers, New York. This time the operational plan was for six carloads of agents to seal off the block and then await Sontag's signal to move in for the arrest as soon as he was satisfied that Johnny Peanuts was at home.

But Johnny Peanuts was out walking his miniature poodle, and as soon as Sontag saw them he decided to take him on the street instead. Alert to his signal, the other five cars revved up, charged in and screeched to a halt, narrowly avoiding a multiple collision. As ten agents piled out, guns drawn, Johnny Peanuts picked up his poodle with a puzzled frown, and Special Agent John Cotter buried his face in his hands.

As Cotter obviously had no intention of taking any part in this affair, Levine decided to follow Sontag, who was now pushing through the circle of agents surrounding Johnny Peanuts outside his house.

"John Manfredonia," Sontag said proudly, "you're under arrest."

He stretched out his hand to detain him, but snatched it back in alarm as the poodle, yapping defiance, snapped at it viciously. He tried again, with the same result. Nonplussed, Sontag caught the eye of Special Agent Graham Schatz and nodded at *him* to do it. Schatz moistened his lips and tentatively extended his left hand, but the poodle bared its teeth in a low growl and he thought better of it. Putting his gun away, Schatz then tried with *both* hands, hoping to use one as a decoy while he grabbed the dog with the other, but the poodle was too quick for him.

Johnny Peanuts smiled unhelpfully, offering himself and his dog to anyone else who cared to try, and Levine rejoined Cotter in the car.

After several more abortive attempts by Sontag and his men to arrest the poodle, now fired up with success and yapping incessantly, Johnny Peanuts lost patience.

"You fucking guys wait here," he said. "Lemme put the dog away."

Turning on his heel, he marched into the house, shut the door in their faces and did not come out again for half an hour, making them all wait in the street while he got dressed for the ride downtown.

This was still far from what Levine had had in mind. Remembering his conversations with Sante Bario, he tried to move onto a higher plane of enforcement by staging his first undercover operation.

Posing as an art salesman, he conned a shoeshine boy he knew as "Junior" into introducing him to Sam, a neighborhood bookie serving the area around 21st and 22nd streets, between Fifth and Sixth avenues. By pretending to know that a certain race had been fixed in favor of a horse named Son of Roman, he induced Junior to back it as well, and then volunteered to place the bets for both of them so that Junior would not have to lose any business by leaving his stand.

Bookie Sam could have doubled for Buddy Hackett. He had the same hoarse, cross-eyed intensity as that globular comic, and the moment Levine put his head around the door of the shack he used as an office, Sam erupted in voluble frenzy.

"Who are you? What do you want? Who sent you? No, don't look at me. Turn your back. Go sit in the corner and tell me what you want. And don't look. Just tell me who sent you. Who was it?"

When Levine explained who had sent him, he placed Junior's bet and his own on Son of Roman to win. Then he picked Golden Shoe for the second race and bet on them both for the daily double. Having thus risked $30 of his own money to further the investigation, he went back to the office and called for Sam's tax returns.

Confirming his faith in Providence, both horses romped home to win comfortably. Two days later he returned to the neighborhood to find Junior ecstatic and Sam rather less so.

"Oh, yeah," he said, when Levine called to collect his winnings. "I owe you money."

He pulled a grubby bankroll from the pocket of his pants, grudgingly peeled off $70 and pushed it across the counter.

"What's this?" Levine demanded. "I bet Son of Roman and Golden Shoe. You owe me like eight hundred."

"What?" Bookie Sam bounced up and down like a misshapen rubber ball, sputtering with rage. "You didn't bet Golden Shoe. You didn't. You told me another horse. You bet Orsinet's Due. I heard you."

Resisting an impulse to grab him by the shirt and drag him bodily over the counter, Levine blinked at him reproachfully. "How can you *say* that?" he asked. "I bet Golden Shoe. You *know* I did."

"You didn't. You didn't." He disappeared suddenly, and when Levine leaned over the counter to find out what he was doing he saw Sam rummaging through a garbage bin, pulling out paper bags with writing on them. "I'll show you. I'll show you," he said. "I got that day's work right here."

Levine was highly gratified. Here he was, working undercover for the first time, and the guy was showing him his whole operation.

"See? See?" Sam brandished a bag under his nose. "I wrote it down. I write all my work down on bags. So you better be careful. Eight hundred dollars? You take what you won. That or nothing."

"Then you wrote it down wrong," said Levine. "You made a mistake. But I guess there's nothing I can do."

"Do?" Sam popped up like a sky rocket and came out from behind the counter as if he could not believe his ears. *"Do?* I tell you, kid, you don't know who you're messing with." Though barely up to Levine's shoulder, he wagged a finger at him threateningly. "You don't know. So you better listen. What are you, a salesman?"

"Yeah. I'm a salesman, not a gangster. I'm not looking for trouble, but—"

"Trouble? *Trouble?* Listen, kid." He glanced around and dropped his voice confidentially. "Don't even mention the word. What do you think you're gonna do?"

"I didn't say that. I didn't say I was going to do anything. I just don't think it's right, that's all."

"You saw it," Sam went on, cooling off as he began to see further business possibilities in the situation. "You saw what I wrote on the bag. And there's what I owe you. So don't talk to me about trouble or we'll find out where you live."

"Well, if that's the kind of businessman you are . . . ," Levine said coldly.

He turned to go, but Sam ran around to get in his way.

"Now wait a second. What's your hurry? I never met such an impatient guy. Sit down. Sit down over there in the corner." He examined the bag more closely. "I coulda made a mistake," he conceded. "Because you know, I took a voice bet. From now on, I'll write it down."

"What do you mean, from now on? You think I'd come back after this? You must think I'm crazy."

"Just wait a minute. Slow down. I'll make a deal with you. We'll split the difference." He was figuring it out in his head. "You would have won $792. If you'd bet the right horse. So I'll give you $350 credit. But you gotta bet it."

"Bet it?"

"Well, what else, dummy?" He was stung by Levine's ingratitude. "Take it or leave it."

"I don't know." Levine shrugged. "I don't know what to do."

"*Do?*" shrieked Sam. And off he went again.

After placing several more bets, none of them successful, Levine wrote up the whole episode in a memorandum to his boss, Area Supervisor Jack Wilson.

"Not bad," Wilson said. "Looks like you gotta case here. The schmuck. He's gonna find out where you live? Shit. I'm gonna charge him with threatening a federal officer."

As threats went, it was not enough to keep Levine awake nights. Or even during the day sometimes. But on September 11, 1966, after months of constant nagging, begging and pleading, he was at last moved out of IRS Intelligence Division into the promised land of the Treasury's Alcohol, Tobacco and Firearms division. As a Special Investigator, Grade 7, the transfer brought no improvement in his gross salary of $125 a week, but an ineffable boost in morale, as though, having struggled through the bureaucratic thickets for a year, he had suddenly emerged at the edge of a vast, uncharted plain teeming with fair game. With government money in his pocket, a gun, a badge and a sense of mission, he galloped off in all directions to solve the crime problem.

Oddly enough, his first day on the job, he was sent back to the IRS with Special Investigator Morty Jacobson, aka "Baby Hughie," to help its Organized Crime Division build an income-tax case against Aniello Dellacroce, underboss of the Carlo Gambino family. They were handed a mugshot and told to keep him under surveillance.

"Great," Levine said. He had always known big-time enforcement would be like this. "Then what?"

"Then what? Then write a report. We wanna know where he goes and how he spends his money. Stuff like that."

"Okay."

"Try the Ravenite Social Club. That's where Dellacroce hangs out."

"Okay. Where's that?"

"Jesus Christ. On Mulberry Street."

Armed with the mugshot, Levine and Baby Hughie, who was six feet six but easily impressed, drove over to Mulberry Street, parked opposite the Ravenite Social Club and walked over to see if they could see anything inside. They could not. And as they hovered uncertainly by the door, peering in and debating what to do now, out came Dellacroce with his driver and four heavy-weight bodyguards: Mike Catalano, Louis Palmieri, Tony West and his brother Charlie. They grouped themselves around the two in silence. Baby Hughie tried a careless laugh.

"Who the fuck are you?" Dellacroce asked Levine. "You look like a bomb t'rower."

"And who the fuck are *you?*" Levine reported, trying to sneak another look at the mugshot to make sure. He was distracted by a movement of Tony West's hand toward his pocket. *"Don't,"* he said coldly. "Because if you take something out, I'm gonna stick it up your ass."

"Fucking wise guy." West started forwa out a restraining hand. "You know who you

"You know who *you're* fucking with?" Levi scious of a certain lameness in his repartee.

"Okay, okay," said Dellacroce wearily. "You' , right? Don't say nothing—I know you're on the job. S dn't you just tell me? Instead of acting like some kinda bomb rower?"

"Well, why didn't you just *ask* me?" Levine demanded.

Without deigning to answer, Dellacroce turned and went back inside again, his driver grabbing open the door for him while his escort covered the rear, glaring at them balefully. Levine, in turn, glared balefully at Baby Hughie, who fought to suppress another nervous giggle.

"Get away from that fucking door," said a disgusted voice behind them. It was a cop's voice, and it belonged to a bulky, gray-haired man in a raincoat, whom Levine had noticed ducking in and out of doorways as he approached. "Who you with?"

"ATF."

"Jesus. You know who that was?"

"That's Dellacroce, right?"

"Yeah. That's Dellacroce," he said, shooing them along in front of him. "And you know something? That guy could make a phone call right now and in two minutes you'd be dead. And with all these guys watching, there's nothing we could do to put it on him."

Levine stopped in his tracks. In at least half the cars on the block, two men were sitting in front wearing hats, and were obviously being paid to do so by the city, state or federal government. And they were all laughing.

But he soon got the hang of it. Five different agencies were watching Dellacroce as part of their respective drives on organized crime. Sometimes he would send his driver out to tell them in advance where he was going. Other times he would take them on a mystery tour, running lights, changing lanes without warning, and making sudden, unsignaled turns, just to break their asses in the traffic. Tiring of that, he would then leave his car and driver out on the street all night, so that they would have to stay out all night as well, just in case. But when he needed his privacy, it was another story.

Levine was sitting outside the social club one night at the head of the waiting procession, when a truck ran into his stationary car, throwing him up against the windshield. When he got out to re-

...strate with the driver, several bystanders tried to set a dog on him, and in all the confusion Dellacroce drove away unobserved.

After that, Levine contrived to be too busy to catch the assignment again. Though geared, from force of habit, to investigating liquor violations and tobacco tax evasion, AFT had arrived at a watershed in its history without quite realizing it. Always something of a catchall division in Treasury law enforcement, it was accustomed to helping out other government agencies, including the Secret Service. (With his formidable gifts as a warrior, Levine was often assigned in his early years to act as bodyguard to Richard Nixon, Hubert Humphrey, Governor George Wallace, Lyndon Johnson and other politicians with cause to worry when they visited New York.) Now, with new gun-control laws in prospect to curb the growing use of firearms even in minor crimes, and with drug abuse afflicting every level of society, the old territorial distinctions between federal enforcement agencies were becoming more and more blurred, which suited Levine perfectly. As far as he was concerned, his brief as a federal officer was to arrest anybody committing any federal crime he happened to feel strongly about. And after the winter of 1966–67 there was nothing he felt more strongly about than narcotics.

One cold night, just before Christmas, he was home with Liana and his infant son Keith when his mother telephoned. She was sobbing so hard he could scarcely make out what she was saying, and had a sudden, panicky vision of her having been attacked. Junkies were moving into the neighborhood. Just two days earlier a neighbor had been mugged outside her apartment.

"No, it's not me," she gasped. "Just come. I must show you something."

He took the shortcut, behind the apartment buildings, and was glad he had brought his gun. The neighborhood was going down faster than he had realized. The darkness was full of moving shadows and interrupted whispers. By the time he arrived at her door, he was in a high state of tension, but she opened it at once, obviously unharmed, and without a word led him through to his brother's room. On the bed was a box. In the box was a hypodermic needle and a spoon—a junkie's works. His *brother's* works. She had found them while tidying his closet.

He sat down heavily, trying to take it in. "Where is he?"

She shook her head, and he was glad she didn't know because he was angry enough to have killed him.

"I looked at this shit in the box, and I was sick. Just *sick*. My mother knew what it meant, but had to hear me say it. She was very upset, so I called Liana to tell her I was staying, and we settled down to wait. I just couldn't believe it. I'd been around drugs and junkies on the street ever since I was a kid, and to me only weak-minded scum did that to themselves. It made me sick to my stomach. And now my own *brother?* I couldn't believe it. But there in my hands was the proof. My baby brother David was a heroin addict.

"He had hidden it well. But as we sat there, waiting for him to come home, not talking much, a lot of things suddenly made more sense. The fight with Howard and his boys. David's restlessness. His moods. The aimless way he drifted from job to job.

"After high school he'd worked in a gas station doing grease jobs and learned to be a mechanic. A good one. Bought himself tools, started to build a business, then suddenly dumped that and became a hairdresser. Hated that, went into something else, then back again—it was all part of a pattern I should have recognized, but I was too busy messing up my own life at that point to pay much attention to his.

"Anyway, he finally showed up around three in the morning, and as soon as he saw our faces, he knew. He was just totally down, but in a funny way I think he was glad we found out. 'Are you mad at me?' he said, and we all started to cry. Couldn't help it. 'How long you been doing this?' I asked him. 'Are you an addict?' He didn't like that word. He said he'd started when he was fifteen —around the time I went into the service. He'd been using junk for seven years, and none of us had even suspected it.

" 'You're *dead,'* I told him, furious with *him,* with myself, with everybody. 'Anyone who gets into heroin *dies.'* That's when he promised for the first time to get into a program. Up to then he hadn't really tried, but after that night he fought like a bastard to get off it."

From that time on, Levine found it difficult to talk to his brother, or even be around him, and this was a source of pain to them both. Michael *wanted* to help, wanted to fight this battle for him, too, but beneath the concern, and the twinges of guilt, he also felt betrayed. He still loved his brother, but something ugly, something alien, had taken him over. And it was David's own fault. Aware of their estrangement, and in his anxiety to make amends, David now undermined their relationship still further by appearing meek and submissive when big brother was looking for at least a show of determination.

"I couldn't snap him out of it. Couldn't understand it, to tell the truth. For me, there was always *something* I wanted to do, no matter how depressed I got. The martial arts, for instance. They meant a lot to me then. I could train at it. Work at it. Fight. I tried everything I knew to fire him up, but no good. I got a *life*. Let me *do*. Let me *try*. No good. David was very bright, very talented, but something was missing. He was a victim, and all the talk in the world couldn't change that."

With her gentler nature, and a better understanding of what it was like to live in Michael's shadow, Liana drew closer to David as his brother turned away from them both to vent his frustration on the streets.

"David simply lost his way and couldn't get back," she says. "He was a *good* man. A caring man. And he wanted so hard to be just a *normal* man. He was hurting all the time because he knew what he was doing to himself and the family was horrible, but he couldn't deal with it. He *couldn't* stop. After we found out, he was in and out of every kind of program—Phoenix House, counseling groups, methadone. He really tried. But he was also very unlucky. Every time he seemed to be making headway, something would trip him up again."

Looking back, Levine concedes the truth of this. "I remember one time he was on methadone, and smoking a little grass to help things along, and he had an accident on his motorcycle. Came around a corner too fast and lost it. Hit a parked car, cartwheeled over and broke his pelvis. While he's lying there, in great pain, waiting for an ambulance, a uniformed cop looks in his saddlebag and finds a joint. Next thing he knows, David is waking up in the prison ward of Queens General Hospital. Soon as he got out he went right back on heroin. Had no luck at all, my brother."

New York City's drug traffickers were out of luck, too. Levine was already convinced that Providence had put him into law enforcement. Now it had also defined the enemy and topped up his sense of mission with a craving for revenge—at the very moment when the move to ATF freed him from constraint. Bored with looking for Puerto Rican liquor stills, Levine greeted the 1968 Federal Gun Control Act as his personal hunting license. The day it came into force he set off in his powder-blue Mustang with a government bankroll in his pocket to disarm New York and perfect a technique that would become standard police practice throughout the world. Target the suspect. Get in undercover. Make a buy (or a sale). Effect an arrest. (And as often as not, induce the defendant to turn informer.)

His prime targets under the act were unlicensed gun dealers, convicted felons or fugitives with guns, and anybody committing a federal offense while in possession of a firearm. In practice, that meant working with informers and catching mostly dope dealers, which suited him fine. Indeed, he was one of the first federal agents to realize that the Gun Control Act, enforced by ATF, could be a better weapon against them than the drug laws available to the Bureau of Narcotics and Dangerous Drugs. In some courts, a narcotics conviction might result in little more than probation, but a firearms offense now carried a mandatory minimum jail sentence.

Teamed up initially with Lou Kozinn, who went on to become coordinator of New York's Organized Crime Task Force, Levine made twelve major undercover cases in his first year, in between working routine liquor violations and knocking over after-hours joints to keep the bosses happy. He would pick up on any lead that might give him a crack at another narcotics trafficker.

"An informer only had to come in and say, 'I got this doper with a gun in his car,' and I'd say, 'Okay, let's get him.' And that's what we'd do. I'd set him up, and if the U.S. Attorney didn't want him I'd give him to the city. Made a lot of cases like that. Every spare moment. All the wrongs I saw, drugs were behind them, and I was locking people up for anything."

Area Supervisor Jack Hollander, his boss at ATF, was happy to let him go. Like many an old-time "revenooer," he was mainly interested in a quiet life, preferring to devote his declining years in Treasury service to the pursuit of the near-extinct bootlegger than to anything actually dangerous. Often without a partner to cover him, and with no rule book to follow, Levine virtually composed his own job description, and was soon making more cases by himself than the rest of the New York office put together.

His first really good informers were Willy Lopez,* a rat-sized psychotic who supplemented his income from stealing cars by giving up other car thieves, and Ray Velez, a sweet-natured Puerto Rican junkie, on parole for attempted grand larceny. Lopez he acquired through Austin "Buddy" Muldoon, an ex-New York

* Not his real name.

detective turned ATF agent, who told him a police sergeant he knew in the Bronx had an informer who could do guns and dope if he had a Spanish-speaking agent to hang out with, while Velez approached Levine on the street to volunteer his services. And when Levine demanded to know how Velez knew he was the Man, he was even more surprised to learn that Lopez had told him. Lopez, apparently, was telling everybody.

When he cooled down, Levine decided to let it pass for a while, despite the obvious dangers. Riding around with Lopez, he had made gun collars, dope collars, bought stolen drivers' licenses and credit cards and made all sorts of cases—often five or six at a time —and he had yet to squeeze him dry. But it was soon clear that Ray Velez was even better. Quick-witted and inventive, he liked Levine and liked the work.

They soon fell into a daily routine. Levine would pick Velez up in the morning at his mother's house on Fox Street; they would then review the day's possibilities over coffee and doughnuts, and finally move off like a pair of hunting dogs. Velez would set up the target, bring in Levine as his partner and "cousin," and as soon as they had a case, Levine would call in a squad to make the arrests.

On one such day Velez connected with a junkie named Pete at the corner of Tompkins Avenue and Ellery Street in Brooklyn. Pete had heard that Velez was looking to buy a gun, and for $20 undertook to introduce him to a guy who could get him anything he wanted. Velez replied that he and his cousin both needed guns, and took him over to meet "Cousin Miguel," who was sitting in his car nearby.

At Pete's direction they drove over to Hopkins Street and Delmonico Place, where Levine parked in front of a schoolyard and Pete got out to look for his contact. When he came back he said the guy would be there soon, and would they wait?

"Fuck that," said Cousin Miguel. "*You* wait. When he shows, come and get us."

He led Velez across the street and into a pool hall on Delmonico Place. It never paid to seem anxious.

Half an hour later, around 4:00 P.M., Pete called them out to meet Papo, another skinny little Puerto Rican junkie.

"You wan' guns?" he said. "Whatchoo wan' guns for?"

"I need one for a geese, man," said Levine, meaning a stickup. "And like right now."

Papo was unimpressed.

"After that," Levine went on, before the other could turn him down, "after that, I throw it away and maybe come back and buy some more. *If* I like the price."

Papo nodded, and led him aside for a private word. "Last week I had a lot," he said, "but I sold 'em. I got more coming, but the best I can do for right now is a .38."

"What make?"

"EIG. It's a good piece, man."

"Shit," said Levine. "How much?"

"Hundred dollars."

"Shit." He sighed and half-turned away, but then changed his mind. "You wanna show it to me?"

"Yeah. Butchoo gotta wait for my frien'. He took my car to pick up some dope."

"Yeah?" It was too easy. Levine almost yawned. "I didn't know you did dope, man. Whatchoo got?"

"Nickel bags."

"Okay. I'll take five."

"Okay. But get off the street, man. People are lookin' at you."

"Yeah, yeah. I'll wait in the car."

Noting Levine's annoyance, Pete waited until Papo was out of earshot and set about protecting his $20. He knew somebody else who did guns, he said. He might be quicker at closing a deal. Now with two leads for the price of one, Levine sent Velez off with Pete to investigate while he waited for Papo to return with his friend.

Five minutes later an old brown Chevrolet drove up and parked directly opposite, across the street. Several minutes after that, the driver got out carrying a brown paper bag, which he locked in the trunk. He then walked slowly away in the direction of Flushing Avenue.

He was hardly out of sight before Velez came back with Pete. They had failed to find the other gun connection. The three of them now stood on the corner, waiting for something to happen. Another five minutes passed. Then Papo returned on foot and seemed relieved to see the brown Chevrolet. Yeah, that was his car, he said. He had told his friend to lock everything in the trunk if he wasn't there to meet him.

"Orright, orright." Levine grabbed his arm to walk him across to the car. "Let's get this thing over with."

"Well, yeah," said Papo, resisting. "But my frien', he still got the keys."

Levine stopped in his tracks and struck his forehead with the butt of his hand. "Then fuck you," he said. "And fuck your stoopid friend. I ain't got no more time to waste."

He had no intention of leaving. He was simply bedding the hook deeper, so that in the end they would be pleading to do business with him. As he turned away, he caught sight of the driver of the Chevrolet standing in a doorway farther down.

"That him?" He asked Papo, jerking his head in that direction. "The guy lookin' at us?"

"Yeah, that's him," Papo said. "Come on."

But as soon as he was close enough to read his friend's expression, he slowed down, and motioned the others to wait while he went on ahead. The two then conferred in an undertone for several minutes, each breaking off from time to time to give the others a hard stare. Levine meanwhile fidgeted about in circles, muttering to himself. Eventually, and with obvious reluctance, the driver of the Chevrolet reached into his pocket and handed the keys to Papo, who trailed back thoughtfully.

"My frien', he thinks you're the Man," he said.

"Pa' Carajo!" Levine made to go after him, then abandoned the idea with a gesture of contempt. "You just ain't smart, man. If I was the Man, you already be busted. So do it or don'. Jus' stop wastin' my time."

Papo hesitated, shaking his head doubtfully, then set off toward the car. "If he is the Man," he told Pete, "I'll fuckin' kill you."

He looked back over his shoulder, and his friend, still standing in the doorway, shook his head with heavy disapproval. Now distinctly worried, Papo slowed down again.

"He says we shouldn't do business with you."

"Well, I don' wanna do business with him," Levine retorted. "If it's his piece, you can tell him to shove it up his ass."

"No, no, it's my piece." Stopping short of the car, he turned to face them. "And I don' want all you guys standing around the fuckin' trunk when I open it. I'll give the stuff to your boy here." He nodded at Ray Velez. "But first I wanna see the money."

Levine scowled and reached in his pocket. Licking his thumb, he counted off $125 from the government's roll and gave it to Velez. Then he strolled back across the street to wait in his car, and Pete drifted away to the corner.

With a last look around, Papo unlocked the trunk and rummaged inside. First, he handed up a large pistol, which Velez stuffed hastily into his belt under his T-shirt. Then he removed the brown paper bag, and in full view of Levine shook out five small packets, which he gave to Velez in exchange for the money.

Hurrying over to Levine's car, Velez handed the evidence in through the window and went back to pay Pete his $20. With the smoothness of regular practice, Levine then picked Velez up on the corner, the car still rolling, and the two drove off to 120 Church Street to lodge the gun and the dope in the ATF evidence locker . . .

"And that was pretty typical of the way I worked Velez," he said, bringing them back to the Quantico classroom. "We'd do four or five of those on a good day, sometimes more. Working undercover, you soon learn to be an aggressive conversationalist. Doing somebody is like a seduction—and I got to be pretty good at that, too."

The agents all laughed, and even harder when somebody asked if he gave lessons in that as well.

"You're getting one now, man," Levine said amiably, although it always disturbed him when they took what he had to say too lightly. "See, there's a flow to it. Push too hard and it's over. Relax too soon and it's over. Give her a chance to think and you give her inhibitions a chance as well.

"Same thing in fishing. You've got to keep a certain tension on the line while you're playing a fish. If there's a slump in the conversation and the line goes slack, chances are you lost him. Or her. You can tell from the eyes. Always watch the eyes.

"Anyway, we test-fire the gun, and it's in working order. BNDD tests the five nickel bags, and they check out as heroin. Okay. So now I go to Eastern District to get warrants for Papo and his friends, and away we go with a bunch of guys to take 'em off. Two cars. This is

the routine part. Only all of a sudden, it's
not so routine anymore . . ."

He took Special Investigator Sammy York with him in the Mustang because, once again, Sammy's was the only black face available. As in the Archie Dent case, alarm bells would have sounded all over the Williamsburg section with a white agent in the car. For the same reason, the two backup cars had to hang back out of sight several blocks away, keeping in touch with events by radio. (As an unlooked-for honor, one of them was manned by Area Supervisor Steve Dutch* and Levine's supervisor, James Collington.)

Around three-thirty that afternoon, October 9, Levine and York spotted Papo hanging out on the corner of Tompkins and Park avenues, Brooklyn, with a group of blacks and Puerto Ricans, whose purposes were not entirely social. Almost at the same moment, Papo caught sight of Levine, who pulled up just short of the corner and waved him over to the car.

With no hint of alarm, Papo took a few steps toward them, and Levine smiled. This was one of the rewards, watching a defendant's face as he realized how completely he had been destroyed. It was the undercover equivalent of a standing ovation. But what Levine did *not* know then was that Sammy York, the sick man riding beside him, bore a strong resemblance to a black detective who worked in the 90th Precinct. As soon as Papo saw him clearly, he stopped dead. He had a leather jacket folded over his forearm, concealing his right hand, and a fistful of money crumpled up in his left.

"Hey, Papo," Levine called out encouragingly. "Come over here, man. I wanna talk to you."

"Yeah, yeah. Just wait a second, man. I got some business to take care of."

He turned, as if to go back to his companions, but instead started to run down Tompkins Avenue like a groundhog making for his hole. Cursing violently, Levine and York struggled out of the car and set off in pursuit.

York ran twenty feet and stopped, clutching his side, but Levine, always dauntingly fit, was enjoying the exercise. Loping along, gun drawn, getting closer with every stride, he yelled out three or four times, "Halt! I'm a federal officer. You're under arrest." But Papo

* Not his real name.

had no intention of halting, even with Levine breathing down his neck. At the corner of Ellery Street, he paused long enough to fling his jacket at Levine's legs and widened the gap to twenty or thirty yards again before his pursuer recovered his rhythm. Laughing with delight, Levine accelerated, running him down like a dog. Though vaguely aware of others behind him, he paid no attention, assuming York had used his portable to call in the backup.

Some sixty yards down the street, with Levine again at his heels, Papo suddenly dived for a narrow hole in the wire-mesh fence to his right, and wriggled through. Eluding Levine's despairing lunge, he slid down feet first into the schoolyard on the other side, having obviously been making for this spot from the moment he started to run. As Levine clutched at the wire, chest heaving, sweat running into his eyes, his quarry jogged nonchalantly across the yard, laughing at him over his shoulder.

Holstering his gun, Levine turned—to find what looked like half of black and Puerto Rican Brooklyn grouped around him in a silent semicircle.

The surge of adrenaline wiped his slate clean. There was no sign of York or his backup, and no sense in going for his gun until he had to. It was a tough neighborhood. Some of these guys could be carrying a piece, and most would have a blade. Nor was there a lot of point in showing them his badge or invoking the protection of the Constitution. If he was going to get out of this, he would have to be quick.

"Hey, whatchoo chasin' that man fo'?" asked the boldest of them. He was a black guy, about Levine's size, and hardly out of breath.

"Yeah," said some of the others, edging closer. "Whatchoo wan' with him? Why you chase him like that?"

"To bust his mother-fuckin' ass," Levine snarled, and to his considerable relief, Steve Dutch's car turned the corner and rolled slowly up toward them.

Still calm, he strode forward so confidently that those in front moved aside, unwilling to stand their ground and raise the stakes so soon. If he could just keep going, Levine figured he would reach the curb to coincide with the arrival of the car. There could be a tricky moment when he turned to climb into the back, but there was probably time to get away with it while they digested the change in the odds.

As he sidled around the car, and the crowd closed in, growing abusive, he saw Dutch look up at him through the window, sightless with panic, and punch the button to lock the door.

"Hey," Levine protested. He took a few quick steps to chase off some who had come too close, and returned to bang on the window. "Open the goddamn door."

But it was obvious that Dutch could neither see nor hear him. He could see only the faces of the crowd, which now had the scent of blood. The second backup car turned the corner.

"What the fuck's the matter with you?" Levine shouted. "Open the fucking door." When still nothing happened, he turned to face the mob as it edged in.

"You see what he did?" he demanded, in furious street Spanish, as though looking for sympathy. "That's my *boss*. He sees what's happening here, and what does he do? He locks the fucking door. Would you believe that sonofabitch?"

Bemused by the fact that he now seemed to be one of them, and on *their* side, the crowd hesitated—and the second car moved up fast, its driver recognizing trouble.

"Who the fuck needs you?" Levine shouted at Dutch, still in Spanish. "Just get the fuck outa here."

This dismissive gesture brought him conveniently close to the second car, which had pulled up behind Dutch's. Motioning to the four men inside to stay where they were, he dragged open the rear door and paused long enough before climbing inside to bestow on the crowd a dazzling smile.

As they drove away, the guy who had challenged him first shook his head and laughed.

Levine shook his head as the class murmured appreciatively. "Any agent of mine who pulled a stunt like that would get his fool ass kicked around the office, so don't do like I did, just do like I tell you.

"I got out of it because I knew I could die but it didn't worry me. You know what I'm saying? I'm no more anxious to die than the next man. If you go undercover, you've got to be ready for anything. One moment everything's cool, everything's routine, then, boom! You're alone and running your ass off on a strange street, blood thumping in your ears, eyes bugging out, heart getting set to explode through your chest, and maybe bullets cracking around your head.

"That's happened to me. You got to be ready for that. But there's more. You got to *love* the idea of flirting with death. In the middle of everything, you got to *enjoy* knowing that your life depends on your ability to *outthink* the danger. To be calm. Manipulative. You understand what I'm saying? Unless the idea of death makes you feel more alive, stay out of undercover. It's not for you."

He sighed, uncertain of their response. "You ever read Carlos Castaneda? Here's a quote, 'The warrior's courage is unassailable, but more important are his will and patience'—and that's exactly true for the undercover. 'He lives every moment in full awareness of his own death . . . and in light of that awareness, all complaints, regrets and moods of sadness or melancholy are but foolish indulgences.' Am I making any sense to you guys?"

. . . The few months in which Levine ran Ray Velez in tandem with Willy Lopez came to an end one day in a junkyard at Hunts Point, in the Bronx.

Levine and Velez had been hanging out there for weeks, on and off, getting in tight with a gang of Puerto Rican stickup artists with a view to taking them off as soon as Levine was reasonably satisfied that he knew all their associates. Their boss, Tito, had even cut him in on their plan to hold up a big Spanish supermarket using automatic weapons.

Summoned to Hunts Point by a call on the undercover phone, Levine drove over with Ray Velez to make the final arrangements, and as they turned into the junkyard Willy Lopez drove out in one of his stolen cars.

"Hey," said Velez. "That mother-fucker saw us."

"Yeah? So what?"

"I don' know." Velez shrugged. "Like I tol' you, he's a treacherous little mother-fucker. If he gets jealous . . . I hope he don't do nothing, that's all."

"Do? What *can* he do?"

Levine put it out of his mind. Indeed, he forgot about Lopez altogether when he discovered that the stickup was scheduled for the following day. Although he pressed him as far as he dared, Tito still would not say where. It was a big bodega, that was all. Told to meet them on Vyse Avenue just before the hit, Levine had to be satisfied with that.

Next day he drove out alone in his Mustang to keep the appointment. Unable to stake out the target bodega in advance, and unwilling to risk moving surveillance with a group as cagey as Tito's, he was relying on his wits and the portable radio under his seat to stay on top of the situation.

A few blocks short of the meeting place, as he slowed for a red light, he suddenly spotted Tito, stepping into the street to wave him down. And something told him it was no chance encounter. Tito had been waiting for him.

With a premonitory flutter of excitement, he pulled over to the curb, and Tito retreated across the sidewalk.

Levine frowned. "Hey," he called through the window. "Somethin' wrong? What's happenin', man?"

Tito motioned with his head toward a doorway, as though to speak with him in private. Levine pulled at his ear, listening to a still inner voice that said, No, no, *no*. He stepped out onto the sidewalk, and the voice exploded in a soundless scream. Apprehension socked him in the gut. He ducked back into the car without a word and drove away.

Next morning Levine sent Velez to Hunts Point to find out what had gone wrong.

"Nothing," he reported upon his return. "They don' trust you, that's all. Or me neither. So if it's okay with you, I don' wanna go there no more."

Levine shrugged. Such things happened. It was a waste, after all the time and effort they had put in, but there was no shortage of gun-dealing dope traffickers. Still unable to account for his spasm of fright on Vyse Avenue, he turned the case over to the police department and set off with Velez for another day's garbage collection. Business as usual.

Two weeks later, as he was tidying his desk, he came across a routine circular from the office of the Bronx District Attorney. It described an unnamed undercover cop whom the DA was anxious to talk to, and whom Levine recognized at once as himself. When he called in, he learned that Tito had been arrested and on deciding to cooperate, had told investigators about "some cop" (answering to Levine's description) who had managed to penetrate his group. When they found out, the group had decided to blow him away. Tito had called the guy over for a meet, and stopped him on Vyse Avenue, right opposite a building where one of his people was waiting on the roof with a rifle. But before his man could get off a shot, the cop had climbed back in his car and driven off . . .

". . . Dumb, dumb, dumb. Dumb to go after those guys alone. Dumb to let an informer run around loose when you know he's telling everybody you're the Man. Dumb to think an informer can be your friend. Anybody that dumb *deserves* to get wasted. But there was nobody around in those days to tell me what *I'm* telling *you*. I just got lucky. That little voice spoke up, and Levine lived to make an asshole of himself another day."

"What about Lopez?" the FBI agent in front asked helpfully.

"Yeah. Now I had another mission in life. . . ."

To smoke him out, Levine sent Velez up to the Bronx to find where Lopez hid his stolen cars. Protected by the Bronx police sergeant for whom he informed against other car thieves, Lopez worked the parking lots at Kennedy, La Guardia and Newark airports with a suitcase full of ignition keys. Once he had identified the make and model he needed to fill an order, preferably with out-of-state license plates, he would go through his keys until he found one to fit and then simply drive the car away, more often than not finding the parking ticket tucked in the sun visor.

Velez discovered that Lopez kept his cars on Jennings Street, and that same night he and Levine went up to see what there was in the inventory. Armed with the list, Levine then called Special Agent Jeremiah Smith, of the FBI's Stolen Car Squad, who sent a team to dust the vehicles for prints. When these matched the specimens with Lopez's rap sheet, Smith applied for a warrant and

Levine went home feeling better. But he had reckoned without the Bronx police sergeant. To protect himself as much as his informer, the sergeant promised the FBI to bring Lopez in on the federal charge, and when he did so got him out again, vouching for his subsequent appearance in court.

When Levine heard, he drove up to the Bronx in a fury to set the sergeant straight.

"You can't *do* that," he raged. "That little mother-fucker tried to get me killed."

"Bullshit," said the sergeant. "He wouldn't hurt pussy. And you just fucked up my best informer."

"Yeah? Well, if I see him I'll *kill* him."

The other smiled. "Well, if I see him I'll *tell* him."

It came as no surprise to either of them when Lopez failed to appear for his hearing. Nor was he to be found on Jennings Street or at his last known private address.

Teamed up now with a young Puerto Rican agent named Ray Martinez, one of the first to be hired by ATF, Levine scoured the Bronx from end to end for two months. And when Martinez complained mildly about the hours they were spending on the search to no apparent purpose, Levine explained that it was like hunting woodchuck. Lopez had holes all over the place, he and his wife and six kids. Using a different car every day, they could move in or out of a building in around forty seconds, all of them running with cartons.

"Human beings don't live like that," he would say. "But Lopez does, because he knows I'm after him."

One day he got a tip that Lopez was moving into a tenement building on Third Avenue, and immediately dropped everything to stake out the block, stationing Martinez in a car at one end and himself in a second car at the other. Sure enough, after about an hour's wait, a typical Lopez pimp's model Buick in crushed strawberry drove cautiously onto the block and pulled up outside the building. Mrs. Lopez got out at once and ran across the sidewalk with a carton. After that, nothing happened for several seconds but both Levine and Martinez could see another little head in the car. Then Lopez himself got out with a carton and started walking nonchalantly toward the building.

"That's *him,*" Martinez shouted over the radio.

"You're *right,*" agreed Levine, exultant. "Let's *get* him."

Starting their cars, they converged on Lopez sedately, making no sudden moves that might frighten him, but Levine could see from the set of his head and the controlled fear in his walk that he had spotted them.

"Let's go, let's *go!*" he yelled. "He's *made* us."

Following his lead, Martinez drove straight up on the sidewalk as Lopez reached the door. Getting out of their cars almost together, the two agents pounded into the hallway after him, with Martinez slightly in the lead. He was therefore the first to trip over the carton that Lopez had dumped just inside. Moving too fast to avoid a collision, Levine fell across his partner and slammed his right knee against the tiled floor, but in the lust for blood, he hardly noticed it. Picking himself up, he sprang at the stairs, closely followed by Martinez, and hurled himself triumphantly through an open door on the second-floor landing.

Confident they had Lopez trapped, both agents charged through the apartment, through rooms full of screaming people, and ended up in the back bedroom. The window was wide open at the bottom, and there below them, running away across the yard like a gopher, was Lopez. He had jumped about thirty feet onto a mountain of garbage.

Pounding the windowsill with his fists, in agony now that he had time to think about his knee, yet half-admiring Lopez's grasp of Bronx topography, Levine found himself screaming impotently, "I'm gonna get you, you mother-fucker. Just you wait. I'll get you, don't you worry. . . ."

". . . And *did* you?" asked the studious agent.

"Yeah, but I'm getting a long way off the point here," he said. "I'm gonna talk about informers later. I only told you that story because, like I said, I did a dumb thing and nearly got myself killed. It's an unforgiving game we're talking about. I don't care how good you are, or how much you trust your boss and your backup crew, there's always something you gotta deal with off the top of your head."

Patrolman Michael Paolillo found out how capricious death can be while waiting his turn to be served in a gunsmith's store at 3356

White Plains Road, in the Bronx. The customer ahead of him was a tall, slim black man, aged about twenty-five, with a brown-tinted Afro and a black T-shirt, who wanted the grips fixed on a .25 caliber automatic pistol. When the gunsmith asked him for identification, he pretended to fumble through his pockets, then snatched back the gun and ran out of the store.

Though off-duty, Patrolman Paolillo immediately gave chase, and that was the last time anybody saw him alive, except for his murderer. He was found dead shortly afterwards in the hallway of a nearby apartment house with seventeen stab wounds in his chest. His gun had been fired, and the evidence suggested that he might have wounded his assailant in the left arm. Questioned afterwards, the gunsmith also recalled seeing a pronounced scar on the suspect's right arm.

Around this time Levine was buying guns and heroin from Velton Ellis, a tall, slim black man, aged about twenty-five, with a tinted Afro and scarred right forearm, who lived in the South Ozone Park section of Queens. Some weeks earlier an informer had introduced Levine as a member of the Young Lords, the Puerto Rican revolutionary party, and this had pleased Ellis, who bragged of supplying handguns, shotguns, rifles and silenced weapons to the Black Panthers.

Looking into the truth of this claim, Levine bought a variety of firearms, often three or four at a time, and as a serious buyer, was eventually allowed out to the house to choose what he wanted from the racks in Ellis's basement. Around that time Levine's informant reported that Ellis had bragged about "icing a cop," and when Levine himself later steered a conversation with Ellis in that direction Ellis admitted taking part in a recent shoot-out with cops before abruptly changing the subject.

Back at the office, Levine turned up a NYPD circular about the murder of Patrolman Paolillo. The sketch and description of the suspected killer looked and sounded a lot like Velton Ellis, aka "Youngblood." As the visit to the gunsmith also fitted Ellis's M.O. —he was known to burglarize gunstores, and could have been "casing" the place—Levine took the circular to his supervisor, Nick Angel, and together they went to Anthony V. Lombardino, the Assistant U.S. Attorney in charge of the Criminal Division of Eastern District, New York, for arrest and search warrants.

"Hey," said Lombardino, lighting up like the Fourth of July. "A cop killer? This is *major.*"

Working for ATF in Brooklyn, Levine had already seen enough of Lombardino. Never a great admirer of ambitious attorneys stopping over in government service on their way to more lucrative positions in private practice, he had a particular aversion to prosecutors who liked to play cop. When the FBI eventually refused to indulge him Lombardino had transferred his affections to Brooklyn's ATF agents, and made them "his boys," deriving particular pleasure from busting after-hours joints. Many times Levine went on raids with Lombardino at the head of the group, carrying a gun, but that was nothing compared with the headline-grabbing potential of a cop killer's arrest, and Lombardino took charge of the case immediately.

To plan the raid, he convened a meeting with representatives of the New York Police Department, the Eastern District of New York Strike Force, the U.S. Marshal's Service and the DA's office as well as ATF. It was already clear that General Lombardino would be in command of a force about sixty or seventy strong, and as generals do, he outlined his plan of attack before inviting questions.

"As soon as Levine gets through the fucking door, as soon as we know he's inside, then that's when we hit."

"No, no, Tony," Levine said politely. "Not right away. Not with me inside. You could start a fucking war. When I walk in there I don't know how many guys I'm gonna find. There may be just Ellis. There may be ten people—and they got wall-to-wall guns in there. If he's a cop killer, he'll use 'em. What's he got to lose? No, you gotta give me time to get in there and then get out again so we know what we're up against."

Annoyed that a mere private should meddle with strategy, Lombardino was still more irritated when the cops around the table seemed inclined to agree.

"No, I wanna execute the warrant with *you* inside and the *guy* inside."

"Why? I don't understand."

"Legally, it's better," he snapped.

"Look," Levine said reasonably, "what's the difference if I go inside, buy six or seven guns and get him to help me carry them out to the car? He'll do it. I've seen him. Fucking guy sells his guns right out in the open like he's got a license. So let me make the buy, get him to help me, and you take him off on the street with his arms full. The guns are not loaded. No problem."

"Makes sense, Tony," said his right-hand man, Bill Gallinaro.

"I think so." Levine got in quickly. "And take me off as well."

"What the hell for?" Lombardino demanded, transferring his glare of disapproval from Gallinaro. "What's the point of that?"

"Put me in jail with the guy and we'll see. I'll say to him, 'Hey, they say ju keel a cop, meng. I no wanna get involve in da' shit'— and we'll see what he says."

"Yeah, well. Okay. But it's still better legally if we execute the warrants with everybody inside."

They argued it back and forth for an hour and finally agreed to do it Levine's way. The arrest would go down with him and Ellis on the street, and the signal for the hit would be when Levine took off his beret. With that, the raid was set for the following Wednesday, and the meeting broke up. Having won his point, Levine left the logistics to the others. Between them, they shared enough expertise to mount a D-day landing, although his previous experience in combined operations, with five or six agencies vying for the bodies, had not been encouraging.

On Wednesday afternoon, having made sure, via the radio, that everybody was in position, Levine drove up and parked a few yards from Ellis's door. As he got out of his "new" car, a 1967 Plymouth Fury bearing all the evidence of a hard life, he took a good look around but saw no sign of surveillance, which, on the whole, was encouraging.

Velton Ellis himself came to the door, greeted him cordially and asked him inside. They had picked a good time, because the only other people in the house were Ellis's brother Robert and his wife, who lived there with their kids, and a man later identified as Vincent Wise, who evidently worked for Ellis. He was standing at the window of the living room, watching the street, and remained there when Ellis led Levine to the basement to choose what he wanted from the gun racks.

He took his time, as a genuine buyer would, and after half an hour had set aside a sawed-off shotgun, two pistols and four long guns.

"Okay, meng. Das it. Ju hep me carry da shit to my car, okay?"

"Sure," Ellis said easily, with never a doubt in his mind. Tucking two of the rifles under his arm, he led the way out to the street and helped him stow them in the trunk.

"Das cool, meng," said Levine. Taking off his beret, he wiped his forehead on his sleeve.

Nothing happened.

He replaced the beret, his stomach doing twists and turns.

"Okay, then," said Ellis. "You wanna beer?"

"Nah. I got t'ings to do, meng." Again he removed his beret to give his forehead another wipe. And again, nothing happened. "Lemme pay you, and I'll be on my way." He began to seethe.

They set off back to the house. Something had obviously gone wrong. If so, Plan B was for him to pay off Ellis inside and split with the guns, after which everybody would wait until Ellis next left the house before moving in to make the arrest.

He sat down in the living room to count out the money. But the roll was hardly in his hand before the guy at the window stiffened, took another hard look and screamed, "Cops!"

Not waiting long enough to show a reaction, Velton Ellis took off through the door toward the back of the house as brakes squealed outside. Frozen momentarily by the realization of what Lombardino had done, Levine stuffed the money back into his pocket and was a fraction late in following. He was not much concerned about it because he knew the backyard would be covered.

It wasn't. And Ellis was already straddling the fence.

"Hey, bro', wait for me," he yelled urgently, but Ellis wasn't waiting for anything. He was halfway across his neighbor's yard and approaching the next fence like an Olympic hurdler.

Muttering savagely to himself, Levine set out in pursuit, and immediately had to fend off the neighbor's dog, which evidently knew Ellis but objected to *him*. This proved to be true in the next yard also, when an irate Doberman came close enough to rip the leg of his pants as he cleared the fence.

At this point Levine pulled his gun from its bellyband holster. What with the dogs and Ellis's unexpected turn of speed, the gap between them was opening up, not closing. For the first time in his career, so enraged was he at Lombardino for putting him through this, he thought about shooting Ellis and maybe claiming the gun had gone accidentally. He was wanted in connection with a cop-killing, after all. And he was getting away.

He couldn't do it. Stuffing the gun back into his belt, he took the next fence just ahead of a crossbred German shepherd plunging about at the end of its chain, and landed on the other side *without* a gun. He had felt it drop out as he strained to take off.

"Hey, bro'," he panted. "Where ju fockin' goin'?"

But Ellis just kept on running and widening the gap.

Still in touch, but only just, Levine saw him break away to the left and dart down an alley. Pounding along behind him, with his knee starting to act up, Levine found himself suddenly out on the street, just as Ellis dived into another alley opposite. Brakes screeched. Lights flashed. Somebody shouted, "Stop! Police!" And the shooting started.

With bullets cracking around his head, Levine pushed on as best he could, and started to cry. Was this what he'd been saved for? To get killed by a cop? The entrance to the alley across the street looked miles away now, as though God were dragging it backwards to torture him. More people joined in the shooting. More bullets whacked and whined about him. As the tears ran down his cheeks, he kept sobbing to himself, "Oh, no. Oh Jesus, not like this . . ." Because in one more second he'd be dead.

Then he was into the blessed sanctuary of the alley, and still running. More backyards. More dogs. More fences. After a full half-mile of this, his chest hurt and his legs were almost gone when suddenly, out of nowhere, ATF Agent Kenny Coniglio appeared at his elbow.

Levine waved him on, unable to speak, and Velton Ellis turned, balked for a moment by a higher fence than the rest. Levine saw the gun in his hand and threw himself into the dirt. He was finished anyway. He watched Coniglio, on the run, fire once and miss, and Ellis drag himself over and drop down on the other side. Closing fast, Coniglio tried to jump the fence, but hit it with his front foot and fell back heavily. He didn't get up at once. A former world-class high hurdler for Villanova University, he, too, had nothing left.

Velton Ellis had gotten away.

When he recovered his breath Levine limped back to the street, now full of cars and uniformed officers standing around, smelling one another's guns so as to have witnesses, if they needed them, that they had not been fired. He declined to acknowledge Lombardino, and never spoke to him again, even refusing to recognize him when they passed by chance in the hallways of the Brooklyn federal courthouse. Next day he applied for a transfer to the Bronx ATF unit, and Nick Angel, his supervisor, made no attempt to talk him out of it. The only other agent besides Kenny Coniglio to have joined in the chase, Angel had been badly bitten by one of the backyard dogs.

But first, Levine had a score to settle. So far in his career no one had escaped him, and Velton Ellis was not about to set a precedent. When Vincent Wise was charged with conspiracy, for acting as Ellis's lookout, Levine arranged for his release in return for his help in tracking Ellis down. Then, in his customary implacable way, Levine haunted South Ozone Park and Jamaica night and day, handing out leaflets on the street with Ellis's picture (printed at his own expense), pressuring informers and leaning on Ellis's family, friends and neighbors until he was the prime topic of conversation in every bar, pool hall, and bodega in that section of Queens. "Fucking guy's *crazy*, man."

Levine generated so much heat that all kinds of people started to call in with information: some scared he would find out they knew Ellis and jump to the wrong conclusion; others just tired of Levine's churning up the neighborhood and making it tough to do business. Sooner or later he knew somebody's nerve was going to crack, and that somebody turned out to be a young man who had seen Velton Ellis going in and out of a basement apartment in South Ozone Park. He had recognized him from the photograph on the leaflet.

"Look, I know where the guy's stayin'," he told Levine, "but I don' want no trouble. If I tellya, you gotta keep me out of it."

Ellis, he said, was not only hiding out in the basement, he was also receiving visitors—among them, Vincent Wise, whom he recognized from the mugshots Levine showed him.

"The sonofabitch," said Levine, without surprise.

"He's not gonna know I turned him in, right?" His informant was beginning to realize what he had done. "Is he gonna know?"

"Fuck, no," Levine said truthfully, and put a reassuring arm around his shoulders. "Don't you worry, man. I'm gonna fix it."

He managed to rope in enough agents to man three cars, and they all drove over to Vincent Wise's house.

"Hello, Vincent," he said winningly. "This is your lucky day. You're supposed to be helping me find Velton Ellis, right?"

"Yeah, yeah. That's right, man." Wise surveyed the agents in the other cars uneasily. "I ain't heard nothing yet, but I'm gonna help you."

"Good. Then get your coat."

Blinking in bewilderment, he accompanied Levine to his car, and as they drove off, laughed uncomfortably.

"Where we goin', man?"

"I told you, man. You're gonna help me find Velton Ellis."

Levine's tone was encouraging, but as they drew steadily closer to Ellis's basement apartment and Wise began to realize where they were going, he turned gray. When they stopped a block away from the house his teeth were chattering.

Levine patted his cheek, and got out to deploy his forces. Then he motioned Wise to join him on the sidewalk, and taking his elbow, led him gently up to the door of the basement apartment.

"Now, Vincent," he said. "Ring the bell."

"Listen, I—" Wise rubbed the sweat from his eyes. "Gimme a break, man. He's gonna think *I* told you."

Levine drew his .357 Magnum. "Ring the fucking doorbell, Vincent," he said patiently.

Shoulders slumped, Wise obeyed, and Levine stepped out of range of the peephole, pointing a silent warning. They heard footsteps approach the door and stop—Wise still held immobile by that pointing finger. Then chains rattled and locks clacked, and Velton Ellis opened the door.

"Wha's happenin', man?" he said.

"You wha's happenin', man," cooed Levine, sticking the gun in his ear.

Ellis ultimately pled guilty to federal gun charges. There was insufficient proof to tie him to the cop killing.

"Why didn't you just shoot the sonofabitch when he started to run?" asked an FBI agent at the back, and several others snickered.

"Well, I thought about it." Levine could still feel the pressure of his finger on the trigger as he eyed the base of Ellis's spine. "And I've thought about it a lot since then, because after that I had even better reasons to shoot, and I still didn't. I don't know. I guess the answer is that having to kill people kind of spoils the effect. It's like I was trying to tell you this morning: working undercover is so full of danger and unexpected twists that if you *can* do it without killing then it's more satisfying. It's a bigger achievement. You've mastered everything, including the presence of death. The two Treasury Special Act Awards I got for *not* killing people when I could have—and maybe *should* have—mean a lot to me. They're like Oscars."

Some of them seemed to understand. Most plainly did not, and he shrugged.

"Anyway, a lot of the time your body just seems to react without even consulting your brain. I remember working in Brooklyn once, around this time, with Murray Shaw. I'd hidden my gun and handcuffs in the trunk while I did an undercover bit, and I was just getting them out again—Murray and the stool were already in the car—when I heard a woman scream. Like a wounded animal. She must have seen her death coming because as I looked up I saw a car plow into her. It was like something in a dream. She was a big, fat woman, and her body came hurtling up in the air toward me like a huge, floppy rag doll. The DA told me later she 'flew' a measured eighty-six feet. And the car's not stopping. It's accelerating up the block.

"And there I am in the middle of the street, aiming my gun at the driver. I don't know how I got there. I swear to God, there wasn't a thought in my head. It was like some kind of trance. The car's coming at me. I'm aiming and squeezing, and everything's in slow motion. I can see the driver's face above my front sight. He's got chinky little eyes. I can see the hammer back on my gun and I'm waiting for it to fall. Then the car swerves up onto the sidewalk and smashes into a garage door.

"Next thing I know, Murray's screaming at me and the stool's split. They both think I'm crazy, and now my brain's back in charge I can't say for sure they were wrong. Anyway, four guys stumble out of the wreck, drunk on their ass, and we hold 'em at gunpoint until the cops show up. By then, a big crowd is gathering and I don't want to blow my cover, so I point out the guy who was driving and leave 'em to it.

"Around four in the morning I got a call from some assistant DA out in Brooklyn. The woman was a mother of four, and he wants to charge the driver with vehicular homicide, only the cop can't remember which guy I'd pointed out, and all four deny driving the car. Well, the face of that sonofabitch above my gunsight was so etched in my brain that I picked him right out of a holding cell with about fifty people in it, and the bastard got seven years. But four kids had lost their mother, so maybe I *should* have killed him. I don't know. After all these years I've only got to close my eyes and there he is . . ."

Levine shook himself.

"A lot of things like that kept happening to me around that time. I'm not especially religious, but it felt like I was being tested—you ever get that feeling? Like the night I was out with Ray Boylan and we stopped to eat at Katz's Delicatessen on Houston and Ludlow. In those years they had a side door onto Ludlow Street, and I'd just bitten into a huge pastrami sandwich when we hear screaming and yelling and running feet outside.

"So out I go, with my mouth full of pastrami, just in time to see this guy smash another guy over the head with an axe. A squad car whizzes up, with its dome light spinning, but the guy ducks and it goes right by him. Next thing I know he's running full tilt toward Ray and me and my gun is out.

"Now what the hell is *this?* I aim square at the center of his white shirt. I'm screaming at him to stop, spraying half the street with pastrami and rye bread, but he keeps on coming. People told me afterwards he had the axe raised over his head like fucking Lizzie Borden. Now I'm on automatic, practicing breath control, sight picture and trigger squeeze, and all of a sudden he's right there, in the lights of the store, and I'm expecting the gun to go off.

"That's when he froze. A yard away. And dropped the axe.

"I don't think the margin between him and death was even measurable, but the crowd loved it. Out comes the owner of Katz's. 'Greatest thing I ever saw in my life,' he says. 'From now on, you guys eat here for free. Anytime you want.' That lasted about a week."

Everybody laughed, including the guy at the back, but he was shaking his head.

"Too close, man," he said. "You got away with it that time, but why take the chance?"

Levine scratched his head. How *did* you explain to the percentage-playing civil servant with a pension in his sights that this was *art?*

FOUR

". . . the only Jewish Nazi in America."

"Okay," Levine said, starting out briskly after the break. "We talked about the risks and what can go wrong. Now let's take a look at what undercover's all about, and how to do it right. To stop me from rambling off again, I got a few slides to show you."

He nodded at the FBI operator, who put the first one up on the screen.

"Here we go." Levine rapidly read off the text. 'Definition. Undercover work is an investigative process in which disguises and pretexts are used to gain the confidence of criminal suspects for the purpose of determining the nature and extent of any criminal activities they may be contemplating or perpetrating.' "

He looked at them over his shoulder. "Any problems with that? Okay. Let's have number two.

" 'Purposes of undercover work. One. To determine if a crime is being planned or committed.' Also to check up on informers. You gotta know if what they're telling you is reliable, exaggerated or just bullshit.

" 'Two. To identify all persons involved.' That means not just the active participants, but also the banker, the chemist, the weapons and equipment suppliers—everybody.

" 'Three. To obtain evidence for court.' All kinds. Not just the obvious physical evidence, like when you make a buy or get a sample, but anything else you can get hold of. Like guns or counterfeit or stolen property. Or you may go in wired with a Kel set or Nagra to make recordings. And then there's documentary evidence, like phone numbers, addresses, notebook entries and buying or selling instructions.

"Stop me if you got any questions. 'Four. To locate contraband or stolen property.' In dope deals, that generally means finding the stash, or the mill where they do their cutting and bagging.

" 'Five. To determine a suitable time to execute an arrest or search warrant.' Very important. We just got through talking about that. The best time is obviously when you're gonna pull in the most contraband and the most defendants, but you also gotta think of the *safest* time. Like when they're unarmed or off their guard.

" 'Six. To collect intelligence on drug-trafficking methods of operation.' How many people in the group? What territory do they cover? Where do they get the stuff, and how do they distribute it?

" 'Seven. To develop confidential informants.' That's the key to the whole thing. Mostly, you do it by arresting the guy and flipping him. Other times, if you're smart enough, you can run him as an unwitting informer, and that's great because then he's never gonna do a Willy Lopez on you. And then you got the guys who do it for money and all kinds of other reasons. We'll look at them later.

" 'Eight. To penetrate major trafficking organizations and identify and neutralize the highest echelon of traffickers.' Okay. There you got my mission in life. Who are the top people? How am I gonna take 'em off? That's what it's all about."

He twisted around, and saw most of them taking notes. Now they were happy. Somebody was telling them how to succeed, and they were writing down the recipe.

"Right." He waited until they had all finished. "Let's have the next one. 'General qualifications: Intelligence. Self-confidence. Courage. Good judgment. Mental alertness. Initiative. Resourcefulness.' Hands up anybody who doesn't have all of those."

No hands went up, and they laughed.

"Okay," he said. "That's good. Those guys who really *do* have all these qualities are well equipped for the job. And those who are lying and cheating, well—they're even *better* equipped for the job. See, working undercover is the ultimate form of seduction. Even the terminology is sexual. 'I *did* the guy,' you'll hear an undercover say. First the winning of confidence. Then the penetration. But in this seduction it's his *life* you're after. It's the kind of seduction that *always* ends in betrayal. And up close. Watching it in his eyes. As time goes by, you tend to forget the faces of people you send to rot in jail, but they'll never forget *yours*. In every betrayal both sides have a price to pay."

Some of the older agents seemed to know what he was talking about.

"All right, back on track. Anybody got any

questions before we get on to planning an operation?"

"Yeah," someone called out, "what about Willy Lopez?"

Levine sighed. Then he looked at his watch. "You guys wanna hear this?"

There was a generous murmur of assent.

"Okay. I'll make it fast. Willy's last seen winning the downhill garbage mountain race. Now two months go by, and we get another tip. He's moving his family into a basement on Fulton Avenue, in the Bronx. So right away, me and Ray Martinez drop everything and set up the same way as before. Two cars, one each end of the block. And sure enough, there he is. Willy comes up from the basement, sniffs the air and ducks back in again.

" 'That's him, that's him.'

" 'You sure?' says Ray—we're using our portables.

" 'Oh, man. I see that little ferret in my dreams. Next time he comes up for air, let's grab his ass.'

"And we did. Up pops the head. It swivels around. Now he's up on the sidewalk, twitching. Now he crosses to his car, and we *go*. Wham-bam! Up against the car. Cuffs on. I finally *got* him.

" 'Hey, listen, you guys,' he says. 'I talk to the FBI. I work for them now. They know I'm here. They know.'

" 'Yeah, yeah. Let's go, Willy.'

" 'No, *really*,' he says. 'Call 'em up. Call 'em up. I tell you, I talk to the FBI. Please call 'em up.'

"So I look at Martinez, who shrugs. I know it's not likely, but maybe the little weasel's telling the truth. And what harm can it do? This time I got him handcuffed.

"So we drag him into the basement, and there's got to be twenty or thirty people down there, all screaming. Mothers with children. Dogs barking. Pandemonium. And I'm yelling at him, 'You mother-fucker. You almost got me killed.' 'Oh, no, no, no,' he says, but his face is tellin' me, yeah, yeah, yeah. 'Not me. Not me. It was Ray. Ray Velez set you up. Ray's the one that nearly got you killed.'

"Now I know for *sure* it was him, and I take him by the throat.

" 'No, no, no,' he says. 'You call the FBI. You'll see. They'll tell you. Just lemme put on my clothes. I'll go there with you.'

"So I put him down and tell Ray to go with him while I make the call. And when finally I get through to somebody who knows about stolen cars, the guy tells me, no. Willy Lopez is *not* working for 'em. What's more, he didn't show up for his hearing.

" 'Great,' I tell him. 'I got the little mother-fucker right here.'

" 'Great,' he says. 'I'll call the U.S. Attorney's office.'

"Fine. I hang up, go out, and there's Ray standing in the hall by himself.

" 'Where is he?'

" 'He's in there,' he says. 'In the john. Changing his clothes.'

" '*What?*'

" 'No, it's okay. He can't get out.'

Levine clutched at his brow, and staggered back dramatically.

"Didn't even have to look. I *knew*. And sure enough, there was a tiny little window that only a tiny little rat could get through. And outside was an airshaft with a sheer wall that only a fucking beetle could have climbed up. And no Willy. Willy Lopez was gone again, and I didn't talk to Ray for a week."

He was working them now like a stand-up comic.

"Fucking guy *deserved* to beat the rap," someone said.

"Not in *my* book. A few weeks later the little scumbag's luck ran out. He wound up doing time, and I didn't even think of him again for fifteen years. Then a guy working for me comes in with a stool who's talking about a death hole full of bodies out in Jersey—and you guessed it, it's Willy." Levine smiled at them wryly. "Too soon to tell you the end of that one, but if you're missing a late-model Merc with out-of-state tags, ask for Willy."

He consulted his notes. "O-kay . . ."

"You always do spicks?" asked a new voice. "Like *me*," he added, seeing he had everybody's attention.

Levine spotted him on the aisle, a neat young man in a dark suit and glasses, with an attaché case across his knees.

"Man, I'll do anyone I can get over on." He lavished a lot of candlepower on his smile.

"No, I mean as a cover. You always José or Miguel?"

"Ah. Okay. I speak Spanish so I get to do a lot of Spanish-speaking people, the dope business being the way it is. But I'll do anybody they aim me at. How about this for Italian?"

He strutted up and down a few paces, straining the seams of his suit. "Meet Mike Pagano . . ."

. . . the only Jewish Nazi in America.

An ATF informer had reported that the National Renaissance Party was planning to send an armed squad to Washington to disrupt a peace rally outside the Pentagon, and to Levine's mind the only sure way to check this out was to put on the lightning-bolt armband as one of the boys. Six weeks before the planned demonstration, the informer took him along to the regular weekly meeting of the party's section leaders at 10 West 90th Street, and introduced him to James Madole, who had taken over as führer of America's ultra-right after the death of George Lincoln Rockwell.

Impressed by the quality of his new recruit, Madole invited Mike Pagano to join the party's Security Echelon, the uniformed branch responsible for his personal protection, the distribution of hate literature on the streets, and "special assignments" like the mission to Washington. Pagano, naturally, accepted at once, volunteering in the same breath to drive one of the two station wagons that the party planned to rent to carry its squad to the capital. Beaming with approval, Madole then assigned him to John Ryan, the blue-eyed, fair-haired Irish "Aryan" in charge of that section, and went on to outline his plans for breaking up the rally.

On the day, they would meet at his apartment and leave in twos and threes, starting around 4:00 A.M. Uniforms would be worn, but only the pants until they reached New Jersey. To avoid any problems on the road, banners, armbands and leaflets would be issued upon their arrival in Washington and returned to him there before they left. Before the rally, there would also be a mass meeting in Alexandria, Virginia, to coordinate tactics with the American Nazi Party, the White Party, the Ku Klux Klan, the Minutemen and other action groups.

Madole said nothing about guns, but in the general discussion that followed, Gary Smith, another of his section leaders, told Pagano that "the day is going to come when these niggers see our guns come out." (Madole had introduced Smith as Rockwell's former bodyguard in the American Nazi Party.) When the meeting broke up, several members remained behind after Pagano left, including his informer, who told him later that Ryan had said he would definitely be carrying a gun to Washington.

At the next weekly meeting, Pagano foamed at the mouth with the best of them. While considering the text of a new leaflet for street distribution, the members got into a general discussion about the best method for disposing of Jews after they took over the country. As gas chambers had been brought into disrepute, somebody suggested the electric chair.

"Naw," said Pagano. "That's no good. They'll die too fast, and there ain't enough chairs anyway. Why don't we just load 'em onto those mothballed ships they got in the Hudson, tow 'em out to sea and sink 'em? So like then we could sit around barbecuing and drinking beer, listening to 'em scream and watching the boats sink for fucking days . . ."

They turned this over in their minds. "You know something?" Ryan said. "He's *right*."

Having agreed on Levine's final solution, the meeting turned to the proposed leaflet and eventually settled on the headline, "JEWS ARE NIGGERS TURNED INSIDE OUT." The text below warned how dangerous Jews were to white Christian America because you couldn't always tell them by sight. Another passage that made Levine smile was to the effect that Jews often changed their names to fool people. "But turn a Jew inside out," the message ended, "and his insides are as black as any nigger's."

Madole and his section leaders were so pleased with Pagano that they asked him to join the Security Echelon when it started distributing this new material on the street the following Saturday afternoon. Puffed up with pride at this unexpected honor, he agreed at once, though reminding them that he had yet to be formally inducted into the party. The ceremony, as he knew from his informer, involved dressing up in the NRP's black and gray uniform and, in front of the full membership, kneeling before a candle-lit altar decked out with incense burners and statues of Nordic gods to swear an oath of unconditional obedience to the party and its National Socialist ideals.

This seemed the best way to identify, and possibly photograph, everybody associated with the NRP before the Washington rally, but Madole was noncommittal, seeming to suggest that Pagano should first prove himself in action. And since all the hints and overheard snatches of conversation tended to confirm his informer's reports that the NRP was massing guns, Pagano found himself on the corner of 86th Street and Third Avenue two days later, handing out copies of "JEWS ARE NIGGERS TURNED INSIDE OUT" under the watchful eyes of Section Leaders John Ryan, James ("The Pope is a Jew") Wagner and Louis Mostacchio.

He was not enjoying it much.

"Go mother-fuck yourself," snarled a black man, slapping the leaflet out of his hand as he continued on his way to the corner.

"Hey, wait a minute," said Pagano, trailing after him. *"Read* it. The Jews are exploiting you, too." People on the sidewalk stepped around him elaborately. "Don't you wanna know about that?"

The black man's middle finger went up in the air as he turned south on Third, and Pagano nodded. The guy had balls. Most people either took the leaflet and laughed nervously or crossed the street to avoid him.

"Hey," he shouted. "Don't run away. We only wanna send you back to Africa. We gonna send the fuckin' Jews to the ovens."

He smiled wolfishly at a middle-aged couple, probably Jewish, who happened to be passing, and they actually smiled back.

He kept it up for an hour, and nobody really gave him any trouble. A few people crumpled up the leaflets and threw them away as soon as they were safely past him, but that was all. It was now easier to understand how the Nazi Party had taken over in Germany. Then, with the last few leaflets in his hand, the worst happened, the thing he'd been dreading all afternoon.

He had seen the kid approaching. He was short, dark, curly-haired and carrying an armful of books. If he had noticed it earlier, he would have chosen that moment to harass someone else or cross the street to ask for more leaflets, but it was only when the kid drew level with him that he saw he was wearing a yarmulke on the back of his head. And Section Leader Ryan had seen it, too.

"Oh, *shit,*" he said, as he handed the kid a leaflet. He couldn't have been more than seventeen or eighteen.

The kid accepted it automatically, but faltered and stopped as he took in the headline. Then he started to tremble, and his books dropped on the sidewalk. His eyes swimming with outrage and fright, he forced himself to retrace his steps, crumpling the leaflet in his fist. Unable to speak, he tried to spit in Pagano's face, but was so unused even to the idea of such a thing that most of the spittle ran down his own chin.

Section Leader Ryan was already signaling his colleagues to come across the street. Passersby were slowing down to watch. Pagano's backup was moving in closer, just in case. Pagano really had no choice.

Wiping his face with the back of his hand, he took a menacing step forward. The kid hesitated, trying to stand his ground, but began to back away before Pagano reached him. That was good, but he knew exactly what sort of turmoil was going on in the kid's mind. In the old days he had lived through many a scene like this, with himself as the victim, and learned the hard way that dignity was not worth risking your life for. As one of a dwindling band of Jews in a changing neighborhood, he had fought all comers, luckily being equipped to do it, but in the end it had been easier to let himself pass for something else. With his black hair and dark skin, it had been easier just to blend in, to be accepted as something he wasn't. In that sense, working undercover was just an extension of childhood.

He grabbed the kid by the front of his shirt and kicked his feet out from under him. It was pathetically easy, and he despised himself. The kid sprawled on the sidewalk, his face contorted with shame, and as he scrambled, blushing, to his feet, Pagano booted him hard in the ass and sent him down in a heap again, the ring of spectators moving back hurriedly out of the way. Some of them laughed.

Ryan and the others showed no sign of joining in, which was good. None of the bystanders seemed inclined to help the kid either, which was good in one sense but bad in another. All he had to worry about now was the possibility of a cop showing up.

With no thought of resistance left, the kid ran, leaving his books on the sidewalk. Pagano let him go, but caught Ryan's eye and thought better of it. He was Mike Pagano, Jew-hating psychopath. Screaming abuse, he gave chase, caught the kid with another running kick, though not hard enough to bring him down, and continued in apparently mindless pursuit until the kid fled for his life around the corner and disappeared in the throng on Third Avenue. Then he stalked back to the scene of his triumph, muttering and cursing to himself, threw off the congratulations of his party comrades, and kicked the kid's books savagely into the street.

He was *in*. He could tell by the warmth of brotherhood in which Ryan and the others enfolded him.

"Did you see how that little kike ran? Left a shit stain on the sidewalk . . ."

His backup was also pleased with his performance. It was obvious from the way they hung back when Ryan drove his gallant storm troopers up to the Bronx to celebrate their victory in his apartment.

It was several hours before they let Pagano go. They discussed weapons, agreeing that the NRP should standardize the training of recruits on the M-1 carbine. They drank a lot of beer and listened to old German 78 rpm records of Nazi rallies at Nuremberg, joining in the chorus of the *Horst Wessel* song. And they dyed several dozen uniform hats to be worn on the Washington mission.

"One way and another, it was quite an evening," Levine said. "Never saw the kid again, but my insides still hurt when I think about him."

"I hope it was worth it," somebody said distantly.

"Worth it?" Levine pulled a face. "Wasn't for me to judge. Kid didn't deserve that, but if I hadn't done it I'd have blown my cover and maybe the whole investigation. As it was, I was all set to go to Washington with those psychos in my black uniform. They had guns, and they were going to cross state lines. I was happy as a pig in shit.

"Then Washington pulled the plug. A few days before the demonstration, the chief of enforcement decided it would be bad for ATF's image if it got out in the media that one of its agents was masquerading in a Nazi uniform. No arguments. Just close the case."

Several grunted in sympathy, and Levine nodded.

"I know I keep saying you shouldn't make value judgments, but that's not to say you can't be touched. It won't take long in this job to shake your belief in everything—in God and country and the value of human life. But who knows? If I hadn't had to rough up the kid a little, maybe I would never have made the case of the smuggling rabbis."

"The *what?*" The clique of Southern agents laughed in disbelief.

"We'll get to it. What I'm trying to say is, you can't afford to get emotionally involved in a case but sometimes it's hard as hell *not* to. To go undercover and seduce people out of their lives, you've got to make them like and trust you. And it's hard to do that without finding something in them that you like, or convince yourself to like. If you don't, the act's not real, and they'll know it.

"But it's still an *act*. And it's a scummy, treacherous world you've chosen to work in. I've had to dump a pregnant woman on her ass when she tried to pull a gun on me. I've turned son against father and brother against brother, each of 'em trying to save his own skin. I've even locked up two DEA agents for selling me the names of informers—when they thought I was a Mafia guy who wanted to kill the people they named. If there's a limit on treachery I still haven't found it.

"So don't get involved any more than you have to. What happens after you've done your job is none of your business. Fuck what happens in the courts. The plea bargains. Ambitious prosecutors. Political judges. Bad verdicts. Wrong sentences. Fuck it all. It's none of your business. If there's anything you can learn from me, it's how to survive."

One virtuoso performance was quickly followed by another. Irving Pierce, ATF's Area Supervisor in Buffalo, New York, was faced with a law-enforcement problem new in his experience. Three powerful motorcycle gangs were wintering in the city and generally running it ragged with street crimes, rapes, burglaries, dope dealing and sporadic outbreaks of violence, sometimes involving guns, bombs and automatic weapons.

With no witnesses or victims willing to testify, the only answer seemed to be to get somebody in undercover. After asking around, he wrote to Jack Hollander in New York, on behalf of the Buffalo police and the Erie County Sheriff's office, asking for help from the one man in government service thought to be capable of pulling it off (and crazy enough to try).

"You know how to ride a motorcycle?" Hollander asked.

"Sure," said Levine.

"Okay. You wanna go to Buffalo? Join a motorcycle gang?"

He thought it over. For at least five seconds.

"Sure," he said.

The planning took longer. They had an opening in the shape of a five-time loser named Blackie, who faced a life sentence following his fifth felony conviction unless he agreed to cooperate. Blackie was a vice president of the Night Riders, the largest of the Buffalo gangs, whose winter lodge at 65 Oak Street was regarded by local citizens and law-enforcement officers in much the same light as a foreign embassy is seen in Washington, D.C.—as somebody's else's sovereign territory on U.S. soil.

Levine spent three full days with Blackie before deciding how to

handle the assignment. They got along fine. The vice president of
the Night Riders not only could have passed for his brother—he,
too, was big, dark and Latin-looking—but they also shared the
same background of growing up hand-to-mouth on the streets. Levine saw a lot of himself in Blackie, and could well have acquired a
comparable record for violent crime. The main difference between
them was that Blackie claimed to be the illegitimate son of Meyer
Lansky and a $100-a-trick hooker who had farmed him out at
birth.

Both agreed there was nothing to be gained from Levine's shav-
ing his head, climbing into rivet-head leathers and rolling up on a
Harley Davidson. The main traffickers were fringe members and
hangers-on who drifted in and out of the lodges and orthodox
criminal circles with the ebb and flow of supply and demand. For
the sake of flexibility, Levine decided to be one of these.

"All right," said Blackie. "I'll take you in to the club, and that's
it. That's all I can do. I'll tell 'em you're my cousin from New
York, but after that, it's up to you. You're on your own. Sink or
swim."

"That's all I need," Levine said grandly, although he was beginning to wonder. Unlike the short-term street cases he was used to,
this one made no allowance for a backup team or any cover at all,
for that matter. Once he moved in with the gang, he would be
working without a net for days, perhaps weeks at a time. If he
made a mistake, the chances were that nobody would hear about it
(or him) again. The local case agent, William Mallery, promised to
do the best he could, but there were clearly limits to the protection
he could provide while huddled in his car in the depths of a Buffalo
winter a good hundred yards from the clubhouse.

With this in mind, Levine took Blackie carefully through the
membership with a view to finding out in advance about as many
of its quirks and foibles as possible.

"It was like a guided tour through a human zoo," he remembers.
" 'This guy's a killer. That's guy's a killer. Watch out for this
fuckin' guy, he's totally crazy. That guy drops acid all the time.
This one's always stoned in the afternoon.' Talk about a rogues'
gallery of fucked-up human beings. I never in my life, before or
since, found people so totally alien to the Judeo-Christian concept
of normalcy as bikers. They're crazy. All of 'em. All the way up
the scale from eccentric to fucking berserk."

By the end of the third day's briefing, Blackie had begun to enter into the spirit of the thing. Growing to like Levine as he sensed the common ground between them, he talked about various bars he would take him to in Buffalo, and guys he would introduce him to in the other gangs, the Kingsmen and the Chosen Few. After all, it was the kind of thing you would just naturally do for your cousin when he came visiting from New York. And because he spoke Spanish and wanted to buy guns, Mike Pagano would be half-Cuban this time, and ravening after anybody with a kind word to say for Fidel Castro.

Wound up to concert pitch by all these preparations, Pagano was almost totally ignored when he at last made his debut. Having believed Blackie was in jail, the Night Riders, with their women and hangers-on, were more concerned with welcoming back their vice president than checking his cousin's credentials. By morning, Pagano was the only one still conscious in the clubhouse, and as the others struggled out of their comas of booze and drugs during the day, they accepted his presence without question. Mike Pagano was in.

Fascinated by the anarchic squalor of their communal life, he hung around for several days to get them used to him, and then, to test his acceptability as a floater like Blackie, he drifted off without a word to confer with Pierce and local enforcement officials about what he had learned so far. When he returned to the clubhouse several days later, hardly anybody seemed to realize he had been away.

That evening Blackie introduced Pagano to Joseph Anderson, better known as Castro, an introduction they had all been looking forward to in view of Pagano's fanatical hostility to the Cuban regime. In the course of several six-packs, Anderson claimed he could, if needed, supply enough handguns, long guns and auto-matic weapons to launch another Bay of Pigs, but all he had in stock right then was a sawed-off shotgun.

"Yeah?" said Pagano. It was time to start making cases. "Well, I might be interested in that. I gotta little job to do tomorrow."

They arranged to meet again the following afternoon at Kubik's Bar, around the corner on Eagle Street, and although Anderson remembered to keep the appointment, he had evidently forgotten the rest of their conversation because he again assured Pagano he could supply him with machine guns, grenades and anything else he wanted, but all he had available for the moment was a sawed-off 12-gauge shotgun, about eighteen inches long. When Pagano asked patiently if he could buy it, Anderson said he wasn't sure because Eddie Reichert of the Kingsmen was its co-owner. Then could he rent it for the night? Pagano persisted. He was willing to pay $20. Again Anderson didn't know, but he said he would ask Eddie. Pagano sighed. Dealing with bikers was really hard work.

They met again at five-thirty in the Night Riders' clubhouse. Anderson led Pagano through to the back room where his partner, Eddie Reichert, sat waiting on the pool table. After the usual exchange of fraternal grunts, and with all the solemnity of a secretary of state negotiating the sale of a Trident missile system, Anderson declared their willingness to part with the gun and its five remaining shells.

"How much?" asked Pagano.

"Sixty dollars?" Reichert suggested.

"Sold."

Reichert went out to fetch the gun and ammunition from his car. He and Anderson then vied with each other to show Pagano how it worked and the best way to carry it concealed in his clothes, advice which suggested the weapon had seen some service in their hands. Pagano thanked them gravely and drove off to Ellicott Street to lodge it in the ATF evidence vault.

The following week he bought a .45 caliber automatic pistol from one of the Chosen Few, and as the gang looked to be a promising source for weapons in quantity, arranged afterwards for a story to be planted in the Buffalo *Courier-Express* about a .45 caliber pistol lost by a suspect fleeing the scene of a robbery. This was to explain why he needed another one so soon.

As the weeks went by and Pagano came to move freely in and out of all three gang lodges, so the flow of intelligence about their activities improved. Always with money in his pocket, whenever anybody showed up with guns or drugs for sale, he would buy them, lodge the evidence with ATF, do his paperwork while supposedly visiting with his people in New York, and add the case to those already on the back burner awaiting the day when he applied for warrants.

Through frozen Bill Mallery, still sitting out in his snowbound car for up to twelve hours at a stretch, he also kept the police and county sheriff's office supplied with leads and early warnings of crimes or trouble brewing, and even managed to achieve results on a national scale. Just from listening to clubhouse gossip, he was able to pass on information that led to the closure of labs producing hallucinogenic drugs out west on Indian reservations, and nomadic bikers passing through with drugs or firearms were now being nailed in increasing numbers on the roads between Buffalo and California. But after four or five weeks, there was still nothing really *big*. The gangs were simply not very businesslike.

Conscious of having cut a sorry figure as an arms supplier, "Castro" Anderson now tried again, this time with an introduction to Wendell Corcoran and Donald Frackowiak, aka "Spick," of the Kingsmen. Running true to form, he arranged for Pagano to meet them at the Night Riders' lodge, but neither showed up.

With some fast talk about machine guns and dynamite, Castro then persuaded Pagano to attend a second meeting, and almost two hours after the appointed time, Spick telephoned to say he was waiting with Corcoran someplace else. Breathing heavily, Pagano drove over with Anderson to the Surfside Lounge on Niagara Street, where the four of them had a promising discussion about the technical specifications of the equipment Pagano needed for the job he had in mind. On the strength of this, he ordered two Thompson submachine guns at $150 each, and sat back expectantly.

Well, now they had to wait for the guy who was bringing the guns, Spick explained. But meanwhile, he had a sawed-off .22 rifle for sale, and was he interested?

Pagano sighed. Yeah. Well. Maybe . . .

Sensing a certain lack of enthusiasm, Corcoran stepped into the breach and asked Pagano if he ever dropped acid.

"Hey, man," he replied, with the air of a ballplayer asked if he ever chewed gum.

"Then you gotta try this." Corcoran fumbled in his pocket and produced a small black pill. "Go on. That's black magic. Ain't nothing else like it. You'll see. Try it."

"Yeah, I will, man. I will." This was another occupational hazard of undercover life. "But I'm flyin' already, okay? I'll save it for later."

He put the pill away carefully, and Corcoran beamed. "Be my guest, man. Right there's the best trip you ever had, I guarantee you. And I got a lot more if you wanna buy some."

"Yeah. Okay. But right now I need the guns."

The guy with the guns never showed.

Next day Anderson called Pagano at the motel where he was staying. (Whenever possible, he avoided the night at the clubhouse so as not to be drawn into the seamier side of the Night Riders' social life. This was not so much on moral grounds as to deprive defense counsel of potentially damaging ammunition when the cases came to court.) Wendell and Spick, he said, were on their way to the lodge with the tommy guns. Pagano drove over at once and waited with Anderson for several hours, but they never showed up.

"Look," he said wearily, "find out what happened. Tell Wendell I'll take a hundred of his black pills, but I won't pay more than two dollars each. And I still need the guns."

Four days passed. Then Anderson called to say that everything was at the club.

"You mean it?"

"I swear," he said. "Spick and Wendell are right here with me. You wanna talk to 'em?"

"No, no. I'll be right over."

Anderson met him at the door and led him through to the back room, where Spick and Wendell were waiting—not just for him but for the guy with the guns.

"No, listen," Pagano said warmly. "You guys are just jerkin' me off."

"No, no. He's coming," said Wendell. "No shit. Any minute. And I got your pills right here."

"Fuck your pills. I mean, I'll take 'em, but I really need those guns."

"Well, how about my sawed-off .22?" Spick suggested. "Thirty dollars?"

Pagano breathed out gustily. "Yeah. Okay . . ."

He bought the gun and the pills for $230, but the guy with the tommy guns never showed.

Then, out of the blue, he hit the jackpot.

One of the favorite haunts of the Chosen Few was the IBM Bar, where Pagano had squandered barrels of government beer soliciting guns and dope. As a result of his missionary work on behalf of the Cuban exiles, word had spread among the gang that he was up from New York with money to spend, and he now received an unexpected call in his room at the Ramada Executive Motel in Cheektowaga from Walter Posnjak, who was waiting in the lobby with his partner, Alex Koschtschuk. Though he had never spoken with them before, he knew these Chosen Few by sight as a formidable pair of thugs, and asked them to his room with a twinge of reluctance. Bill Mallery was off-duty for once, and rip-offs were not unknown among bikers.

But they were all business. "What are you lookin' for, man? What d'you wanna buy?"

"Anything I can make money with," he said. "Handguns. Carbines. Grenades. Machine guns. Anything you got I can sell in New York City to my uncles. They need all this stuff to fight Castro."

"Okay. We can do machine guns. How about dynamite?"

Pagano frowned. Without referring to the National Firearms Act and the Gun Control Act of 1968, he was not entirely certain that his brief included dynamite.

"Sure," he said. "If you got blasting caps and fuses." That surely had to fit the act's definition of an explosive device. "And if the price is right. They use a lot of that stuff to blow up buildings and cars. Things like that."

"Okay. No problem." The two exchanged a satisfied glance. "We can get you all the dynamite you want. Two dollars a stick."

"How about the caps?"

"Caps included. But fuse is extra."

"How extra?"

"A dollar a foot."

"Okay." Pagano searched their faces unsmilingly. "Only don't try to flake me, man. Don't sell me no bad stuff or phony sticks or nothing like that because these Cubans don't kid around. If the stuff is bad, first they'll kill me, and then they'll come looking for *you.*"

"Hey, Mike." Their feelings were hurt. "Don't worry about it. The stuff is fresh, okay? We get it right from the factory. Show him, Walt."

Posnjak reached into his leather jacket and produced a New York State License for Transporting Dynamite.

"See that?"

"Okay." Pagano took their word for it, as gentlemen. "When you're dealing with Cubans, you don't fuck around. You know what I mean?"

"Listen, the stuff's guaranteed. You wouldn't believe where we get if from. And if you want, we can get your people some really special shit from the Army. I mean, like it's experimental, right? *They* don't even got it yet."

"Well, I'll see." Looked like good times were just around the corner. "You bring the stuff with you?" he asked, rather hoping they had not.

"Fuck no, man. You crazy? Give us an order and we'll bring it tomorrow. As much as you want."

"Okay." He was figuring out the logistics. "This is what I'm gonna do. I'm gonna take a hundred sticks for openers. If my uncles like the stuff, then I'll come back and buy every last stick you got."

"Man, you couldn't *use* that much dynamite," said Alex cheerfully. "You could blow up the whole fuckin' world."

After a few beers to seal the contract, they arranged to meet in the parking lot behind the motel at seven o'clock the following evening. And as the two set off down the hall, Pagano heard Alex remind Walt to call "Kelly" as soon as they got to a phone, as though to place the order.

Levine now had some telephoning of his own to do. He was more comfortable with guns than explosives, and given the standard of driving among bikers, who were usually drunk or stoned, and the condition of the roads, which were slippery after several days of snow flurries, he was far from happy with the prospect of Alex and Walt, or himself for that matter, driving around with a load of dynamite big enough to blow up most of Buffalo.

The local police were not enchanted with the idea either. Levine and Mallery had to rant at Pierce and the others for almost an hour to prevent them, first, from pulling the plug on the whole operation, and then, from arresting Alex and Walt as soon as they delivered the hundred sticks. Failing to endear himself to any of them, Levine swore he would take it up directly with Washington if they blew the case before he found out who Kelly was and where the Chosen Few were getting the stuff. He willingly agreed, however, that the Army should take immediate charge of the explosives, but not until he gave the signal that Alex and Walt were safely out of the way.

Promptly at seven o'clock the next evening, a Pontiac sedan drove slowly into the lot behind the motel and parked alongside him. Blowing on his hands, Pagano scampered out of his car and into the back of theirs.

"Jesus, it's cold," he said, shivering as much from elation as from the blizzard outside. "You got the stuff?"

"Yup," said Alex. "In the trunk. We got *two* hundred sticks in there. You can have 'em all if you want."

"The caps are right here," added Walt. He took a box of them from the glove compartment. "And we got a fifty-foot roll of fuse. If you want more, we can get it."

"Okay," Pagano said cautiously. An undercover agent playing a part would be tempted to take the lot. A half-Cuban biker buying untested dynamite for a terrorist group from an untried source would not. "I'll take the fuse. But like I say, I'll take just the hundred sticks for now. And it better be good, I'm telling you. Because if they put that stuff under some guy's house and it don't go off, I'm dead."

"Hey, man." Alex was showing signs of impatience at having his integrity questioned like this. "I told you. The stuff is factory fresh. There's a date on the box. Now do you want it or don't you?"

"Right," said Walt. "You got enough back there to level the whole fucking place." He jerked his head at the sprawl of the Ramada just visible fifty yards away through swirling curtains of snow. "So make up your mind."

Pagano sucked his teeth thoughtfully. "Okay. If it's good, I'll be back. If it ain't, I won't be. Not *ever*."

"Fuck," said Alex, laughing. "Just pay us the money, man. Don't worry about it."

"I'll give you the money when I got the stuff in my car," he said, and they both laughed indulgently.

He helped them transfer one of the two boxes of dynamite sticks to his trunk, placed the detonator caps and coil of fuse under his front seat, and carefully locked the car before rejoining them in the Pontiac. That was the signal that the deal had gone down. The next move was for him to pay them and propose a drink to celebrate, so that while they were gone, the Army could remove the explosives.

With his money in their pocket, Alex and Walt relaxed over a few beers at the IBM Bar to the extent of admitting that the dynamite came straight from Du Pont, which had already seemed likely from the logos and dates on the boxes. They also claimed to have good contacts for grenades and machine guns, and promised to bring him samples, but the only hint Pagano could glean of their source was in a story Walt told about breaking into a railroad boxcar full of military equipment. Tottering down the tracks under the weight of a case of Army .45 caliber pistols, he had been forced to drop it and run when a railroad cop gave chase. Brooding over this anecdote, Pagano exchanged phone numbers with them, and as they dropped him off by his now-empty car, promised to get in touch as soon as he returned from New York.

A check on the serial numbers of the dynamite showed not only that the box had been stolen from a local Du Pont plant (which also undertook experimental work for the Army), but that Du Pont was unaware of the theft. Intrigued by the implications of this, Levine now called for a council of war. As he saw it, the sensible way to proceed would be to place a really large order with Alex and Walt, for several thousand sticks, to test the scale of their operation, and then, if they filled it, to track the shipment back to the hole in Du Pont's defenses. This would also buy him enough time to run down their connection for grenades and automatic weapons, which worried him almost as much, for he now saw no reason to doubt their ability to supply these as well. But Pierce, unwilling to make the decision on his own, telephoned ATF headquarters and was told it was too much money to spend on a buy.

"But that's crazy," Levine said, when he called Pierce from New York to get the decision. "Forget about the grenades and machine guns—what about this guy Kelly? What about their connection at Du Pont? You can't take 'em off until we get some answers here."

"What do you want from me, Mike?" Pierce complained. "They're the bosses. That's what they say. And besides, Du Pont's security is doing a complete investigation."

"Okay, okay." He could hardly believe it. They were going to screw him again. "So what are you saying? Are we gonna do 'em for just the hundred sticks or what?"

"No, I talked to the U.S. Attorney. We'll take 'em with the rest of the stuff. I want you to set 'em up for whatever you think they got left."

"Oh, man. I mean, that's really *stupid.*" Levine kicked the filing cabinet he was leaning on, and everybody around him looked startled. "These guys aren't gonna give up their connection. They're bikers, for Chrissake. They don't have enough fucking brain cells left to cooperate."

"I'm sorry, Levine, but that's it." Pierce was now very distant. "We'll take 'em off when they deliver."

"And leave their fucking guy in place inside Du Pont?" he demanded furiously. "Whoever he is, he's not the fucking janitor, not if he's moving this much stuff through their security. If he can do it with these guys, what's to stop him from doing it with somebody else? This is just so fucking *dumb* I can't believe it."

Pierce was silent for a moment. "What would be *really* dumb," he said eventually, "would be for you to question your orders. You were sent up here to work for me undercover. Not to take over the fucking office."

Four days after buying the sample box of dynamite, Pagano called Alex and Walt to order 4,000 sticks at $2 apiece, complete with detonator caps, and 4,000 feet of fuse at 50 cents a foot. Sure, they said. No problem. They could fill the order tomorrow. No, no, he said. He didn't want the stuff tomorrow. First, he had to go to New York to get the money.

A few hours later, Alex called him back to say that their contact had raised the price. Four thousand sticks would now cost him between $14,000 and $16,000, but it was better stuff than the first lot: 60 percent nitro instead of 40 percent. Pagano said he would ask his people. It would probably be okay, but he would call the following Sunday, one way or the other.

For the rest of the week Levine lobbied everybody he knew at ATF's New York headquarters to get them to change their minds, but all he succeeded in doing was hardening opposition to the point where he was actually denied permission to use "real" money in a flash roll.

"Use a Jewish bankroll," Pierce suggested (a $100 bill wrapped around a roll of singles).

"You bastards are trying to get me killed," said Levine, and Pierce shrugged.

On the Sunday, Levine called Alex and Walt from New York, as arranged, and learned that the delivery would be in 40 percent nitro sticks after all, priced at $12,000. He told them that was fine with him, and he'd talk to them again next day, as soon as he arrived back in Buffalo.

Checking in at the Ramada around noon, he called as promised, and was told what he had to do. He was to rent a truck and meet Alex and Walt at noon the following day in front of Sattler's Tire Center. They would then take the truck and leave him there while they went to fetch the load. After Pagano had satisfied himself it was all there, he would pay them and they would then go their separate ways.

Finding no fault with this plan, Levine spent the rest of the afternoon trying to dissuade Pierce, the Buffalo police and the county sheriff from attempting a moving surveillance on the rented truck after Alex and Walt took it over.

"These guys are no dummies," he said. "You burn 'em, and you'll leave four thousand sticks of dynamite out there someplace. They're not gonna tell you where. You'll find out one day when the stuff gets unstable and blows up half of Buffalo. Just leave 'em alone and they'll bring the load in like good little boys and dump it in our laps."

Next morning he took Joe Rodrigues with him from the ATF office to rent a truck, and drove over to Sattler's Tire Center just before noon. A few minutes past the hour Alex and Walt drove slowly by in their Pontiac, checking out the neighborhood, and returned even more slowly to park alongside the truck.

"Who the fuck's that?" demanded Alex when he saw Rodrigues.

"Nobody. Just one of the Cubans." Pagano sounded annoyed he should even ask. "They sent him up with the money."

"Wouldn't trust you with it, right?" Walt suggested, with a slightly nervous laugh. They both seemed jumpy.

"They don't trust nobody," said Pagano, unamused. "Including you. Are we all set?"

Alex was still eyeing Rodrigues suspiciously. "You didn't tell us about him."

"It's okay," Pagano said. "Forget it. He don't even speak English."

To demonstrate this, Levine spoke to Rodrigues in rapid Spanish. Being Portuguese, Rodrigues failed to understand a word, but replied at once in his own language, which was equally incomprehensible to Levine. Though neither knew what the other had said, Alex seemed satisfied.

"Our guy's running late," he said. "Got tied up in Syracuse."

"Fuck. So when's he gonna get here?"

"He says around four."

"Okay." With his usual detachment, Levine wondered if a touch of paranoia on *his* part might help to steady them. "But not here. I don't wanna meet here again. Not twice in one day."

"Yeah. All right." Alex thought for a moment. "You know Carrol's Drive-In? It's a restaurant. On Broadway. At Woltz Street."

"I'll find it."

"All right. See you there at four."

With another long look at Rodrigues, they got back in their car and drove away.

Something had spooked them. Some inept attempt at surveillance, probably. There were too many people in on the act. As the

afternoon wore on, Levine could think of no better way to disasso-
ciate himself from whatever threat they might have sensed than to
be even more nervous than they were. He was also concerned that
if left too long to themselves, their jumpiness might feed on itself to
the point where they jumped right out of the deal. Around 3:00
P.M. he called Alex's number.

"Hey, listen, man," he said. "I gotta problem. These fucking
Cubans are giving me a hard time. You hear from your man yet?"

"He's coming. I told you. He got tied up in traffic."

"Yeah, well, my people say he *ain't* coming. They say the deal
shoulda gone down by now, and you're just stalling. They think it's
a rip-off. They're telling me to drive right back to New York with
the money."

"Shit, man. You can't *do* that." Alex sounded really alarmed.
"You ordered the stuff and it's coming. The guy's on the way with
it. I can't tell him to take it back. Shit, you don't know these
people. I mean, to them, Cubans are just fucking waiters."

"Hey," said Pagano. "My old lady's Cuban."

"You know what I mean, Mike. We made a deal. So the guy's a
little late, so what? You can't call it off just for that. Fuck, he'll *be*
here. Call 'em. Tell 'em that."

"I did already. But they don't think he's gonna show. They
think you're just gonna try and take us for the money."

"Oh, for Chrissake, Mike. I don't even wanna *see* the fucking
money until you check the load. First you look. Then you pay."

"Well, that's all right with *me*, Alex, but these guys are something else. See, they don't know you. They only got my word. I
told 'em they can trust you, but—well, you know how it is. I'll see
if I can stall 'em a bit longer, okay?"

"Yeah. I mean, for Chrissake . . . And listen. Let's change it
back to Sattler's, okay? Carrol's gets kinda busy."

"Okay. What time?"

"Gimme the number you're at. I'll call you when we're set."

Pagano gave him the number of the undercover phone at the
ATF office. By sweating out the delay there, he felt he would at
least have a chance to head off any bright ideas that might occur to
his colleagues.

At four o'clock he put his feet on the desk, looking determinedly
casual. At five o'clock Pierce looked in, and when Levine shook his
head, sighed heavily and pretended to punch the doorframe.

"You know we got a hundred men out there, standing by?" he

said. "Maybe thirty cars. Trucks. The bomb squad. Plus special services. Plus helicopters. And that's not counting the Army. They got another thirty or forty guys, plus vehicles. And they're all just sitting there."

"Yeah," said Levine. "I know."

The undercover phone rang about half an hour later. Everything was ready, Alex said. And they would meet at Carrol's after all.

"Sure," said Levine, who recognized professional caution when he saw it, but failed to see how Alex and Walt could guard against the risk of a stakeout at Carrol's when they returned with the dynamite. Unless they had someone watching the place . . . Or unless they switched again and took the stuff to Sattler's, planning to phone from there.

Arguing around these possibilities. Levine managed to persuade Pierce and the others to stakeout both locations but keep their main forces in reserve until they were sure of the final delivery point. This discussion lasted half an hour, so that it was around six-fifteen before Levine and Rodrigues at last arrived at Carrol's with the truck.

"Where will you be?" Walt asked, as he settled behind the wheel, and Alex climbed in beside him. "You got a couple of bars over there."

"Nah, I'm gonna wait right here," Pagano said. "Get something to eat. How long you guys gonna be?"

"As long as it takes, man," Alex said coldly.

It took until eight o'clock. When Pagano saw the truck coming back, he left Rodrigues inside at the table with their bankroll—a $100 bill wrapped around 150 singles—and went outside to meet them. He was sorry it had to be this way, but it was still the biggest dynamite seizure in ATF history. In honor of the occasion, the lot was half-full of undercover cars and plainclothes officers gagging on their fifth or sixth hamburgers.

"Thought you got lost," he said cheerfully. "Any problems?"

"No problems." Neither of them was in any hurry to get out.

Pagano came around easily and opened Alex's door for him. "It's all in there?" He nodded toward the back of the truck. "You get all the stuff?"

"Yeah, it's all there," Alex said. "Forty cases of sticks. Four thousand blasting caps. Four thousand feet of fuse. Where's the money?"

"Inside. The Cuban's got it. He's sitting in there waiting for you."

"Okay." Neither of them moved.

"Why don't you go get it, Walt?" Pagano suggested, watching intently for the first telltale flicker of trouble. "Me and Alex'll check the load."

The two looked at each other. They knew something was wrong, but could not pin it down. They also knew they were committed anyway. As Walt got out and headed for the entrance to the restaurant, Pagano stepped back to let Alex lead the way.

"Come on," he said. "Let's see what you got in there."

Alex looked at him for a long moment, and as he stepped down, Levine drew his gun and showed him his badge . . .

" . . . and that was it," he said. "Big headlines in all the papers. 'U.S. TREASURY AGENTS RECOVER 40 CASES OF DYNAMITE BOUND FOR TERRORIST ACTIVITIES IN NEW YORK CITY. Area Supervisor declined to release details of his three-month-long investigation in the case, but this reporter learned blah, blah, blah.' Usual bullshit."

The class murmured sympathetically.

"Three months out of my life. Two more nails in the coffin of my marriage. Half a case instead of a whole one. And all I get is a nod from the regional director, plus a week on the witness stand with defense counsel trying to tear me to pieces.

"See, the big problem with deep undercover, where you go in and *live* with the people, is that you got three things to do at once. It's like a circus act. You're juggling eggs in one hand, china plates in the other, and walking a high wire singing 'The Star-Spangled Banner.'

"The first thing is getting over—taking on the role, getting accepted, keeping it up. Second, while you're doing that, you got to be recording everything in your mind, every little thing, because that's how the case is go-

ing to be won in court. You're gonna have to
swear to every detail under oath. Maybe an actor can afford to lose himself in a part, but
you *can't*. And third, you gotta work like you
were on a football team. To score, you gotta
have a game plan and set plays. Each guy goes
his part, the undercover included. The supervisor is the quarterback. If a player starts
improvising, or getting away from the plan,
the game falls apart. And in an undercover operation, people get killed.

"But if you do it *right,* then the only way defense counsel can beat a good undercover case
is by making you out to be a bigger scumbag than
his client. He's *got* to discredit you or he
loses. So anything you do while you're getting
over, while you're getting yourself accepted
as one of the bad guys, is more than likely to
come back at you on the witness stand. This is
the high-wire part of the act. It's *easy* to be
bad. That's why we got a crime problem in the
first place. For an undercover, it's easy to be
too bad, and wind up getting fired or busted
himself. And it's just as easy to be *so* bad,
trying to get over, that the jury winds up liking the defendant better than you.

"That's why I tried not to spend too many
nights with the Night Riders. Comes the trial,
and the prosecutor takes me through all the
dry shit—all the open-and-shut detailed testimony of names, dates and places—and now
it's the defense attorney's turn. And he's
good. Very dynamic. A real actor, with a lot of
courtroom presence. And he's got a big audience of motorcycle bums and their girls.

" 'Officer Levine, how long were you up here
in Buffalo?'

" 'About three months, off and on.'

" 'You a married man?'

" 'Yes, sir.'

" 'And where do you live?'

" 'In New York City.'

" 'And you were away from home for three months, living with these Night Riders, is that correct?'

" 'On and off, yes, sir.'

" 'Isn't it a fact that they had parties? In the clubhouse?'

" 'Yes, sir.'

" 'And isn't it a fact that they would have girls at these parties? Some of them young?'

" 'Yes, sir.'

" 'As young as thirteen?'

" 'I don't know.'

" 'Well, *fourteen?*'

" 'I don't know, sir. Possibly.'

" '*Fifteen?*'

" 'Yeah, I would say some of them were as young as fifteen, yes, sir.'

" 'Very well. Now did you ever see sex, open sex acts, at these parties?' "

Levine looked along the rows of faces in front of him and laughed. "By now, he's got the jury on the edge of their seats, right? Just like you. And I certainly had seen some sex acts.

" 'Yes, sir, I did.'

" 'And when these open sex acts took place, were they with multiple partners?'

" 'Er, multiple partners?'

" 'Was it a lineup, Agent Levine? A gang bang?'

" 'Well, yes, sir. Sometimes.'

" 'Okay. Now you said you'd been away for three months. Did *you* ever have sex with anyone?'

" 'No, sir.'

"Uproar in court, right? The bikers all moan and hold their heads, like I'm the biggest liar in the world. The girls all go, 'Ho, ho, ho.' You understand? The guy had set me up. Did it well. All I could do was sit there with a straight face, with my ears feeling like they were gonna explode, until the judge quieted 'em down. Then I said, 'I want to take a polygraph test.'

"More uproar. Defense attorney goes batshit. 'I want that answer stricken. I want the witness to be warned not to volunteer information. I want that stricken from the record.' 'Yes,' says the judge. 'Don't volunteer information. Just answer the question.' 'But, your honor,' I say, all wounded and innocent, 'I'm not volunteering information. I'm just asking for a lie-detector test.' The judge threatens me with contempt of court. I shut my mouth, but from the look on the jury's faces, I got my point across. It's all part of the game, part of the way of the undercover. And Alex and Walt, they both got convicted. Only then the Second Circuit Court of Appeals decided that dynamite, detonators and fuse was *not* an explosive device as defined by the Gun Control Act of 1968, and turned 'em loose."

"Oh, boy." Levine's friend in the front row seemed personally dismayed.

"Yeah. And around that time, I also found out that Bruce Jensen, the agent in charge of the BNDD office in Buffalo, wanted to have me arrested for buying drugs undercover without his permission." He laughed. "I thought that was pretty good. Just about the only official recognition I got."

It was true. Though the case was a milestone for ATF, and perhaps the most spectacular deep-cover operation in federal law-enforcement history up to that point, Levine received not a word of commendation from any quarter.

"What about Alex and Walt?"

Levine shrugged. "Who knows? That was my swan song with ATF. Now I just wanted to do narcotics."

"Any special reason for that?"
"Oh, yeah. I had a reason."

The reason was his brother.

He had been fifteen when Levine enlisted in the Air Force, and with his father gone, it had felt like a second desertion. Always more reserved than Michael, and until then always under his protection, David was suddenly left to cope with life on his own and found it beyond him. Too proud, and too withdrawn to admit it, he looked for comfort on the street and found it came in nickel bags.

What may have tipped him over the edge was the brutal collapse of the only other relationship that seemed to mean much to him. He had been going with a girl named Linda, who was also fifteen, and who now discovered she was pregnant. When she broke the news to her parents, both Polish immigrants of peasant stock, they shrieked and tore their clothes and invoked a curse on their daughter's seducer that certainly frightened Caroline Levine-Goldstein. Linda was sent to Florida to have her baby, which was then given up for adoption, and when Michael came home on furlough, his mother insisted on making a ritual incantation over him and his brother to ward off evil spirits. At the time Michael found this rather funny, but, thinking back, wonders now if the breaking of still another emotional tie might not have set David completely adrift.

"I tried to kid him out of it, but I could see he was really disturbed by this weird turn of events. Later on, I found out he started on drugs around this time, so maybe the problem with Linda had something to do with it. But I think it was what starts most kids off—the people he ran with. Peer pressure. He was a sweet and lovely guy, but you didn't have to scratch too deep to find a really bitter and resentful streak. I made a mistake once, when I was home on a pass. Still playing the big brother, I smacked a cigarette out of his hand in front of some guys he was hanging out with. He went crazy. Attacked me with a knife, and really tried to cut me with it. I should have guessed then he was on drugs, but the thought never crossed my mind."

By the time Levine left the service in 1961 and returned home for good, the pattern of his brother's addiction was established, but Levine was also too preoccupied with his own untidy life to pay much attention to David, except for emergencies like the battle of

Alley Pond Park, which Levine later realised, had more to do with Howard* as a pusher than as a pimp.

Liana was now taking up most of his free time, although in some ways this drew him closer to David, whom she had known and liked before she ever met his older brother. Though dazzled by Michael's looks and his smooth line with girls, she found it easier to talk to David, who, in turn, seemed to relax more readily in her company than with anyone else. He was often included, therefore, in their outings to the movies or, in summer, to the beach. And after Michael and Liana were married, David was always a welcome visitor to their apartment in Bayside, around the corner from where he lived with his mother.

To Liana, he became even more welcome in the months before and after the birth of her son Keith in the following year, for she now found herself more and more housebound at precisely the time when her husband was trying his hardest to find whatever it was that Providence had saved him for.

"Right from the start, Michael and I used to fight a lot," she remembers. "We were both very young and very stubborn, and I never saw myself as a submissive little wife. I knew he was not the sort to sit around the house playing Scrabble. He was a high-energy person, and difficult to get close to, however hard I tried. But I wanted *him* to try as well, and he didn't. I wanted him to *share* his life, but he couldn't. What I didn't understand then, at twenty, was that Michael's life was a constant challenge to him. Every situation he was in, every person he met, had to be mastered in one way or another, and where women were concerned, that usually meant in a sexual way. And it wasn't enough to rise to a challenge just now and again. He had to do it every day. Twice a day. Which is the perfect motivation, I suppose, for a cop, but absolute hell on one's private life. And anyway, I hadn't married a cop. I'd married an accountant.

"So it was a long way from what I wanted. Like any nice Jewish girl, I wanted a nice conventional sort of life. I wanted to have a good time and laugh a lot. Instead, I cried a lot. Once we almost separated, but I learned how to block things out and generally make life tolerable. And David helped. He helped me through some really bad times. I could always talk to him. And because he knew Michael as well as I did, he would always understand."

* Not his real name.

In spite of her disappointment, she never tried to put a brake on Michael's erratic hours or his unpredictable comings and goings, not at least in the early years of their marriage. At that stage, she had no real conception of what being a government agent, or the wife of a government agent, actually meant. She just wanted him to settle down to something and be happy. But he didn't. And he wasn't.

Toward the end of his four-year apprenticeship with ATF, what with all the cases, the paperwork, the court appearances, the martial arts, the cultivation of informers and life on the street, there was no time left for living with anybody. Liana, now pregnant again, was treading the edge of desperation, and David he hardly ever saw at all, mainly because he had now moved the family to a garden apartment in Monsey, New York. This was as far from drugs as he could get them, but it had cut Liana off from her friends, relatives—almost everyone she knew. With an absentee husband, and another baby on the way, she tried for the first time to put a brake on Levine's runaway commitment to the streets, but he was too caught up at this point even to consider changing his ways. But for David, who visited her as often as he could, her son Keith and the unborn baby, the marriage would certainly have collapsed long before it did.

"What do you *want*, Michael? Is it me? Don't you like me anymore? Can't you talk to me? Have I done something wrong?"

"No, no," he would say uneasily, and head for the refrigerator. "It's not you, doll. It's me. It's my fault."

And she would frown, expecting more. "Well? Is that supposed to make me feel better? And don't walk away from me, Michael. I'm trying to talk to you."

"I'm just getting a soda, okay?" He hated it when she took off after him like this. He hated to see her get hurt. He hated not having the answers she wanted.

"Michael, you're like a stranger to me," she would say, trailing after him. "You're gone most of the time anyhow, but even when you're home I get the feeling you can't wait to get away. I just don't understand you anymore. And I don't understand what's happening."

"I know. I'm sorry, hon." Popping a can of Diet Pepsi, he tried his smile of boyish contrition. "I'm tired, that's all. I got a lot on my mind."

"Then *share* with me, Michael. Make me feel wanted. I want to feel like I *mean* something to you." She pushed him away, anguished enough to resist his usual method of shutting her up. "I *don't* feel that anymore. I don't ever feel close to you now, and I want to know why. I've tried to be a good wife. I've tried very hard to make a home for you and Keith, and I don't think I've done so badly, have I?"

Her voice broke. He reached for her again, meaning it this time, but she shook him off.

"No, be honest with me, Michael. I don't think you *care* anymore."

"Oh, for God's sake, Liana."

"Sometimes I wonder if you *ever* cared. Sometimes I think it was all just an act, and now you're bored with it."

"Look, will you get off my back? I love you—and that's the truth. But don't ask me to stop doing what I'm doing. Don't ask me to change, because I can't. This is me. Right here. What you see."

"Yeah? Well, you look like my husband and you sound like my husband, but I don't know you anymore."

"Baby, I am what I do. That's all. There's nothing else to know."

"Well, that's what I said. You don't need *me* anymore."

"Oh, I need you, baby." He rested his forehead on her shoulder. "You're all I got. But you gotta give me room. I gotta keep moving. You know I don't *mean* to hurt you. It's just the way I am."

It was almost the literal truth. Like a shark, he knew he would suffocate if he ever stopped moving. As incomplete, as *unfinished,* as any other kind of actor, Levine had been making and remaking himself since a boy, since the day he had first understood he was on his own. Having never fully known who he was, he was forever losing track of himself in the maze of sometimes contradictory personalities he was capable of projecting, a potentially dangerous liability in most walks of life, but a positive, cultivable asset in *his* line of work. Going undercover was stepping out of one life into another life impossible to share with anyone. What he did was not pretense. Performance, yes—all life was performance, and he was a performer, first and last—but not pretense.

As a performer, he tended to become whatever the circumstances, professional, social or domestic, seemed to require. Some roles, the riskier ones, he lived out under the tight, central control of a detached intelligence he even thought of as "The Producer/

Director"; others, mostly the private or domestic ones, he sometimes performed like a sleepwalker.

And sometimes that stillness at the core, the eternal watching and calculating, could feel as cold as death. Then he would try to warm it into life, flesh against flesh, or in the affection and applause he could usually milk from others, and still again draw no comfort from it, for "The Producer/Director" could no more stop producing and directing than the shark could stop swimming. Providence had so arranged things that the impulse to be whole—to be seized by a passion or conviction too strong to manipulate—required him to live in the vicinity of his own death. In the neighborhood of everything or nothing.

He also needed the professional recognition that the old-timers in charge of ATF could not bring themselves to offer a cocky young Jewish agent who preferred working guns and narcotics to alcohol and cigarettes. Promoted, unavoidably, to a Grade 11 agent, he set his sights on the Bureau of Customs. Headed by Myles Ambrose, a Nixon appointee with access to seemingly limitless funds, Customs was making better cases than the Bureau of Narcotics and Dangerous Drugs, and was said to be looking for aggressive, streetwise agents, prepared to stay out.

After finagling an introduction to John Fallon, the agent in charge of the Port of New York, Levine formally applied for a transfer to Customs in March 1970, and was duly assigned to the Hard Narcotics Squad in September.

FIVE

". . . justice is none of our business."

"**A** couple of weeks ago the FBI asked me down to Quantico to lecture on undercover tactics," Levine said, and a hundred cops laughed heartily.

Drawn from a dozen different police departments in New York State, they had packed the room for his two-day seminar at the Westchester Police Academy, and the off-duty spirit kept breaking through. Which was all right with him. Cops were his favorite people.

He waited for them to settle down, but then somebody at the back chimed in, "Was the first lesson on how to take off your tie?"

Levine again waited patiently. He had intended to compare the FBI's attitude toward undercover work favorably with that of most other agencies, but the FBI evidently had few friends in *this* group.

"You guys heard the news?" he said. "J. Edgar Hoover is dead. It's a whole new ballgame now. These days, you've got a lot more in common with FBI guys working serious crime than you've probably got with your own bosses. It's the old-timers who are still suspicious of undercover, and think the guys who do it are cowboys and hotshots. If we're going to make a dent in serious crime—especially in narcotics—then it's got to start with us. With guys who work the streets. That means teamwork—and that's what undercover is all about. Planning and teamwork. Work together and stay alive."

He surveyed them, unsmiling, and in the silence the screech of a chairleg on the polished floor turned every head like a gunshot.

"Okay. Now I've got some opaques to show you, just to kind of keep me on track."

He nodded to the operator at the back of the room, and stepped aside as the headings came up on the screen behind him.

" 'Preliminaries before an Undercover Meeting.' Now we're talking narcotics here, so either you or your undercover is going in to meet some doper. And either you got a regular informer who can get you in or you busted some low-level creep with the stuff and flipped him. Now you gotta decide how far you're gonna go with it. Maybe you can flip the next guy as well and move on up the line toward the source. I've run cases like that months—years sometimes—and locked up dozens of people, starting with one little undercover buy. You just don't know until you see what you got. But you gotta plan it, step by step."

He turned to the message on the screen.

" 'Review Informant Files.' That's if you're using a regular stool. What's his track record? Is he hard to handle? What's his motivation? What's his relationship with the target? All important questions.

" 'Review All Intelligence Reports Relative to the Subject.' Common sense, of course, but you'd be surprised how many undercovers can't be bothered. And wind up on a slab. How can you know too much about a guy you're trying to con? What's his record? What kind of crimes? Is he known to be violent? Where does he hang out? Is the neighborhood known to be dangerous? Don't be shy—check with other units. See what *they* know. Vice. Organized crime. What's his financial status? Can he really do what the stool *says* he can do?

"And that's the next thing—'Completely Debrief the Informant.' Make sure the sonofabitch isn't holding out on you. Or making things up so he looks important. How does he know what he *says* he knows? What's *his* stake in the deal?

"Okay. Now we get down to the details. 'Consider Personal Protection.' What kind of backup and surveillance is possible? Are you gonna use body armor? How do you get in and out of the meeting place? Where are the entrances and exits you gotta cover? How long are you gonna let your undercover operate out of sight before you move in? What are the emergency signals?

" 'Consider Selection and Use of Weapons.' In other words, if you decide to carry a weapon into an undercover meet, take something exotic. Not a standard police firearm. An automatic is good."

With some surprise, the audience found itself looking at a pistol in his hand.

"These days I use a 9mm 13-shot Smith & Wesson," he said, putting it away again. "Takes a 20-round clip when you need the extra firepower. And working undercover, I normally use an ankle holster. If you think about it, most of the time you're sitting down on these deals. In a hotel room, maybe, or a car. Then it's just inches away from your hand. And you gotta think about that. It's the worst-case scenario, right? Suddenly your cover's blown, your backup's downstairs on the street, and you gotta go for it. Well, practice that. In front of a mirror. And never mind what your wife says. If you *don't* practice, you could make her a widow.

"And it's not just your gun that can give you away. Don't go in with your badge and credentials. No, don't laugh. I've known guys who did that. But not for long. Going undercover means you abandon your identity. Clean out your pockets and your car. Get rid of everything. No credit cards. No letters, No notebooks. Nothing that could cause suspicion or be traced back unless it's consistent with your cover story. And make sure your license tags and undercover driver's license can't be traced.

"Okay. Next. 'Consider Use of Body Transmitter or Recorder.' Well, that sort of depends on how effective this is likely to be. You gotta watch the law covering the use of recordings. I don't like wearing a wire myself, but there are times when you ought to consider it. And also the risk. If there's a real danger of it being found, don't do it. Have the informer wear it. He's expendable.

" 'Record Money.' Right. *Always.* Serial numbers. Denominations. And I mean, *always.* Just look in your manuals. If it says anything at all about working undercover, you'll find more about protecting the money than protecting your lives. So keep the record on file, checking off the serial numbers of the money as you use it. Cover your ass. That's the number one rule in narcotics enforcement.

"Next. 'Discuss Predictability.' Well, again that may seem pretty obvious, but talk it over with your team. How does this type of deal usually go down? What are the chances of a rip-off? Will the subjects be armed? If something goes wrong, will they run or shoot?

" 'Discuss the Limits of the Operation.' Okay. Here's the bottom line. The undercover, the case agent, the supervisor—everybody's gotta be very clear about this. How much money can be spent? When, and if, should another meeting be set? How much time can be spent on the subject? Is he worth it? Can the undercover *travel* with the subject? This is all very important because nothing damages a case more than an undercover saying he'll do something and then having to break his promise because he didn't clear something up front with his bosses.

"So if it's a first meeting with a subject, know in advance how far you can go. Rehearse your background story with the informer so there are no inconsistencies. If you or the informer can influence the choice of location for the meet, make it a public place, like a restaurant or bar. Or out in the open, on a street corner or in a park. Surveillance can do a better job, then. It can protect the undercover better and corroborate the deal better. And if somebody's wearing a wire, there's less chance of them finding it. Less chance of a rip-off, too.

"But if it's gotta be in somebody's apartment or hotel room, then try to find out where you're going before you go, so your backup doesn't have to follow you around everywhere and risk getting burned. If the deal is gonna take time, then the undercover should try and keep in touch by phone. Or by going out to buy cigarettes or something. And remember, always have plenty of surveillance on hand in case the subject moves or other subjects show up. For want of another car, you could lose the main man.

"If you gotta move, a good undercover can always slow things down so he doesn't lose his surveillance. 'Hey, what's the rush? Lemme finish my coffee.' Or, 'Jesus. Hold on a minute. I left my fucking lights back in the room.' That kinda thing. If you keep on your toes and stay loose, you can run the whole deal the way you want to from start to finish."

He sized up the room with a practiced eye. It was time for a story.

"I remember a case I had in Customs once that pretty well touched all those bases," he said, reversing his chair and straddling it. "Started off at Kennedy Airport and took me all the way to Bangkok, Thailand, via a Florida swamp. . . ."

It was the Fourth of July, and Customs Inspector Elliot Kaplan would rather have been broiling hamburgers in his backyard than checking the baggage of passengers arriving on TWA Flight 741 from Bangkok.

Somebody lifted three Samsonite suitcases onto the table in front of him and, when Kaplan met his eye, made the mistake of smiling at him in a nice, frank, open sort of way. The kid looked to be in his early twenties, and with his doeskin bucks, flounced shirt and little pink-rimmed glasses, could have passed for Pat Boone's brother.

"Will you open that one for me, please?" said Kaplan, in a studiously colorless tone, determined to be fair.

"That one? Sure," said John Edward Davidson, in a nice, frank, open sort of way.

As Kaplan bent over to look inside, he caught a faint but unmistakable whiff of glue, and smiled for the first time that day.

Michael Levine did not, when he heard about it. With Liana and Keith, he had driven over to his uncle's house on Long Island for a daylong party in honor of a cousin from Israel, and when the call came, he was firing up the barbecue. Although he had drawn "the duty," he had not expected anyone to be unpatriotic enough to smuggle in hard narcotics on July Fourth (or inconsiderate enough to intercept them if somebody did). Muttering under his breath about the traffic and other evidence of moral decay, he drove over to Kennedy with the idea of locking somebody up as quickly as possible and getting back to the party.

By the time he arrived at the airport, there were *three* cases:

Davidson and two Latin American women caught with cocaine. The other agent on duty, who had gotten there first, had already taken a statement from Davidson, but when he heard that Levine was eager to get back to his family, offered to give him Davidson for processing while he took "the two Spanish broads." They would almost certainly take longer because they were ready to flip and turn informer, in which case the whole squad would probably have to be called out to make a controlled delivery.

Levine accepted the favor gratefully, but as he read Davidson's statement, his impatience ebbed away. Inspector Kaplan had found over three kilos of heroin hydrochloride in the false-bottomed suitcases, and according to his passport, Davidson had made seven entries into the United States in the previous two years. That suggested a total of around twenty-two kilos, with a street value of maybe $20 million.

The statement itself was the usual one-page bullshit. Somebody had paid him to carry the bags. He didn't know who the guy was, or what was in them. When he got to New York, somebody was supposed to contact him, he didn't know who.

Pretending to be absorbed in this rigmarole, Levine wandered into the interview room where Davidson had been left to stew on his own for a couple of hours, and sat down without bothering to look at him. When it came to exerting psychological pressure on subjects with a view to having them cooperate, Levine now had few equals in government service. He had made a study of it. In many cases, his appearance alone was sufficient, for he had cultivated a manner so impersonal and deadly, so far removed from any ordinary human impulse to compassion that, to some, compliance with his wishes seemed to offer the only hope of survival, let alone of lenient treatment.

He looked up suddenly at Davidson across the table, taking in the fresh-faced, all-American health and youthfulness, the flounced shirt and pink glasses.

"John," he said, his expression belying the friendly tone, "if this is the truth, you don't have a whole lot to worry about."

"Oh," said Davidson, pleasantly surprised. "Okay. That's great."

"Yeah. Of course, I gotta check out everything you say because this is a serious case. That means I'm gonna tap every phone number I find on you. I'm gonna visit every address in your notebook. I'm gonna go down to Florida and check out your house the same way. I'm gonna talk to everybody you know. Everybody linked to you by any stretch of the imagination. And why am I gonna do that? Well, you can *see* why." He tossed Davidson's passport on the table. "Seven trips overseas? In two years? We could be talking twenty kilos here."

"No, no." Davidson's eyes widened. "Those were just vacation trips. I never did anything like this before."

"Well, that's good. Because if I find out you've been lying—just one little lie in anything you say to me or that's written on this piece of paper—you know what I'm gonna do?"

Unable to face such concentrated, impassive malevolence, Davidson looked down at his hands.

"Well, I'll tell you. If you lie to me, I'm gonna make sure you go to that part of the jail where they keep guys doing life. *Big* guys. Guys who haven't had sex with a woman in years. You know what I mean? To them, you're gonna look like Marilyn Monroe."

"Oh, Jesus," Davidson muttered.

"And you know why I'll do that? Just so you know I'm not kidding."

Davidson shook his head numbly.

"I'll do it because my kid brother is a heroin addict. And as far as I'm concerned, it's *your* fault."

That was usually the clincher. Levine let it sink in. Then he placed Davidson's statement alongside his passport.

"So what do you want to do? Start again?"

Snatching up the statement, Davidson tore it to shreds. And it was four days before Levine returned home.

Once he started to cooperate, Davidson hardly knew how to stop. First, he gave up Alan Trupkin, his twenty-three-year-old employer and financier, who supplied an extensive network of traffickers in Chicago and the Midwest. A graduate of Miami University, then living in Gainesville, Florida, Trupkin had given Davidson $7,500 to bring back three kilos of 98 percent pure Dragon-brand heroin from his connection in Bangkok.

The price in Thailand was $6,500. Landed in the United States, it would be cut once, to double the quantity, and then sold to wholesalers, as 50 percent pure, at $2,000 an ounce—to show a profit of around half a million dollars per trip. And that was just the beginning. They were building up toward shipments of six to eight to ten kilos a time.

Next Davidson gave up his Bangkok connection.

"His name is Liang Sae Tiew," he said, "but everybody calls him Gary. And he's always with his partner, who doesn't speak English. A guy named Thirachai Pluksamanee. Mr. Geh, for short."

"And who introduced you to Gary?"

Davidson hardly hesitated. "A guy I know named Tom Simmons. We—ah—did a couple of deals together."

"We'll get to that later. How did Simmons know him?"

"He met him when he was in Vietnam."

"Okay. How big a dealer is this guy Gary?"

"As big as they come," said Davidson proudly.

"How big is that? And how do you know?"

"Listen, Gary can do a hundred kilos, two hundred kilos—anything you want." He stared at Levine earnestly. "He took me up to Chiang Mai, which is like where all the stuff comes from. Showed me his uncle's factory. And his uncle is like the biggest heroin maker in Thailand. You should *see* the setup they got there. So we were trying to work up to where we'd be doing that kind of weight."

"Okay." Levine eyed him thoughtfully. "Then I guess it's time to call Alan. I want you to pick up that phone, John, and tell him you're coming."

"No, I can't," he said, then added hastily as Levine's expression changed, "If I call from New York, he'll know something's wrong."

"Why? What were you supposed to do?"

"When I got to Jacksonville, he told me to call him from there."

"Then that's just exactly what you're gonna do."

First, there were a few preliminaries. Levine drove Davidson into the city for processing, and to prepare a new statement in the squad's offices at 120 Varick Street. By the time this was done, it was July 5, and he booked Davidson in for the night at the Sheraton on 42nd Street. Next morning they drove over to the Eastern District courthouse, where he was arraigned and released into the custody of U.S. Customs against a personal recognizance bond of $25,000. The three false-bottomed suitcases were then returned to him, along with a half-kilo of heroin, and the rest was sent for analysis. The stage was now set for the classic procedure in smuggling cases, a controlled delivery.

Accompanied by George Sweikert, one of the airport agents, Levine and Davidson flew down to Jacksonville, where they were met by agents from the local Customs office. It was now around midnight, and after Davidson tried unsuccessfully to get Trupkin on the telephone, Levine decided they should all drive out to Davidson's trailer home in Alachua and try again from there.

Without Davidson to guide them, they would still have been searching for it at daybreak, for he lived in the middle of a swamp. Approached from the highway via a dirt road, then a grass track, and finally over open country, his trailer was nevertheless fitted out with every conceivable luxury, including piped-in electricity, a telephone and a ten-foot boa constrictor, which lived in Davidson's clothes closet and took care of any local wildlife that came out of the swamp.

It was now July 6.

"Okay," said Levine. "Try his number again."

"But it's one-thirty in the morning," protested Davidson, who had stayed up late two nights in a row.

Levine held out the phone without a word, and he took it reluctantly. It wasn't just tiredness, as Levine well knew. This was the moment that would mark Davidson for good as an informer. So far, they had just talked about Trupkin. Now came the actual betrayal. He watched Levine hook up his tape recorder to the phone as though watching him heat up a branding iron, and dialed the number, wincing each time he pressed a button.

A girl's voice answered, sleepily. "Hello?"

"Louise," said Davidson, relieved it was not Trupkin.

"Yeah?"

"How are you, dear?"

"Fine. How are you?"

"Pretty good. Is Al there?"

"Yeah. Just a minute. Lemme see. I don't know. He stepped out for a minute."

"Okay."

"Who *is* this?"

Even Davidson was surprised, after all that. "This is John. Don't you remember? Don't you recognize my voice?"

Silence. Then, "You're *kidding.*"

"No, I'm not kidding."

"John, how *are* you? *Where* are you?"

"I'm at my house. I've been trying to get ahold of you people all night."

"Really?"

"Yeah. I called from Jacksonville, and I couldn't get though, so—"

"Hello?" A male voice came on the line, evidently Trupkin's.

"—so I went ahead and rented a car and came on home."

"Huh?"

If the conversation so far had seemed a touch surreal, the next few exchanges might have been scripted for Abbott and Costello.

"Howya doin', Al?" asked Davidson glumly.

"Huh?"

"Howya doin'?"

"All right. How *you* doin'?"

"Pretty good."

"Huh?"

"Pretty good."

"Where are you?"

"I'm at my house."

"Huh?"

"I'm at my house—I told you."

"You're at your *house?*"

"Yeah."

"How'd you get *there?*"

Davidson blinked at the phone, as though expecting something more cogent from a university-trained boss of an international dope ring.

"I tried to call you," he said patiently, "but I couldn't get ahold of you, so I went ahead and rented a car and came on in."

"Everything's okay?"

"Everything's beautiful." He glanced up at Levine, who nodded approvingly. He was monitoring both sides of the conversation on the earphone of his recorder.

"Really?"

"Just fine."

"Well . . ." Trupkin hesitated, evidently torn between bed and business. "Then why don't we get together?"

"Okay." Eyeing Levine, Davidson saw his last chance of postponing the inevitable slip away. "Why don't you come on out?"

"Hold it." Trupkin covered the mouthpiece while he conferred with someone beside him. "Well, John and Madeleine are here, and we'll come on out."

"Do me a favor," Davidson said urgently, and Levine frowned.

"Yeah?" said Trupkin.

"Don't bring them."

Levine scowled at this obvious attempt to limit the carnage, but Davidson pretended not to see.

"Just John?" Trupkin suggested.

"No. Just you."

Levine tapped Davidson on the forearm and bunched a fist under his nose. But Levine needn't have worried.

"I don't know how to get there," Trupkin said.

"Huh?"

"I don't know how to get there."

"You *don't?*"

"No."

Another male voice broke in. "I can bring him."

"He just wants *me* to come right now," said Trupkin.

"Okay." Davidson nodded helplessly, transfixed by Levine's dreadful stare.

"You want John to come in, too?" With three kilos in the offing, Trupkin was ready to indulge him in anything he pleased.

"Ah, sure." Having bitten into the Judas apple, there was no way to repent of it now.

"Okay. Just the two of us will come."

"Okay."

"Okay. Outa sight."

"Okay."

Davidson hung up. Then he hung his head.

Levine stared at him for a while, lips pursed, but decided to let it pass. Once a defendant flipped and turned stool pigeon, it was important to keep a finger on the fear button, but Davidson, he judged, was close to the point where he might no longer care what happened to him, and he still had work to do. The telephone conversation with Trupkin had provided no real evidence of anything, including brains. To tie him securely into a conspiracy to smuggle narcotics, Levine needed to hear some incriminating face-to-face exchanges before making an arrest.

"How long will it take 'em to get here?"

Davidson shrugged listlessly. "I don't know. Half an hour maybe? Something like that."

Levine huddled with his crew. As there was little or no cover around the trailer, their four cars had to be backed off into the swamp, or Trupkin would be bound to see them in his headlights as he drove up. Levine, the case agent, was the logical choice to join the boa constrictor in the closet, but there was nowhere else inside the trailer for anyone to hide. For immediate backup, he would have to rely on Sweikert and one of the Jacksonville agents, who could just about fit under a planter attached to the outside of the trailer, and be in its shadow to anyone approaching by car. The others would have to flatten themselves in the swamp and rely on Levine to signal for the hit with his portable radio.

After some discussion it was agreed that three deliberate clicks would mean, go! They then dispersed to their positions, leaving Levine alone in the trailer to coach Davidson for the final betrayal. Once they started to tear into the suitcases, the deception would be obvious at once, so that it was important for Trupkin to implicate himself in this and previous deals within moments of his arrival.

At 1:50 A.M. Levine's portable crackled, and his lookout reported, "They're coming. I see their lights."

"Okay." Levine crossed to the closet. "Everybody quiet now. Heads down until they're inside."

He stirred the boa constrictor with his foot. It made no response.

"All right, John," he said pleasantly. "This is it. Make or break time. Do this right, and I'll get you the best deal I can. Mess up, and I swear I'll bury you in the shit so deep you'll never see daylight again. Believe me."

Davidson nodded, believing him. "Just don't frighten my snake, that's all," he said.

Levine climbed into the closet, and then, as a thought struck him, climbed out again. Switching on his tape recorder, he placed it out of sight beneath the couch, and with a last minatory wag of the finger, returned to his hiding place, leaving the door open a fraction, the better to hear what went on.

Davidson greeted Trupkin and John Clements, his hanger-on, in such a subdued tone that Levine ground his teeth. Any fool would have realized at once that something was wrong, but Trupkin was evidently too greedy to get at the heroin to pay attention to anything else. After listening to Davidson itemize his expenses and limply explain how much the three kilos had cost, Trupkin brushed him aside to get at the suitcases.

"Would you say it was better than the last lot?" he asked, and Levine relaxed.

"Yeah," said Davidson.

"*Much* better?"

"Much better."

"Dragon brand?"

"Dragon brand."

"Brother, I love you," said Trupkin fervently. "I'm really happy . . ."

His happiness was short-lived. As he burrowed into the first suitcase, and their conversation died, Levine clicked his portable three times, slowly and deliberately.

At the third click, there was a tremendous thump outside, and the whole trailer rocked on its springs.

"What the fuck . . . ?"

Set back on his heels with surprise, Levine was marginally slower getting out of the closet than was Sweikert in bursting through the door.

As the trailer filled with armed men shouting, "Federal officers," "You're under arrest," and "Up against the fucking wall," Levine noticed they were one short, and looked outside to see where he was.

The Jacksonville agent who had been hiding with Sweikert in the shadow of the trailer was sprawled on the ground, unconscious. At the third click, he had bounded up so eagerly that he had driven his head right through the planter and knocked himself cold.

". . . so now I try to flip Trupkin. He's got a book in his pocket with names and addresses and phone numbers all over the U.S. This kid's a main distributor of heroin, but he won't talk. I try everything, including the rabid bit, foaming at the mouth. Nothing. He's tough, right? 'If you wanna do time,' I keep telling him, 'I'm just the guy to get it for you.'

"Now it's Clements's turn. He's a nothing. Just hangs around Trupkin. But a guy like that can be valuable because he knows who the customers are, and they know him. 'I can see you're a flunky,' I tell him. 'You drove him out to Davidson's place, that's all. I know that. But technically you're as guilty as they are, so why not make it easy on yourself? I don't even wanna lock you up. Just tell me everything you know, and I'll let you take a walk.' And I meant it. The case against him was so weak I knew the magistrate would dismiss the charges. And he did. Later that morning. I tried to take the credit for it—'Okay, now you do something for *me*'—but Clements wasn't talking either. Which was *really* dumb, because now I made a point of talking to the U.S. Attorney down there to make *sure* he got indicted.

"I told him that. 'You're twenty-four years old,' I said. 'If you don't work for me, they're gonna put your case before a grand jury and I'm gonna tell 'em what you did, and they'll indict you for conspiracy. Doesn't take much to do that. Just *knowing* these guys is enough. After that, maybe you'll beat the case when it goes to trial and maybe you won't, but why take that chance?' 'I don't know nothing,' he says. And he's right. He don't know enough to save his own skin, so down he goes with Trupkin.

"Now I'm thinking, in all these Customs cases, the sons of bitches sending the shit into our country never get touched. In those days I was too inexperienced to know what I was getting myself into, but I wanted their Bangkok connection real bad. So I lay it on Davidson. 'About this guy Gary,' I says to him. 'You have his address?'

" 'Sure,' he says. 'I have his phone number, too.'

" 'Okay. Then suppose I wanted to go over there, as your partner or something, to pick up the next load. By myself. What would I have to do?'

" 'Well, first I'd have to introduce you,' he says. 'I'd have to write him a letter explaining why I couldn't come. And I'd have to send him a picture of both of us together—torn in half, so you could match your piece with his piece when you got there.'

"Now I'm hungry for the case. My head is full of visions of reaching around the other side of the world and smashing the shit out of the *real* enemy. It was something no one had ever done before. The next thing Davidson knows, we're having our picture taken against the wall of the Jacksonville courthouse. Arm in arm and smiling. Then he writes a letter. 'Dear Gary, Things are very busy here. I can't come myself so I'm sending my partner Mike. Please let me know if that's okay.' He puts my home address on it. We tear the picture in half and send Gary the bit with our happy, smiling faces. I figure it's worth a shot. So I mail the thing off and forget about it. Davidson stays in Florida with the others. George Sweikert and I fly back to New York, and that's it. Next case. . . ."

The letter from Davidson to Liang Sae Tiew in Bangkok was mailed on July 12. On August 25 Davidson received a reply asking when Mike was coming.

Levine took it into Al Seeley, Assistant Special Agent in Charge of the Hard Narcotics Unit, a former New York City detective and, as far as Levine is concerned, "the best boss I ever had in narcotics law enforcement."

Seeley read it and handed it back. "So what do you want to do?"

"Well . . ." Levine could feel his mind being read. "Davidson was up at their factory in Chiang Mai. He says they're knocking out hundreds of kilos a month. He was supposed to graduate to bigger things. I think it's worth a shot."

Seeley considered him thoughtfully. "Think you can do it?"

"Fuck, yeah," said Levine, still not sure which way this was going.

"Then go get your passport, kid."

Levine stepped off the plane in Bangkok with a tourist visa, $200, and no doubt in his mind that Providence would show him the way. He was met at the gate by the U.S. Customs Attaché for Thailand, Joe Jenkins, and Special Agent Tommy O'Grady of the Bureau of Narcotics and Dangerous Drugs, neither of whom shared his confidence. Spiriting him out of the airport, they explained why as they drove downtown.

"Officially, you don't exist," O'Grady said. "If we tell the Thais you're here, the case is dead. The head of the Thai narcotics squad is on the payroll of every major doper from here to Cambodia. On the other hand, if we *don't* tell 'em . . . If they catch you doing a dope deal here when we haven't told 'em you're officially in the country"—he exchanged a glance with Jenkins—"well, then they're gonna throw your ass in jail, and I don't think there's a fucking thing we could do to get you out."

"Okay." Levine looked from one to the other, slightly puzzled. "So what am I supposed to say now?"

"You still wanna do it?" asked Jenkins.

"Well, I sure as hell didn't come all this way just to go to a fucking massage parlor."

"All right." O'Grady nodded, laughed and punched Levine lightly on the arm. "Then let's do it. Let's jam it up their fucking asses."

But now they came to the next and still more serious problem: U.S. government regulations.

"It's a bitch, Mike, I know," said Jenkins sympathetically, "but they just won't allow you to front any money."

"No *money?*" He looked from one to the other incredulously. "Then what am I supposed to do? Ask 'em if they take American Express?"

"I don't know, Mike. But that's the way it is."

"But that's how Davidson always did it. He'd give 'em the money and they'd come back with the stuff. I'm supposed to be his partner. They're expecting me to show up with $6,500 cash, give it to 'em and wait. Just like *he* did."

"I know," said O'Grady. "That's how all the big Chinese dopers do it. That's why they got us over a fucking barrel out here. They know we don't front money. Everything the Thai cops know about us, the dopers know. In fact, once you make contact with these guys, you better not be seen with us. I'm serious, Mike. This is their fucking country. You could wind up dog meat—and there wouldn't be a fucking thing we could do about it."

"Well, thanks a lot," Levine said gloomily, thrown forward as the car braked sharply. Half the population of Thailand seemed to be out practicing for Indianapolis. "Welcome to Bangkok, right?"

"Look, you make contact with these guys and I'll start pushing in headquarters," Jenkins suggested. "But I gotta wait till around ten o'clock tonight to call. That's ten A.M. in Washington."

Levine sighed heavily.

"Hey," said Jenkins lightly. "You're the con man. A couple of Chink dope dealers ought to be like a walk in the park for you."

Levine stared out the window and grunted. "Some fucking park," he grumbled.

His opinion of it improved after he checked into the Siam Intercontinental, the best hotel in town. He called Gary from his room, and next morning two young Chinese arrived at his door.

Gary looked hardly old enough to be out by himself, but at least he spoke basic English. His companion, Thirachai Pluksamanee, whom he introduced as Mr. Geh, was about the same age but gave off weightier vibrations. Though Gary explained that his friend would not understand a word of their conversation, Levine could already see that Mr. Geh was the one he had to convince. Gary was the Thai version of John Davidson.

Fighting down a sometimes irresistible tendency to lapse into "Me Michael, you Gary" pidgin, Levine ordered up two Cokes and a Canadian Club from room service, and launched into an airy account of why he had come so far to buy three kilos of pure white, grade four heroin without actually having any money. This was not easy, because in their previous transactions Davidson had simply arrived, handed over Trupkin's money, and waited at his hotel for Gary and Mr. Geh to return in due course with the dope already secreted in their brilliantly constructed false-bottomed suitcases. But for Davidson's impatience to return on July Fourth, when he had supposed the vigilance of Customs would be at its lowest, and the consequent lingering smell of glue, the procedure might have been followed without variation for as long as they continued to do business. To want to change it now would represent an inexplicable attack of mistrust unless he could offer a convincing explanation.

As there had been talk of Gary himself carrying the next load to New York, Levine tried first for a simple misunderstanding. Davidson, he said, had assumed he would pay for everything when Gary arrived in the States. Oh, no, Gary said. The stuff came from Mr. Geh's uncle up north, strictly in return for cash. No money, no dope. John knew that. John always paid first.

"Oh, gee," said Levine. "You see, he thought you were ready to leave, like today or the day after. But if you can't do that then I guess I'd better call John tonight and have him wire the money tomorrow."

Gary explained this to Mr. Geh, who seemed to think it might do. The conversation then turned to general gossip about narcotics and mutual acquaintances, including the whereabouts of Davidson's friend, Tom Simmons, who had introduced Davidson to Gary, and who was now wanted in Florida on a hash-smuggling charge. Gary thought he was probably in India, which jibed with Levine's information, but the missing money was evidently still irking Mr. Geh, because he suddenly broke into a spate of irritable Chinese.

"No understand why money not here," Gary said, as Levine looked at him inquiringly. He tried to sound stern. "How long they send the money?"

"Well, if I call tonight . . . See, when it's eleven o'clock nighttime here it's eleven o'clock in the morning over there. That's when I call. John not easy to find, but I keep calling. After I get him, it will take a telegram maybe eight hours."

"And then you pay?"

"Yeah. I go telegraph office," Levine said, backing this up with sign language. "They give me the money. Then you come back here tomorrow, and I give you."

Knowing the pace at which Washington worked, Levine prepared the ground for further delay by telling Gary that another reason John had not sent the money but kept it for him in America was because he and Trupkin were plowing all they had into a Thai restaurant they wanted Gary to help them with when he arrived. They had customers waiting for the heroin they thought Gary was going to bring, and would have paid for the load out of the money they got for it. But there was no problem. When he called them about the change of plan, he was sure they could get these customers to front the money if necessary and wire it out to him. But the stuff would have to be as good as the last load. These new people had liked the quality and trusted John to get them more just like it.

As Gary hastened to reassure him, Levine was fairly confident he had roped him into this fantasy, but there was no way of telling with Mr. Geh, who hardly once took his eyes from Levine's face. After they left, promising to return around eight o'clock the next morning, Levine called the embassy to find out about the money.

"You're not gonna believe this," said Jenkins tiredly. He sounded as if he had been on the phone all night. "They say you should order only one kilo. They won't let you front more than $2,500. O'Grady even tried to get the money from BNDD, but they told him, 'Fuck you. It's a Customs case.' They're pissed that you're even here. I don't wanna *begin* to tell you the trouble *that's* causing."

Levine controlled himself with an effort. "They got any ideas how I'm gonna explain that?"

"Hey, that ain't all. Now they gotta cable the embassy to release the funds. Because the embassy won't *do* that without a cable. And that's gonna take twenty-four hours at best."

"How about at worst?"

Jenkins laughed. "How long you say you worked for the government?"

"Jesus. If we put this on TV, you think anybody'd believe it?"

Promptly at 8:00 A.M. Gary called up from the lobby, and Levine answered in his half-asleep, half-hungover voice. There was no word yet from Washington—he had already checked with the embassy—so that a further exercise in undercover histrionics was now required to keep the case afloat. Yawning and scratching, he invited the two young Chinese up to his room and launched into a rambling account of how some bar girl had rolled him for his money at the Na Na Bar the previous evening. All he had going for him was whatever credibility he could load into the role he had chosen for himself. With no money, all he had to offer was technique. But Mr. Geh was more interested in the money.

"Yeah. Well . . ." Levine looked at him as though trying to be sincere, only his eyes hurt. "John say this. It's very tight in the business, the restaurant. He's gonna send—by tomorrow, he's gonna send money. From Bank Americard. For one key. One kilo. He want you bring the other two. *You* bring two. *I* bring one. Understand?"

Obviously they did not.

"When I go back to U.S.," he said patiently, trying again, "he will call you direct. Send you money. Send everything to you direct. He said to me last night, it's stupid that I even come like this. From now on, he will try to deal directly with you. But for now, one key. By tomorrow, I expect money for one key."

"He send money?" Gary asked.

Levine nodded ruefully. It was hard enough anyway, trying to make a case out of thin air. Having to do so when neither subject could even understand what he was saying, let alone respond to the finesse of his pitch, would place an altogether unnatural strain on anyone's salesmanship.

"Yes. He send through Bank Americard. See, what happens is, he goes to Bank Americard in the U.S. and gives them money. And it's transferred to Mike Levine in Bangkok, Thailand."

"Siam Hotel?" asked Gary, determined to get this straight.

"Siam Hotel. Bank Americard, when they get the money, they send it here. By tomorrow. The latest, Wednesday."

"And then you go?"

"I go to U.S."

"And he call me?"

"When I get there, he'll sell that key. Then you do same thing. You know? He'll send to you the money, and you bring two kilos when you come. Okay?"

They were making progress. Gary now began to worry about the problem of having to identify himself by his real name when the money arrived. He was not at all comfortable with the idea, but as Levine pointed out, he would be traveling on a passport in his real name, so what difference did it make? They then agreed, without difficulty, that the price for one kilo, including the false-bottomed suitcase, would be $2,500. And all the while Mr. Geh watched Levine's face unblinkingly.

"Now let me ask you," Levine said, with a nod to Mr. Geh, to show he was including him in the conversation, "when I give you the money tomorrow, or whenever, how fast do you get the stuff? 'Cause I have to make, you know, reservations."

"Yes," said Gary. "Take me three days."

"You mean I have to wait three *days?*"

"Yes."

"Oh." He pulled a face. "Okay."

He was concerned because he was now being followed when he went out, and even at the hotel he sensed he was being watched. His first thought had been that perhaps the Thai police used stools to keep an eye on the guests, but O'Grady felt it was more likely to be the dopers. "That's the way they do business here," he said. "They don't take too many chances."

Either way, Levine had decided he would have to start acting more like a tourist. If he was under surveillance, a more concentrated study of Thai massage parlors was probably the answer, a thought that led him to describe his unfortunate visit to the Na Na Bar the previous evening.

This was an important part of the pitch, as he tried to explain later playing the tape of this conversation to Jenkins and O'Grady. So far he had been asking Gary and Mr. Geh to accept what they didn't want to hear—a deal scaled down from three kilos to one, and still with no money on the table. To help make it palatable, he first had to treat the situation as though everybody knew that such difficulties were commonplace in the American dope market, so that they would appear naïve and inexperienced if they questioned it. To strengthen this psychological barrier, the next step was to scale down the significance of the whole affair to the point where any further discussion of its details would seem petty compared with the more serious matter of where to go for the best bar girls. The only way to keep things going, in short, was to manipulate Gary and Mr. Geh into a position where any move toward breaking off negotiations would make them appear foolish in his eyes, and thus lose face, a matter of some importance to most Chinese.

"They steal your money?" asked Gary, catching on finally. "How much they steal?"

"A lot. I'm not sure."

"A few hundred dollar?"

"A couple of hundred. Three or four hundred. I don't know. I was drunk."

"You go out by yourself? Or somebody take you?"

"Somebody told me to go there. Americans, staying at the hotel. They say they went there. Had a good time."

Gary shook his head and looked wise. "If you go out I forget tell you one thing. If you go out, and somebody take you out by yourself, then they can steal your money."

"That's right." He was finding this very hard work.

"Tonight, if you go, you never can see that girl again. Don't go there again."

"No. No more. Next time I get girl here, when I do, I do it with my money in my mouth."

He gripped his wallet between his teeth and made riding motions. They all laughed merrily. Even Mr. Geh.

"So now I lost a lotta money, I wanna go back as fast as I can," he said. "As soon as money come, I would like you to go quick to get me the stuff."

This almost persuaded Gary to feel that *he* was to blame for all the delay, and on that note, Levine took them both downstairs for breakfast, in the course of which he noticed Jenkins taking surveillance pictures of them from the kitchen. Despite all the difficulties, the seduction was going well. Levine could see that Gary now really liked him and, as usual, had to fight an impulse to pity. The enemy was still human, after all, and the day he ceased to feel *something* for seducing a victim out of his life would be the day he turned in his badge. But meanwhile, to keep up the pressure, he insisted that Gary offer him a choice of suitcases in which to carry the stuff back—this effrontery buying him another twenty-four hours at least.

But by late afternoon on Day 4 there was still no word from Washington and he was forced to resume his balancing act. When Gary and Mr. Geh arrived at the hotel around four-thirty, expecting to hear good news, Levine seized the conversational high ground as soon as he opened the door and held it until they parted late that night, allowing them no opportunity to inquire about the money without appearing impolite and mistrustful.

First, they settled the matter of the suitcase. Offered a choice of gray, green or black, Levine chose black, and right away began to crowd them with his misgivings about people at the hotel seeing Gary deliver a brand-new suitcase to his room. He had been worrying about it all night, he told them.

"I know that." Gary looked reproachful. "We have a plan. When package come, I take to my home. Then you come. Get suitcase with package and go to different hotel."

"Oh. I get it. Yeah. Sounds good. I check in someplace else. Wait for the glue to dry, and then fly out. Yeah. That's good. Okay."

"We do this when John come. Same now."

"Yeah. Right."

That settled, he urged them downstairs for something to eat before taking them out for an evening of Thai boxing. Between bouts, after a swift exchange with Mr. Geh, Gary asked tentatively if Levine had heard from Davidson.

"No," he said distantly. "I told you. John say last time, something go wrong, he call me. If he don't call, everything okay."

"Oh," said Gary. "Okay."

Day 5 brought new problems. First, the cable had still not arrived.

"Oh, shit," said Levine. "These guys are getting pissed. You mean you can't get twenty-five hundred out of embassy funds? Now they know it's been cleared?"

"They *don't* know—not until they get the cable. That's not how it works. That's the State Department. What can I tellya?"

"Oh, *shit.*"

"Listen," said Jenkins. "Right now we've got a *bigger* problem. We got no arrest powers here. And as soon as the Thais know we're working on Gary and Mr. Geh, then forget it."

"What do you mean? You trying to tell me they *won't* arrest 'em?"

"Mike, I'm trying to tell you it's going to be tricky. Gary and Mr. Geh are big, which means they're paying part of the salary of the colonel in charge of the narcotics unit. So I talked to O'Grady and we figure the only way is to *embarrass* the Thais into doing it. As soon as we know the dope is on the way to your hotel, we'll call and tell 'em to rush right over because we got a drug deal going down in the parking lot. That's all. No names. Nothing. Just that. So when Gary and Mr. Geh get there, the cops'll have no choice. I *think.*" Jenkins rolled his eyes up to heaven. "But keep your head down because is the shit gonna hit the fan!"

"Sounds good to me," said Levine. "Don't see any problem with that."

"Wait," said Jenkins. "There's more. The problem is that the dope has got to be in *their* hands, not yours."

"Huh?" He looked for some sign that Jenkins was joking.

"No, I mean it. That's the law."

"You gotta be fucking kidding."

"Wish I was. If the shit is in *your* hands, they'll love it. Because that'll make *you* more guilty than Gary and Geh."

"I don't believe this. They're selling the shit to *me.* How am I gonna make 'em keep it in *their* hands?"

Jenkins waved his hands airily. "Just tell 'em to deliver the stuff to the hotel and we'll get the cops to bust 'em before they get out of their car."

"And if they don't have it with 'em?"

"Did I say it was going to be easy?"

When Gary and Mr. Geh checked in a few hours later for their daily visit, Levine could see they were in no mood for another runaround.

"Money come?"

"Yeah, it's on the way over now," he said, drawing them inside as if all their troubles were over. "I talked to John last night. He had the money in his hand. He was going right out to send it when I called. So everything's safe. Now we do business, okay?"

"When money come?"

"Yeah. When money come," Levine said, misunderstanding him deliberately. "And John say to me, stay in hotel now because he sending more money in two, three days. Maybe fifty, sixty thousand dollar. For big load. So I stay now, and then we go together. Understand?"

"Yeah," said Gary, bewildered. "But no money come?"

"Yeah. John send money last night. Maybe here now, but bank will call. And John say to me, Mike, you be very careful. No one know you there. But he think maybe police watch you and Mr. Geh. Okay? Tell me if you don't understand. John say, maybe police watching."

"Yeah."

"Okay. Then this is what I want to do. Me and you, we go get suitcase. Empty. Nothing inside suitcase. Then we go in your car for drive around town."

"Yeah. I know."

"Okay. If police grab us, nothing. They find nothing."

"Yeah."

"Understand? That's what I want to do, then. We bring suitcase here. Empty suitcase. Leave here, okay? And when you get stuff, you bring here. We put in suitcase here. You bring glue. Okay? Understand?"

They went around a couple more times before Gary finally grasped what he meant, and Levine started to lose him. He could feel it.

"See, John sending big money now," he said winningly. "He want twenty, thirty kilos. He tell me, be very careful. Stay in hotel. Wait for money. Nobody know you there, but maybe police know Gary and Mr. Geh. So you stay in hotel. You safe there. You tell Gary, bring stuff to hotel. Understand?"

If Gary understood, he wasn't saying. "Money come. You pay me first, okay?"

"Sure. I told you. Maybe money here already."

"Okay. You want Mr. Geh call uncle? In Chiang Mai? Tell uncle send package?"

"Yeah. One kilo now. Maybe twenty, thirty kilos next week."

By the time he had finished with them, he barely had the strength to drag himself to a massage parlor.

Day 6 began more promisingly.

"Hey, listen," said Jenkins. "I just got through talking to Washington. They swear the cable is signed, approved and on the way."

"Okay." Levine checked his watch. "I better not come by the embassy. Last night I had little men on bicycles following me all over town."

"Yeah?"

"Yeah. It's gone on too long. I don't know if they're cops or Gary's people getting itchy or what. If it's Gary I guess the money'll take care of it."

"Yeah. And if it's the cops God knows you don't act like a government agent. More like a massage-parlor freak."

"Yeah. If I go to another one I'm gonna have permanent footprints on my back." Relief had put him in a better humor. "Can you send the money over? Give it to room service. They can bring it up with my breakfast."

"Hey, slow down a minute. I said the cable was on its *way.* By the time it's routed through channels, we'll probably have it tomorrow."

"Tomorrow?" Levine sat down heavily on the bed. "You know what you're doing to me? You and those assholes in Washington? I'm losing these fucking guys, you know that? I've been stalling for a week. The only reason they're still around is because Gary likes me. He thinks I'm his friend. He even wants to take me up to Chiang Mai to meet Mr. Geh's uncle. He asked me last night."

"Oh, no," Jenkins said promptly. "That's *out.* The company just lost a guy up there. Some guerrilla outfit snatched him."

"Well, I wish they'd come down here and snatch *me.* Get me out of this shit. What am I gonna tell 'em now?"

"Well, if he likes you so much, just give him a big kiss and tell him you'll give him the money tomorrow."

There was nothing else Levine *could* say when he met the two Chinese later that day. The bank had called him, he said, to confirm that the money would be there the following morning. If Gary and Mr. Geh came to the hotel at noon, he would give them $2,500 in cash and settle the delivery arrangements.

"When I go out, people follow me," he said. "I no like that. Maybe police watch you. They see me with you, now they watch *me.* John tell me, stay in hotel. You safe there. You go with Gary to get stuff, maybe you get arrested with him. You tell Gary, bring stuff to you. Give him the money, and he bring stuff to hotel. Okay?"

Gary looked at Mr. Geh. "You pay money. Then we see. And you don't worry too much. No trouble with police."

"Okay." He would have to talk to Jenkins about that. "Tomorrow we fix everything."

Day 7 was a breeze compared with what had gone before. Jenkins counted $2,500 into Levine's hand. Levine went away and counted $2,500 into Gary's hand, reflecting that, if he had been a real trafficker, the outlay would have netted him at least a quarter of a million back in the U.S. Everybody was all smiles, even Mr. Geh.

"When package come?" Levine asked.

"Tomorrow. Mr. Geh call Chiang Mai, and uncle say tomorrow."

"Okay. You bring here? Like John say?"

"No. You take taxi. You go Dusit Thani Hotel, ten o'clock. We meet you outside with suitcase in car. Then we bring you back Siam Hotel and everything okay."

"Well, wait a minute. Let me think about that." Levine poked around the idea, looking for flaws. His problem was to make sure they had the heroin in their hands when the waiting police picked them up at the Siam Intercontinental parking lot. If they brought him back there, as Gary said, after he picked up the dope at the Dusit Thani, then it would amount to the same thing. "Yeah, okay." Jenkins and O'Grady would simply have to adjust. "Yeah. That way it'll look like I just went out and bought a new suitcase."

But Jenkins and O'Grady were less than happy about the change of plan when they met Levine later that night in a tourist bar to settle the final details.

"Why don't we get the Thais to take 'em off at the Dusit Thani?" Jenkins suggested. "That way you don't even have to *be* there."

Levine shook his head. "How do I know what's in the suitcase, Joe? If I was Mr. Geh, after all the bullshit he's listened to, I think I'd try a dry run with fucking flour first. Wouldn't you? You ought to see the way that bastard just sits and studies me. I know *I* would."

"Well, that's because you're a devious, double-crossing sonofabitch. How am I supposed to explain to the Thais why we employ a lowlife like you?"

"Just give 'em a big kiss and say I qualify to work for *them*. See, I *know* these two now. They're not gonna show up with the stuff and just wait like sitting ducks. I've put 'em through too many changes. Now I'm pretty sure they'll do the same to me. And if we have the Thai cops show up at the Dusit Thani and these guys have nothing . . ."

"Don't even *think* about it," said O'Grady.

"Well, Gary says they'll drive me back to the hotel, and I'm gonna hold them to that. Wherever they take me, I'll insist they bring me back. So the minute you see me leave, you guys tell the Thais the deal's going down, like we said. At the Siam Intercontinental. And as soon as I show up there with Gary and Mr. Geh, I'll step out of the car without the dope. That puts it in *their* hands, right?"

"What if they *won't* drive you back?" asked O'Grady, after a pause.

"Don't even *think* about it," said Levine.

On Day 8 it was Gary's turn to stall. He came around to the hotel unexpectedly early to join Levine for breakfast.

"Hey, I was just gonna call you," Levine said, as he let him in. "I talked to John again last night. You know, to tell him we're all set. He needs the stuff bad."

"Yeah? What John say?"

"He say, if stuff good, like last time, he send you money for big load when you come."

"Okay. But package not here yet Chiang Mai. We wait now. Take one more day."

"Yeah?" Levine tried to read the signs, but Gary just smiled and looked twelve years old. "You got problems?"

"No. No problems. Just late. Get here tomorrow."

"Oh. Okay." After stringing him along for a week, Levine was in no position to complain. "Same time?"

"Yeah. Outside Dusit Thani Hotel. Ten o'clock."

"Okay. That's what I was gonna call you about. John say I gotta see the stuff first. Before you glue up the suitcase, okay? Make sure it's good, like before. So you bring suitcase and stuff in car. *Not* glued, understand? You give *me* glue, and I fix suitcase back at hotel. Okay?"

Gary's smile turned vague. When he at last understood, he looked hurt, but Levine blamed everything on Davidson and his customers, and after a lengthy breakfast they parted the best of friends again. Levine then called Jenkins to postpone the operation for twenty-four hours, and with a whole day now before him, decided to keep up the good work as a tourist.

Day 9 began according to plan, except for a headache and weakness in the knees. As Levine drove away in his taxi, he caught sight of Joe Jenkins on the grounds of the hotel, and suddenly realized it was his last look at safety. From this point on, he was completely on his own. He could neither speak to nor understand anybody (except Gary, whom he did not trust anyway). There was no one he could turn to for help if he needed it, including the police, who would lock him up forever if they caught him now. And already he had no idea at all of where he was in this totally foreign and bewildering city.

His sudden sense of isolation touched off such a tingling shock of excitement that he laughed out loud, startling the cabdriver into an answering guffaw, which tickled him still further, so that they both laughed at everything all the way to the Dusit Thani, where Levine overtipped him heavily, having made at least one friend in Bangkok.

He then stood outside the hotel for several minutes before Gary approached on foot, having obviously kept him under observation until satisfied he had come alone. Beckoning Levine to follow, he led the way down a side street and then doubled back and forth for a while, stopping repeatedly to look over his shoulder. Levine made no attempt to hide his amusement at these precautions, and eventually Gary grinned back. Turning another corner, they came upon Mr. Geh sitting behind the wheel of a small blue Toyota. On the backseat were a shopping bag and a black suitcase.

Motioning Levine to get in beside Mr. Geh, Gary climbed into the back and they drove off at high speed through a maze of narrow, twisting lanes. Then they slowed to a walking pace and actually stopped several times before turning around and heading back the way they had come. Eventually, they reached the edge of the city and drove down long stretches of straight road, with the jungle on one side and waterways on the other, again stopping several times to watch for signs of surveillance.

After almost an hour of this, Mr. Geh looked back at Gary and nodded.

"Okay, Mike," Gary said. "You look now."

Twisted around in his seat, Levine watched as Gary showed him how the suitcase worked. The heroin, packed very flat in sealed plastic bags, was already in position, and all that remained to be done was for the false bottom to be glued down.

"You get more than kilo," Gary said. "Same money, okay?" He really liked Levine. He was giving him a present. "This for you, too," he added, opening the shopping bag to show him a pair of expensive-looking silk shirts.

For a moment, alone with them in some unknown part of a foreign city, sitting in a car with a kilo of heroin and two gift shirts, Levine felt guilty.

"Hey, that's great," he said warmly. He liked Gary, too, but that had nothing to do with anything. "We go hotel now?" He put on his sunglasses. If he was wearing them when they arrived back at the Siam Intercontinental, that meant the deal had gone down and Jenkins should signal the Thais to move in. "Have drink? We celebrate, okay?"

"Okay." Gary beamed.

Levine settled back contentedly. He was unarmed, but pretty certain they were, too. If the Thai police now did their stuff, he would have pulled off a grand slam unequaled in Customs history. Not content with flipping a major smuggler, he had gone back all the way down the line to nail the guy's financier and associates in Florida, and then on halfway around the world to collar their source. Nobody else had ever done that, not as far as he knew.

"Why are we stopping?"

"You get out here," Gary said, smiling but surprised he should ask. "Take cab. Then we meet at hotel."

"Now wait a minute." Levine sat up straight. "That's not the deal. You mean, you're gonna leave me on the sidewalk? With a suitcase full of dope? No way. Forget it."

"It's okay, Mike. No problem. Cab come. He take you hotel. We come later. No worry."

"Uh-*uh*." He shook his head emphatically. "You no leave me here. I hear stories. I get out with suitcase. Thai police come. No way. You take me hotel, like we said."

Gary looked hurt. In a rapid burst of Chinese, he explained the situation to Mr. Geh, who glanced at the suitcase. Levine hugged it to him, in case they should think of throwing it out, and sat tight. If they *did* have guns, he was done for.

"We know police," said Gary reproachfully. "They not come. Nothing bad happen."

Levine again shook his head. "*You* careful. *Me* careful."

"John trust. Everything okay. Why you no trust?"

"John say, be careful. He tell me, stay in hotel. But I come with you, okay? I trust you. Now you take me back."

Caught between the two of them, Gary shrugged and lapsed once more into Chinese, after which they both fell silent, appraising their chances of ejecting him by force. Abandoning that idea, Gary proposed a compromise.

"Mr. Geh say, we take you near hotel. Very close. Two blocks. Maybe less. Okay? Don't worry."

"Okay," said Levine, easing them back step-by-step. With too much strain on the line, *they* might get out and take a cab, leaving him holding the baby.

Talking nonstop in agitated Chinese, the two then drove off again, with Levine clutching his heroin and starting to sweat about the possibility of their taking him someplace quiet, where they could count on finding help. But he soon saw they were heading in toward the center of the city, and eventually recognized a major intersection that he knew to be no more than a couple of blocks from the hotel grounds. Day and night, it was busier than Times Square, with a more or less permanent traffic jam clogging the streets and a sea of humanity filling in the spaces.

Spotting an opening, Mr. Geh pulled over to the curb and stopped. Ignoring Levine, he twisted around in his seat to harangue Gary again, then abruptly got out of the car and disappeared in the crowd.

"Where's he going?" Levine demanded, watching the main man slip through his fingers.

Gary came around to take Mr. Geh's place behind the wheel. "Don't worry," he said, misunderstanding the cause of Levine's anguish. "He come back later. Say goodbye. *I* take you now. Keep cool."

Without further hesitation, he drove onto the hotel grounds and pulled up outside the main entrance, where Joe Jenkins was waiting with a squad of Thai police. Levine stepped out immediately, leaving Gary with the dope as local law required, but nobody else moved. He could see from the faces of the police that they were being asked to arrest somebody they were not supposed to. It was only when Jenkins stepped in front of the car to prevent Gary from driving off again that the uniformed lieutenant in charge of the police ordered his men to surround it and make the arrest.

"Where the fuck's the other guy?" demanded O'Grady, from the back of an unmarked Thai police Mercedes as it pulled up along-side.

"He got out," Levine shouted, making for the door as O'Grady threw it open. "A couple of blocks back."

"Shit."

O'Grady yelled in Thai at the driver, and the Mercedes took off with Levine neither in nor out. Grabbing at his arms, Paul Samaduroff, Jenkins's partner, managed to pull the door shut behind him, but then the car screeched to a halt at the parking lot entrance, balked by the wall of traffic on the street outside.

Fuming with frustration, Levine almost missed Mr. Geh. He was standing near the front of the crowd that had already begun to mass across the street from the hotel to watch what was going on.

"That's *him*," he breathed incredulously, ducking down in the seat, so that Geh wouldn't see him and bolt. "Next to the guy in the pink shirt."

O'Grady bellowed at the Thai cop in front, who apparently could not see anybody. Cursing him in English, O'Grady then leaped out himself and plunged into the traffic like a matador crossing 42nd Street.

By the time Mr. Geh saw him coming, it was already too late. As he turned to run, O'Grady tackled him hard and held him facedown on the sidewalk at the feet of the crowd until two Thai cops, who no longer had a choice, strolled across the street to take over.

"And that about wrapped it up," Levine said, as a hundred cops returned to their Westchester classroom with an audible sigh. "Now it was over, I really had to hand it to Jenkins and O'Grady. Those two guys had taken chances I had no right to ask of anybody who had to stay in Thailand. The local cops were definitely not happy. But now they had no choice, they leaned on Gary and Mr. Geh to give up the suitcase maker, and next day the Bangkok papers were full of it. And not all that friendly either. Going on about how drugs were really an American problem, and it was our fault for corrupting innocent Thai citizens.

"Didn't say anything about innocent Thai

cops, though. Before I came home, the colonel in charge of the narcotics unit asked to meet me, so I went over. And you should have seen the place. Looked more like a BMW dealership in Beverly Hills than a police station."

"Pretty mad at you, right?" said a fat deputy sheriff in front. He had been distracting Levine for almost an hour with his attempts to get comfortable on a plastic stackable chair.

"Yeah, I guess you could say that. Just looked me up and down and said, 'You very smart,' like he really didn't mean it, and that was that. End of interview. Short time later, they busted him for corruption and found more than a million dollars cash in his safety deposit boxes."

"What about Gary and Mr. Geh? They take a walk?"

"Oh, no. No, they all went down. I flew back a couple of times to testify and they each got seven years, which is like a death sentence out there. No, I did what I wanted. I went full circle. Right around the world and got 'em all."

As an exercise in sustained improvisation, undercover on unfriendly ground, without money, props or backup, the case had no parallel in U.S. Customs records, and yet the feat went largely unrecognized. While the bureau could hardly deny him a Treasury Special Act award for his conduct of the investigation, virtuosity of Levine's sort rarely wins friends in government service, being hard to manage, or even contain, within a tidy bureaucratic framework. And most of the time, Levine did not mind. "By then," he says, "I was used to violating the laws of gravity and getting nothing to show for it." As long as he was allowed to apply his unique blend of tenacity, imagination and bilingual histrionics to worthy cases, the work was its own reward.

Though greeted more often with suspicion than encouragement, Levine's ability to snare high-level targets in webs of persuasive fantasy had not only become his greatest single asset as an undercover agent but would also find expression later in cases that permanently changed the face of South American politics as well as the essential character of narcotics law enforcement.

"How about the guys in Florida?" somebody asked. "Davidson and that bunch. How did they make out?"

"Well, now, that's kind of interesting. Davidson pled guilty to one count—that was the deal—and drew four years, which is like nothing. Parole board probably let him out in two. Trupkin—the main man, the financier and brains of the outfit—he keeps his mouth shut and goes to trial, along with Clements, his gofer. But in the middle of the trial, after they play the tapes of the phone conversations and the one from the recorder hidden under the couch in the trailer, Trupkin's attorney asks for a recess and changes Trupkin's plea to guilty on one count. The judge allows it and gives him fifteen years."

From the grunts of approval, everybody seemed to think the sentence was about right.

"Okay. Now Clements, the asshole, continues on trial by himself—though I'd warned him from the beginning. Sure enough, the jury convicts on two counts of conspiracy and the judge locks him up for thirty years. Didn't even look up from his papers."

Several people whistled, and Levine was silent for a moment.

"Well . . . like I always say, justice is none of our business. We're paid to lock people up, that's all. What happens to 'em after that has got nothing to do with us. It's up to them, their attorneys, *our* attorneys, public opinion, politics, the media, God, the weather, the Dow Jones average—you name it. Juries convict people, not agents. And judges decide sentences. But that's not to say you won't face real dilemmas about guilt and justice.

"I remember another case I had where a guy sold me a pound of heroin, hand to hand, and took a walk. Would you believe the judge sentenced him to time served? Two or three months, okay? Walks out of the courtroom and he's back in business on the streets that same afternoon. And yet Clements, who only drove Trupkin over to collect the dope, he gets thirty years."

Levine looked around expectantly, but nobody seemed to have anything to say.

"Well, those are the breaks, right? *I* didn't put him in the trailer that night. I even showed him a way out. Clements was a big boy, and I don't think I lost a minute's sleep over what happened to him. In fact, him and Davidson, they gave me one of the best tools I got for flipping defendants. Davidson worked and got four. Clements wouldn't work and got thirty. Strong argument. You wanna use it next time you make a seizure, be my guest. But what would you say if I told you I locked up a guy once and then spent as much time and effort getting him *out* as I ever did putting somebody *in?*"

The fat deputy shook his head, more interested in an experiment with *two* chairs to see if he could distribute his weight more comfortably.

"Happened right after I got back from Thailand," Levine went on. "Al Seeley calls me into his office and hands me a piece of paper. 'Some guy just tried to smuggle two kilos of cocaine out at the Lufthansa terminal at JFK,' he says, 'I want you to take care of it.' 'The guy gonna work?' I ask him. 'No, they got no bodies,' he says. 'Looks like he escaped on foot. So will you get over there and find out what the fuck is going on?' "

Inspector William C. Shaw was on duty in the Lufthansa cargo building at Kennedy Airport when Sergio Espinoza Ibarra arrived to claim a suitcase he had shipped through as air freight from Santiago de Chile. Around forty years old, five feet ten, medium build, clean-shaven, and with long dark hair, he presented a carrier's certificate for one piece of luggage, listed as personal effects, and consigned to himself at the Hotel Stanford, New York City. Unable to speak any English, Ibarra was accompanied by Oscar Camacho, a cabdriver who had picked him up outside the TWA terminal and agreed to act as interpreter.

When the cargo agent, Theodore Moritz, located the suitcase, he called over Inspector Shaw to examine it in the presence of Ibarra, who, through Camacho, confirmed that the contents were his personal effects. Inside were a pair of pajamas and eleven pairs of cheap men's shoes, in a variety of sizes.

With the studiously blank expression assumed by all good Customs men when their suspicions are aroused, Shaw removed one of the shoes to examine it more closely. Seeing nothing obviously wrong, he then flexed it experimentally, and with a faint pop, the sole split open to reveal a white powder inside.

"Well, well," said Inspector Shaw.

He looked up in time to catch a brief glimpse of Ibarra sprinting through the door.

When Levine arrived an hour or so later, the inspector showed him a total of nearly two and a half kilos of cocaine hydrochloride recovered from the hollow soles and heels of Ibarra's eleven pairs of shoes. But there was still no sign of their owner, despite an airportwide alert, and after taking statements from Shaw, Moritz and Camacho, Levine drove back to the city to see if anybody knew anything about Ibarra at the Hotel Stanford. Having no great hopes of this, he was considerably surprised to find that somebody named Ibarra had checked in a few days earlier, signing the register as Jaime Ibarra. Even more astonishing, he had not as yet checked out. And there in his mailbox with the key was a Lufthansa notification of arrival of baggage.

Satisfied that this Ibarra's description tallied with that of the airport Ibarra, and that his bags and possessions were still in the room, Levine settled down to wait. Spelled by George Sweikert, the agent who had accompanied him to Florida on the Davidson case, he waited for the rest of that day, all night and all next morning. Then, at about 12:30 P.M., a male Hispanic, around forty years old, five feet ten, medium build, clean-shaven, long dark hair, and just about the ugliest human being Levine had ever seen, minced into the lobby, collected his key and the Lufthansa envelope, and swung his hips into the elevator.

Levine allowed him enough time to get up to his room before he and Sweikert followed and banged on the door.

"Yes?" said a voice, in English. "Who is it?"

"Federal agents," Levine said. "Open up."

As the door opened a cautious crack, the two agents pushed their way in, guns drawn, propelling Ibarra backwards, squawking with alarm. In his hand was the Lufthansa envelope.

"Jaime Ibarra?"

"Yes?" he quavered.

Levine holstered his gun. "Were you out at JFK Airport yesterday?" he demanded. In English.

Ibarra flinched at his tone. "Me? No. Why? What I do?"

"What's that in your hand?"

"This? I don't know. It was with my key."

"Is it for you?"

"What? Oh." He seemed frightened to take his eyes off Levine in case he attacked him while he wasn't looking. "No. Not for me. This is for Sergio Espinoza Ibarra."

"Well, that's you, isn't it?"

"Me?" He was clearly startled. "No, no. Not me. My name is Jaime Ibarra. Look. I show you my passport. I don't know this name. This is some mistake."

Levine thought so, too. He could usually tell in the first couple of minutes if he was on the right track or not. Although the guy's English was terrible, Ibarra knew enough to collect a suitcase without needing a cabdriver to interpret for him.

Levine looked around the room. On the dresser at his elbow was another envelope, already opened, with a letter folded up inside. It was addressed to Jaime Ibarra at an address in Bogotá, Colombia. The sender had written his own name and a New York address in one corner of the envelope. The sender's name was Sergio Ibarra.

"Okay," said Levine. "Get your coat."

They had a reasonable complaint, what with the coincidence of name, the matching descriptions and the Lufthansa notice. Although Ibarra is a fairly common name in Spanish, and the desk clerk would naturally put the envelope in Jaime's box if he was the only Ibarra staying at the hotel, there was enough to hold him while they found out if anybody recognized him as the guy who had legged it across the airport.

Arriving downtown, Levine processed his prisoner and continued to question him, with a growing certainty that they had the wrong man. According to Jaime, the Sergio Ibarra who had written to him in Bogotá was his nephew, whose full name was Sergio Ibarra Merlano. He knew no one by the name of Sergio Espinoza Ibarra, and certainly nothing about his shoes.

Sensing that Levine was disposed to believe him, he began to unwind, and before long, was launched unstoppably on his life story. He was a dancer by profession, he said, and had worked for Federico Fellini in *La Dolce Vita*. Only a tiny part, but significant. While in Rome, he had fallen in love with an Italian policeman, but the affair had gone badly. When they quarreled, he had tried to kill himself by jumping off a high building, only he had lost his nerve at the last moment. He had always been afraid of heights. To prove he was telling the truth, he produced a tattered newspaper clipping with a picture of himself clinging to the dome of a church. Eventually, the Rome fire department had been called to pry him loose.

Levine interrupted this saga to drive Ibarra over to the Eastern District courthouse for his arraignment before U.S. Magistrate Vincent Catoggio, and at this point the system started to go wrong.

Catoggio was celebrated among federal agents and prosecutors for his occasionally eccentric views and wayward sense of humor. Unimpressed from the start by Ibarra's general demeanor, he suddenly leaned forward on hearing the drugs came from Chile, and fixed him with an intense glare. As Levine remembers it, the exchange then went something like this:

"Chile?" Catoggio thundered. "You Chileans make me *sick.*"

Ibarra, who had wisely chosen to have a court interpreter translate for him, started to protest in Spanish, *"Pero, pero, pero,"* but Magistrate Catoggio under full sail was not easily deflected.

"Just who do you people think you are?" he demanded.

"Pero, pero, pero . . ."

"First you have the gall to nationalize Anaconda Copper. You take stock away from poor retired people who need their dividends to live on, and now you send *drugs* to this country?"

"Pero, pero, pero . . ."

"Bail is set at $50,000."

"Pero, pero, pero . . ."

"Judge, I think the defendant wants to say something," said Jaime's court-appointed attorney.

"Yes?" The magistrate surveyed Ibarra from a great distance. "What do you want to say?"

"I'm a Colombian," said Jaime diffidently.

"Oh." Catoggio considered this. "Well," he said, "I don't like Colombians either."

". . . You wanna hear my other favorite Catoggio story?" Levine asked, when they stopped laughing.

"Okay. Well, we get a tip that a couple of Colombians are coming in with cocaine hidden in their wooden legs. Some wise guy's hiring people with artificial limbs to bring the stuff in. And sure enough, here they come, hobbling through Customs with coke in their legs. We know because we drilled a little hole and white powder came out, but we couldn't get the goddamn legs off because they were the old-fashioned kind with suction cups. You needed a special key to release them, and their boss had kept that. So we take 'em over to St. Vincent's Hospital, in Greenwich Village, and the doctor on duty hasn't seen a leg like that since the Spanish-American War. He makes each guy grab hold of the heating pipes while three of us—the doctor, me and another agent, Joe King—try to wrestle it off. We're twisting and pulling. The guy's screaming. There's blood all over the place. And finally his leg pops off like a cork out of a bottle. And inside each leg, there's a kilo of cocaine.

"So now we find 'em each a pair of crutches, because the legs are evidence, and take 'em over to Eastern District to be arraigned in front of Magistrate Catoggio. He looks at the evidence, listens to an outline of the case, stares at the defendants for a minute. Very solemn. And then he says, 'Seems clear to me they don't have a leg to stand on.' "

As Jaime Ibarra had about as much chance of making $50,000 bail as of joining the Bolshoi, he went to jail for ten days to await his next hearing, and Levine conferred with Joan O'Brien, the Assistant U.S. Attorney in charge of the case.

"You got enough to hold him for now," he said, "but I'm not so sure he's the right guy. We may have to cut him loose."

"Well, unless we can tie him in directly with the shoes, you're probably right," she agreed. "If this is all there is, I'll move to dismiss next time. But you got ten days. And I don't like coincidences."

As soon as he could, for he was also working a dozen other cases, Levine took Ibarra's mugshots out to the airport and showed them to Inspector Shaw and the cargo agent, Theodore Moritz. Both were quite positive that Jaime was *not* the man who had fled from the Lufthansa cargo building. Levine then went looking for Oscar Camacho, the taxidriver, and he, too, failed to identify Ibarra as the fare he had picked up outside the TWA terminal.

All that remained now was the possibility of a conspiracy. As Jaime had obviously not gone to the airport himself, perhaps he knew who *did*. As a first step, Levine obtained a list of the telephone calls Ibarra had made during his stay at the Stanford Hotel, and began methodically to track each one down.

After eliminating the inconsequential calls, he was left with six possible co-conspirators, including Jaime's nephew, Sergio Ibarra Merlano. The others were old friends Jaime had known in Colombia, including two who had gone out to the airport with Sergio to meet him upon his arrival from Bogotá, and another, Malmgren Restrepo, whom he had not seen for ten years. Each of these now had to be interviewed and photographed for possible identification by Shaw, Moritz and Camacho. With other, more urgent cases intervening, Levine was still working on this when Ibarra came up for his hearing after ten days at West Street, and as all Levine had succeeded in doing was weaken an already flimsy case, the charges against Ibarra were dismissed.

So far, so good. If the worst that happened to Jaime Ibarra in his life was ten days' wrongful imprisonment, he would be better off than a lot of people sucked into the system, including John Clements. But having started an investigation of Ibarra's associates, Levine was obliged to complete it. And after three weeks of low-level, routine police work, he had eliminated everybody but Malmgren Restrepo, a Colombian artist with a permanent resident's visa and a clean record, who lived on Jones Street, in Greenwich Village.

Unlike the others, Restrepo proved uncooperative and disdainful when Levine approached him.

"This is very boring," he said. "Why are you bothering me with this? Go away."

After ten years' residence in the U.S., Restrepo spoke English as well as Levine, and would have had no reason at all to ask a cabdriver to interpret for him, but his refusal to answer questions or have his photograph taken led to an official, written request for him to appear at Varick Street for an interview. And when he reluctantly showed up there for questioning, he lied.

Flustered, perhaps, because Levine and Sweikert formally read him his rights at the outset, he denied knowing anyone named Jaime Ibarra, and claimed not to recognize him from his mug shots.

"You sure?" asked Levine. "The guy's an actor. A dancer from Colombia. You're an artist. Maybe you know him from the theater or something back there?"

"No. I've not been back to Bogotá in ten years. And I never saw that man before in my life."

Before letting him go, Levine gave him several more chances to change his mind, but each time, and with increasing vehemence, Restrepo denied all knowledge of anybody named Jaime Ibarra.

Faced with this new problem, Levine now called Ibarra for an interview, ostensibly to pick up some personal effects held at Varick Street since his release. As standard procedure, he again advised him of his rights before asking him if he remembered making any telephone calls while staying at the Stanford Hotel. Ibarra thought for a moment, and then remembered them all, except for the one to Restrepo.

Levine sighed. There was not a doubt in his mind that Ibarra and Restrepo knew nothing whatever about the cocaine in the shoes, but between them they were making it very difficult for him to prove it.

"Is that all?" he asked. "Didn't you also call a Malmgren Restrepo? At 691-4689?"

"Oh, yes," replied Ibarra without hesitation, impatient with himself. "Malmgren. That's right. I forgot him."

"How long have you known Restrepo?"

"We were friends in Colombia. Before he come live here. Long time now. Maybe ten years."

"Why did you call him?"

"Why?" Ibarra looked surprised. "Why I call him? I told you. Old friend. I want see him."

"Okay, so then you got together with him, right?"

"No. Not yet. Maybe soon. Malmgren very busy. Then this happen. Maybe he hear about it. I don't know."

Levine showed him a ten-year-old photograph of Restrepo supplied by Immigration. It had been taken when he applied for his green card, and Ibarra recognized him at once.

"Yes," he said. "That's my friend. Why you ask me this? Malmgren in trouble?"

They both were. Although Al Seeley was inclined to agree that the two were probably innocent, he was more interested in facts than in hunches. There was no question of dropping the investigation at this stage, and in the absence of any other lead, Restrepo was now the best suspect they had.

"All right," said Levine. "But that old Immigration shot is no good. He looks a lot different now. Lemme take Sweikert and Jesús Muniz and we'll get some surveillance pictures of this guy. Then I'll try 'em on the airport witnesses, like the others, and close this thing out. I'm getting really pissed off with this case."

For three days, the three agents stood watch outside Restrepo's house and his place of work on East 45th Street. When finally they had a few good pictures, Levine put them in an envelope with ten other surveillance photographs of other subjects, and drove out to the airport to settle the matter once and for all.

Inspector Shaw looked through the collection several times and gave up, shaking his head. "Tell you the truth," he said, "I didn't pay that much attention to the guy until he ran off. And then I only got a look at the back of his head."

Having, as he supposed, disappointed Levine several times already by failing to recognize anybody, Theodore Moritz, the cargo agent, was now anxious to please. He studed each photograph closely, going back for a second look at some of them, and finally seized on a picture of Restrepo.

"That's him," he said. "That's the one."

Levine groaned. "You sure?"

"I'm positive. Definitely him."

That left Oscar Camacho, the cabdriver, and the best of the three witnesses in that he had been with the smuggler longer than the other two. Levine drove over to show him the pictures—and found he had moved since his last visit. No one knew where.

"Nothing *I* can do," Seeley said. "The U.S. Attorney's got it. Talk to Joan O'Brien. If she thinks she's got a good enough case for the grand jury, that's all there is to it. It's up to her."

Next morning Levine arrested Restrepo on Jones Street and took him downtown for processing. He was then arraigned before Magistrate Catoggio, and held in $25,000 bail. A subsequent search of Restrepo's apartment turned up little of interest except two Columbian passports, one expired, which showed that contrary to what he had told Levine at the Varick Street interview, he had been back to Bogotá twice since settling in New York.

"So he lied," said Levine. "He's nervous about his green card. He thought Ibarra was in trouble and wanted no part of it."

"Ibarra *is* in trouble," said Joan O'Brien. "The minute I saw his face, I *knew* he was wrong. Now Moritz puts Restrepo in the cargo building. Restrepo lies about knowing Ibarra. And Ibarra's the name on the waybill. What more do you want?"

Levine sighed. "Well, Restrepo speaks English. Why would he need an interpreter?"

"To throw us off? Who knows what goes on in people's minds."

"No, no. And anyway, he didn't have time. He was working that day."

"He was out to lunch. The times fit. You told me yourself."

"It's too close, Joan. Much too close. The people he works with say he was only gone an hour at most. How's he gonna make it out to the airport and back in an hour?"

But Joan pointed out that his co-workers could easily have mistaken the time.

"Well, I dunno. I'm not that sure about Moritz. He's too goddamn anxious to please. How about a lineup at least?"

"Okay," she said. "Let's do it. You'll see."

After failing to identify Restrepo from the surveillance pictures, Inspector Shaw also failed to pick him out in the lineup three days later. Theodore Moritz, however, applied himself to the problem with ominous diligence.

"Will you have Number 2 turn around slowly, please?"

"Sure," said Levine, willingly enough, for Restrepo was Number 3.

"Now will you have him look up?"

Number 2 looked up, as instructed.

"Now will you have him stand with his back to me."

"Sure." Joan O'Brien was getting nervous.

"Okay. So please have Number 2 face me again."

Moritz stared at him, long and hard.

"Yes," he said. "It's Number 3. Definitely Number 3. I would know him anywhere."

O'Brien clapped her hands. "I knew it, I knew it," she said. "You satisfied now?"

Levine was satisfied that Moritz had identified Restrepo as the man in the photograph he had picked out three days earlier, and that Ibarra was probably guilty of no more than ugly in the first degree, but there was nothing to be gained by belaboring the point. Ibarra and Restrepo were probably booked for fifteen years each in a federal penitentiary. Unless he could find Oscar Camacho.

He had already started to look for him when the federal grand jury indicted the two later that afternoon. And he was still looking when Ibarra was rearrested by federal marshals on a bench warrant four days later.

Camacho had been living with a welfare client but she had kicked him out, she explained, when she heard he was sleeping around, and if Levine found out where he was she would like for him to tell her so she could go stick a knife in his neck.

Unfortunately, no one had thought to make a note of the cab company Camacho worked for, and the last address the hack bureau had for him was with his homicidally inclined girlfriend. But as Camacho had picked up his fare at the TWA terminal, it was reasonable to assume he had been driving a medallion cab, and all Levine had to do now was check every cab company in the five boroughs. In between working night and day on all his other cases.

It took him three weeks to work through the list, and while several dispatchers knew the name, none of them knew where he was. At this point, Levine was tempted to give up. The guy could have left town. Taken a different kind of job. Gone on vacation. Dropped dead. And nobody was prepared to help out. O'Brien felt she had a good enough case without Camacho, and neither Customs nor the New York Police Department was interested in pursuing a case that was already "solved," not with hundreds more piling up around their collective ears.

As a last resort, Levine took to asking every Hispanic cabdriver he came across if he knew Oscar Camacho—and the long shot paid off. One rainy night someone *did*. Sure he knew Oscar. He'd just started driving nights for a guy who owned his own cab. Finding him after that was routine.

"Yeah," Camacho said. "That bitch. Didn't want *her* to find me, so when I split I took off for a couple of days. Dropped a bundle at Belmont, and went in with this guy who owns his own hack. Family man. He pushes daytime. I take it nights."

"Yeah, yeah," said Levine, producing a mugshot of Restrepo. "Look at the picture. You recognize that guy?"

Camacho took a second, closer look. "No. Never saw him before."

"Is that the guy you picked up at the TWA terminal and took to the Lufthansa cargo building?"

"Him? No way. Nothing like him."

" . . . And that blew it. We already had a witness who couldn't identify the suspect. Inspector Shaw. Now we had another one who was ready to *swear* Restrepo was not the guy who went for the shoes. Two out of three. No jury in the world was gonna convict on Moritz alone, and Joan O'Brien knew it, although she didn't give up easy.

" 'Well, how do you know *Camacho* isn't lying?' she says to me. 'I'll bring him in.'

" 'Yeah, I think you should do that,' I tell her. 'Talk to him, because you're not gonna win this case. He's solid. Everything checks out. He's a good witness. And you can't *hide* the guy.'

"So she finally drops the charges, gets Ibarra and Restrepo out of jail, and doesn't speak to me again for a year. In fact, everybody's pissed off with me except Jaime Ibarra.

"Jesus, was he ugly! I know I saved *his* fucking life. One look at that pan and any court in the world would have put him away forever. If we're gonna talk philosophy, I think I could prove a pretty good case that there's absolutely no fucking justice for the ugly."

They all laughed, but Levine was serious.

SIX

"My God, I love this life. It's fantastic. I love it."

Before actually meeting Levine, Al Seeley had been reluctant to take him on. He needed a good street agent for the Hard Narcotics Group, and whoever heard of a street agent with a name like Levine? When he got him anyway, he proceeded to work Levine's tail off, as though determined to find the flaw that had to be in there someplace, and in failing to find it, played *his* part in extending the range and versatility of the Customs Bureau's secret weapon.

Levine had arrived precisely on cue, in the year when, for the first time, cocaine seizures by federal agents exceeded the volume of heroin seized. Now the focus of President Nixon's so-called War on Drugs began to shift from Asia and the Middle East, from the sleazy, sniveling world of the heroin addict, to Central and South America, to the sleazy, self-adoring world of the coke-snorting swinger. With Cubans, Colombians, Puerto Ricans and blacks beginning to dominate the supply lines, and Hispanic agents being rarer even than Jewish ones, the best hope the bureau had of scoring a few token victories against the mass invasion of cocaine traffickers was a dark-skinned, Spanish-speaking undercover artist of inexhaustible energy.

Not that Levine was remotely interested in the political mileage the Nixon administration hoped to gain from a hard line on drugs, or ever less than deadly serious in his vendetta against dopers: he hated them all implacably. And almost everything that happened went to reinforce his conviction of being singled out as an instrument to strike them down, including his timely transfer to Customs, Seeley's demanding management, and even the disintegration of his marriage. He was in the right place at the right time, sharpening his claws on the toughest cases that came along. He loved his family, but there was no way anybody could meet *two* full-time commitments.

By the time Levine hit his stride, any serious attempt to suppress the cocaine traffic would have required an act of God rather than an act of Congress.

In effect, Customs and the other federal agencies involved had been called out in a blizzard and told to keep the snowflakes from hitting the ground. Cocaine was pouring into the country through every port of entry, through every crack and chink and loophole in its mostly unmanned frontiers and coastline. It came through in tourists' baggage and postal packages; in body cavities and swallowed condoms; in diapers and girdles; in cans of spray deodorant and toothpaste tubes; in Cadillacs and baby strollers; in game fish catches and baseball mitts; in hollowed-out books and teddy bears. People even saturated their clothes in cocaine solutions and *wore* it in.

Smuggling coke didn't even feel like breaking the law. Pastors, priests and rabbis did it. Diplomats and politicians. Little old ladies, who insisted on itemizing every purchase made abroad, right down to the packet of Alka-Seltzer (with its highly unorthodox tablets). Worried professionals and businessmen did it, with another year's tuition to find for their ungrateful children. Aspiring actors needing new noses. College kids, bored with waiting on tables. And these were just the amateurs.

Almost anybody could buy a kilo of 90 to 98 percent pure cocaine in, say, Bogotá, for $2,000 to $3,000, and watch their investment grow to $25,000 to $30,000 on walking it through Customs a few hours later. For professional smugglers, this kind of arithmetic was even more stimulating than the product itself, particularly after a kilo had taken a full hit and become *two* kilos of 50 percent pure, worth $50,000 to $60,000. If sold off in ounces, it would fetch even more, for the demand was such that street-level dealers could step on 50 percent pure coke another three or four times and still sell it, only 15 to 20 percent pure, to the sucker market for $50 to $100 a gram.

For coke was status. Glamour. Coke was life in overdrive for globe-trotting high achievers. A reward for being so bright and beautiful, knowing and rich. It was caviar for the nose. Pleasure without guilt. An endlessly repeatable, twenty-minute orgasm for the brain. The purest expression of self-love, since it required no partner. Available anywhere, anytime, without tiresome preliminaries or tedious complications, coke was a sprinkling of stardust. And coke was here to stay. Although not if Levine had anything to do with it.

Customs cases almost always began with a seizure. If the smugglers were amateur, bringing home the stuff for their own use or to finance their vacation or mortgage arrears, then the buck usually stopped there. But if they were professional couriers, the specialized skill and the standard procedure of the Customs agent was to flip them, as in the case of John Davidson, and carry out a controlled delivery with a view to arresting their employers, and perhaps moving on from there, widening the net, to pull in the whole operation, from source to final customer.

In his first year with the Hard Narcotics Group, which was never more than thirty agents strong, Levine made or took part in 240 such arrests. With the follow-up investigations these demanded, many of them undercover; with the cases that did not pan out, like Ibarra's; with the paperwork, the conferences, the court appearances, the testifying, often for days on end—with the general, disordered frenzy of the workload, his private life dwindled away to eating hamburgers in the car, and sleeping on desks, with occasional opportunities for working out at the martial arts and flying visits to Monsey to see Liana, Keith and his new baby daughter, Nicole. He could not have wished for a happier life. Liana could have, and *did*.

She had hoped that his move to Customs would lead to a more settled routine, and to begin with, it did. His first few days with the bureau were spent walking the Brooklyn piers with two Customs patrol officers, learning the ropes. As a Customs investigator, he was now equipped with wider powers than any of his colleagues in other federal agencies, including the right to carry out searches without a warrant and, subject to State Department rules, to operate overseas (which would allow him to take on the Thais later on). On reporting for duty with the Hard Narcotics Group, he was given a cash advance of $500, a book of government vouchers exchangeable for airline tickets to anywhere in the world, and told to go to the Sheraton Hotel on Eighth Avenue, where Richard Berdin was being held, and wait for two hundred kilos of heroin to show up.

As Berdin's bodyguard, companion and debriefer, Levine not only kept regular-shift work hours for two weeks, but also received a postgraduate tutorial in international drug trafficking.

Berdin, a thirty-one-year-old Frenchman, was U.S. sales manager for the French Connection. In his eighteen-month career he had sold around a thousand kilos of uncut heroin from the Marseilles laboratories to the American Mafia, which had, in turn, moved the merchandise on for around $500 million. Most of it had been brought in by sea, packed into the bodywork cavities of imported automobiles, and as often as not, Berdin never saw it. He simply received a commission on sales that was either banked for him in Europe or reinvested in subsequent shipments.

For Levine it was a revelation. He was used to dealing with street-corner dealers and junkies who lied, cheated and knifed one another over nickel bags. The idea of dope trafficking as a formal business with a corporate structure, employing white-collar executives who trusted one another not to make off with the dope or the money was entirely new to him. He found himself admiring Berdin's style, and studied him like an actor learning the part.

Faced, on the one hand, with an eight-count indictment, each carrying a twenty-year term, and, on the other, with the number one slot on the Corsican and Mafia hit parade, Berdin had chosen to cooperate with the federal government and to testify against his former associates in return for plastic surgery and a new identity in another country. Yet no one would have guessed his predicament from the calmness and assurance of his manner. Looking a little like the pop star Tom Jones in dress and appearance, Berdin was accustomed to traveling first-class, with a $30,000 wardrobe, $10,000 in his pocket, and no talent whatever for self-denial. Dealing in millions, he was cavalier about money and possessions. If anything made him nervous, or suggested he was under observation, he would simply abandon his hotel suite and everything in it, and resurface somewhere else. The one time he failed to follow his instincts in this way, he was caught.

Unlike most street-level dealers, Berdin also found "shop" talk about drugs and drug experiences distasteful. Levine was going through a particularly sticky period with his brother David, who had relapsed yet again into mainlining heroin, and toward the end of another long day with Berdin, Levine asked him if he had ever tried it himself.

"Me?" Berdin looked at him in unfeigned astonishment, more than slightly offended. "I *sell* ze stuff," he said.

Levine would use Berdin's manner, and that response in particular, at least a hundred times after that, when passing himself off undercover as a trafficker. It became his standard counter to any invitation to try the dope he was there to buy or sell, collect or deliver, when an outright refusal might have risked his cover. He was also in Berdin's debt for raising his sights above the skyline of Brooklyn and Queens, although others seemed to think that the real importance of Berdin's arrest was that it effectively broke the French Connection.

As a result of his testimony, twenty high-level traffickers went to jail, a murderous gang war in Marseilles drove the rest of their customers away, and the whole pattern of illegal drug movements changed. The Far East and Mexico succeeded Turkey as principal sources of opium for heroin production, and most of the surviving Corsicans in the business settled in Central and South America. From there, they could take advantage of the cocaine routes pioneered by Cubans and Colombians into the soft, southern underbelly of the gringo market.

Levine began to learn about these global shifts of supply when he accompanied Al Seeley to Kennedy Airport with a small army of Customs and BNDD agents to meet Christian David, Michel Nicoli and Claude Pastou, who were arriving on an early-morning flight from Rio de Janeiro. They had not come willingly. Expelled from Brazil as a result of American pressure, the three Frenchmen now faced trial on multiple charges of large-scale drug trafficking, much of it under the aegis of El Commandante, Auguste Ricord, a wartime French collaborator with the Gestapo, who was also awaiting trial in New York after his extradition from Paraguay.

Ricord was probably the biggest dope dealer ever to be arraigned in the United States. He was certainly the most significant, for it was he who had personally organized the Corsican invasion of Latin America in the sixties. But David and Nicoli ranked only just below him in the executive hierarchy of the Corsican cartel, and had been separately indicted, with eighteen others, on conspiracy charges involving five hundred kilos of heroin. In this company, Pastou was relatively small fry, although as a courier for Ricord, he had walked through U.S. Customs with a load strapped to his body at least thirty or forty times—everybody had lost count. More recently, he had been hired by David and Nicoli as their New York salesman and troubleshooter.

Normal procedure now, for both sides, was to consider the possibility of a deal—lenient treatment in exchange for information—but Ricord, David and Nicoli were in no position to hand over anybody bigger, and, in any case, lacked incentive. All three were wanted in France: Ricord to be guillotined for war crimes, David to be executed for the murder of a Paris police chief, and Nicoli to serve twenty years with hard labor for armed robbery. Next to asylum in South America, they were better off doing time in American jails.

Pastou's problems in France, however, were relatively minor. He also knew as much about the ramifications of the Corsican empire as anybody. And on alighting from Pan Am Flight Number 202 at 6:30 A.M. on a cold November morning in New York, Providence and Al Seeley placed him in the persuasive custody of Michael Levine and BNDD agent John Coleman.

For more than a month Levine spent twelve to eighteen hours a day in Pastou's company, coaxing out a statement that eventually led to Operation Springboard and the Great Heroin Panic of 1972. Still one of the most spectacular busts in American history, Springboard resulted in scores of arrests and indictments, and virtually eliminated the French from the American market (much to the satisfaction of their Southeast Asian, Mexican, West Indian and Central and South American associates, who felt quite capable of handling the business *without* their help).

Often on weekends, and in the middle of the night, when Pastou, feeling lonely, would start throwing dishes and fits of Gallic temperament at his safe house in Valhalla, New York, Levine would be summoned to calm him down. He would drive up from the city, or occasionally, when he happened to be home, from nearby Monsey, and sit with him for hours, listening to some new and spectacular twist in Pastou's remarkable story.

His three-year career as a courier and bagman for Ricord had ended with his arrest and imprisonment in Spain in 1967, but not before he had established a reputation for reliability and honesty among most of the Corsican traffickers. After escaping to Brazil in 1971, Pastou was approached by Christian David, who wanted to know if he would be interested in going to New York to check through a fifty-kilo delivery of heroin for a Mafia customer of Michel Nicoli's named Carlo Zippo. The load was due to arrive by sea from France in a Volkswagen camper accompanied by one Roger de Louette, traveling on a French diplomatic passport, who would be staying at the Park Sheraton Hotel. Zippo would pay $550,000 in cash for the heroin, from which Pastou would give de Louette $25,000 before bringing the balance back to Rio, where he would receive his own commission of $30,000 ($600 per kilo).

Accepting the assignment gratefully, Pastou went first to Uruguay to buy a new passport and driver's license in Montevideo, returned to Rio to collect $2,000 for expenses from David, and then took a Pan Am flight from São Paulo to Los Angeles, where he changed planes for New York.

Arriving some days ahead of the shipment, he checked in at the Hotel Edison, near Times Square, and made contact with Carlo Zippo, who lived at the Hotel Woodstock on West 43rd Street, to confirm the price and make sure he was paid in $100 bills. Two nights later he presented himself, as David had instructed, at the Park Sheraton and waited in the lobby until he recognized de Louette from the description he had been given. The two men then walked downtown as far as the Taft Hotel, where they sat in the bar and discussed the delivery arrangements.

De Louette had packed the Volkswagen himself with forty-eight kilos, not fifty, and supervised the loading at Le Havre aboard the M/S *Atlantic Cognac,* which had now docked at Port Elizabeth, New Jersey. He would clear the camper through Customs next morning and meet Pastou at the Taft, either between noon and 1:00 P.M. or, in case he was delayed, between 6:00 and 7:00 P.M.. After unloading the heroin he would drive on to Mexico, a trip he had planned long before agreeing to bring in the shipment.

Pastou had already guessed that de Louette was not a professional smuggler. Something about him suggested the military, and the fact that he was traveling on a diplomatic passport meant he was well connected. Next day he waited in the bar at the Taft until 2:00 P.M., and then again from 6:00 to 8:00 P.M., but de Louette did not appear. With a Gallic sigh for his lost commission, Pastou returned to his hotel, packed his bag and left that night for Montreal. From there, he returned to Brazil via West Germany.

Levine was entranced by this story.

Pastou's instincts had served him well. When Roger Xavier de

Louette arrived in Port Elizabeth to claim his camper, the Customs inspector assigned to check the vehicle found a half-kilo bag of heroin hidden behind the dashboard. A more thorough search uncovered ninety-five more bags, and de Louette was arrested, touching off the most celebrated narcotics case of the decade. Customs agents kept watch on the Park Sheraton for the next two days, waiting for de Louette's contact to show up, but the bird had flown. And it was not until Pastou told his story to Levine that the bird was at least identified, and the whole deal traced back to David and Nicoli.

By then, the de Louette affair had blossomed into a diplomatic scandal that had grumbled along for almost a year and severely strained Franco-American relations, not least between the CIA and its French counterpart, the SDECE. Though de Louette had said nothing about meeting Pastou, he had not felt obliged to protect his associates in France. Arraigned on May 11, 1971, before a U.S. magistrate in Newark, New Jersey, and held in lieu of $500,000 bail, he told the case agents that he had been recruited to smuggle the heroin into the United States by Colonel Paul Fournier, a high-ranking official of the SDECE in Paris.

The uproar set off by this revelation made headlines around the world. The idea of an intelligence agency of a friendly power trafficking in narcotics in the United States incensed even French public opinion, although Michel Debré, then Defense Minister, poohpoohed the importance of the incidence, and later, when Fournier was indicted with de Louette by a federal grand jury for heroin smuggling, an internal investigation by SDECE "cleared" Fournier of the charges.

De Louette thereupon insisted on taking a polygraph test, and in the course of a three-day interrogatory conducted by a French examining magistrate in the presence of Justice Department officials, laid out every detail he could recall, not only of Fournier's complicity in the affair, but, as a former contract agent of the SDECE, of the agency's other illegal activities, including the use of counterfeit American currency in its overseas operations. Why, he was asked, would senior French intelligence officers wish to engage in heroin trafficking in the United States? Because, he replied, municipal elections were soon to be held in France, and Fournier and his friends needed funds to support politicians friendly to the SDECE.

What he was not able to tell the Justice Department was that the

SDECE was hand-in-glove with the Corsicans who then controlled the world's supply of illegal heroin; that the shadowy figures to whom Fournier had introduced him in France and who had organized the whole affair, including Claude Pastou's fruitless trip to New York, were Christian David and his associates. It was left to Pastou to make that connection in the course of a midnight conversation with Michael Levine.

Later on in his career Levine would turn up evidence of working arrangements between intelligence agencies and criminal syndicates without surprise, and even allow for them as a background factor in any complicated overseas investigation, but this was the first such case he had come upon directly, and the first of many such cases when the agencies concerned would plead that their participation in narcotics trafficking was in the national interest. For a kid from the Bronx, this was heady stuff.

After several weeks in the company of Richard Berdin and Claude Pastou, Levine's whole conception of the job had begun to change. From then on, a controlled delivery or a successful buy-bust could never be an end in itself but simply the bit that showed of a much larger case behind it. From then on, every arrest he made posed more questions than it answered. Where does it lead? Who else can we get?

In this frame of mind, he traveled to Bangkok to follow up the Davidson case, and later to Portugal, Israel and England to bring back fugitives. But it was the three weeks he spent debriefing Manuel Noa, in February 1973, that turned his attention primarily toward Central and South America. He was assigned to the Noa case just when Spanish, as an agent's second language, became more important than French, and the ability to pass undercover as an Hispanic more important than anything. Manuel Noa, in effect, completed Levine's postgraduate education and set him on the road that would one day lead him to cross swords with South America's feudal cocaine barons and bring down Bolivia's Minister of the Interior.

Noa was a Cuban brothel-keeper who had learned the pimping trade as a second class cook at the U.S. Guantánamo Naval Base. Settling in the United States in 1962, he soon realized there was more money in dope than in prostitution, and by 1967, when he broke through to the big time as a wholesaler of heroin and cocaine, he had already done well enough to own a house and boatyard in Miami, another house in Puerto Rico, and three apartnents in Manhattan. When Levine met him, however, Noa's permanent address was c/o the Atlanta Federal Penitentiary, where he had begun a twenty-five year sentence that he hoped to reduce substantially by giving up his former associates and customers.

His heroin sources were Roberto Arenas, whom Levine would later arrest, and Segundo Coronel, partners in a Cuban smuggling group that moved prodigious quantities of dope around the country on domestic airlines. Besides his heroin business, Arenas also enjoyed a substantial income as a *santero,* a high priest of *santería,* a cult similar to voodoo, which claimed many followers in the drug trade, particularly among Cubans. When Levine and his partner, Hector Santiago, arrested Arenas in his temple, they found among the weird and grisly trappings of a black magician a record of what he charged for his spells and potions. As to their efficacy, that same night Levine and Santiago arrested one of Arenas's *santería* clients with a bag of herbs around his neck, for which he had paid $500. When asked what it was for, he replied, "To keep from getting arrested."

Noa's first big deal with Coronel and Arenas was for fifty kilos. With Coronel sitting beside him, he followed Arenas in his car out to JFK Airport, where he was told to wait outside the Eastern Airlines terminal while the others went in to meet a flight from Chicago. They emerged eventually with a tall, thin man who spoke Spanish with a French accent, and two Samsonite suitcases, each containing twenty-five kilos of heroin, which they carried back to the city and stashed in one of Noa's apartments, on West 47th Street.

Over the next several days, Noa delivered about half the load to customers of Coronel and sold the rest to customers of his own, establishing a pattern they would follow for three vastly profitable years. Their second deal, about a month after the first, had Noa driving Coronel to Philadelphia to pick up another fifty kilos, which he again stashed, some on 47th Street and some uptown in another apartment, on Audubon Avenue.

A month after that Coronel called Noa in Miami, and they drove up to Savannah, Georgia, to pick up sixty kilos. The next trip was to Texas for forty-two kilos. Then to New Jersey for fifty kilos, and so on, regular as clockwork. In their first year of business together, Noa and his partners dealt over three hundred kilos of heroin, grossing between $10 million and $15 million wholesale.

The loads then got bigger still, including one of 124 kilos, and Noa had to rent two more apartments to cope. He was also beginning to feel invincible, and as neither Coronel nor Arenas was interested, branched out on his own as a cocaine wholesaler, buying from Roberto Gonzalez, a smuggler with Colombian government connections who operated a travel agency in Bogotá; a Dominican woman in Miami, who smuggled between fifty and seventy kilos a year from Santo Domingo in hollowed-out dolls; and José Cuadrado, who sent couriers up every month from Quito, Ecuador, with as much as twenty kilos a trip. Run as a sideline to the heroin business, Noa's cocaine agencies also prospered, to the point where, in 1970, he engaged in a 110-kilo deal with a Chilean named Rodolfo Quintanilla worth well over $1 million wholesale.

What fascinated Levine about Noa's three-year bonanza, apart from the numbers, was his attitude toward the business. Most traffickers and users are drawn to drugs as Eve to the apple. The mystique, the danger, the allure of the forbidden, the promise of arcane pleasures and wealth transcending the ordinary limits of double-entry bookkeeping, the sense of life in the fast-forward mode—all this tended to invest drugs with an aura of romance to which not even Levine had been immune. Narcotics agents lead racier, more glamorous lives than ordinary cops. But the magic of drugs entirely escaped Manuel Noa. He treated his merchandise with all the delicacy and awe of a pork butcher setting out a tray of sausages. Dope was a commodity. If he could have made more selling dogshit, he would have bought a kennel.

When Coronel called one day to say he was waiting at the corner of 46th Street and Twelfth Avenue with a twenty-five-kilo package, Noa decided it wasn't worth getting the car out for such a short distance and walked over from his 47th Street apartment to meet him. Coronel was furious, but Noa simply picked up the suitcase, and in broad daylight, through crowded streets, humped fifty-five pounds of 95 percent pure heroin several blocks east to the stash, regardless of cops, neighborhood bums, stoolies, rip-off artists, muggers or anyone else. The elaborate caution of a Claude Pastou and the B-movie outlook of most major drug dealers were entirely foreign to his nature. And when BNDD agents finally did get to him, it was not because *he* had drawn attention to himself through lack of discretion, but because one of his customers had aroused suspicion and unwittingly led the agents to him.

The three weeks Levine spent with Noa completed the course of demystification that had begun with the discovery of his brother's heroin works. Behind the self-serving propaganda of the libertarian lobby, the cant theology of the counterculture and the other windy humbug of the social avant-garde, he now perceived the reality of parasites like Berdin, Pastou and Noa gorging themselves on human weakness.

It was a shame in a way, for until then he had rather enjoyed the idea of narcotics law enforcement as a dual of wits and tactics with the bad guys. He now saw it was an idea that did them too much honor. It suggested an equality in status that might easily inhibit his actions against them or lead to some fatal hesitation in a crunch. Here was no white knight sallying forth to do battle with the ungodly in accordance with the laws of chivalry. A better attitude was that of an exterminator setting out to gas rats in their nest.

Levine was not the only one to see himself in a clearer light at this stage of his career. Liana did, too. The joys of being a policeman's wife had always escaped her, but she knew he loved the work and generally managed to keep herself from reproaching him for the hours he kept, for the times he failed to appear when he had said he would, for the ruination of her social life, the near-total absence of family activities, his inadequacies as a parent, his neglect of household chores and routine maintenance, and her virtual exclusion from 80 percent of his life. She did not even begrudge him—at least, not often—the time he spent on the martial arts when he might have been with her and their children.

For Liana, the move to Monsey had amounted to exile. Cut off from her old circle of neighbors and family, she found it difficult, as virtually a single parent with a young child, to get out and make new friends. After Nicole was born, in July 1968, her life became even more cloistered, allowing her plenty of time to wonder if the move from the city had also been calculated to provide her husband with another excuse for not coming home nights. Almost her only regular visitor was his brother David, particularly after he helped them move into the new house Levine bought for his family in Bardonia, New York, in 1971. Now there was room for David to stay for the night or the weekend to help with the children and keep her company.

Levine encouraged this. It was good for all of them, he thought. Good for Liana and the children to have someone to talk to. Good for David, who kept slipping in and out of drug programs, to have somebody to think about besides himself. And good for Levine, who still felt uncomfortable around David and could now feel less guilty about neglecting everybody.

There was no clear distinction between his private and professional life. "I could see what I was doing to her, but I didn't know how to separate what I did from who I was. I'm not sure I know even now, and it's not just *me*. I never knew a good undercover with a happy home life. Or, look at it another way, if a guy's not happy at home then very likely he's good on the job. Working undercover is like riding a motorcycle. Your life is really in danger unless you concentrate all the time, and not being able to think is a luxury when you're carrying around all the fucking guilt in the world for screwing up your family's lives and not knowing how to fix it.

"Undercover consumes everything. Dominates everything. You can't share it. People around you are all living their lives, but you're not. You're watching. You're manipulating. You're remembering everything. Nothing about you is real. You're a performance, and it had better be a good one or you're dead. And that, man, is *pressure*.

"Narcotics enforcement is *all* pressure. Normal police work is varied, but in narcotics it's all-out constant war. You're pushed night and day to get out and make cases, and when you're out there's a million ways to make a mistake. But all you need is one. One mistake, one little error of judgment, and it can cost you everything. Guys crack under that kind of pressure. I knew another guy who blew his brains out in the office. Came in, smiling. Sat at the desk with his gun out—a lotta guys do—and the next thing, boom! No warning. Nothing. A lotta people knew a lotta reasons for it afterwards, but there's no one normal in this job. The divorce rate is 85 percent in the DEA. And the average agent has a life expectancy of fifty-five years, assuming he survives to retire at fifty.

"The statistics got so bad the bosses hired stress-management consultants. Guys were supposed to be able to talk to 'em in confidence and iron out any problems they had. Except nobody trusted that. Confidential or not, they figured that anybody who went to see a consultant was as good as admitting that he couldn't cope, and would find himself out on his ass. And I'm not saying they were wrong. In every headquarters of every agency I ever worked for there's always some coldhearted sonofabitch with twenty-twenty hindsight, ready to do you.

"My salvation was to work out physically. And not always in the gym. If one little mistake could snuff me out, then I figured I oughta enjoy life while I had the chance. I was very fatalistic in that way, about accepting what can't be altered. I'll go when it's time, neither sooner nor later. I also leaned heavily on Bushido, and drew a lot of strength from that. I'm comfortable around violence. It doesn't worry me. I feel really alive when dangerous things are happening. Many a time I've gotten out of some strange, hairy situation and started to laugh and say to myself, My God, I love this life. It's fantastic. I love it. When I'm an old man people will see me sitting in my rocking chair just laughing to myself as I remember those times."

The two years he spent as a Customs agent were, in retrospect, "the good old days," before bureaucracy, due process, budget cuts and percentage-playing management combined to cramp his style with the 1973 merger of all federal narcotics agencies into the Drug Enforcement Administration. Until then, Al Seeley had managed to screen the Hard Narcotics Group from meddling superiors by producing results. Once an agent proved himself, he was allowed to run on the loosest of reins, and invariably responded with a level of performance that had almost nothing to do with the agent's contract of employment and almost everything to do with esprit de corps, camaraderie and the sheer satisfaction of being the *best*. One of the strongest reasons why Levine rarely went home was because he was afraid he would miss something.

December 12, 1972, was a fairly typical day. After taking part in a late-night arrest at Kennedy Airport on the 11th, he had finished helping to process the prisoners around two in the morning. Too tired to drive home from Varick Street at that hour, particularly as he was due in court in Brooklyn at 10:00 A.M., he settled for a nap on the office couch, and around 6:00 A.M. made a start on the stack of paperwork he had been trying to get at for days.

With a container of coffee and egg salad on a roll to eat on the way, he then drove over to the Eastern District courthouse, where he spent all morning at various arraignments, hearings and conferences. Around 2 P.M. he was called out to JFK Airport again. A Colombian woman who spoke no English had been intercepted in Customs with two kilos of cocaine. Routine case. Happened every day. After listening to the details he went through to the interview room, where she had been waiting alone for nearly two hours, and sat down at the table, looking her over as impersonally as a butcher appraising a side of beef while he read her her rights. Nemesis in a crumpled suit.

Levine's success in breaking people down and converting them into believers, into "cooperating individuals," had a lot to do with first impressions. Just by sitting there for a minute or two, offering as little comfort and humanity as the north face of the Eiger, he could usually get his message across without saying a word in any language.

Lady, I have your life in my hands, his attitude said. I'm gonna fuck it up completely, and doing it won't mean a thing to me because you interrupted my lunch. So right after I make sure your life is in ruins, I'm gonna go out, get something to eat, come back and do this again to somebody else. And it still won't mean a thing because I got more important things to do. Like getting a shoeshine.

As soon as he judged this had sunk in, it was time to strike the hook, in bored, impatient, flawless Spanish.

"Lady, come here and sit down," he said. "I know they told you we'll only throw you out of the country, but that's not so. You've broken the laws of the United States, and for that you will be tried and punished. So don't give me any shit. If you want to talk, talk. If you don't want to talk, don't talk. But let me tell you this. If you *don't* talk, you are going to jail. You're going to do seven or eight years of very hard time. You understand?"

She shook her head, and he shrugged.

"All right. I'm not going to say another word. You've got one chance to help yourself, and that's by giving up everybody you know. I'm going to walk out of here now, and it's up to you to stop me. Because if you let me go through that door, you will never see Colombia again."

Unless the victim was very stupid, it usually worked. On the other hand, it never paid to place too much trust in these instant conversions, particularly where Latin American women were concerned, because as soon as the shock wore off, the clever ones would tell themselves they had just bought a little time to try to outsmart the system.

She stopped him at the door and agreed to make a controlled delivery. Her instructions had been to take a cab to Times Square after clearing Customs and check into the Holland Hotel.

Levine drove her into the city himself, and by the time they arrived, the group had the hotel staked out. He then briefed the other agents with a description of the man who was supposed to meet her there, and with agent James Healy, took her upstairs to wait in her room. It was still just routine.

Half an hour later one of the agents in the lobby advised them by radio that a man answering the description of her contact had just entered the hotel.

"Okay," Levine said to his prisoner. "This is it. When the phone rings tell the desk clerk to send him up."

The phone rang. She told the clerk to send him up.

"Good. Now we're going to get in the closet. When he comes in I want you to talk about the drugs a little bit. Just act natural, and as soon as we have heard enough we'll come out and arrest him. You understand all that?"

She understood all that. Levine set his tape recorder going, hid it under the bed and joined Healy in the closet, pulling the doors behind him. The usual routine.

Somebody knocked discreetly. They heard the door open, and then a low murmur of voices, too low for them to make out what either was saying. The conversation lasted for about a minute and a half, and then silence. Nothing. Levine waited a few more seconds and took a peep. The woman was still there, by the open door, but the man had gone. Levine snatched out his portable, eyeing her malignantly.

The agents downstairs collared the fugitive on the street. He was armed with a .38 caliber revolver. And when Levine played back the tape, they could all hear her quite clearly warning her visitor that two agents were hiding in the closet.

"I had a funny feeling when I heard that," Levine recalls. "It's not beyond a Colombian doper, when he's told a thing like that, to go boom! boom! boom! into the closet. Well, later that night, after we'd taken 'em downtown and I was on my way home, all of a sudden, there's holy hell on the radio. Two agents had been shot by some Latinos at the Sheraton Hotel, a few blocks away from where we'd been. One was dead, and the other had a bullet in his spine. And I could still hear that woman warning the guy with the .38 that we were hiding in the closet."

Approaching the George Washington Bridge, he was then diverted by radio call to join a squad of agents and uniformed police waiting at a New York Thruway exit to intercept a smuggler on his way down from Canada with ten kilos of heroin. And at four o'clock in the morning of December 13, when he tried to explain all this to Liana, she wouldn't believe a word of it.

His last few months with Customs before the merger into DEA were among the busiest of his career. Besides the "normal" caseload, he was also appointed liaison officer with the BNDD, Customs' arch-rival in narcotics enforcement, which was no more enthused by the prospect of pooling resources than the Hard Narcotics Group. With an eye to the future, Levine was also grooming some of his better informers for the move to the new superagency, and working on several promising cases that he also intended to take with him as part of his dowry.

The most challenging of them involved Stanton Freeman, famous during the sixties as owner of the Electric Circus, New York's glitziest hard-rock disco—and Levine enjoyed busting celebrities almost as much as busting attorneys and diplomats. Two weeks before the merger, he picked up the scent at Kennedy Airport with the late-night arrest of Marilene Tombini, an attractive, twenty-two-year-old Brazilian arriving from Buenos Aires with two kilos of cocaine in her false-bottomed suitcase. A check of the passenger list showed she had been traveling with her boyfriend Francisco Rudge, Hermano Albuquerque, and Roselys Rudner, daughter of a prominent Brazilian banker. The other three had apparently cleared Customs and Immigration without incident, and were now hiding somewhere in the city.

Levine had to do little more than scowl before Tombini was telling him where. Rudge and Albuquerque had booked two double rooms for the four of them at the Albert Hotel, on East 10th Street, in Greenwich Village. When Levine arrived there, around 3:00 A.M., he found both men asleep and arrested them, but there was no sign of Roselys Rudner, who had bought the two kilos in La Paz and recruited Tombini as her courier. After arranging for the hotel to be kept under surveillance in case Rudner returned, Levine took his prisoners to Varick Street for questioning.

Albuquerque had nothing to say. He was plainly determined to protect the missing Rudner, but it hardly mattered. Rudge caved in as readily as Tombini had, and between them, their statements thoroughly incriminated the other two. All Levine had to do now was wait for Rudner to surface, which she did—briefly—around 5:00 P.M. that afternoon. The agents on surveillance at the Albert called in to report that a telephone message had been left for Rudge: "Room 1815. Hotel Paramount."

Levine arrived at the Paramount ten minutes later, but the bird had flown again, leaving only her luggage, which contained, in addition to her clothes, a few grams of cocaine and a handful of coca leaves. Now there were two hotels to watch, at a time when the group was already overstretched. After three days Levine had almost resigned himself to calling off the dogs when the Paramount surveillance unit reported that some guy had just shown up to pay Rudner's bill and collect her luggage.

Levine intercepted him on the street with agents Jay Silvestro and Joe King. His name was John Spencer Davis, he said, when he recovered enough to speak. He was a musician. And he had been sent to collect Rudner's bags by Stanton Freeman, who ran the Le Jardin disco at the Hotel Diplomat.

"Well, well, well," Levine said contentedly. He was no great student of the society pages, but he certainly knew the name. "Then we'd better not disappoint him."

After a few minutes' coaching Davis got out of the car with the luggage and continued on foot to the Diplomat, where he found Freeman in the hotel restaurant. But when he tried to hand over Rudner's bags, it was clear that something had gone wrong. Freeman not only refused to take them, but could hardly bring himself to say a word. After the briefest of exchanges, he walked out, leaving Davis at the table.

"What was that all about?" Levine demanded.

"He knows," said Davis miserably.

"Knows what? That you've been arrested?"

"Yeah."

"Yeah? Well, *how* does he know?"

"There were two of us. Stanton sent two of us. Kim must have told him."

Levine breathed out heavily. "Who's Kim?"

"Kim Ornitz. He's a friend of mine. In the record business. He must have seen us when you picked me up."

"Then why the fuck didn't you *tell* me there were two of you?"

"You didn't ask me," Davis said nervously.

Without another word, Levine took him by the elbow, and with agent Jay Silvestro, went in search of Stanton Freeman.

They found him in his office, nervous but disposed to be haughty, which prompted Levine to try his Peter Falk–Colombo routine. As though sorry to trouble him, he read Freeman his rights, and when assured and reassured that these were understood, asked him about the bags with the half-apologetic air of a man required to do this against his better judgment, and listened to the answers with a dogged, anxious-to-be-fair bewilderment that Freeman obviously found infuriating.

No, he didn't know any Brazilians. He knew nothing about any luggage. He knew no one staying at either the Albert Hotel or the Paramount Hotel. He had never seen John Spencer Davis before in his life. Yes, he knew Kim Ornitz, but until Kim stopped by earlier that day to say hello, he hadn't seen him in months.

Levine thanked him politely, and after a long, Colombo-type pause for reflection, produced a number of photographs of Roselys Rudner, taken from her boyfriend, and a set of mugshots, taken downtown, of Tombini, Rudge and Albuquerque. Did Freeman recognize any of these people? No, he said. He had never seen any of them before in his life.

Pleased with himself for trapping Freeman into so many demonstrable lies, Levine took John Spencer Davis downtown to add him to the others. But before leaving for the day he was rather less pleased to learn that the noted defense attorney Gerald Lefcourt had appeared at the Eastern District courthouse to represent Tombini and Rudge, and had advised them both to make no further statements. To Levine, it seemed a pretty long coincidence that a member of the Lefcourt family, which owned the Hotel Diplomat, in which Stanton Freeman's disco was located, should show up out of the blue to muzzle his two cooperating defendants.

Next morning Levine drove Davis over to Eastern District, where he made a full statement to Assistant U.S. Attorney Bernard Fried, who had been assigned to present the case to the grand jury. Rehearsed by Levine, Davis then made a tape-recorded telephone call to Kim Ornitz, which amply corroborated his story about Freeman sending them both to collect Rudner's bags, and on the strength of this Fried applied for warrants to arrest both Freeman *and* Ornitz. He did not have to explain to Levine that the case against Freeman was flimsy. To show he was part of a conspiracy to import cocaine, they needed at least to prove a closer connection with one or more of the smuggling foursome, and, ideally, to find some collateral evidence of his involvement with drugs.

"Don't worry," Levine said. "We got enough to hold him. Just lemme get my hands on his diary or address book, and that'll do it.

Trust me. I know these suckers. They never think it can happen to *them*. And another thing. I want you to lay a grand jury subpoena on Gerald Lefcourt.

"*What?* You crazy?"

"I wanna know what a guy like that is doing, trying to screw up the case."

"Isn't that what defense attorneys are *supposed* to do?"

"Yeah, but who hired him? Tombini and Rudge didn't. They don't know him. So who's paying? And why?"

"You can't get into that. That's privileged."

"Bullshit. A grand jury can get into anything. Just gimme a subpoena. *I'll* serve it."

"Well, let me think about it."

While Fried was thinking about it, Levine and Joe King went to look for Stanton Freeman.

They arrested him around five o'clock that afternoon as he came out of his house on Perry Street in Greenwich Village, accompanied by an attorney, William London. After reading him his rights, Levine ordered Freeman to turn over all his valuables to London, but seized his address and telephone book. As the significance of this dawned on Freeman, he became agitated to the point of incoherence. On his arrival at Varick Street for processing, he made a rambling statement, in the presence of his attorney, to the effect that he had been asked by some Brazilian he hardly knew to recommend an immigration lawyer. The only reason he was in trouble, he said, was because he had tried to do someone a favor. In fact, he said this several times, and although Levine tried to tempt him into further indiscretions with another display of earnest incomprehension, Freeman resisted the bait and spent the night in the West Street House of Detention pending a bail hearing.

As Levine had suspected, Freeman's address book offered the necessary connections with the other defendants (and also with their attorney, Gerald Lefcourt). Two days later, with the arrest of Kim Ornitz, the case looked stronger still. Ornitz admitted at once that he had witnessed the arrest of John Spencer Davis on the way to the Hotel Diplomat with Rudner's bags, and had gone ahead to warn Freeman about it. (Later that summer, before the case went to trial, Ornitz also admitted buying cocaine from Stanton Freeman at prices ranging from $1,200 to $1,500 an ounce, and agreed to testify to that.)

Meanwhile, Levine was following his usual practice whenever a case got under his skin. Sensing some sort of cover-up in progress, he fastened onto Freeman, leechlike, and spent every minute he could spare on running down the phone calls made by the defendants from the Albert and Paramount hotels, and other leads suggested by entries in Freeman's address book.

One of these led him to Freeman's ex-wife, Dawn Freeman, and her live-in boyfriend, Richie, who declined to identify himself further when Levine stopped by to interview them, but who turned out to be Richard Rosenblatt, better known as rock music composer Rich Cordell, who wrote many hits for Tommy James and the Shondells. Taken by surprise, Dawn Freeman identified photographs of the fugitive Roselys Rudner as one of three Brazilians she had met at Freeman's house on Perry Street the night before his arrest, but then realized that this was probably unwise and refused to say anything else. Piqued again by this obvious desire to protect Freeman, Levine descended once more on Assistant U.S. Attorney Bernard Fried and had Dawn and Richie subpoenaed.

Succumbing to Levine's persuasive powers, as most people did in the end, Fried had also agreed to bring Gerald Lefcourt before the grand jury, but Lefcourt moved to quash the subpoena. At a hearing of the motion, Gerald Lefcourt was represented by the even more illustrious attorney Leonard Boudin. When the judge acknowledged Boudin's presence by saying, "It's an honor to have you in my court," it came as no surprise to Levine when the Lefcourt subpoena was thrown out on the grounds that it infringed client-attorney privilege.

Rather more surprising was Dawn Freeman's spirited attempt to beat *her* subpoena on the grounds of insanity, citing in evidence the fact that she had once been institutionalized. Unable to avail himself of the same excuse, her boyfriend, Richard Rosenblatt, aka Cordell, was forced to appear, but proceeded to demonstrate another form of insanity by lying under oath to the grand jury in his efforts to protect Dawn's ex-husband. Now distinctly peeved, and not a little puzzled by the loyalty Freeman seemed to inspire in his followers, Levine obtained a warrant for Rosenblatt's arrest on a charge of perjury.

A few days later, on June 29, the grand jury made him feel better by handing up an indictment.

"ROCK BIG & 5 INDICTED
IN $1M COCAINE CASE"

wrote Robert Kappstatter in the *Daily News.* "The owner of a once popular East Village discotheque and a record producer were indicted with four Brazilian nationals yesterday on smuggling charges involving $1 million worth of cocaine."

Arraigned before Judge Jacob Mishler, Freeman was held in $200,000 bail, Kim Ornitz in $50,000, and three of the four Brazilians in amounts ranging from $150,000 to $250,000. The fourth, Roselys Rudner, had apparently succeeded in getting away and was thought to be hiding in Lisbon.

Without her, the case against Freeman was entirely circumstantial, as Assistant U.S. Attorney Bernard Fried never tired of pointing out. And as Levine never tired of serving subpoenas, he kept coming up with potential new witnesses, and occasionally with a consolation prize for all the legwork. One such reward for perseverance came when he and Joe King pounded at the door of the Chelsea apartment of one David Duffy and his roommate, Rosanna Polizatto, to serve them with grand jury subpoenas.

"Who is it?" someone cooed winningly.

"Federal agents," replied Levine, in a bad temper.

Gengis Khan at the gates of a ladies' seminary could hardly have caused a greater flutter. Pandemonium broke out on the other side of the door—muffled shouts, screams, the slap of bare feet running down the hall, and then the incessant flushing of a toilet. In absolutely no hurry at all, Levine and King smiled at each other beatifically. When Duffy at last opened the door, he was still in bare feet, buckling the belt of his pants and cringing like a dog expecting the whip.

Levine handed him the subpoena. Duffy stared at it, then at Levine, and then at King. Nobody moved.

"Is that it?" Duffy wrinkled up in pain. "You mean, you don't want to come in?"

Levine patted his cheek consolingly, and turned to leave. "Not this time, sonny," he said. "Just be in court on the day it says."

When they reached the street door they could still hear the wails and curses from upstairs.

But with that small victory, Levine had to be content for a while. The Stanton Freeman case now looked set to go to trial in the fall, and there matters stood on July 2, 1973, when Levine and 749 other Customs agents were transferred to the Department of Justice as Special Agents of the Drug Enforcement Administration, and ordered to report to their new regional headquarters.

Levine was testifying in court that day, but when he did finally check in at 555 West 57th Street, he found himself the only Spanish-speaking agent in Billy McMullen's group, which suited him fine. McMullen was an ex-Customs group supervisor with plenty of street experience, and to celebrate, Levine went out to make his first undercover case as a DEA agent on July 13. Bearded, mustachioed, wearing dark glasses and a new Puerto Rican outfit, he slipped into the traffic on West 109th Street as effortlessly as a shark reentering the Gulf Stream, and bought half a pound of cocaine from a Colombian dealer at the Ideal Restaurant for $4,700.

Meanwhile, the Stanton Freeman case continued to bug Bernard Fried, who continued to bug Levine, who in turn bugged everybody he could think of who might tie Freeman more closely into the conspiracy. With the case scheduled for trial in September, Freeman, who had made bail, volunteered to take a polygraph test, a development which Levine assumed to mean that Fried had agreed to prosecute or move to dismiss on the strength of the result. With no doubt in his mind about Freeman's guilt, Levine did not entirely approve of staking the case on a polygraph readout, but, with no new evidence to throw in the pot, held his peace. And to his intense satisfaction, Freeman flunked the test.

For reasons best known to themselves, Freeman and his attorneys then waived their right to a jury trial, and the prosecution of the government's case, such as it was, began before Chief Judge Mishler the day after Rudge, Tombini and Albuquerque had each pled guilty to the same charges.

Taking the stand in his own defense, Freeman continued calmly to deny all prior knowledge of his co-defendants and of the cocaine they had admitted trying to smuggle into the country. It was only when he came to Levine's part in the affair that he began to lose his composure. After describing his arrest, he quoted Levine as saying, "Give all your valuables to your attorney, but that is *mine*"— referring to his address and telephone book. In a voice often trembling with emotion, he went on to contrast Levine's attitude unfavorably with that of agent Jay Silvestro, whom he complimented for his gentlemanly conduct during the case.

"Silvestro is an honest man," he said, "and treated me very well. But Mike *Levine*"—he drew a shuddering breath—"Mike Levine is a man I wouldn't want to meet again in broad daylight, no less in a dark alley."

Allowing him to continue in this vein a little longer, Judge Mishler finally insisted he get to the point.

"The point, your honor, is that when they arrested me, Mike Levine and this other agent, Joe King, threw me into the back of their car. They took my wallet, which had a hundred dollars in it, and gave it back to me without the hundred dollars."

Levine was disappointed in him. Sitting as case agent at the government's table, he looked at Fried expectantly, and waited for him to challenge this crude attempt to discredit his principal witness. But Fried just shook his head slightly and Levine deferred to his judgment, assuming he would take it up with Freeman on cross-examination. When Fried's turn came to question the defendant, however, he made such heavy weather of the circumstantial details at the heart of the case—the phone numbers, the lies, and all the other suggestive ins and outs of the evidence—that Judge Mishler grew visibly impatient. Rattled still more by defense counsel's frequent objections, Fried struggled on through as many points as he could remember, then abruptly said, "No further questions," and sat down.

Levine was flabbergasted. He leaned across to snarl in Fried's ear, and in a moment the two were arguing in furious whispers. Judge Mishler watched them for a moment, then demanded to know what was going on.

Fried stood up reluctantly. "May I put one more question, your honor?"

With the judge's permission, he turned to Freeman and asked: "Did you not testify that Mike Levine and Joe King took your wallet and removed a hundred dollars from it?"

"Yes, I did," agreed Freeman, with a pitying smile.

"But didn't you also say, in your earlier testimony, that Levine told you to give all your valuables to your attorney on the street? And that you did so? Didn't you say Levine just took your address book?"

Freeman opened and closed his mouth several times, saw everyone was looking at him, and finally shrugged helplessly.

Thinking back, Levine is certain that this was the moment when Freeman was found guilty as charged. Judge Mishler subsequently sentenced him to two years' imprisonment on each of the four counts, but Levine's satisfaction at having finally worried the case through to a conviction was not shared by the Circuit Court. On appeal, the verdict was overturned on the grounds of insufficient evidence, the first and only time such a thing ever happened to the Chief Judge of the Federal Eastern District of New York.

Levine had better luck, however, with the other interesting case he brought with him from Customs. Beginning in a small way with a one-pound heroin seizure in Chicago, it led on to a massive conspiracy involving several interrelated smuggling and distribution networks, provoked an international incident, proved a link between American and Israeli organized crime syndicates, and took him to Tel Aviv to bring back one of the leading figures in the case of the smuggling rabbis.

A routine check of airmail parcels by Customs in Chicago had turned up a package from the Middle East containing a pound of heroin. Addressed to Barry Nadell, in Adel, Iowa, it offered no clue to the sender, but after Nadell and a fellow conspirator, David Supera, were arrested, a search of Nadell's safe deposit box produced receipts for large sums of money wired at frequent intervals to one Samuel Shapiro, of Monsey, New York. Telephone company records showed that Nadell had also called Shapiro long-distance on many occasions, and there were references to "Sam" in Nadell's correspondence that were highly suggestive of Shapiro's involvement with illegal drugs.

These suspicions were then confirmed when David Supera admitted that he had bought hashish from Shapiro, who was said to be bringing in about five kilos a week from Israel, as well as heroin and other drugs. Neither he nor Nadell was prepared to testify against Shapiro, however, and at this point the Chicago office handed the case over to Al Seeley in New York, who assigned it to Levine. Shapiro was a rabbi. Levine was a Jew. They both lived in Rockland County.

Though less than diligent in his religious observances, Levine found it hard to match his conception of a rabbi with any of the standard smuggler profiles. As a matter of routine, he arranged for the chief of the mail section to alert "All import specialists, Mail specialists, Segregators, Foremen, Dog Handlers, SNIF and X-Ray" to examine any parcel sent by or to Rabbi Sam at any of the three addresses Levine had managed to trace, and he set up a Customs lookout at all points of entry, requesting a full search and notification of entry if Rabbi Sam, traveling on his Israeli passport, showed up anywhere from overseas. But he didn't really *believe* in the case at this stage. Nor did it seem any more credible when, driving around with his son one Saturday afternoon, he finally spotted the highly respectable figure of Sam Shapiro outside his home on Maple Avenue in Monsey, in the heart of the Orthodox Jewish community.

"Hey, Keith," he said. "See that guy? In the black suit? He's a big dope smuggler."

As the car drifted by the house, his eight-year-old son looked at Shapiro and then at his father.

"Aw, come *on*, Pop," he said scornfully.

After following Shapiro around a few times without result, and with nothing to show for the Customs alerts, Levine began to wonder if Keith was right.

A few weeks later a businessman named Eliezer Becker was arrested at Kennedy Airport with two kilos of cocaine. Although the case agent was Gus Fassler, Levine was assigned to be the "street general" as usual, and the following morning found that a night in the West Street House of Detention had already persuaded Becker of the need to cooperate. Almost eagerly, he told Levine that he had flown in with a man named Ramón Torres, who had cleared Customs without incident, and was probably now sitting home in his apartment at 288 Lexington Avenue, waiting to hear what had happened. Torres was crazy and dangerous, he said, but no fool. He had not told Becker where the cocaine was going. It was for a big customer known only to Torres.

"In that case," said Levine, "you're gonna call him up and say you were stopped and questioned but they didn't find the dope. Understand? Tell him you didn't want to take any chances, so you waited a day before getting in touch. Just to make sure you weren't being watched."

"Well, I don't know," Becker said doubtfully. "This guy is really *crazy*. He got arrested in Chicago for taking a bomb into some hotel out there. So they sent him to the funny farm for observation, and he just walked away one day."

"Listen," said Levine, "I'm sure you've read about the problems of overcrowding and homosexual rape in the federal prison system. Next to where you're gonna spend the night, Torres is gonna look like Momma and apple pie."

Becker finally got through to Torres with a taped telephone call the following afternoon, and after convincing him that all was well, arranged to pick him up at his apartment. Wearing a Kel T-2 transmitter hidden in his clothes, he arrived there around 5:15 P.M. in a cab driven by Special Agent William Schnakenberg, and followed by Levine and Special Agent George Caraviotis in an undercover car. When he judged he had heard and recorded enough of Becker's conversation with Torres, Levine pulled in across the path of the taxi and placed Torres under arrest.

He soon saw what Becker meant by crazy. Torres was a good-looking Colombian with the air of a moody fanatic. It seemed he had married a prostitute to gain American citizenship, and described himself as a part-time teacher of "Oriental Meditation" at Columbia University in New York. His principal qualifications seemed to be his ability to stick pins and sharp objects through various parts of his body.

Though he insisted at first he had nothing to hide, as Levine bore down hard with his lurid account of what the Neanderthal population of federal prisons was liable to do to good-looking Colombians, Torres eventually admitted that he was the only one who knew the customers for the two kilos Becker had tried to bring in, and that if he failed to call them by 7:00 P.M. they would not answer the phone after that.

"Well, you better call 'em right now," Levine said, "because I make it six fifty-five."

"Don't ask me to do that," said Torres. "Because if I make the call, I must kill you."

Levine laughed good-naturedly. "Now, come on, Ramón," he said. "Let's cut the bullshit. This is your last chance. If you don't make the call, I'm gonna put you away for fifteen years, and that's all there is to it."

"Okay." Torres threw up his hands, disowning responsibility for what would inevitably follow. "I'll make the call. But understand, then I must kill you."

"Yeah. Well, make the call first, okay? It's six fifty-seven."

Shaking his head, Torres telephoned David Klein, owner of Dav-El Limousine Service, and told him he was running a little late, but was on his way over with two keys of coke.

"Now I must kill you," he said flatly, as he hung up. "I warned you. You have made me an informer, and for that I *must* kill you."

Levine considered him for a moment, never one to encourage such talk. "Well, you don't have time now," he said. "Dave is expecting us."

As street general, he chose Gus Fassler to go in undercover with Torres to deliver the cocaine, and told them he would wait five minutes before raiding the place to give them time to hold incriminating conversations with whomever they found there. A former schoolteacher and Customs agent from Maine, Fassler had never worked undercover before, and seemed far from certain that this was the moment to start, but Levine urged him along cheerfully, and after setting them down with the suitcase at Klein's apartment house on East 63rd Street, had a final word of encouragement for him on the sidewalk outside.

"Let Ramón do the talking, okay? You just listen and remember what they say. And when we come in, I'm gonna arrest the both of you. That way, they won't know Ramón's been helping us. So make it look good. Okay, Ramón?"

"Okay. But I must still kill you. Remember that."

Levine took him lovingly by the throat. "Ramón, if anything happens to Gus here," he said, *"I will kill you."*

Not much comforted by this assurance, Fassler rode up in the elevator with Torres, Levine and the rest of the group (except for two agents who remained downstairs to cover the exits and make sure the doorman's first loyalty was to his government). With his men flattened against the wall of the hallway on either side of Klein's door, Levine positioned Fassler and Torres in clear view from the peephole, smiled at them affably, rang the doorbell and stepped out of the picture.

In a moment the door opened wide and someone drew them inside with screams of delight, closing it behind them without so much as a glance in the hallway. Levine knew from Torres that Klein's roommate was a South American ballet dancer, and it sounded as though they were throwing a party. But he could make out nothing intelligible from the hubbub, and after allowing them the five minutes he had promised, he rang the bell and hammered on the door.

The noise stopped instantly, as if a switch had been thrown.

"Open up," he bellowed. "Federal agents."

Not a sound.

He pounded on the door again, even more heavily. "Federal agents. Open up or I'll kick it in."

The threat provoked a volley of muffled shrieks and squeals, and as the agents massed behind him for the charge, they heard a frantic exchange of whispers at the door before it opened a cautious crack.

Levine and his men hit it like a phalanx of linebackers running amok. Galloping into the apartment, guns drawn, scattering all before them, they found the living room full of panic-stricken ballet dancers desperate to get away. With their only exit plugged by armed men, they fluttered about as vainly as caged birds trying to elude a clutching hand. As Levine and his colleagues watched in amazement, one of them actually ran up a wall and did a back flip, crying hysterically. Another was climbing the drapes, while a third tried to squeeze into the six-inch space under a sofa.

Seeing no sign of the suitcase or of drug paraphernalia, Levine went through to the rear bedroom, chuckling to himself, and arrested Jairo Mejia, Klein's roommate, as he was trying to find somewhere to hide a set of scales with a quantity of white powder in one of the pans. He offered no resistance. Indeed, only two people in the apartment put up a struggle and had to be forcibly subdued—Gus Fassler and Ramón Torres, who had previously warned Levine that he was into Kung Fu. Before those agents still able to keep a straight face could pin Torres to the bathroom floor, he had kicked in a full-length mirror and half wrecked the apartment.

"It's all right," said Dave Klein gallantly. "You can let those two go. They just came up here to order a limousine."

When he recovered, Levine asked Klein's permission to search the apartment, explaining that anything he found of an incriminating nature would be used against him in court. Klein replied that he would like to talk to his lawyer first, whereupon Levine called the U.S. Attorney's office to get a search warrant, and was advised to remain in the apartment while they tried to find a judge. Knowing how long these formalities could take, Levine sent the rest of his squad across town with the prisoners and settled in to wait with Bill Schnakenberg.

They were not bored. Among a number of visitors to Klein's apartment, were Peter Frescia, who identified himself as a BNDD informer, and said he had come to buy cocaine, and a personable, nicely spoken young man who identified himself as Michael Arlen, and said he had come to order a limousine. He clearly did not expect them to believe this, but a body search provided no reason to detain him, and he wished them good night. Without knowing it, Levine had just met the prince of informers who would one day give him Rabbi Sam Shapiro and a dozen other major violators.

Levine as "José with the cigarettes," a disguise that gained him entrance to the toughest black after-hours joint in St. Albans, Queens, in a "sting" that nearly cost Levine his life.

While an agent with the Bureau of Alcohol, Tobacco, and Firearms (ATF), Levine received the U.S. Treasury's Special Act Award for disarming an ax-wielding felon "without resorting to the use of firearms." Pictured with Levine, second from right, are ATF supervisors, left to right, Gene Martin; Mr. Buckley; Levine's partner, Ray Boylan; Mike Laperch; and Jack Hollander, the area supervisor.

Levine began to study the martial arts early in his career and was fascinated by the code of Bushido, the way of the warrior. Now a *shodan,* a first-degree black belt, Levine believes the rigorous training has helped him survive a life undercover.

In 1970, Levine was the center of the most spectacular deep-cover operation in law-enforcement history. For three months he lived with Buffalo, New York, motorcycle gangs and ultimately seized forty cases (four thousand sticks) of dynamite headed for terrorist gangs in New York City.

Levine, sitting with his back to the surveillance camera, at the Siam Intercontinental Hotel bar in Bangkok with heroin smugglers, Mr. Geh, right, and Gary, left. The 1971 case was the first in history in which one undercover agent managed to snare the courier, the traffickers, *and* the source in the case—in New York City, Florida, and Thailand, respectively.

In Thailand to testify against Gary and Mr. Geh, Levine stands outside the Hall of Justice, Bangkok, with the Thai prosecutor, right, and the interpreter.

Levine, left, takes into custody Claude Pastou, celebrated "French Connection" heroin and cocaine smuggler, in 1972. Used to dealing with the nickel-and-dime world of street dealers and junkies, Levine found these white-collar executives, who dealt in tons, a revelation. They viewed narcotics trafficking as an ordinary business.

In a 1975 surveillance photo, Levine, left, buying heroin from Billy Yellowhair in Chinatown. At the time of the photo, Yellowhair was a member of Chinese street gangs. Later indicted for homicide and extortion, he eventually became a murder victim himself.

Levine, center, undercover on the streets of Buenos Aires in 1979 with Pedro Castillo, left, a drug trafficker who in this meeting first mentioned the name Robert Suarez. The most powerful cocaine dealer in the world, Suarez handled a thousand kilos a month. Levine eventually negotiated with Suarez in what became the biggest sting operation of the decade.

The Billy Kwastel Case. In a case starting with a routine pill bust, Kwastel, the "unwitting" informant, was so brilliantly manipulated by Levine that he led the DEA to more cases with a higher body count than any other undercover "wheel" conspiracy in the agency's history. Through Kwastel, Levine had undercover dealings with twenty-six defendants.

Above: Left to right, defendants Kwastel and Sussman with Levine.

Kwastel, left, Derek Williams, another defendant, center, and Levine, concluding a heroin deal.

Derek Williams, left, sells heroin to Levine.

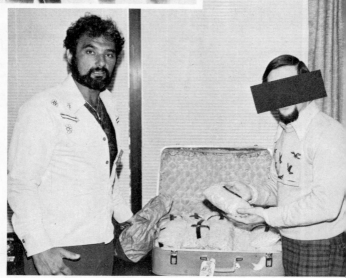

Levine, with agent "Skippy" Garcia and the pills seized from defendant Barney Rebackoff's luggage.

Above and right: A typical day in Spanish Harlem during the years of the Alimony Boys, Levine's record-breaking narcotics squad.

Michael Levine, Group Supervisor, Drug Enforcement Agency,
U.S. Department of Justice.

At 3:20 A.M. the next morning, an Assistant U.S. Attorney called to say he had finally obtained a signature for the search warrant. And when Levine at last arrived home for breakfast, Liana went straight into the bedroom and slammed the door.

SEVEN

"To get the best out of a stool, you gotta train him like you train a dog."

In front of a big crowd, he favored the lecture-performance technique—"An Afternoon with Michael Levine," complete with coffee and doughnuts at intermission. Generally speaking, the larger the numbers, the smaller the contribution from the floor, and at State Police School in Albany, the audience was large, its collective experience formidable, and its attitude to start with as genial as a state trooper's approach to a drunk-driving suspect. As he got to his feet, their silence said, Show me.

"He that goeth about as a tale-bearer revealeth secrets, but he that is of a faithful spirit concealeth the matter. The tale-bearer is an abomination to the Lord."

He waited to observe the effect of this text on the congregation, and turned again to his notes.

"The words of a tale-bearer are as wounds, and they go down into the innermost parts of

the belly. . . . Therefore meddle not with him
that flattereth with the lips."

He paused again and was rewarded with a puzzled stir. "That's from the Bible," he said.
"And it just goes to show how people have hated
mother-fucking stool pigeons right back
through recorded history."

This time the stir was of general relax-
ation.

"I despise them myself," he went on cheerfully. "I can't conceive of a lower form of
life than slug-junkies who think nothing of
informing on their own families after they've
managed to entrap them in their miserable
lives. But good police work, especially in
narcotics enforcement, depends on good information. On good informers. And that's what
I'm here to talk about. The art of squeezing
these vermin dry, like you're juicing an orange, then junking what's left.

"Now I can't teach you how to do that, any
more than I can teach you how to work undercover or con people out of their lives. But I
can tell you how it works for me. And I can
teach you how to do it safely.

"Okay? Then this is it. There's not a stool
that I've dealt with—and we've got to be up in
four figures by now—who didn't believe I really *cared* about him. Or her. They all really
believed that I was interested in their lives
and their problems. That I was really concerned about their families and their welfare."

He paused, wrinkling his face in disgust.

"Well, the truth is, after I'd used 'em up, I
couldn't possibly have cared less whether
they or anyone spawned by them or anyone that
would lay in the same bed with them lived or
died. In self-defense, in this most treacherous of subworlds, the narc must be the most
treacherous of all to survive. The trick, if

it *is* a trick, is to learn how to immerse yourself in shit for varying periods of time—in my case, for twenty-two years—and still come up clean, healthy and sane enough to live alongside 'normal' people."

He was off and running, the Levine machine accelerating smoothly through the gears.

"So where do we start? If we're gonna be scientific about this, let's understand first of all what informers can do for us.

"Number one, he can tell you stuff you can't get any other way. Who's doing what to who and for how much? What's around? Prices. Sources. All the things they talk about among themselves on the corner of 92nd Street and Columbus. Street gossip. A good stool can be your eyes and ears.

"Number two, he can keep people under surveillance in situations where a strange face would either frighten 'em off or invite trouble. He can also negotiate for you with a cautious suspect if you can't get in yourself, but we'll talk about that in a minute.

"Number three, he can help you identify suspects, locations, cars—he can save everybody a hell of a lot of time and legwork. I mean, why send out a four-car surveillance team for days on end to find out where a suspect keeps his stash when an informer can maybe tell you right off the bat?

"And number four, he can help get you into trafficking organizations undercover. That's the biggie. In all the years I've been doing this, I can think of very, very few cases were a guy went out undercover by himself and managed to get in cold. Guys like me who work undercover nearly always have an informer to take 'em in.

"And most of the time that's all I want him to do. Get me in. If you use him for anything else, for surveillance or to make a buy or to sit in on some deal, then he'll probably have to testify to it later on, and that can cause problems. Like, he won't do it. And even if he's willing, he's probably got a worse record then your average war criminal, and defense attorneys like that. Gives 'em something to work with. Besides, if you make him testify, he's gonna get burned as an informer and maybe get himself killed. So either way, he's not gonna be much use to anybody after that. You gotta do it yourself. Whenever you can. That's the golden rule.

"It pays in other ways, too. If you don't get in yourself, he may try to con you or hold back some of the stuff for himself or take off with the bankroll he was supposed to use for the buy. He could also work a switch and act as informer for them against *you*. I've seen all those things happen. Many times."

He had also lost count of the times he had asked himself how many of these guys were really *listening*.

"So a stool is usually your first connection with the bad guys. He's gonna get you in. Now, *why*? This is important. What's his motive? Ask yourself, can you trust him? Knowing what a treacherous sonofabitch he is, can you trust him not to blow your cover in what is already a goddamn dangerous situation? Well, I'll tell you the answer. No, you can't. But you can usually manipulate the mother-fucker so it isn't worth his while.

"How do you do that? You gotta understand what makes him tick. A stool works for one or more of these reasons. First, out of fear. You arrest some guy carrying dope, lean on him a little, get him to flip. Okay. He's afraid of what you can do to him. He's afraid of going to jail. And you gotta keep pushing those fear buttons because he's also afraid of the guys he's dealing with. If he ever gets to be more afraid of them than he is of you, the minute that fear balance tips the wrong way, then you got a treacherous informer. So no Mr. Nice Guy. But that don't mean you gotta beat the shit out of him either, because that sort of fear doesn't last. What I mean is, he's gotta see in you all the power of the government to crush him like an ant. You gotta get the guy behind you, saying, 'I'll do it, I'll do it. I wanna work. You got me convinced.'

"Okay. Number two. A stool can work for revenge. Maybe somebody crossed him up. Sold him bad stuff or won't pay what he owes. Maybe his boss or his partner or his source or his customer doesn't love him anymore. Maybe he's jealous. Maybe somebody's moved in on his girlfriend or boyfriend or wife or whatever. Maybe somebody's undercutting his prices or he just wants to wipe out the competition. Who knows? The details don't matter too much. Just remember to squeeze him dry up front if he's got a grudge, because you never know when he's gonna get back together with whoever it is he's informing against. If you're going undercover with the guy, get in and out fast. And make sure you check out what he tells you before you act on it because an emotional stool can get pretty careless with his facts.

"Right. Number three. There's the stool who works for what I call perverse motives. Not just neurotics and psychos, although you get plenty of those, but guys looking for some kind of personal advantage. Like maybe he's trying to divert suspicion from himself to somebody else. Or maybe he thinks if he makes himself super-useful you'll straighten out some other problem for him, or help him with some other beef. You know the kind of thing. Guys like that often start off with a load of crap, thinking they can outsmart you, but if you handle 'em right, if you keep 'em off balance, they generally wind up outsmarting themselves.

"Then there's the informer who does it for the money. The mercenary. The Judas stool. You know where you are with him. He gets paid by results, so his information is usually on the ball. You just gotta be careful he doesn't get greedy or you could have problems with entrapment. And make sure he's not holding back any part of the evidence for resale. The sonofabitch would melt his children down for soap if he thought there was a market for it, but he's still the best weapon you got. Behind every successful cop stands a good professional stool.

"Next, you got the breast-beater. The born-again stool. The stool who's seen the light. All he wants to do now is repent, to atone for his sins and repay. So naturally you're gonna encourage him. You're gonna tell him how hard he's gonna find it to break away from the old life until he gets rid of all his former associates. *All* of 'em. And you can help him with that. You *know* you can.

"And then you got the law-enforcement buff. You're the coach, and he's desperate to get on the team. Loves the work. Loves to hang out with the guys. Makes him feel good. Helps him live with his own nasty, backbiting, larcenous nature if he can tell himself he's doing it for *us*. Makes him feel like James Bond. A guy like that can be worth his weight in arrest warrants if you keep him on the leash. If you don't, sooner or later you'll find he's using you, using his connection with the Man to protect himself as a trafficker. If he gets caught he'll either say you know about it or you let him do it. And either way, you don't need the problems *that* can bring you."

He looked them over reflectively. A lot of solid stuff there. It was story time again.

"Had a stool like that once named Chano. Puerto Rican. Used to call me boss. 'The boss is sending me out,' he'd tell the other agents, and I'd play along with that. But a lot of the guys wouldn't. They'd try to bring him down. 'You're a stool. You're no fucking good. Get outa my face.' Well . . . okay. But if you wanna use these guys, you gotta understand that stool complex. All his life he's been recognized for the lowlife dirtbag he is. I saw what he was *really* hungry for was acceptance. 'I'm somebody. I work for the DEA or the state police or whatever.' And if you wanna get the best out of him, you gotta cater to that. A lot of stools work for me and won't work for anybody else, because I make 'em feel welcome. Like I said, they feel I really care about 'em. That I really care about their home life or their love life, or whatever's important to 'em.

"Chano came to me after working with several other groups because I encouraged him in his fantasies. 'Where do I work today, boss?' 'Hey, Chano, I was just gonna call you. I got an assignment for you.' No harm in it. Guy worked like a bastard and made a lot of good cases for me. But he was a buff. The problem with Chano was he'd get *too* involved.

"Time and time again I'd go out undercover with him, we'd do a deal with some guy he'd introduce me to, and then he'd go back without telling me and hang around where we'd done it— which was really no good for his health *or* mine. He'd done so many people in his time that the minute you got an introduction you had to get him out of the way, because if you didn't, if you left him out on the street for twenty minutes, sure enough somebody was gonna come by who wanted to kill him.

"Anyway, we hit a lean spell, and Chano's the kind of guy who's unhappy unless he's got something going all the time. He needs that. He's gotta keep feeding his ego, so he starts in with a little entrapment. He asks some cabdriver, 'Hey, can you get me some dope?' And the guy says, 'Sure. I know three or four guys doing dope.' Now right away that's entrapment. He's my stool and he's entrapping this guy. So Chano comes to me and says, 'Hey, boss. I gotta cabdriver doing dope.' Thinks it's great. Hell of a lot safer for him to get some clown to act as an unwitting informer and then come up on payday to collect. But it's bullshit, and I wasn't gonna let him get away with it. With informers you gotta have a bottom line, and he'd reached it.

"Happens once. I go out undercover with Chano, and when we get there, the cabdriver says, 'Oh, yeah. I'll take you to the guy.' No good. I pull Chano out and wag a finger at him. Few days later, he does it again, and I blast him. 'Listen, you mother-fucker. I *told* you. When you get a doper with the stuff in his hand, *then* you come to me. Unless you got a live one, don't call me. Don't come in. Don't have nothing to do with me, understand? Because I don't have time for this bullshit.'

"Okay. He gets the message. No word from Chano for maybe a week, and I know he's gotta be dying. Because he and I share a secret. We both know that his whole fucking life, from the air he breathes to the guys and broads he goes to bed with, means absolutely *nothing* without the feeling he gets from me of being *somebody*. Then suddenly he's on the phone, chattering like a cage of monkeys.

" 'Boss, boss. I got 'em. I got 'em. I really got 'em this time. I got Colombians. I got Puerto Ricans—and they're big. I mean, *big*. They're doing a shitload of stuff and—and—'

" 'All right, all right, all right. Slow down a minute . . .'

" 'No, boss, you don't understand. Just call me in, okay? We gotta move on this fast. They gotta store out in Queens, and I told 'em we're coming. We gotta go meet 'em right now.'

"He's talking a mile a minute, but I'm kinda leery of him after this bad streak we've been having. Anyway, we drive out to Queens and meet this guy Emilio, who runs a topless bar in Manhattan. 'Follow me,' he says. 'I'll take you over to the guy that has the stuff.' And right away I'm saying to Chano, 'You mother-fucker.' Looks like he's done it to me again. But we go to this house and there's Hector, a Colombian who can't speak a word of English. 'Okay,' he says. 'So what do you want?'

"Well, to them I'm a Puerto Rican, so I give him one of my bullshit business cards. This one says, Miguel Garcia, La Plata Agency. The story is it's a gambling agency. We take gamblers to Las Vegas and Atlantic City. It's got a beeper number and a phone with an answering machine that says, 'I'm sorry. There's nobody here. Our representatives are in Las Vegas now.' And so on. If these guys wanna check up on me and they hear this, they're gonna say, 'No shit. It's a company.' But it's just a phone with a recorded message. I mean, if these guys were *smart*, we'd never catch 'em, right?

"Anyway, Hector takes the card and I give him the rap about the agency—this is all in Span-ish, of course. 'Lemme see what you got,' I say. 'I'm heading down to Atlantic City to-night, so gimme a sample. I'll give it to these people I know, and if they like it, if it's real good quality, they'll front me the money and I'll come back and take all you got.'

"So Hector says, 'You wanna sample? Okay.' And he pulls out a plastic bag with maybe four or five pounds of cocaine in it. 'Put it on the table,' he says. 'Help yourself.'

"Just then I caught sight of Chano. He was

like having an orgasm of joy, and I couldn't watch. I thought I was gonna have to get a tongue depresser out.

"So I took about an ounce of coke. Always get a sample if you can. If the deal goes wrong later you still got that as evidence. So I took the coke, and when I said, 'Okay, you want I should pay for this now or what?' Hector says, 'Don't worry about it. I don't want your money. Take it.' Then I knew Chano was right. These guys were big. They got coke coming out of their ears.

"Now we're driving away, and I'm telling my backup guys over the radio how it went down. 'Yeah, I gotta sample. Looks good. Real good.' And Chano's going crazy with pleasure. To get the best out of a stool, you gotta train him like you train a dog. Instant reward, instant scolding. It's all you need. So I'm patting him on the head. 'Yeah, right. This is it. This time you really did it. Looks like you hit the jackpot. So don't fuck it up, okay? I don't want you to go to Queens. And I don't want you to go within ten blocks of Emilio's topless bar. Just keep away. You understand what I'm telling you? Keep away.'

" 'Yeah, boss,' he says. 'Don't worry. This is the big one, right? I did good, right?'

" 'Yeah, Chano,' I tell him. 'You did good.'

"Next day he comes into the office to listen while I telephone Hector in Queens. I'm supposed to be in Atlantic City, so in case they have to call back, I've set up a call-forward number to the undercover phone in the office. But he gets on the line right away and I start the recorder.

" 'Hey, listen,' I say. 'I'll take seven kilos for starters. And it's very important that you tell me how much you got of this exact same merchandise. My customers have chemists, and they want it to be exactly like the sample, okay? So how much you got?'

"And the guy says, 'I can guarantee you two hundred kilos of the exact same merchandise.'

"Two hundred *kilos?* Break for five milliseconds to adjust. I guess some guys would have said, 'Okay, I'll take the lot,' and I was tempted. But it didn't feel right. How many wise guys running a gambling agency could come up with like six million in cash without batting an eye or even asking his customer? So I said I'd take everything he had at the rate of seven or eight kilos a week, and Hector agrees. We're all set. I figure we'll take these guys off after the first or second buy—just as soon as I know where the stash is. And Chano is busting.

"The minute I hang up, he explodes. He's fuckin' ecstatic. The man was ricocheting off the walls, his eyes bugging out like golf balls, his face all red and full of blood. He looked like a monkey's erection. But finally I calm him down and get rid of him, telling him to go straight home. This is Sunday night, and the deal is set to go off Monday. I'd told Hector I would be coming back from Atlantic City with the money.

"Two o'clock in the morning I get an hysterical phone call from Chano. Fucking guy didn't go home. The idiot did just what I told him *not* to. He went to Emilio's topless bar. Aside from the fact that he's a cokehead beyond belief and thought he'd get himself a free blow, the sonofabitch couldn't resist acting out the fantasy of being a big-time operator. With a 200-kilo deal going down, he figures Emilio's gonna treat him like he was Al Capone. And so he does—until some scumbag comes in who Chano did a couple of years before. The guy recognizes him and whispers in Emilio's ear. Next thing you know, Emilio's aiming a gun at Chano, and Chano's setting a new Guiness record for running the hundred-yard dash while screaming all the way.

" 'Guy wants to fucking kill me,' he wails on the phone.

" '*He* wants to kill you?' I say to him. 'Forget it, mother-fucker. *I* want to kill you.'

"But I don't have time. I round up some of the guys and we lock up Emilio. Then we go running out to Queens to hit Hector's house, but Hector's long gone. And so is the two hundred kilos."

Levine paused to soak up the warmth of approval. He had done it again, and it was like taking on fuel. By using different voices and accents and sketching out the parts, he had moved on from the polite inattention of the lecture hall to directly involving an audience in his one-man show: from classroom to theater with the easy authority of twelve years' regular practice. This was his best shot at maybe helping someone to save himself from disaster someday.

"What now? Well, to keep the case going, we flip Emilio, who tells us Hector's gone to Vegas. He even knows which hotel. And by now, Hector's had enough time to get there, so I make Emilio call him on the phone, and I record the conversation.

"Always do that. A tape recorder is one of your basic tools in narcotics enforcement. Soon as you flip somebody, make him call his contact, even if they only talk about the weather, because the minute a stool sees you put that cassette in your pocket with his conversation on it, he knows you've got *him* in your pocket. Never fails. You got physical proof of the guy's treachery, and you've bought him with that. He's *yours*.

"Anyway . . . Turns out Hector was with a guy that the DEA had been working on for years.

This guy was involved in air smuggling, and the Vegas office thought he might be building an airstrip out in the desert someplace, only until I called, they didn't even know he was in town. So after I played 'em the tape of Emilio's conversation over the phone, they got search warrants for the room and took 'em both off with a kilo of coke. And that was that. End of story.

"Except that Chano shows up next day in the office and says, 'See, boss? We made a good case, right?' Damn near kicked him out on his ass. I was really pissed off. Still, I got him a thousand dollars for the introduction, which isn't much for a kilo and two Class 1 dealers, and I didn't hear nothing for a couple of days. That's how long it took him to spend it. Then he calls me at home.

" 'Boss,' he says, and his voice is all broke up with emotion. 'Listen, boss. I know I fucked up. I've been thinking over my life, and I gotta tell ya—I'm in love.'

" 'Huh?' I mean, it's like two in the morning.

" 'Yeah,' he says. 'And I gotta do something. It's driving me crazy.'

" 'Ho, wait a minute. What are you talking about?'

" 'I'm talking about this girl, boss. I been a shithead all my life, and nothing but a stool, but there's this girl I met, and I'm in love, and I wanna—'

" 'Hey, Chano. Hold on. Back up a minute. What girl? Who are you talking about? *Where* did you meet her?'

" 'I just got through talking to her on the phone, boss, and I—'

" 'On the *phone?* You met her on the *phone?*'

" 'No, boss. I knew her from years ago in New York, and now she's in L.A., and I really love her. And she loves me. We're in love.'

" 'Yeah, okay. I get the picture. She's out there and you're here, and—'

" 'Yeah, and we want to have kids. We want to get married and have kids. I really want that. And she does, too.'

" 'Well, that's—that's fine, Chano. Congratulations.'

" 'Thanks, boss. I was on the phone. I was talking to her out there, and we both realized we're in love and want the same things outa life. This is the break I been waiting for, boss. All my life. I wanna get married. And have kids.'

" 'Okay. That's great. But what are you calling *me* for?'

" 'Well, boss, I'm broke. And she's in California.'

" 'Oh. Okay.'

"So I went and had a word with my boss, Joe Maloney, who knew Chano the way *I* knew Chano.

" 'Okay,' he says. 'But don't give him any money. Buy him a one-way ticket. And have a guy take him out to the airport and put him on the plane.'

"And that's just fine with Chano. 'Oh, boss,' he says, 'I knew you'd come through for me. I'm gonna name our first kid after you.'

" 'Yeah, yeah.'

"So now the bridegroom gets on the plane and flies off to a new life in California. Couple of weeks later, I get a call from the DEA office in Los Angeles.

" 'You know a guy named Chano? He gave us your name.'

" 'Yeah, I know him. He's a real good stool— if you handle him right.' And I told the guy all about him. I always do that. Whenever you get another cop working a guy you've handled, give him everything. So after I get through filling him in on Chano, I say, 'So what's going on?

He's only been out there a couple of weeks. Who does he want to give you?'

"And the guy says, 'Oh, just some broad he's living with. . . .' "

Levine waited until the laughter died down.

"Had another guy once. Sam Rochester.* Looked a lot like Woody Allen, only older, and had an even bigger mouth. Never stopped talking. Lived in a filthy one-room apartment in Greenwich Village with two of the ugliest, smelliest dogs I ever saw. He was a piss-poor jazz musician, but he knew everybody in the business, and we made a few cases. Nothing big. In fact, the most interesting thing about Sam Rochester was the Jewish star tattooed on the end of his penis.

"I kept hearing about it from various police departments around the country. Tampa. New Orleans. Galveston. He'd get drunk in some bar, flash his tattoo and get arrested for indecent exposure. And the first name he'd give out would be his buddy Mike Levine. Did a lot for my image in the South. . . .

"Then there was Roberto. One of my best informers. Made a lot of good cases with him. Roberto was cute. He was a Cuban bisexual with dyed orange hair who lived with a female Jewish butcher. One time he took me and another agent, Bobby Joura, in undercover with a bunch of Mexicans dealing dope on the Lower East Side. Broke up a major operation. Four arrests, plus a kilo of heroin. Good bust, so I gave Roberto a thousand-dollar reward.

"Shouldn't have done it. First thing he does, he buys himself a $300 Gucci umbrella. Then he gets trashed out of his mind, picks up some boy and takes him back to the apartment he shares with the Jewish lady butcher. She comes home early, catches him in bed with the boy and

* Not his real name.

chases him into the street with a cleaver. Next morning Roberto shows up at the office with all his worldly possessions. The clothes he stood up in, and his Gucci umbrella."

Again he waited, patient but unsmiling, until they fell silent.

"Yeah, it's funny," he said. "And you could die laughing. A lot of these worms can be likable. After all, they gotta have something going for 'em or they'd never get *close* enough to anyone to do 'em. But it cuts both ways, and that's what you've got to watch out for. The few you *do* get to care about—like Roberto and Ray Velez—they're the ones who might just seduce you into crossing that bottom line that must never be crossed. And as for the rest of the scum, well, don't get careless. There's no limit on treachery in *our* world, gentlemen.

"Chano, Sam, Roberto—whoever it was—they each had their different acts, and I noticed how other agents treated 'em. Like they were funny, dumb little monkeys sitting in a corner waiting for their banana. Pretty soon they'd be like part of the furniture, and that's when somebody, with his guard down, would say something in front of 'em that they shouldn't have heard. About his family or his private life, maybe. Maybe he'd taken an hour off the day before to take his wife to the doctor, and used his government car. Or maybe he complained to another agent in their hearing about his partner's drinking problem. That's all it takes. You get careless with these monkeys and you'll find out the hard way that they ain't so dumb. They got eyes, ears and a memory, and they'll fucking do *you*."

He took a long pause, looking somberly along the rows of faces. By now he felt he could separate at a glance those who might make it from those who might not.

"I knew an informer once," he went on, "who

was smarter, more manipulative and definitely better looking than—well—most of us.
Had five or six felony arrests on his sheet and
never did time—not more than a month or two,
anyway, when his bail was set high. I've
watched him work a jury when he was on the
stand, and watched their faces. Would have
been standing room only on Broadway. I saw how
judges treated him, and sometimes wished
they'd treat me half as well.

"His name was Michael Arlen, and he gave me
the smuggling rabbis."

For Levine, Michael Arlen validated his theory that justice is fo
the good-looking, Jaime Ibarra representing the converse. Arle
was fair-haired, handsome and charming; Ibarra, dark-haired, ugl
and awkward. Arlen was a polished professional cocaine deale
Ibarra, an innocent victim of circumstance. Arlen never serve
time; Ibarra would have drawn fifteen years if Levine had minde
his own business.

Arlen was also a very good talker. Six months after meetin
Levine at the door of Dave Klein's apartment, the two met again a
the DEA's New York office, where Arlen was once again talkin
his way out of trouble. He had been arrested in the Bronx on
state narcotics conspiracy charge, having been previously arreste
in Paterson, New Jersey, when a search of his car after a traffi
accident produced a glass jar of cocaine rocks. Already deepl
implicated in the continuing DEA Becker-Torres-Klein case, h
was now trying, with three strikes against him, to trade off hi
extensive criminal acquaintance.

Gus Fassler, as case agent, had begun the debriefing, and whe
Levine took over, Arlen had already sketched in the outline of
massive conspiracy centered around Howard Zachary Fuchs,
short, red-haired social worker whose parents had survived th
Holocaust and seemed blissfully unaware that, besides his globa
narcotics network, their only surviving son operated businesse
ranging from a brothel on West 18th Street to a shoe factory in E
Salvador. Though as menacing to look at as an overweight rabbini
cal student, Fuchs scared the daylights out of Michael Arlen, wh
seriously believed there was a contract on his life. At Fuchs's tria
he and other witnesses testified that Fuchs had also plotted th

deaths of at least two former associates, although Fuchs was never charged with their murders.

Arlen was a cokehead. He had become a dealer because that seemed the sensible way to finance his habit, but it was a sketchy, hand-to-nose existence until he met Fuchs in the spring of 1972. On hearing that Arlen had scored a backstage pass to a Rolling Stones' concert at Madison Square Garden, Fuchs fronted him four ounces of cocaine to sell behind the scenes. They had then lost touch for a while and were subsequently reintroduced to each other by Carol Richner, a low-level dealer from Greenwich Village to whom Arlen had turned that fall to help him out with a cocaine bonanza.

A friend of his worked for Pan Am at Kennedy Airport as a jet mechanic. Though not involved in smuggling himself, he put Arlen in touch with a group of Colombians who were—in particular, with Emil Pantoja, who also worked in Pan Am's maintenance department. Pantoja had evolved a virtually foolproof system for bringing in cocaine with a cousin who serviced Avianca aircraft in Bogotá.

Every Sunday his cousin would load two or three kilos of 98 percent pure cocaine into the nosewheel housing of the Avianca jet about to leave for New York. And every Sunday, after discharging its passengers and freight at Kennedy, the Avianca aircraft would be towed to the Pan Am hangars for routine servicing. And there, every Sunday night, Pantoja would remove the package from the wheel housing and take it home after work to Paterson, New Jersey. As an airport worker, he was not required to go through Customs.

At their first meeting, in a parking lot opposite the Pan Am terminal, Pantoja offered Arlen a full kilo, which was about thirty-five times more than Arlen could afford or knew how to dispose of. To preserve his dignity, he asked loftily for a sample and agreed to pay $100 for it next day if it proved to be of the requisite quality. Scarcely believing his luck, he scampered back to the city to ask his friend Carol Richner if she could help him finance the deal and market the stuff. After trying the sample, she agreed to do both, and a week later Arlen bought four ounces. He met Pantoja and his friend, Juan Gonzalez, a.k.a. John, at 168th Street and Broadway; they drove him over the George Washington Bridge to Paterson to collect the package, and sent him back by bus. Richner then sold it for him, and he made several more such trips in the course of the next three weeks.

But it was like working a gold mine with a toothpick. Arlen and Richner needed financing and a distribution network if they were to exploit the source properly, and Howard Fuchs had both. The only problem was that Howard was not prepared to front the money, and Emil and John were not prepared to front the cocaine. And until they got to know him better, the compromise Arlen worked out proved so exhausting that he subsisted on a diet of cocaine, amphetamines and tranquilizers and eventually drove his rental car into a pole on Interstate 80.

"It was a progression," he explained to Levine. "I had about $6,000, which I'd made from doing these small pieces with Carol, and when Howard came in I drove out to Paterson to buy my first half-brick—my first half-kilo. Got there around three in the morning, went upstairs to this second-floor apartment they had on Pennington Avenue, gave them the six thousand for the half-key, which meant I still owed them $4,800. Drove back and worked the brick to Howard that night. He looked at it, liked it, told me to leave it. Assured me I'd have the money in the morning.

"Sure enough, first thing in the morning, he called me, told me he had the money. About thirteen thousand. I called Emil to tell him the news, and he said to come out. So off I went again, paid them in full, and they gave me another half-brick. Turned around and came right back to Howard, who got rid of it immediately, and back out again I went later that night, or the next day. Kept that up from October through May, picking up two or three keys of coke every week and turning it all over to Fuchs, or to Eddie Cohen, who worked for Fuchs. Every Monday morning Emil or John would call me to say they had another shipment. Then I'd go out and rent a car and start in again with the Paterson–New York Cocaine Shuttle.

"Toward the end, Emil and John finally decided they would trust me with the whole shipment, but these guys, man, I swear to Christ, they were amateurs. They may have been good smugglers, but they'd weigh out the coke on a postal scale, spilling the stuff all over the place. They didn't even know my last name. Didn't know where I lived. Just my phone number—which is an incredible thing, when you think about it. I'm doing $2 million worth of business with these guys, and they don't even know my last name."

It was too good to last. Unlimited access to pure cocaine inevitably went to his head. By March 1973, he found it hard to breathe. He also had a problem with Emil and John. In late February he had picked up a kilo that started white but quickly turned brown when exposed to the air. As usual he sold it to Fuchs, who sold it on, but complaints started coming back, and when Pantoja produced another kilo of the same stuff Arlen balked at taking it.

"I'd heard it was making people sick, and I became very scared, and worried that I was poisoning people. But they insisted I take it. Otherwise, they said, they couldn't get me any more product, so naturally I took it. But Fuchs couldn't get rid of it, not even to his Detroit people or his people in Ohio. Finally, I picked out all the rocks I could find—about forty grams—and took the rest back. About one and a half pounds. *Made* them take it. But I was so wired from doing cocaine, I took a pill to calm me down, and on the way home drove into this pole."

The Paterson police found a pill and some speed in his pockets, and took him in. "I passed a test for drunkenness," Arlen said, "but I was very stoned. Talked a lot. Finally, they realized I was on drugs. They searched the car—illegally—and found the bottle with the rocks between the front seats. Arrested me. $2,500 bail."

With no time to explore a moral code that seemed to condone the poisoning of coke sniffers in Detroit and Ohio but not in New York, excused the driving of a car on a public highway while the driver was too stoned to avoid hitting things, but condemned a search of the car wreck as illegal, Levine pressed on with the interrogation.

Bailed out by his friend David Klein, Arlen returned to Paterson next morning to appear in court. After pleading guilty to a lesser charge, the movingly contrite defendant was fined $150 for the speed, $50 for the pill (which Arlen rather resented as it was a prescription drug), and $55 for reckless driving. The cocaine possession charge was dismissed.

"That was slick," Arlen observed appreciatively. "I don't know how I got out of it, but it was a warning sign. I had a lot of warning signs, man, but I was so coked up, I didn't realize. I couldn't think straight. Things were very foggy for me."

Sooner than risk driving through the fog again, Arlen relied on David Klein's Dav-El limousines after that to ferry him back and forth to Paterson. He could afford it. And as far as the drivers were concerned, it was just another job. They would drop him off at a shopping center parking lot, where another car would pick him up.

Then they would wait until he returned and drive him back to New York.

Did Klein know what was going on?

"David had an idea I was doing something, but he didn't know what. He was a better friend than he was smart. He didn't even realize I was getting him involved in something he had no idea about. And then, when Emil and John forced me to take back the bad coke, he insisted, against my better judgment, he *insisted* on putting it in his safe deposit box."

"You mean, it was *your* stuff we found in it, after he got arrested?"

"Right. Next time out, after I hit the pole, Emil and John said, 'Take it back.' They accused *me* of fucking it up. They said, 'It's yours. You gotta take it. And you owe us the money for it.' I didn't know what to do with it, so Klein insisted he put it in his safe deposit box."

"Is that what you wanted when you came to his apartment? When we were there?"

"No, I wanted my money. I didn't know he was busted. Although I thought he was going to be. See, the day before, he told me he heard from somebody that Becker and Torres got busted at the airport."

"He *what?*" Instead of bursting in on Klein and his ballet dancers, Levine could as easily have blundered into an ambush. "Who the fuck told him that?"

"I don't know. All I know is, he called me next day to say it was all a mistake. 'Somebody was kidding me,' he says. 'It's a bullshit story.' So *I* said, 'David, it smells bad. I can't tell you what to do, man, but I'm out of it. I want my money.' And I went over to get it."

"You were fronting him money?"

"No. No, I *never* front money. He just kept it for me. I was afraid he was going to get popped and they'd find it. See, right after the thing I had in Paterson, I flew down to St. Thomas for a week, and while I was gone, somebody broke into my apartment and stole $35,000. After that, David held my money. And then I found out who did it."

"You found out who broke into your apartment?"

"Yes. Eddie Cohen did. Him and Howard's man in Atlanta. *They* did it. On Howard's orders."

"Oh, yeah," said Levine admiringly. "That's cute. But we'll come to Fuchs in a minute. First, I wanna get these Colombians."

"Okay. But Emil and John are lying low. I got a feeling they know I got popped. I tried to circumvent it by saying I broke my back. Left word I was in the hospital after an auto accident, but I don't know if they fell for it. I'm expecting John to return my calls. He said he'd be in touch with Emil and have him call me. And maybe he did. I haven't been around to take any calls."

Levine brooded on it. "Maybe we oughta take a ride out there," he said. "Take a look around. See what's going on."

"To Paterson?" Arlen lost a little of his poise. "Well, I'm ready to help you, man. But when I go out there to meet them, I'm going out with a gun. Because I owe them $25,000, and they're gonna expect me to pay them, or put out my life. I know these guys. I know they used to have me followed out of Paterson every time I picked the stuff up. They had a guy follow me in a car. It was a warning to me not to fuck around."

"I'd still like to catch 'em with the stuff in their hands."

"Okay. But I told you people a long time ago, I said, 'If we're going to make a buy out there, we got to do it fast.' But up to now, all this bureaucratic bullshit has stopped us doing it."

"I'd like to do it tonight," Levine murmured, tightening the screw. "If we can set it up."

"Well, I tell you, man." Arlen laughed unconvincingly. "I feel safe with you. I'd go out, I'd take you out there, but we're like two sitting ducks. If anything happened, believe me, man, you know how much less of a human I'd feel than I feel now?"

Levine patted his head consolingly, and next day drove him out to Paterson with Special Agent Michael Kane to locate the three apartments to which he had been taken to collect and pay for cocaine. There was no one home at Pantoja's apartment on Pennington Avenue. Levine had already established that Emil had quit his job with Pan Am two weeks earlier, and nobody seemed to have laid eyes on him since. They had no better luck with the second apartment, at 684 East 28th Street, and after keeping the building under observation for an hour, Levine drove them back to New York.

A few days later he went out again with Special Agent Jay Silvestro to check on the third apartment, at 694 East 28th Street. Around 2:00 P.M. a man answering to Arlen's description of John came out with a woman and a young child, and drove off in a tan

Chevrolet. A license plate check by radio established that the car was registered to Juan Gonzalez, at that address, and a check with the phone company turned up one of the numbers that Arlen had often called before going out to collect the week's care package from Bogotá.

Levine followed John and his passengers to a house on Market Street where they got out and went inside. Levine and Silvestro settled down to wait. Five hours later, John came out by himself and crossed the street to the Grand Union supermarket, in whose parking lot Arlen had regularly switched from his Dav-El limo to Pantoja's green Chevy. When John came back again a few minutes later, with nothing more dramatic than a carton of milk, Levine got out of the car on an impulse to bar the way.

"Excuse me, sir," he said politely, showing his credentials. "We're federal officers. And I wonder if you can help us."

He then produced a mugshot he happened to have with him of a defendant in another case, and explained that he and his partner were looking for this man, who had been seen earlier in the area with someone answering to John's description.

John relaxed, studied the picture and finally shook his head. No, he said. He had never seen the man before. Levine, who had no cause to doubt the truth of that, then asked him for some identification, and John, eager to be helpful, invited them both into the house, where he showed them his green card. They had just moved in from 694 East 28th Street, he said. They had not even had time to change the phone listing, which was still in the name of Arturo Romano, the previous occupant, (who had also been investigated by DEA in the past.)

After a few more questions, Levine thanked him for his cooperation and broke off the surveillance. All he needed to do now was to prove that John and Juan Gonzalez were one and the same and to connect him with Arlen, and the grand jury would have enough to indict them all for conspiracy.

Next morning Levine telephoned Gonzalez on the pretext of confirming the details he had written down the previous day and taped the call for comparison with an earlier tape of a phone conversation between Arlen and John. Laboratory tests confirmed that the voices of Gonzalez and John were the same. A routine examination of the toll records for the Market Street phone and Gonzalez's previous number showed a pattern of Monday morning calls to Michael Arlen in New York. Now they were all strung together, and it remained only for the grand jury to tie the bow.

As for Emil Pantoja, Levine had asked the Newark office to see if any of its informants knew where he was, and the next day learned he had just missed him. While Levine and Silvestro had been sitting outside Gonzalez's house, Pantoja had been catching a plane to Puerto Rico. He had told an informer he was going on from there to Colombia, and had no plans to come back to the U.S. Not ever. But he had thoughtfully provided his address and telephone number in Puerto Rico in case anybody wanted to get in touch with him.

Levine wanted to very much, but there was nothing he could do until the grand jury concluded its deliberations. At four-ten the following afternoon, Emil Pantoja-Donado was formally indicted in the New York Eastern District for conspiracy to possess and distribute cocaine, and four hours later he was arrested in Guaynabo, Puerto Rico, with his bags packed. But then the luck ran out. As soon as the warrants came through, Levine took the rest of McMullen's group to round up the other conspirators, but now *Gonzalez* had gone missing, and was next heard of, weeks later, in Colombia.

To make sure of Pantoja, Levine himself flew down to San Juan to bring him back, but even that did not hold. Despite his vehement lobbying, Pantoja's bail was set at a paltry $150,000, hardly more than loose change for a runaway Class 1 violator facing a minimum of fifteen years. A bench warrant was issued for his arrest when he failed to appear for his arraignment, but by then he had joined Gonzalez in Colombia.

Levine took the news phlegmatically. There was no shortage of Colombian dopers. If he felt like locking up a few, all he had to do was put on his beret, shades and purple shirt, and drive out to Queens. What the system chose to do with them then concerned him only if incompetent prosecutors or irresolute judges combined to turn really dangerous criminals loose after he had gone to the trouble of catching them. Considerations of justice now influenced his conduct of a case only to the extent that they helped make the game more interesting. The more intricate the course, the more satisfying it was to negotiate.

Where a less seasoned, less professionally detached investigator might have felt discouraged by the outcome, Levine derived the same sense of fulfillment from the Pantoja case as a chess player closing out a well-judged game. The satisfaction lay in winning, in the successful exercise of skill and imagination. It was a personal matter. Nothing had been "achieved" in any tangible sense, and the world would go on pretty much as before, but Levine had learned to insulate himself against that kind of bottom-line accountancy. He was engaged in an art, not a business. Having eliminated Pantoja and Gonzalez as traffickers, he lost no sleep when the system fumbled the ball and lost possession. In the words of his former boss, Al Seeley, "We get paid to put 'em in. Judges and U.S. attorneys get paid for letting 'em out."

By then, in any case, Levine had turned his attention to the more important quarry of Howard Fuchs and his smuggling rabbis. Unlike the Colombians, Fuchs was going nowhere. He was detained on Rikers Island pending trial on a state narcotics charge, which gave Levine, Assistant U.S. Attorney Dave DePetris and the federal grand jury ample time to adjust the noose to a perfect fit—again with the help of Michael Arlen, whom the jury had named as a co-conspirator with Pantoja, Gonzalez, Fuchs, Eddie Cohen and several lesser lights. The deal Arlen and his attorney had worked out with DePetris required Arlen to plead guilty to the charges and testify against the others in return for the prosecutor's promise to draw the judge's attention, before passing sentence, to Arlen's heart-rending air of contrition and his no less persuasive performance as the government's chief witness.

"Tell me about Fuchs," Levine would say, pulling Arlen in for questioning whenever his caseload allowed it. "I wanna know about Fuchs." And Arlen would tell him.

"Well, Howard *used* me," he complained. "I didn't realize it at the time, but he was *cutting* the coke" (the only really serious crime in Arlen's book). "I was making a profit, no doubt about it, but he was making three or four times more—although he'd never admit it. Whenever I challenged him, he'd say all he was making was twenty-five dollars an ounce."

"Was he buying from anyone else? Did he tell you?"

"In California. I know he had a connection in California because a lot of times he asked me to go out there. He told me about a special place where his people crossed the border. In Arizona. Sonoita, I think he said. And I know he had a courier killed out there after she got caught."

"Did you take him up on that? You ever go out there?"

"No. I wasn't interested. He saw I was making a lot of money, and wanted to get me involved in all his businesses. Then he wanted me to go down with him and meet these people in some lab outside Bogotá. Thought it would be smart to get their product. Told me he could get fifty kilos fronted to him, but he'd have to stay there. They'd hold his body as collateral. They'd send the stuff up. Guarantee it got here. Give it to me. I get rid of it and send the money down. Half a million dollars. But I never got involved with that."

"Why not?"

"I'm not that greedy. I didn't want to get in that deep. Howard makes me nervous. There's nothing he won't do, if he has to."

"Hey, you got about six felony arrests yourself."

"Yes, I know. But Howard, he's a real *criminal.*"

Levine sighed. "Okay. Now tell me again about the people Fuchs sold to. Not deals you heard about. Deals you saw go down with your own eyes."

"Mike, we did all that. Several times."

"Right. Now we're doing it again." Given the intricacies of the conspiracy laws, there was no room for lapses of memory.

Arlen slumped back in his chair resignedly and started to check them off on his fingers.

"Gary Winkel. Gary worked for Howard. I didn't see it myself, but I know he took a load of hash oil up to Montreal one time and traded it for cocaine. He was in tight with some guy up there named Isaac somebody, who got his stuff from Europe. Then there's Carol. Carol Richner. She helped me out when I was getting started, but I had to drop her. Found out she was selling the stuff to Fuchs and taking a percentage from him as well as me. Real cokehead anyway. Okay—José Cruz and John Manacheo. Howard's people in Detroit. He sold to them, and he bought from them, too. I was there in May when an eleven-kilo deal went down at the Sherry Netherlands hotel."

He snapped his fingers. "Yes. Now I remember. The name of the guy Gary went to see in Montreal was Isaac Ashkenazi. Did heroin, too. Got his stuff from Paris, France. Then there was Rabbi Sam. Bought and sold with him, too. And Eddie Cohen. He was—"

"Hold on. Back up a minute. Rabbi Sam?"

"Yeah." Arlen laughed.

"What was his last name?"

"Rabbi Sam's last name? Not sure he told me. Spiro? Shapiro? Not sure. Can't remember."

"What did he look like?"

"He looked like a rabbi, okay? Little guy—five six, five seven. Chubby. Brown hair. Dark clothes. Mid-thirties. Lived upstate someplace."

"And you *saw* him do business with Fuchs? You were there?"

"Sure. Several times. With Cohen, too. *And* Gary Winkel."

Levine smiled. He couldn't wait to tell Keith. The guy he had pointed out to his son that Saturday afternoon on Maple Avenue was now squarely in his sights as a big-time doper. "That's what life is all about, son," he would say. "The cover of the book is what these guys are trying to sell you, and as often as not, it's bullshit."

With Arlen and Fuchs, he finally had the makings of a case against his elusive neighbor in Monsey. Among other interesting connections in Fuchs's telephone toll records, he found a splendidly revealing sequence of calls to Rabbi Sam, to Nadell in Iowa and to several unidentified numbers in Israel. But Fuchs himself was still refusing to cooperate, and Levine decided to leave him on ice until after the trial, now scheduled for January. A guilty verdict and a fifteen-year sentence often focused the mind wonderfully. He homed in instead on Eddie Cohen, whom he had arrested as a co-conspirator with Fuchs in the Pantoja-Gonzalez case.

A graduate of Rutgers who worked in his father's furniture business in Hackensack, New Jersey, when he was not trafficking dope, Cohen crumbled easily and testified at Fuchs's trial as a government witness. Thus initiated as a true believer, he then insisted on describing everyone of the fifteen separate occasions on which he personally had bought hashish from Rabbi Sam, and referred Levine to Gary Winkel for corroboration.

In deep trouble himself, Winkel was happy to oblige, and went further, recalling one deal in particular when he bought $250,000 worth of hash from Rabbi Sam and his close business associate, Rabbi Avraham Safrai. He also confirmed his dealings with Isaac Ashkenazi in Montreal and named several other Israelis, including two more rabbis, with whom he and Fuchs had done business, buying and selling hashish and cocaine. Anxious to please, he then accompanied Levine on a drive around town, pointing out the places where the deals had gone down.

With this, Levine had enough to raise a DEA case number. Until now, he had run the investigation on his own time under the umbrella of the Fuchs-Pantoja-Gonzalez case, but he now had clear evidence of another major conspiracy, with Sam Shapiro at its center, and Cohen, Winkel and, possibly, Fuchs as government witnesses. Assistant U.S. Attorney Dave DePetris thought so, too, when he heard about it, and undertook to find grand jury time as soon as Levine was ready.

But they were not the only ones who wanted Rabbi Sam. Among his other duties, Levine had been appointed liaison officer with the Israeli national police, then represented in New York by Colonel Eli Malki. When Levine stopped by for a chat about this emerging Israeli Connection, he was astonished to learn that Malki already held an Israeli arrest warrant for Shapiro. He had also been in touch with the State Department and the Department of Justice in Washington to arrange for his extradition.

"Fuck that," said Levine. "Excuse my Hebrew, Colonel, but I got Shapiro, I got Safrai—I got a whole bunch of Israelis doing hundreds of kilos of hash, cocaine and heroin. And if you think I'm gonna let 'em go home to serve a couple of weeks for nonpayment of parking tickets, you're crazy."

Malki smiled slightly. "It's more serious than that, my friend. Shapiro is wanted for fraud, embezzlement—for many financial crimes. He swindled hundreds of small Israeli investors out of millions of dollars. If we send him home to stand trial, who knows? Maybe they will get some of it back."

"Fine. When he's done time for the dope, *then* you can have him. With my blessing. And good luck to you."

Malki's smile broadened. "I was about to suggest the same thing," he said. "But the other way around. After all, he is an Israeli. So we have first claim."

"No, Colonel. I don't think so. He's committed serious felony crimes here in the United States, and *we* have jurisdiction. I've got enough on Shapiro, Safrai and others to get 'em indicted right now."

"If you say so, Mike." The colonel spread his fingers and shrugged. "But my instructions are clear. We gave you Meyer Lansky. Now we want Sam Shapiro."

While no more impressed than Levine by Israel's "interference" in a federal narcotics case, DePetris cautioned him against any premature move to detain Shapiro and Safrai until they had cleared it at a higher level. A week later Tom Puccio, head of the narcotics section of the U.S. Attorney's office, called to tell Levine to lay off.

"Forget it," he said. "Washington doesn't want 'em arrested. We're gonna kick 'em out."

"What?"

"You heard me. Washington says, give 'em back."

"Well, that's great. That's really wonderful. So why the fuck do we arrest Colombians? Or Cubans? Or Mexicans? Why don't we just kick *them* out as well? What's so special about Rabbi Sam?"

"Don't ask *me,* Levine. I'm Italian. The Israelis want him bad, and that's that. They don't believe Shapiro and Safrai are into drugs anyway."

"Well, how the fuck would *they* know? Tom, I've been working this case for a year, okay? Brought it over from Customs. I got three co-conspirators putting both these guys in a major hash and coke conspiracy—*four,* if I flip Fuchs. I got more'n enough to arrest 'em right now, and you're telling me you're gonna let 'em take a *walk?"*

There was a brief silence at the other end, and Levine smiled. Puccio hated dope dealers almost as much as he did.

"What kind of weight are they dealing?"

"As of right now, for a conspiracy indictment, we can prove a pound of heroin, three kilos of coke, five kilos of hash oil and about 240 kilos of hash. But these guys are doing *tons.* Since when do we let guys like *that* go?"

There was another silence.

"Okay," Puccio said. "Come in tomorrow with everything you got. I'll get the warrants ready."

Levine hung up before he could change his mind, but it made no difference. As soon as he saw Puccio's expression next morning, he knew he was thwarted again.

"No go?"

"Sorry, Mike. Washington says no way. We gotta clear everything through State, and they say no arrests."

Levine thumped his forehead with the butt of his hand and turned away, muttering to himself.

"Since when does State tell the Eastern District who to indict?"

"Now don't start on me, Mike. Take it up with the Israelis."

"Okay. I'll talk to Malki."

"Yeah. He wants to see you anyway. You got 'em all bent out of shape over there. Not about Shapiro so much, but Safrai. They just don't buy it."

"Wait till I play 'em a couple of tapes."

"Okay. But leave your stuff here. I'll find some grand jury time. Maybe if we get an indictment, that will do it."

Again, the sheer weight of cases demanding attention pushed Shapiro aside for a time. Ten days before Puccio's grand jury was due to begin hearing testimony, Levine and Special Agent Jim Montagne went to see if they could persuade Colonel Malki that the U.S. had the weightier claim.

"Colonel, I don't wanna give you a hard time," Levine began insincerely, "but cooperation's a two-way street. When you bust Americans for doing dope in Israel, *you* got the right to lock 'em up. No squawks from us. And if we bust Israelis doing dope over here, then *we* got the right. Now, if you want 'em afterwards for something they did back home, that's fine. Same thing goes for us. But these guys are *here*, and they're breaking *our* laws."

"So you say, Mike." Malki threw up his hands. "So you say. But Shapiro is a swindler. A loan shark. A con man. Drugs are not his thing. And as for Safrai . . ." He shook his head. "It's not possible. Safrai comes from one of the most prominent, one of the most religious families in Israel. Why would he do this? Nobody I talked to, nobody in the government can believe he is trafficking drugs. A little financial hocus-pocus, maybe—the connection with Shapiro is unfortunate. But not drugs, Mike. It's out of character. Completely out of character."

"Yeah, I thought you'd say that. Listen to this."

He placed his recorder on Malki's desk and played a fifteen-minute extract from the tape of Gary Winkel's debriefing. After describing the $250,000 hash deal with Shapiro and Safrai, Winkel went on to outline the rabbis' connection with Ashkenazi's Canadian group, and Howard Fuchs's operations in the U.S., naming eight other co-conspirators.

When Levine switched off the machine, Malki sat in silence for a moment.

"Is this man Winkel a reliable witness?" he asked.

"He's talking to save his neck," Levine said. "If he lies to me, he's down the tubes for fifteen to twenty years. He knows that."

"Yes, but—"

"Colonel, I got two other cooperating co-conspirators who made the same deal he did. Everything he says checks out. And sooner or later, I'm gonna get Fuchs to testify as well. Rabbi Sam and Rabbi Safrai are Class 1 violators, Colonel. And I *want* them."

Malki sighed. Then he scratched his head. "The tape," he said. "Is that a spare copy?"

"Come on, Colonel. Will having the tape make any difference?"

"Well, I'll talk to Tel Aviv. Tell them what you've got. Perhaps they'll change their mind, perhaps they won't. But I can see you've got a case, Mike. If there's anything you want me to do, anything you need from our records, just let me know."

Two days before the Shapiro grand jury was due to be sworn in, Levine took a call from Dave DePetris.

"Sorry, Mike," he said. "Washington just iced the whole deal. We won't be taking the Shapiro case to the grand jury. Not yet, anyhow."

Levine had allowed for the possibility of further argument, but not for this.

"They *iced* it? Can they *do* that?"

"They can, and they did. I'm sorry, Mike."

"Well, shit. I know the system works pretty bad sometimes, but I didn't know you could just turn it off if it gets to be inconvenient. I mean, not even the fucking *President* can do that. *Who* iced it?" It was like discovering he was badly wounded without knowing how it had happened. Defendants taking a walk was one thing; that usually happened *after* the trial. Now, for the first time in a major case, he was being robbed of the satisfaction of "putting them in," his first lesson in what would become a postgraduate course in the politics of drugs. "These guys are fucking criminals. *I* know it. *You* know it. Washington knows it. We got the fucking evidence. And now somebody comes along and says *no*? I don't fucking believe this. We can't even *indict* 'em?"

"Not yet. Not until they're back in Israel. I don't like this any better than you do, Mike, but if that's what the State Department wants, that's what it's gonna get."

"The hell it is. You trying to tell me some fucking bureaucrat, not even in the Justice Department, has only gotta say no to some case, and right away, we just junk it? That's bullshit."

"Nobody's junking anything. You'll get your fucking grand jury —just as soon as they're out of the country."

"Well, some fucking difference. What the hell's the point of taking it to a grand jury if we can't lock the mother-fuckers up?"

"The point is we'll extradite the sonofabitch when the Israelis get through with him. And will you get off my back? Go yell at Kissinger."

"Well, there was no way I was going to let Rabbi Sam take a walk," Levine told his Albany class. "Apart from anything else, I had something to prove to my eight-year-old son. I wanted him to see that the sonofabitch would go to jail, rabbi or not. I also knew Malki was too good a cop to let it pass, so I went to work on Howie Fuchs. After he'd been inside for a couple of months, I went to visit him in jail, and saw the system had pushed all the psychological buttons *for* me. Steel bars, wooden benches and being surrounded twenty-four hours a day by hairy-legged men can have a definite loosening effect on the tongue, Howie was *mine*.

"It was like turning on a faucet. Talked nonstop for ten hours and gave up everybody. Shapiro. Safrai. The Canadians. His people in Atlanta and Detroit. The California operation. Everything. A week later, the grand jury began hearing the case of the smuggling rabbis, and six weeks after that, Shapiro, Safrai and the rest were finally indicted. Took more than a year, but I did it.

"And it took another three years before I finally got my hands on Rabbi Sam. Safrai they wouldn't give us. Malki said it would be too demoralizing for the Jewish people if a guy like that, from one of the top Israeli families, was extradited for drugs. But Sam we could have. And as soon as we heard they were letting him out, my boss sent me over to get him. Smart move, too, because on the way back I flipped him as well.

"First, he tells me how he got started in drugs. The Israeli mafia supplies him with capital for his loan sharking, and they all make piles of money until one day he lends a bundle to some businessman just before the guy goes bankrupt. The guy's assets and bank accounts are frozen, and now Sam's organized crime bosses want their money back. But Sam doesn't *have* any money. The only way he can pay 'em off is by playing along with an idea they got for smuggling dope through American embassy mails.

"They got Israeli people working in the embassy post office in Tel Aviv who can make ordinary-looking parcels of eight to ten pounds of hash, put American stamps on them and the names of real embassy officials as the senders, and then put 'em through channels to addresses in the U.S. as pieces of embassy mail, knowing Customs won't open 'em. What they need is somebody to set up people over here in the States to receive the parcels, and Sam is it. So Rabbi Sam Shapiro comes over like the ambassador from Israeli organized crime to establish diplomatic and commercial relations with organized crime in America, and that way he can pay back the money he owes.

"Soon they're doing heroin as well. The Israelis know people in the American embassy in Bonn—Marines and clerks and German workers—who can get heroin from Turkish smugglers and send it on down in the embassy mail to Tel Aviv, where their people in the embassy post office intercept the packages, parcel 'em up like the hash, and send 'em on to the States in the same way. It was one of those heroin parcels, addressed to Barry Nadell in Iowa, that gave us our first lead to Rabbi Sam.

"Now this was pretty interesting stuff, and it got better. The connection between Israeli and American organized crime paid off so well that the embassy system was soon being used only for heroin. The hash had to go by containership, in loads of six to eight hundred pounds at a time, mostly crated up as consignments of books. According to Sam, one of the bigger loads, around half a ton, was supplied by a famous Israeli general, who seized it in Gaza, and instead of turning it in, sold it to help finance his antiterrorist group. Seems he didn't get enough money from the government to do the job properly, so he took his organization into drug trafficking to make up the difference.

"They called him Gandhi, but his real name was Rechavam Zehevi. He was one of the world's experts on antiterrorism, and the Israeli government used to loan him out to other countries with terrorist problems. One of them was Ecuador. When he went out there with his team, they took the half-ton of hash with them, traded it for cocaine and maybe heroin—Rabbi Sam wasn't sure—and sent it up to Florida to sell for dollars, using girl couriers.

"Zehevi later denied it, of course, but the debriefing went on like that. One good story after another. Didn't all lead to new cases, but it was great background intelligence and cleared up a lot of questions we had in a lotta different investigations. So when I finished debriefing Rabbi Sam, I wrote up the whole interview as a DEA 6, Report of Investigation, and naturally sent copies around to all the interested DEA offices, including headquarters. Now don't ask me how, but one of those copies wound up in the hands of the Israeli secret service. And stranger still, when Zehevi decided to run for office in the 1979 Israeli elections, my DEA 6 turned up again. On the front page of the Israeli newspaper, *El Ma'ariv*.

"But Sam's real big contribution was proving a link between Israeli and American organized crime. A few months after I brought him back, he took me in undercover to a meeting at the Cafe Metropole, a topless joint on Seventh

Avenue. An Israeli named Sam Nagar, one of the owners of the place, and an Italian mob guy named Frank Negrone offered to sell me five hundred pounds of hash for $375,000. Immediate delivery. And when I asked about the quality, they gave me a kilo sample.

"After that, the case was transferred to another division because these guys were already under investigation for other crimes. But I heard later the Secret Service took Nagar off with half a million dollars in counterfeit hundreds supplied by the mob."

Levine nodded, acknowledging a signal from the front row. He had run well past his allotted time, but nobody was looking at his watch.

"The moral of that story," he said, turning for home, "is, never be complacent. It's the moral of everything I've told you about handling stools. Listen to *all* of 'em. Don't trust *any* of 'em.

"A good professional narc is like a good professional hunter, and the stool is his bird dog. You train him, work the shit out of him, and when he's all used up, you trot him back to the fucking kennel. Before I was done with 'em, bird dog Rabbi Sam and bird dog Howie Fuchs brought me sixteen dead birds—sixteen Class 1 dopers, tried, convicted and sentenced.

"But there the comparison ends. The stool dog is a sick dog that's good for only one thing. He knows how to pretend he's a bird. It's a flawed breed, carrying the seeds of its own destruction. Chano, Michael Arlen, Rabbi Sam, Roberto, Howard Fuchs—they're all the same. They're all addicted to crime and treachery, and when they do finally self-destruct, you don't want to be around.

"Take Howie, for instance. When he got out, I was happy for his parents. They were both in their seventies, and Howie was their only surviving child. When I fixed it so they could see him in a room at the courthouse during the trial, they grabbed my hand and kissed it. And I didn't know how to handle that, not after what they'd been through.

"So when Howard comes to me and says he's going legit, it means a lot to me. 'Look,' he says, 'I'm gonna open a men's clothing store in New York and another one in Buffalo. Why don't you invest? I gotta good business head, and I'm gonna make a lotta money.' 'No,' I said. 'I can't come in with you, but go ahead, Howard, and God bless you. Stay out of this shit. *Do* it.'

"So he does it. In six months Howard Fuchs owns a chain of men's stores. He was right. He had a real head for business. A year later, Howard Fuchs is a millionaire. Then he gets arrested for selling two ounces of cocaine to a Puerto Rican on Southern Boulevard in the Bronx."

EIGHT

"Jesus, Mike . . . You oughta get
an Oscar for that."

While Levine never doubted he
was doing what Providence had called him to do, the DEA was
less certain. His attitude toward authority had not endeared him to
administrators with tidy minds, or civil servants with tidy files, or
embittered career cops with tidy jurisdictions. As far as Levine was
concerned, the function of bureaucrats, however exalted, was to
help him catch dope traffickers, and his regard for them was directly proportionate to their agility in getting out of his way. But a
few of his superiors in the DEA saw their roles in that light.
Levine's name was rarely among the first that sprang to mind when
senior officials sat down to consider recommendations for awards
and promotions. For an agent with Levine's record of accomplish-
ment, he not only had pitifully few citations to hang on the office
wall, he was also well overdue for his next step up the ladder from
Grade 12 to Grade 13.

His biggest fans were group supervisors and division com-
manders who stood or fell on results. At that level of management,
almost everybody, like him or not, would have had to agree that
there was no one else in the region (which effectively meant in the
country) who could match his unstoppable drive and panache. Levine was undeniably the best undercover agent around and argu-
ably the most prolific agent in government service. His division

ader, Wayne Valentine, had watched the body count soar in McMullen's group and, some six months after the merger, called Levine into his office to solve a problem for both of them.

"Mike," he said, in his quiet midwestern way, "you want your Grade 13, don't you?"

Levine felt a prickle of caution. "Hell, yes, Mr. Valentine," he said. "I think I earned it."

"Well, it's the International group. I've just been looking over their reports, and they've got hardly any arrest statistics for the whole damn year."

Levine considered this, trying to read the signs. The International group was famous for starting late every day and making up for it by quitting early, but he liked John O'Neill, the group supervisor, and he could see that Valentine was not inviting him to be critical.

"Well, I guess somebody's got to be on standby," he said diplomatically, and it was true. Most international cases began with a seizure of dope coming in, and whoever had "the duty" had little choice but to hang around like firemen waiting to be called out.

"Maybe so," said Valentine, "but all those double zeros on the bottom line are beginning to attract attention." He eyed Levine ruminatively. "If I put you in there as backup supervisor, you think you can get 'em going?"

Levine had been afraid of that. He certainly wanted his promotion, but not at the expense of what he was best at.

"Well, I don't know, Mr. Valentine," he said warily. "I'm a street guy. Turn me loose in Spanish Harlem or Little Bogotá and I make statistics. But in International . . ." He shrugged.

"That's exactly what I want you to do," said Valentine. "Get 'em off their asses and out on the street. *Make* some cases. You bring their statistics up, and you've got your 13."

Levine was now in a real quandary. It was an offer he could not refuse, but without a streetwise group to cover him, promotion on these terms could mean a one-way ticket to the morgue.

"Okay," he said slowly. "But if you want me to take 'em out, I'm gonna need something to keep me alive long enough to make a dent in those zeros."

"Yeah? What's that?"

"A Spanish-speaking agent. They don't have one, and most of my work is undercover in Spanish. If I go in wired, there won't be a guy covering me who'll know what's going on. They could be saying, 'We goin' to keel ju, meng'—and the group'll be out there sipping coffee.''

Valentine sighed.

And that was how Levine came to team up with Emilio "Skippy" Garcia for three of the most remarkable years in modern law enforcement. Starting from next to nothing, Levine galvanized O'Neill's Group 31 into such a frenzy that they locked up eighty-eight people in three months. In one *day* Levine went undercover four times, made four cocaine buys, arrested four separate sets of violators, and still had time to help out another group that night with a buy-bust in Queens. No federal agent had ever done anything like that before.

A quick study himself, Garcia was soon trying to match him buy for buy, and once he had settled in, they shared the group's undercover work between them, each covering the other, with the other agents either learning how to do it or standing by to tidy up afterward. Within a year Levine had his Grade 13, and Valentine was up to his armpits in statistics. But the Levine-Garcia partnership only narrowly survived Garcia's first night out with the International group.

A Puerto Rican informer who sold hot suits in the Bronx had arranged a cocaine buy with some neighborhood dealers, and in order to protect him Levine had agreed to take them off on the street before they arrived, so that no one would know who had tipped him. It was an ordinary surveillance job. Group 31 would simply follow the dealers' car, and as soon as he was sure they were heading for the informer's house, he would order the group to intercept and make the arrests.

"Okay," said Special Agent Terry Boyle* when Levine had finished his briefing. "I'll take the kid. I wanna see what he can do.''

Boyle was an old-line, Irish law-enforcement officer of vast experience, mountainous bulk and genial disposition. Skippy Garcia was a diminutive, volatile Cuban-American, fresh out of training school with a good opinion of himself. Boyle had had a few beers—it was now late in the evening—and Garcia was twitching with excitement over his first operational outing. Side by side, they were a surrealist version of Laurel and Hardy.

By the time Boyle had arranged himself behind the wheel of his car, the rest of the group was fifteen minutes ahead of them, and

* Not his real name.

Garcia, following its progress on the radio, was beside himself with frustration.

"Don't worry about it," Boyle said, easing cautiously into the northbound traffic on the West Side Highway. "We got plenty of time"—so much time, in his view, that he stopped for a six-pack once they got to the Bronx, and then again, a few minutes later, to relieve himself in an alley. Inevitably, at that moment a babble of overlapping cross talk broke out on the radio. The suspects in the target car had spotted the surveillance and decided to make a run for it. Bouncing up and down in his seat with anguish, Garcia called out, "C'mon, c'mon—the arrest's going down. Right *now*."

Cursing and fumbling with his zipper, Boyle lumbered out of the alley like an irritable rhinoceros, hauled himself into the car and took off in a wild squeal of tortured tires, head cocked in concentration as he tried to figure out from the radio where everybody was.

"My palms were a little wet by the time we ran the third red light," Garcia recalls, "but all things considered, I was taking it pretty well until we hit the Bronx Parkway and started going the wrong way—*against* the traffic. Then I kinda made an act of contrition and got under the seat."

Levine, meanwhile, had directed a high-speed chase that ended abruptly when the fugitives crashed into one of the pillars supporting the elevated highway at a Westchester Avenue interchange. With his prisoners loaded into the group's cars, he was about to drive off with the cocaine and the gun he had seized as evidence when, over the radio, he heard a confused outburst of cries and shouts. As he looked around, frowning, Boyle's car came scorching around the corner, spinning and burning rubber, miraculously missed everything and screeched to a broadside stop just in front of him.

Wide-eyed and pale, Garcia half fell out of the already open passenger door and groped his way over to the roadside parapet to sit down.

"Well?" said Levine cheerfully, in Spanish. "How do you like the job so far?"

"I quit," Garcia said.

But he didn't get the chance. Levine was running so fast to clinch his promotion that it became a matter of honor for Garcia to try to keep pace. Caught up in a whirlwind of on-the-job training, he was soon surprising Levine with his audacity and his instinctive grasp of what undercover work was all about.

When Levine learned from an informant that Jonathan Fried, a fugitive doper from BNDD days, had returned to New York after hiding for years in South Africa, he took Garcia with him to make the arrest to show his protégé how it was done. When he rang the bell of Fried's Greenwich Village apartment, announcing himself loudly, nobody answered, but he heard a patter of running feet inside. Launching himself at the door, he smashed it down with a flying karate kick and saw Fried sprinting for the bedroom.

Levine dived after him, knowing he was going for a gun, but to his surprise Garcia jostled him in the doorway, ducked under his arm and pounced on Fried as he was groping for the loaded Luger automatic under his pillow.

Levine liked that.

"Soon got to be so there was nobody else I'd rather have with me. We took down all kinds of people with guns, just the two of us. Okay, so Skippy's a short, aggressive egomaniac, but when you gotta go through a door after you've told 'em you're coming in, and God knows what's waiting on the other side, it means a lot in this game when your partner is always *there*, pushing to get in first. We broke down a lotta doors in three years, Skippy and me, and I never saw him hesitate. Not once. Never knew him to shut up either. Always ready to tell you why *he* should be running the DEA. But he's the real thing, Skippy. And did we make cases."

With other congenial spirits in Group 31, they settled into a daily round based on paperwork (or court) in the morning, hanging out at lunchtime in a sleazy bar they called the Greeko-Rican (now demolished) on the corner of 57th and Tenth Avenue, followed by an afternoon workout in the gym (or court), more hanging out at the Greeko-Rican or The Library, a restaurant-bar on upper Broadway, and then, as dopers are mostly nocturnal animals, out on the streets until the small hours.

In practice, no spell of duty ever worked out quite like this, but that was the pattern of routine Levine and the younger agents tended to follow when they were not testifying or conferring with prosecutors and other agencies or reviewing cases with their superiors or out on surveillance or traveling out of town or responding to call-outs or making arrests and controlled deliveries or on training courses or qualifying on the range or processing and debriefing defendants or executing search warrants or cultivating informers or assisting other groups. In Levine's case, it was also necessary to find time for the martial arts, as his selection to the U.S. national karate team was imminent. He was such a fanatic by now that even if he arrived home at four in the morning, he would still work out until dawn.

The first real international case that Levine and Garcia worked on together began when Customs discovered seventy-five kilos of prime white heroin concealed in a shipment of French furniture. Special Agent Mike Pavlick was assigned as case agent, and the group camped out on the street to see who came to take delivery. Nobody did. The smugglers had evidently taken fright. But such a load was too large and too valuable not to have set off rumors on both sides of the Atlantic, and little by little, the finger began to point to René Arias, a Cuban dealer who lived in Fort Lee, New Jersey, and Gilberto Otero, who owned the El Quijote restaurant in the Chelsea Hotel, on West 23rd Street.

At this stage, the Otero lead was too tenuous to pursue without supporting evidence, but the case against Arias, although circumstantial, included a positive identification by Howard Fuchs, now Levine's most prolific informer, and that was enough for a warrant. Levine sent the group out to arrest Arias at his second-floor apartment in Fort Lee, but nobody had told them it had a balcony at the back. When the agents pounded on his door, Arias quietly jumped for it, breaking bones in both ankles, but managed somehow to hobble off in the darkness and find a cab. Unaware that he had escaped them until several days later, when word filtered back from the street, Levine flew into a towering rage and embarked on another of his implacable crusades, in which every odd moment was spent looking for Arias. Somebody had only to report that he had been seen at the Château Madrid or La Concha or some other New York Latin restaurant, and Levine was gone. It became a standing joke. If anybody in the group was missing from his desk, his colleagues would shrug and say, "Oh, he's looking for Arias."

But the group was also pressing hard after a dozen other suspects supplied by Fuchs, and the grand jury had at last begun to hear the case against the smuggling rabbis. On top of that, Garcia was developing informers of his own, one of whom now came up with an introduction that provided Levine with the longest running sequence of cases linked by a common, unwitting informer ever recorded by the DEA. Before getting started on that, however, he took a long weekend off and flew down to Panama as one of the twelve-man team representing the United States in the Latin American and Caribbean Karate Championships. (Earlier in the year he had been raised to the rank of *shodan,* first degree black belt in the Gojuryu style of karate by Chuck Merriman, the foremost exponent of that style in the United States.)

Levine had been attracted to karate originally as a means of shading the odds still further his way in a street fight, but had quickly realized how exacting a standard of mental as well as physical discipline was required to reach the first rank as a practitioner of the martial arts. With his appetite for challenges, he had long since worked his way past the knee-jerk machismo of the street fighter, which would almost certainly have gotten him killed by now, and was moving toward a self-mastery that was an end in itself, beyond considerations of winning or losing. He had learned when to stand and when to run, and how to run with confidence, so that confrontations, when they came, were now at times, places, and in circumstances of his own choosing.

His selection as one of the six black belts on the U.S. team was a considerable honor, given the intense competition for places. As guests of the Panamanian government, competitors faced a heavy three-day schedule of individual and team bouts and non-stop partying, from which Levine emerged undefeated, apart from a particularly bloody battle with the Colombian heavyweight champion, in which both were disqualified.

Liana was not impressed. By now, relations between them were so strained, she could take little pride in what he did. He still loved her—and would have loved her to accept him as he was, to be a docile, understanding wife who never complained or asked questions or cared what he did. But she *did* care. She made him feel guilty—and the less he saw of her, the less guilty he felt. The more she railed at him, the longer he stayed away, getting up to more of the things she had railed at him about in the first place. In a sense, he loved her most when he wasn't there, for when he came home the best he could hope for was an armed truce. So he really came to see the children.

He was just as uneasy around his brother, who was now in a methadone maintenance program. With the vague notion of keeping a closer eye on him, he and Liana had installed David in the basement of their house, and Liana's brother-in-law had given him a job in his hairdressing salon, but David was obviously no closer to beating his addiction or acquiring a sense of purpose in his life.

Whenever Levine saw him, he seemed depressed and dispirited, with little to say for himself, so that each, for his different reasons, found it painful to be around the other.

Matters came to a head early one morning when Levine arrived home exhausted and disheveled after thirty-six hours of continuous duty, and found David huddled on the sofa in the den, obviously stoned. And not on methadone. Shocked by his brother's unexpected appearance, David groggily attempted to deny he was shooting up again, but after seven years around junkies, Levine was merely exasperated by his feeble dishonesty.

"You know something?" he demanded, at the end of yet another useless tirade, reproaching himself for ever having started it. "Instead of wasting your money on fucking drugs, you can pay us rent from now on."

It was petty and futile, and he knew it. When David promised, for the twentieth time, he would quit, and started to cry hopelessly, Levine stared at him for a few moments and then went to bed.

In some ways, David's attitude toward his brother was not unlike his brother's toward Liana. Each had hurt, and continued to hurt, the person who meant most to him. Each was guiltily aware of his seeming inability to stop doing so. And each made matters worse by making excuses for himself, by trying to justify the indefensible.

Levine, the extrovert, did so by crowding his days so full of risk and incident that his shortcomings as a husband, parent and brother could plausibly be attributed to the pressures of his job, while David, the introvert, mourned what he conceived to be the congenital flaw in his character that ensured the ultimate futility of any effort he might make toward self-redemption. Neither could be blamed for what they could not help. Levine, in any case, enjoyed what he did too much to stop doing it, and David was not about to give up the absolution he found in being the helpless victim of his own nature.

He was much more at ease with Liana and the children, who were not only less (if at all) censorious in their affection for him, but, in Levine's absence, had come to depend on him for company and a masculine presence around the house. Seeing them together sometimes made Levine feel like a stranger in his own home, which was uncomfortable in one way but a sop to conscience in another. He minded, but he was not entitled to mind, which added up to yet another reason to stay away. Coming off duty, exhausted, in the early hours of the morning, he had nothing to spare for domestic strife as well. It was easier just to grab a sandwich and a cup of coffee across the street and sleep rough in the office. Among his own kind, he had no need to apologize or explain himself. He was admired for what he did.

Three weeks after his return from Panama, Levine arrived home early one morning and found his brother stoned again. This time he did not lose his temper, perhaps because David himself now seemed to realize they could not go on like this. After eight years they had reached the end of the line. Levine put him to bed and spent the rest of the night talking to Liana about what they should do. It was the first time they had discussed anything calmly for almost a year.

David's backsliding was no news to Liana. He had seemed to be holding his own on methadone maintenance, but in recent months the muttered telephone conversations had started again, and the comings and goings at odd hours. She knew the signs and had tackled him about it.

"We were very close. He was there, and Michael wasn't. And I loved him. He was quite a guy. He loved the kids. He was always playing with them and liked to look after them for me if I had to go out. They saw far more of him than they did of their father, and so did I, of course. If I was feeling blue, or angry with Michael, which was most of the time, David would sit up with me half the night, talking and drinking and maybe playing cards or Scrabble or something. He was a really good person, but always in pain. When I knew he was on drugs again, we argued about it all the time, and he'd always end up saying, 'Well, Mike's a survivor, and I'm not.' And I guess he was right."

If it had been up to her, Liana would have given David yet another last chance, and probably more after that, but she was in a difficult position. She loved him, and depended on his company, but the pattern of decline was unmistakable, and his closeness to the children a potential threat to them. He was also Michael's brother, and Michael was no longer willing to have a junkie under the same roof with Keith and Nicole. If, behind his anger and frustration, Michael had loved David any less than she knew he did, she might have insisted that David remain, telling herself she would support him more and somehow protect the children from his example, but she had to allow for a strong element of selfishness in that, and could find nothing selfish in Michael's conviction that

David should go. It was daylight by the time they had talked them-selves to a standstill, and that night Levine took his brother out to dinner.

"I think he knew it was coming," Levine remembers. "He seemed resigned to it. I told him, 'You're gonna die. You're my kid brother, and I love you, but I don't want to watch you die. And I don't want the kids to watch you die. So I really think you got to get out of here. There's nothing more we can do for you. I'm not kicking you out—I couldn't *do* that—but I think you ought to go. Why don't you try Florida for a while? Maybe you can work some-thing out for yourself down there.'

"In two days he was gone. David was a beautiful person, but a victim. Very bright, very talented, quick-minded, and yet some-thing was missing, and all the talking in the world was not gonna help. I knew I'd done the right thing, but it was months before I really believed it."

Liana was not so certain, but had no complaint, even though it meant she was on her own again.

"I would have liked to have done whatever I could for David, although I don't think anything would have turned out differently if he'd stayed. I can't reproach anybody for what happened. Every-body acted sincerely, believing it was for the best. It was right to consider the children first, although they were very upset when he left. We all were. The whole world was falling apart."

A month later the marriage itself fell apart. Levine moved out, technically to a one-room apartment he felt obliged to rent in order to provide himself with a mailing address, and so as not to think about his brother or his family any more than he had to, he threw himself into his work as though there were nothing else in life, which was not far from the truth.

The day before the grand jury finally indicted the smuggling rabbis, Levine made his first undercover telephone call to Billy Kwastel, a plump young college graduate who had carved out a profitable career for himself as a narcotics broker. With a little notice, Kwastel could find a buyer or seller of anything. Marijuana, hash, pills, cocaine, heroin—he would simply check through his mental Rolodex for the right connection, agree on a price (includ-ing his commission), and arrange for delivery to suit his clients' convenience. He was a clever young man, his main weakness being an inability to conceive of anyone being cleverer.

The introduction had come through the first informant Garcia had succeeded in flipping, and although neither he nor Levine had any suspicion of it at the time, the Billy Kwastel saga was to run and run like a soap opera, spinning off into more cases with a higher body count than any other "wheel" conspiracy in DEA history. To start with, however, it looked like just another routine pill bust, and Levine took it because Garcia was busy with the more important-looking leads provided by his informant. After a string of undercover calls with Kwastel and his associate, Rhonda Taffer, Levine agreed to meet them for the first time at the Spuyten Duyvil railroad station in the Riverdale section of the Bronx, where they would sell him 20,000 Seconals for $13,500.

That was going to be the end of it. Levine drew the money as a flash roll, sent the group up to the Bronx an hour ahead of time to hide out around the meeting place, and arrived promptly at 10:30 P.M. with every intention of showing the money in return for a look at the pills and then signaling the group to move in. But as he got out of his car, Kwastel and Taffer came over from theirs to meet him, not with the pills but with a thickset young man who kept his hands in his pockets, and whom Taffer introduced as Timothy Wells. Levine crooked his finger around the trigger of the .357 Magnum hidden in his windbreaker.

In his head, alarm bells were ringing insistently. They had chosen an almost pitch-dark, deserted place for the meet, and his cover was well back in the bushes and trees. If this was a rip-off, Levine was not at all sure the group would even see what was going on, let alone intervene in time.

He addressed himself first to Rhonda Taffer, who asked straight out if he had brought the money. Levine allowed that he had, but politely declined to produce it until he had seen the merchandise. Well, they hadn't brought it with them, Taffer said, because they had to be sure of him first. The connection was waiting somewhere else.

They fenced around this impasse for a minute or two, with Taffer insisting he show them the money and Levine insisting they show him the pills, while he and Wells drifted around each other in a kind of slow-motion dance figure, Wells trying to angle himself on Levine's blind side, and Levine keeping him at the business end of the .357.

As the discussion petered out, Taffer and Wells looked increasingly to Kwastel for guidance, and Levine did the same. It was now clearly up to Kwastel to decide if they were going to try to rip him off or actually sell him the pills.

For a long moment, Kwastel teetered on the edge of extinction. Then he nodded and told Levine to follow them in his car.

They led the group to the Baychester Diner, where Levine got out and waited by his car as his backup drifted into surveillance positions around the parking lot. Motioning him to stay where he was, Kwastel walked off to greet a big, bald man who had come out of the diner to meet him. They talked together earnestly for a few moments and then adjourned to the bald man's car.

As one of Kwastel's sources had now put himself in reach, Levine was beginning to wonder if this was the moment to take them off after all. Certainly, the easiest thing to do was to go ahead as planned, make the collar and explore any further possibilities at leisure. Four defendants and a bunch of pills were not a bad return for a couple of hours' work, and the night was still young. But Kwastel was just the kind of smart, cocky kid who made it his business to know everybody, who wouldn't flip easily, and even if he did, would be a pain in the ass to control as an informer. Levine had a distinct hunch that this might be a case to run with for a while, for in Kwastel he sensed he would have the classic "unwitting" informant.

As he explained to all his undercover classes, "That's the best kind of informant to have—a guy with a lot of knowledge and friends in the druggie world who really believes in you, in your role as a bad guy. If you manipulate him right and, most important, make him like you and trust you as a person, you can milk the sucker dry of every last drop of information he's got without him ever knowing it.

"You manipulate him into introducing you to every fucking dealer he knows—even his own family. 'This is my friend Mike,' he'll say, and the sonofabitch really believes it because you *made* him believe it. When an 'unwitting' is worked by a true artist in manipulation, he won't know you're the Man until you're ready to demolish his little world. It's the ultimate in treachery. You literally destroy the sonofabitch by eroding away his life, inch by inch.

"In the end, when you've made your buys and gotten evidence against every living human, animal and plant he knows, you sit down beside him, and you say, 'Hey, Billy. You and me, we've been friends for quite a while now, and it's time I told you something.

. . .' And as you're saying this, you're sliding your badge out of your pocket. . . .''

The more immediate problem for Levine, however, as he sat in his car outside the Baychester Diner was how to keep the case going when he was not authorized to spend the government's $13,500 flash roll. But then Kwastel showed him how. Package in hand, he climbed into the front seat beside him looking thoroughly disgruntled.

"Sorry, man," he said. "The schmuck fouled up. Says he's got twenty thousand, brings four thousand. Moves the rest someplace else and don't tell me."

"Wow." Though privately delighted, Levine shook his head as though this were a real catastrophe. For that amount, he could make the buy and play with Kwastel a while to see where it would lead him. "Oh, man," he said reproachfully. "Man, I got some very, very big customers that are gonna be very, very disappointed."

"Yeah, I know, man. What can I tellya?"

Still shaking his head, Levine started to press Kwastel's psychological buttons. "You know, Billy, for a minute there you looked a little sharper than most of these assholes," he said. "I thought I finally had a steady connection."

To this day, Levine remembers the look on his face. "I could see I'd hit the sonofabitch where he lived, right in his fucking pride bucket. He's not only greedy, now he's got to prove himself to me. He's got to show me he's *not* one of those assholes.

" 'You were gonna buy those kinda numbers steady?' he says to me.

"That was the moment. I pulled out the wad of hundreds and waved them under his nose. 'What does this look like?' I say, and I thought he was going to faint. It's incredible the effect that the sight and smell of money has on the average asshole. When I was a kid, I used to listen to *The Shadow,* a radio program about a guy who traveled in the Orient to learn the secret of 'clouding men's minds' so he could make himself invisible. Shit, I learned how to do that in the Bronx when I was twelve. Just show 'em money.

" 'Hey, Mike,' he says, and he can't take his eyes off the wad. 'I think *you* are the guy that *I've* been looking for.'

" 'Well, I don't know,' I tell him. 'We had an old saying where I grew up. Money talks and bullshit walks. Right now, Billy, I'm the one doing the talking.'

" 'Okay,' he says. 'No bullshit. I got four thousand pills here. I'll give you the same price you'd get if you were buying the whole twenty thousand. That's twenty-six hundred bucks. And I'll guarantee you, from now on, nothing like this will happen again.'

He was practically pleading with me. I was playing the guy like a saxophone.

" 'You know, Billy, I'm half Puerto Rican,' I tell him, 'and I used to be in the music business. Every Latin musician in New York knows me. And the one thing they all know, and they all say about me is, you can always count on Mike. If he says it's gonna be there, it's always there. You got any idea what that reputation means to me, Billy?'

"Now he looks like he's gonna fucking cry. 'Mike,' he says, 'I didn't know you before, but now I really wanna do business with you. If I could, I'd give you this bunch for nothing, just to make up for screwing you around like this, but it's not my stuff.'

"Well, I'm looking at him doubtfully, like I'm hurt and sad and not sure I should take his word for anything, but I've got the bastard exactly where I want him—liking me, indebted to me and feeling he's got to prove himself to me.

" 'Come on, Mike,' he says. 'Do me a favor. Please. I wanna do business with you. Take the four thousand, and from now on, you can count on me for anything you want. I know a lotta guys in the business, and if one doesn't come through, I got twenty more I can go to.'

"That was what I was waiting to hear. So I smiled and forgave him. 'Okay,' I say, counting twenty-six hundreds off the roll like they were two-cent baseball cards. 'I like you, too, Billy. I think maybe we're gonna do a lot of business together.'

"The sonofabitch had come out that night with the idea of maybe killing me and taking my money and ended up falling in love with me."

But what with looking for Arias, running with Garcia and generally piling up statistics for Valentine, two weeks went by before Levine got back to Kwastel. A check of the bald man's license tags had turned up the name of Barney Rebackoff, and in a series of taped calls back and forth with Kwastel on the undercover phone, Levine made it plain that he was not about to risk another runaround. To test Kwastel's willingness to please, he told him he wanted to talk directly to his connection—just about the ultimate test of goodwill in the drug trade—and Kwastel barely hesitated.

That same night he introduced Levine to Rebackoff, a tough-talking former steelworker, at the Baychester Diner.

They talked shop for a while, taking each other's measure, with Levine leading Rebackoff on to boast about "the organization" behind him. His people could get any kind of pill Levine wanted, he said. And in any quantity. They had manufacturing sources in Mexico. The stuff was then shipped across the border into California, and all Rebackoff had to do was fly out there, rent a car, load up and drive back with anything Levine wanted.

It was clear from their conversation that Kwastel had built Levine up to the skies in Rebackoff's estimation by telling him what an influential figure he was in the Latin music world. From their eagerness to do business, Levine could see no limit to how far he could take them, and decided to go for *all* the marbles—for everybody they *both* knew.

"Sounds good to me, man," he said truthfully when Rebackoff undertook to find out if his people also did cocaine and other drugs. "Why run around town for your groceries if you can get all you want at the supermarket? But I'm gonna need samples. The reds are okay, but I gotta check out anything else you got before I buy."

"Hey, no problem," said Rebackoff. "I already told 'em that. They're sending me samples in the mail."

Levine smiled benignly.

When they left the diner, Kwastel held him back until Rebackoff drove away.

"Listen, Mike," he said, in an undertone. "I wanna protect you, okay? I wanna make sure you don't get screwed around again, because I really like you. I mean, Barney's all right, but sometimes he's not that reliable. Like the other night. And he's only into pills anyway. He doesn't know from coke or smack or nothing. So if it's one-stop shopping you're after, don't ask Barney. *I'm* the supermarket, okay? If you need anything else, come to me. I got people who can get you anything you want."

Kwastel was jealous, which gave Levine yet another button to push, but next day he barely had time to call for Rebackoff's telephone toll records and order a mail watch on his address before heading downtown to set up a heroin buy from Yuk Bui Yee, otherwise known as Billy Yellowhair, a member of the notorious Black Eagles gang, whose main business was homicide and extortion. Though tricky and dangerous, Billy Yellowhair took a liking to

Levine and sold him an ounce on the street, after which Garcia trailed Billy through Chinatown to the building he worked from. Suddenly, Billy looked like their passport into the previously impenetrable world of the Chinese drug networks, and Levine put the case on the back burner to wait its turn.

That night he drove up to meet Kwastel and Rebackoff at the Baychester Diner and collect a sample of Benzedrine pills, which Rebackoff obligingly handed over in a torn envelope with a California postmark. The price was $10,000 for 25,000, and Levine said he would let them know. Before placing an order, he intended to alert the Los Angeles office to watch for Rebackoff's arrival, keep him under surveillance and take down his organization. An analysis of his calls to California had already turned up the number of Kenneth Leroy Parker, a known narcotics smuggler with ties to clandestine pill laboratories in Mexico.

As it happened, Rebackoff was in no hurry to leave. He, too, had taken a shine to Levine and saw no reason now to work through Kwastel. He called the undercover number to set up a private meeting, and Levine joined him at the diner that night.

"I'd made a quick judgment of his character," Levine remembers. "There was a softness about him that belied his tough talk. He couldn't take a bust. He'd collapse and flip right away—I was sure of it. And that opened up the possibility of ordering big, arresting him with the pills, and then putting him right back on the street to work for me without Kwastel being any the wiser. So I ordered 25,000 uppers, and Barney got so excited he said he'd fly out there right away and bring them back himself."

But Kwastel was too jealous not to be on top of Rebackoff's every move. The next Levine heard about his order was when Kwastel called a few days later to say that Barney had sent another guy out to California in his place, and that the pills were due to arrive the following night, which was fine with Levine. Wired with a Nagra recorder, and with most of the group staked out around the diner, he waited with Kwastel and Rebackoff for several hours, but their courier failed to show up.

Both were mortified with embarrassment, expecting Levine to fly off the handle and out of their lives, but he had long since learned how to turn a setback to account. "Kwastel looked ready to commit hari-kari if I didn't forgive him," he said. "And he definitely would have off'ed Barney if I had asked him to. As soon as Barney got out of the car, he starts cursing him and blaming the whole thing on Barney's fucked-up, pillhead connections. Then he starts begging me to meet this cocaine connection he's got. 'It's Merck,' he says. 'Pharmaceutical cocaine. Legally manufactured stuff for hospitals. Hundred percent pure.'

"Now that *really* intrigued me. A tube of Merck was harder to get than a ton of the illegal stuff. The next day he brings me out to Highland Avenue in Queens to meet a tall, good-looking young guy who looks like an American Indian. His name is Bobby Collins, and he's an actor-comedian. He's also cool and slick. Bobby's been around, and he's sizing me up like crazy, but then Billy goes into his act, vouching for me like we'd known each other since we were kids, and Bobby finally promises to bring me a sample of the stuff. With Taffer, Wells, Parker, Rebackoff and Kwastel already in the bag, that made Collins Defendant Number Six."

Still abject and ready to make amends, Kwastel called every day after that, leaving messages on the undercover answering machine pleading with Levine to call him back, but the group was too busy for Levine to spare him any more time for a while. Besides his other cases, he was also preparing to testify at the trial of Manny Gonzalez, the former South Bronx Republican leader. When he did at last speak to him, almost a week later, Kwastel reported he had lined up four more cocaine sources, in case Collins failed to come through. Samples would be available in a few days. And since their last conversation, Barney had gone to California himself and brought back 25,000 uppers, plus fifty pounds of dynamite-quality red Colombian grass.

Levine was pleased with his protégé's progress. With six defendants in his sights, and others pending—all for an outlay of $2,600 —the taxpayer was getting real value for money. But the Gonzalez trial now tied him up for nine days, and he was no sooner through testifying than his division chief, Wayne Valentine, assigned him to work Gilberto Otero. With the fugitive René Arias, Otero had been the main customer for the seventy-five kilos of heroin found in the shipment of French furniture some months earlier.

Dragging Garcia off another promising case, Levine went under-cover and practically lived at Otero's El Quijote restaurant for a week, trying all he knew to get in cold, but Otero was too seasoned a trafficker to exchange much more than the time of day with a stranger. They needed to find some former associate, preferably with a few years of hard time to trade off, who was willing to get in and work as an informer.

Meanwhile, Kwastel's messages on the undercover phone had become ever more urgent and frequent. "Listening to his voice on the machine," Levine recalls, "I sometimes had a pang of conscience about what I was doing to him. 'Mike, are you mad at me?' he'd whine. And then the Producer/Director who lives in my head would remind me: 'The little mother-fucker wouldn't be making the kind of money he does on chemicals worth a few pennies if it weren't for guys like you. *You* make the stuff expensive by making it dangerous to handle. He put *himself* in this business, not you.' And if that didn't work, I'd just have to think of David. These mother-fuckers were killing my own brother—and that would do it."

When Kwastel finally caught Levine "home" some three weeks after the meeting with Collins, he was so anxious to give him a one-ounce sample of cocaine that Levine agreed to drive up to the diner that night. He found Rebackoff there as well, and was relieved to hear that he had sold the 25,000 uppers to somebody else. (It was now December, near the end of the quarter, and Levine was not at all sure there were enough funds left in the group's budget to have made the buy.) But he greeted the news with a pained resignation that soon had Rebackoff almost groveling with apologies. Vying with Kwastel in his anxiety to please, he offered to go back to California next day, if that was what Levine wanted. And not only that, he was ready to guarantee a weekly supply of 50,000 pills of any kind until told to stop.

Levine allowed himself to be mollified. Yes, he wanted the bennies, but he could wait until Barney's next scheduled trip. As for a weekly supply, he would be happy to discuss such a deal once he saw how his clients reacted to the first shipment.

Still mending fences, Rebackoff now offered to cut Levine in on a gilt-edged harness race scam. A trotting horse owner himself, Rebackoff and a syndicate of other owners had perfected a method of fixing triple bets that was like printing hundred-dollar bills.

"I don't know nothing about that kinda shit," Levine said, half interested, half dismissive.

"Hey, Mike," said Rebackoff reproachfully. "After all this, you think I'd steer you wrong? If you wanna piece of the action, just tell me. I'll fix the whole thing. I'll even make sure you buy the right horse."

"Listen, I don't have room in my apartment."

They stared at him blankly for a moment, then fell about laughing as if they had just heard the world's funniest joke.

"No, seriously, Mike," said Rebackoff, wiping his eyes. "All you gotta do is buy a horse at a claiming race. A good one. Cost you ten grand. Maybe twelve. Then we keep him out of the money until we put him in a trifecta with a couple of our other horses. They're out of the money, too. So now, with three good horses in the race, we can box the others, and that's how you win a triple."

"Sure, Barney. Whatever you say. But for right now, why don't you just go back to California and get me those pills like you promised?"

When Rebackoff's trotting-horse scam was reported to the New York State Police, officials in Albany called John Fallon, the DEA's regional director in New York, to ask if they could borrow Levine to break the syndicate. Rebackoff and his fellow owners had been under investigation for some time, but somebody was needed on the inside. They were even willing to buy Levine a horse. Fallon said he would think about it, but finally said no—doubtless to spare his agents the temptation of working with a colleague who knew which horses were scheduled to win at Yonkers, Roosevelt and Monticello.

With so many cases clamoring for attention, Levine decided to run with Kwastel and Rebackoff for a couple more days, then put them on hold again. As soon as the group could spare the time, he had to dust off the Billy Yellowhair connection, and Garcia would soon be needing help with a promising case of his own. But the morning after Rebackoff's invitation to join the horsey set, Kwastel called to remind Levine about the other cocaine connections he had lined up for him, and having gone as far as he dared on the strength of a $2,600 pill buy some two months earlier, Levine drew enough money to pay for a sample. He then drove to the Bronx to pick up Kwastel, and from there to 67th Avenue in Queens, where he bought an ounce of good-quality cocaine from Steve and Anne Friedman, defendants 7 and 8, respectively. With Kwastel vouching for him, they acted as if they had been selling Levine drugs for years.

Next day it was back to the Baychester Diner for lunch to firm up an order for 25,000 mini-white bennies of Mexican manufacture. Right after dessert, Rebackoff left for Los Angeles to fetch them, with Levine's backup team following him out to the airport to make sure he got on the plane. From the office, Levine then called his colleagues in Los Angeles to alert them, and was later told they had trailed Rebackoff to a meeting with his well-known, pill-smuggling uncle, Norman Ramis (defendant 9), at the home of the equally notorious smuggler, Kenneth Leroy Parker.

As far as Levine was concerned, Rebackoff had now reached the end of his rope. The Los Angeles agents were primed to arrest him as soon as he picked up anything that looked like a load of pills—and to do it out on the highway so that it looked like local heat. But the day wasn't over yet. At eight-thirty that evening Kwastel called to say that Steve Friedman, the new cocaine source, also had a great connection for heroin. Two hours later, Levine was back in Queens, buying an ounce of lightly cut smack for $2,000. The Friedmans declined to say who their connection was, other than that he was a black guy who could do "pounds."

Levine was happy to hear it. With defendant 10 now in reach, he drove back to the office and bumped into Ernie Frahm at the elevator.

"Hey, Mike," Frahm said. "Just the guy I was looking for. Warm. Lovable. Articulate. Kind to dumb animals. How'd you like to make a speech at Queens College tomorrow night?"

Levine looked at him suspiciously. "What about?"

One of the hardest parts of Frahm's job as regional public relations director was persuading agents to talk to schools and colleges. "Listen," he said, grabbing Levine's arm and pointing to far horizons. "I want you to go out there"—his voice trembled with emotion—"and save those kids from the evils of drugs, okay?"

"You gotta be kidding." The only reason Levine had not done it before was because no one had asked.

"Hell, no." Seeing he had taken the bait, Frahm moved in for the kill. "All those chubby little co-eds? Right there, in the palm of your hand?" He sculpted one lovingly in the air. "Jesus, Mike, if I was a younger man . . . All you got to do is take a bath and burn those clothes, and you're in for a night to remember."

The following evening, Levine took Garcia with him for moral support, and on the way over made a few notes to remind himself of some cautionary tales. But when he saw his audience, he had to wonder if it might not already be as knowledgeable on the subject of drug abuse as he was. With a few exceptions, it would not have looked out of place in Haight-Ashbury ten years earlier. When he rose to his feet, he was still trying to think of a joke to get himself started, as Frahm had suggested.

* * *

"My name is Michael Levine," he began solemnly. "And sitting over there is my colleague and partner, Emilio Garcia. We are federal narcotics agents employed by the Drug Enforcement Administration."

There was a faint scattering of boos and muffled laughter that gave him an idea.

"As narcotics agents," he went on, with the air of one advising a prisoner of his rights, "whenever we speak at public meetings like this, it's laid down as official policy that we first search the audience for drugs."

With a collective gasp, the room went still. He smiled slightly, anticipating a big laugh when they recovered from the shock. But all he got was a nervous titter, instantly suppressed.

"So, at this time," he continued, broadening his smile expectantly, "my partner, Special Agent Garcia, will pass among you and carry out a body search."

Garcia stared at him, thunderstruck.

There was no doubt Levine had claimed their full attention, but nobody seemed to be enjoying the joke very much, even after he laughed, held up his hands defensively and confessed he was only kidding. Several of the shaggier members of his audience got up and left, shaking their heads, while others sat transfixed, staring at him as though still on the brink of a coronary.

He eventually dug himself out of the hole by suggesting that their reaction to his little joke was no more than an inkling of what they would feel if they ever *were* caught with drugs in their possession, but it remained a salvage operation and the evening ended early, with no chubby co-ed to show for it.

If the talk had been a success, Levine might have felt challenged no further and left it at that, but having fallen so short of his usual standard of performance, he volunteered for all the dates he could fit into his schedule after that. And once he had mastered the techniques of public speaking, he was hooked. Like all performers, his act—private *and* professional—ran on the gasoline of applause. His inauspicious debut at Queens College led directly to teaching undercover as a licensed police instructor, and to a spare-time excursion into semiprofessional film and theater, crowned by a starring role in a television glue commercial.

But there was no spare time at *this* stage of his career, even though several cases suddenly faltered in midstride. Just as he was dusting off the file on Billy Yellowhair, the New York police picked the Chinaman up on suspicion of extortion, assault, the double murder of the owners of the Szechuan D'Or restaurant on East 40th Street, and various other homicides. As that seemed enough to keep him quiet for the time being, Levine put the case back on hold and took a rather puzzling call from Kwastel.

Rebackoff had apparently telephoned Kwastel on the way home from Los Angeles by car to say that the pills came as whites or reds, and he had taken it upon himself to bring 50,000 reds. But if Levine really wanted whites, he would turn around and go back again to get them.

"Tell him to come on with the reds," said Levine. Something very screwy was going on because agents still had Rebackoff under twenty-four-hour surveillance in Los Angeles and had yet to see him with anything resembling a load of pills.

With Christmas less than a week away, Levine started now to duck Kwastel's calls. The group had earned a break over the holidays, and as acting group supervisor in O'Neill's absence, he had no time to work cases. Group 31 was also on standby to help out the FBI and the DEA office in Las Vegas with "Heavy Load," a huge surveillance operation evoking sentimental memories of his first day with ATF, when he had clashed with Aniello Dellacroce, underboss of the Gambino family. Several of Dellacroce's associates, with other mob heavyweights, had installed themselves in the MGM Grand Casino and were said to be awaiting a massive shipment of drugs from Mexico.

To stanch the flow of calls, Levine told Kwastel he had to go out of town for a while, and put off an offer of cocaine from the Friedmans. (There was no need to spend any more money on *them*.) But he did agree to meet once more at the Baychester Diner to hear what Rebackoff had to say for himself. The Los Angeles surveillance team had finally followed him back to the airport, where he boarded a plane for New York, carrying no luggage or anything else that could possibly have held 50,000 pills.

All he had to offer Levine when they met was a couple of sample mini-bennies and a shamefaced account of the runaround his people had given him in L.A. "The problem with those guys is they're too stoned all the time to be reliable," he said apologetically. To keep the pressure up, Levine pounced on Kwastel as soon as Rebackoff left, demanding to know what he had meant by all that bullshit about Barney driving to New York with 50,000 reds and going back to L.A. if he wanted whites instead.

Grinding his teeth, Kwastel swore that Rebackoff had told him to pass on exactly that message. His furious embarrassment was yet another useful card for Levine to play when the time came. On busting either of them, he would find it that much easier to set one to work against the other.

"I'm beginning to think you're right about that guy," he said. "But now I got a problem, Billy. I'm going out of town, and when I get back I'm gonna need a lotta shit. If you're gonna take care of me, man, you better start now."

"You got it, Mike," Kwastel said fervently. "I guarantee it. And I'm gonna take a little trip myself. I got just the guy in mind."

In making excuses for his "absence," Levine had not specified Las Vegas as his destination—nor at the time was it even certain that Operation Heavy Load would need the services of Group 31— but the call came suddenly on New Year's Eve, and the first day of 1975 found him feeding his own money into the MGM Casino's slot machines while he watched Dellacroce's retinue at the blackjack tables.

Sixteen hours later he went to bed showing a heavy loss on the day, and the following afternoon faced up to another long stretch of inactivity, relieved only by the ebb and flow of fortune at the tables. (Again, there was more ebb than flow, and it would take many months of argument before the DEA accountants finally agreed that this was a necessary undercover expense and reimbursed him $30 a day—far less than his actual losses.) After a couple of hours he was trying simultaneously to keep track of his blackjack hand and the conversation of two mob guys on his left when he looked up and saw Billy Kwastel, his eyes shining like a young bride's, heading his way with two companions.

Taken aback by so extravagant a coincidence, Levine threw in his hand and herded them into a more defensible position at the bar. The room was full of agents who knew nothing about Kwastel and might well assume, if they saw them talking together, that Kwastel was an agent himself or, at least, that he knew *Levine* was. Unless he could somehow head everybody off, one careless word could blow a whole string of cases, and more yet to come. It was a coincidence he could have done without, even if it had produced two more defendants, whom Kwastel introduced as Steve and Larry.

The next half hour might have been devised for the Marx Brothers. Every time an agent came within range, either missing or misunderstanding Levine's discreet signals, he had to excuse himself, intercept the intruder at a safe distance, and warn him off with a muttered explanation and a request to spread the word. In such a dense crowd, however, it took time for the warning to get around, and after Levine had broken off his conversation with Kwastel and his friends at least five or six times for one of these subdued, head-to-head exchanges, he was afraid they had guessed what was happening, for they abruptly finished off their drinks and prepared to go. Then he realized it was not out of alarm but respect. Far from arousing their suspicions, the stream of "messengers" had only raised him in their estimation. They took their leave as from the presence of *il capo di tutti capi,* and when he held out his hand, seemed unsure whether to shake it or kiss it.

After a week in Las Vegas with no sign of the "Heavy Load" they had been expecting, Levine and the International group were ordered back to New York. And by another of those coincidences that preserved Levine from boredom, as he left the hotel for the airport, he saw one of Dellacroce's henchmen drive by with two startlingly beautiful girls in his limousine and, of course, decided to follow them.

They led him to where he was going anyway. When the girls boarded Levine's New York flight, he could hardly neglect so clear a sign and chose Johnny Demarco as the agent most likely to succeed. As soon as the seat belt signs were turned off, the two of them moved in and by the time they landed in New York they were not only the envy of every red-blooded male passenger on the plane, but had organized a foursome for a night out at the No Name Club. All in the line of duty.

As mob guys rarely involve their women in "family" matters, Levine ended up learning more about their sexual proclivities than their business in Vegas, "but we developed a lot of useful intelligence," he told O'Neill. And they both nodded solemnly.

A week went by before the group caught up with its backlog and Levine could surface to take a call from Kwastel, who claimed to have found a cocaine connection to replace the Friedmans. Levine met him in a parking lot off the Major Deegan Expressway and drove from there to 174th Street and University, where Kwastel asked him to wait while he made a phone call. Returning to the car, all smiles, he took Levine up to a seventh-floor apartment at

156 174th Street and ushered him in, almost deferentially, to meet defendants 11 and 12: Derek Williams, a big, tough, black former athlete; and Arnold Kerman, a paranoid white hippie who went and hid in the bathroom until they left.

"I bought an ounce from Williams," Levine remembers, "mainly because I saw a chance of converting him into another Kwastel and expanding the whole conspiracy in another direction, into black trafficking organizations. But afterwards, I had to act annoyed with Kwastel.

" 'Billy,' I say, 'I'm only doing these nickel and dime deals because I like you, but this is just not my thing. I need *weight,* for Chrissake.'

"That really threw him. He'd thought I'd be pleased.

" 'You want weight?' he says, ready to cry. 'Well, me and Derek got a guy who'll sell you four ounces right away.'

"Well, in those years, four ounces was a decent case—it makes my head swim to think of what's happened to the cocaine business since then. But I squeeze a bit harder. 'That's not weight, Billy,' I tell him. 'When I say weight I mean *pounds.'*

" 'Yeah, okay, Mike, okay,' he says. 'These guys can do pounds. But they just gotta get to know you.'

" 'Well . . .' I make myself sound grudging. 'How much for the four ounces?'

" 'Six thousand.'

" 'Hey, c'mon. If I was buying pounds the price would be cheaper, Billy. You know that.'

" 'But this is pure, Mike. One hundred percent shit. You can hit it three or four times.' He was desperate. 'Okay, look,' he says. 'I won't make a nickel on the deal. Fifty-nine hundred.' "

Levine had no trouble convincing O'Neill and his new division chief, Tom Taylor, to spend the money. The case still had a long way to go, and he would run faster and farther if he could consolidate his post-Vegas big-shot image with a bigger buy. That night his backup team latched onto defendants 13 and 14—later identified as the brothers Steven and James DiGiovanni—as they brought the four ounces to the meet.

Next day Sister Elizabeth introduced him to ninety girl students at Notre Dame School, who hung on his every word while he explained how drugs could mess up their lives.

"I've got a brother who's a heroin addict," he told them. "And he's in the process of destroying all of us, dragging us with him through one worthless rehabilitation program after another, killing himself and his family inch by inch. He cares more about his habit than he does about destroying the people who love him. Well, if any of you are like that, then go ahead. Take drugs. Destroy your families, too. My brother once said, 'I probably wish I was dead and don't have the nerve to do it all at once.' Well, I'll tell *you* something I didn't have the heart or the nerve to tell *him.* Rather than take drugs, go ahead. Do it. Do it all at once."

Afterwards, he signed autographs, and some of them took pictures.

He then spent a week in the office as acting group supervisor, fielding calls from Kwastel, working cases at night with Garcia and the others, and preparing his end-of-the-month reports. They had been so busy in January that he spent fifteen hours straight on the reports alone. Besides his own dizzy caseload, he was also working the New York end of cases originating in other regions and cooperating with foreign police agencies on matters outside American jurisdiction. On top of that, New York's chronic shortage of Spanish-speaking investigators meant that Levine was frequently on loan to other groups for undercover work, and to crown everything, René Arias chose this particular time to show himself again. For several days after an informer reported seeing him, agents needing to find Levine would automatically put in a call to Mike Pagano at the Château Madrid.

On February 19, Kwastel caught Levine at his most harassed and offered him two kilos of cocaine from Derek Williams and the bashful Arnie Kerman. With everything else going on, six calls a day from Kwastel were at least five too many, and Levine now decided it was time to take him off. After haggling over the price, he finally agreed to $82,000 and set the deal for the following afternoon. But when Kwastel called the undercover number next morning, he had nothing to offer but apologies. Kerman's connection had been busted with the dope before he could deliver it.

Then, after weeks of prompting by Levine, Kwastel called again to say that Bobby Collins, the so-far inactive defendant 6, had a good supply of "unbelievably pure" Merck, prescription-quality hospital cocaine packed in vials.

"Sold," said Levine. "Man, now you're talking. How'd he get hold of that shit?"

"From his boss, I think. The guy owns some kind of construction company, and he's all tied in with the mob and horse racing. You wanna pick me up around three tomorrow?"

Collins met them at their favorite parking lot off the Major Deegan Expressway, driving up in a battered old Karmann Ghia that ill became the bearer of what amounted to the crown jewels of the cocaine kingdom.

"Jesus," Levine said, reverentially fingering the sealed vial that Collins handed to him. "How much you got of this stuff?"

"How much you want? I mean, I only got that sample for right now, but tell me what you need, and I'll get it for you."

"Okay." Levine shook his head in wonderment. "What kinda money am I looking at here?"

"Well, get ready," said Collins. "Because my boss pays thirty-two hundred an ounce for that shit."

Levine whistled soundlessly and flipped his fingers as though he had burned them.

"Yeah, I know." Collins grinned sympathetically. "But this guy —my boss—he owns like his own steel company out in Great Neck, and the money don't mean nothing. He's got like these six or seven racehorses and everything. He just buys this guy a ticket, and he flies down to Florida to get the shit for him. Grass, too, if you want it. And I mean real dynamite weed, man. Much as you want. No limit."

"Okay. Lemme see how this shit checks out, and then we'll talk business."

It checked out as 100 percent pure, and on March 3 they talked business.

Levine's main interest was in identifying Collins's boss, although he already had a tentative make on him. There were not all that many millionaire construction company owners in Great Neck with strings of racehorses. Delicately pumping Kwastel and Collins over dinner at Martell's, he learned that defendant 15 was around thirty-five and liked to hang out with jockeys, most of them "real coke fiends," according to Collins. As for the hospital cocaine, Collins quoted a price of $50,000 for 12 one-ounce vials and confirmed that his boss's source was a doctor in Florida.

Playing for time, Levine pretended to faint into his angel food cake and offered $40,000, observing quite truthfully that he had never before considered paying so high a price for coke, pure or not. Collins looked doubtful, but promised to discuss the offer with his boss.

Two days later Regional Director John Fallon called Levine into his office and instructed him to keep the FBI informed about his dealings with Bobby Collins. Its agents had a prior investigation under way into his boss's connections with organized crime, race-fixing, shylocking and extortion, and the two agencies were anxious not to trip over each other. Levine had no problem with that. He gave the FBI copies of his DEA-6 reports, and they, in turn, showed him surveillance pictures of jockeys sitting with known drug dealers in their cars. Levine was content, in any case, to give them a clear run at Collins for the time being while he attended to more pressing matters.

For one thing, Operation Heavy Load was showing signs of life after death, which meant he was on standby again. For another, he spent the morning of March 10 with officers from the Sûreté Nationale taking statements from various defendants to choke off the last gasps of the now venerable French Connection. Then, after lunch with Colonel Malki, to find out if the Israelis had changed their minds about the smuggling rabbis, he went out with Skippy Garcia to cover him in an undercover heroin buy from Frank Irace and Lenny Demetrio, a case that seemed likely to open up a heavy mob connection.

Though attached to another group, Special Agent Gerry Castillo then requested equal time for a heroin buy from a particularly unpleasant gang of traffickers run by a surly black Puerto Rican named Luis Colón from his apartment on Walton Avenue and 172nd Street in the Bronx. As it was clearly too dangerous for Castillo to work undercover alone, Levine went in with him as the money man, and for two nights they hung out with Colón and his people without getting to first base.

To maintain some link with the outside world, Castillo had provided himself with a limp and a cane housing a miniature transmitter, but it was only when the two returned to base that they discovered it wasn't working. Not that it really mattered. Even if it *had* functioned properly, the entire conversation had been in Spanish, and no one in their backup team understood more than a word or two.

With no more time to spare, Levine decided to bring matters to a head. At the end of their second wasted evening, they were still at an impasse: Colón's man was in one car with the heroin, Castillo in another car with the money, and Levine on the street between them arguing with Colón.

"Okay, Luis," he said. "Here's what we'll do. Gerry's gotta *test* the shit before we pay you, otherwise how the fuck do we know what we're buying? So he'll go with your guy, and you stay with me. If the shit's okay, your man gives him the package and I give you the money. Okay?"

Luis shrugged. "Wait here."

He walked over to consult with his colleague and came back shaking his head. As if suddenly pissed off with the whole deal, Levine shoved him out of the way and went over to talk to the man himself, which was not the safest thing he could have done, given the gang's firepower.

"Hey," he said nastily, as the other wound down his window a few inches. "Fuck you, man. Forget about it."

He then stalked back toward his own car, making washout signals, and Colón was finally convinced.

"Okay, hold it," he said. "I'll work something out. Lemme just see what I can do."

He returned to his colleague, who, after a muttered exchange, got out of the car with a brown paper bag and disappeared into the bodega directly across the sidewalk from where he was parked.

"Okay," said Luis. "It's in the store. You wanna test the shit? Be my guest."

Levine exchanged a glance with Castillo, who seemed willing.

"Okay. Gerry, you go take a look, and I'll stay here with Luis. When I see you come out with the package I'll give him the money."

Levine remembered the buy later, among hundreds like it, because the Assistant U.S. Attorney who prosecuted the case against Colón almost blew it by not insisting on a thorough voir dire of prospective jurors.

"I don't want people to think the government's got anything up its sleeve," he said, and Levine's heart sank. It was mid-December, and sure enough, although virtually no defense was offered to the charges, the jury failed to agree on a verdict.

"Hey, listen, I'm sorry," said the holdout juror afterwards. "I just couldn't send anybody to jail for Christmas. You'll get him next time, fellas."

Levine watched him out of sight. Then he banged his head gently against the wall.

A new trial was set for the New Year. This time the prosecutor made no such mistake and Colón was found guilty in a brief hearing before Judge Constance Baker Motley. But instead of giving him fifteen years, she sentenced him to time served. After selling a pound of heroin to two government agents, he walked out of court a free man, with Levine at his heels remembering how a Florida judge had sentenced John Clements to thirty years for just happening to be around at the time of a controlled delivery.

Meanwhile, Kwastel had reclaimed him for the International group with the news that Rebackoff was back from California with 46,000 yellow downers. Levine said he would believe that when he saw them, and Kwastel did not blame him. Both agreed that if Barney fucked up *this* time he was finished.

On a happier note, Kwastel went on to say that he had tapped another good cocaine connection. The shit was not as good as Bobby Collins's Merck, but Collins was slow in coming through, and at $1,800 an ounce it was not much more than half the price. Levine told him to set things up for the following day. He would buy an ounce to see if he liked it. And he'd take Barney's pills as well—if they were for real and he hadn't already sold them to somebody else.

At 3:30 P.M. on March 20, he met Kwastel at their usual parking lot, and with his backup taking photographs, was reintroduced to Larry Sussman, one of the two men who had been with Kwastel when he appeared unexpectedly in Las Vegas. As defendant 16, Sussman was the kind of softly handsome momma's boy for whom capital punishment would probably have been kinder than what now awaited him in the penitentiary.

Reflecting on this, Levine followed their directions to 66-20 108th Street in Queens, where they were met in a third-floor apartment by Steve Friedman and a guy named Lou, who looked all set as defendant 17. They were expecting their connection to call with instructions for picking up the ounce Levine had ordered, and while they waited, talked up a storm about the deals he would make with this guy. He was real sharp, they said. Never took chances. Never dealt with anybody he didn't know.

"They're never going to catch him," Sussman said shyly. "He's like James Bond, this guy."

Levine looked impressed and asked how they had met him.

"Well, see, like we sell airline tickets," Sussman explained. "Real cheap ones." The others laughed encouragingly. "I mean, people keep bringing us these airline credit cards, and we use 'em to buy tickets. All kinds of tickets to all kinds of places. That's really our main business, you know? And this guy, he sells 'em for us. He's a travel agent, so it's easy for him to do that."

"Yeah," said Levine. "That's very interesting."

When the telephone rang Sussman got to it first, said, "Hi, Don," listened, said, "Okay, Don," and hung up. After huddling with the others for a moment, he then whispered his instructions to Kwastel, who nodded and led Levine back to the car.

"Where we going now?"

"Queens Boulevard," Kwastel said. "And drive slow. I'll tell you when to stop."

With his backup strung out behind them, Levine had no intention of hurrying. He set off with a long-suffering air, watching Kwastel from the corner of his eye for some telltale twitch of recognition that might help him identify Don the travel agent's car. When it came, Kwastel glanced at him sharply to see if he had noticed, but Levine was still looking ahead and showed no sign.

"Okay," Kwastel said, after another two blocks. "Pull over and wait for me here."

Levine did as he was told and watched him out of sight in the mirror, knowing the team would follow.

Kwastel returned smiling and shaking his head. "Now we go to 89th and Parsons," he said. "He's gotta change cars, right? I mean, do you *believe* this guy?"

"Well, he's fucking James Bond, right?"

They chuckled indulgently and drove to the new rendezvous. A few minutes later, Don the travel agent rode by in a different car.

"That's him," Kwastel sighed. "You wanna give me the money?"

Returning with an ounce of cocaine, he persuaded Levine to drive him home to the Bronx.

"So what about the pills?" he said. "You still want 'em?"

"Sure. If he's still got 'em. But I'm getting kinda pissed off with Barney, the way he keeps jerking me around and never comes up with nothing."

"Yeah, I know. Now he says they're uppers, not downers."

"No shit." Levine was disgusted. "Well, you better tell that guy to get his fucking head straight. Because I don't have time for this bullshit."

"Right. Me neither. But he swears on his mother's grave he's got forty-six thousand Mexican whites. Mini-bennies."

"How much?"

"Eight hundred a thousand."

"Okay. We'll do it tomorrow. Right here. Ten-thirty. But if he fucks up again, I'm through with the sonofabitch."

He was anyway. He was bored with Rebackoff. The trick now would be to start making arrests without compromising himself with Kwastel, whose usefulness as an unwitting informer seemed inexhaustible. On returning to base, Levine learned that his backup had not only identified Don the travel agent from his license plates as Donald Ackerman (defendant 18) but had followed him to *his* source and identified *him* as Henry Mayorga (defendant 19).

Levine's inclination now was to go through with the pill deal—as much to consolidate Kwastel's trust in *him* as to perfect the case against Rebackoff—and then set up an out-of-town bust that Kwastel need not even hear about if Rebackoff agreed to cooperate. O'Neill and Division Chief Tom Taylor readily agreed to this strategy, and next morning Levine met Kwastel in the parking lot with $36,800 in his pocket.

Rebackoff, predictably, was late—so late that Levine was driving out of the parking lot when he finally showed up, full of apologies and excuses. But he had the pills, and after Levine had counted the money into his hand, the three sat and looked at one another in a glow of brotherly love.

"Listen," said Rebackoff, "we're gonna get rich together. I got another source. In Canada. He's tied in with some very heavy people up there. They can get you anything you want."

"Yeah, yeah. You said that about your people in California."

"Yeah, I know. But this is different. I mean, they got problems in California. The main guy's in the slammer, and the kids minding the store are stoned out of their skulls most of the time. But these Canadian guys are different. They're Italians—you know what I mean?"

Levine knew what he meant, and told him to go ahead.

For all practical purposes, he had been running the group for some months now, and with O'Neill's long expected departure for Washington, Levine took over officially as acting group supervisor on April 1. This meant that, in addition to his general administrative responsibilities, he now found himself doing double and even triple duty as case agent, undercover agent *and* supervisor—as when Rebackoff called and swore on his mother's eyes that a Canadian courier was due on the 4th with 43,000 downers. On the 3rd, Levine met with Kwastel and Sussman (defendant 16), partly to set up his game plan for Rebackoff's arrest and partly to further the case against Ackerman.

"That was pretty good shit we got from James Bond," he said, as they settled down to business.

"Didn't I tell you?" said Sussman proudly. "The guy's terrific. Dynamite shit, and no hassle. Lemme call him for you."

As before, Levine and Kwastel were instructed to drive to Queens Boulevard, but this time Kwastel knew where he was going.

"Look," he said, "the guy's kinda paranoid or I'd take you in. You wanna give me the money?"

Levine groped for the government's bankroll. "How come we don't have to ride all over fucking Queens this time?" he grumbled, counting out the money.

"Who the fuck knows?" said Kwastel. "Maybe we've seen all his cars now."

Levine watched two of his backup set off after Kwastel on foot, but it came as no surprise when they reported later that the pickup had been made at the Liberty Travel Agency. On returning to the car, Kwastel handed over 1¼ ounces of cocaine in a Liberty Travel envelope.

"That guy," he said. "He's too much. There's nobody in the place, right? But he makes me sit down at his desk and look through his fucking brochures like I'm planning a vacation."

Levine now knew who the connection was and where he worked. The final step would be a direct buy, face-to-face—like the poisoned pill deal he had in mind for Rebackoff.

"Listen, are we all set for tomorrow?" he asked, driving Kwastel home. "You're sure Barney's not just jerking off again, because I got a million things to do. I don't need no more of his bullshit."

"What can I tell you?" Kwastel had his own ass to cover. "He says the guy with the pills is driving down tonight from Montreal and he'll be here in the morning. All I know is what he tells me. Sounds like it's a sure thing, but you know Barney."

"Yeah, I know Barney," Levine agreed gloomily.

"Well, to be fair to the guy, things can always go wrong. Like his man could get a flat or something and a state trooper stops to help him. I known that happen once."

"Yeah. And Barney could be full of shit. I known that happen, too. Tell him to meet us with the load at the diner. At noon. And I don't mean one-thirty."

His plan was simplicity itself. By 6:00 A.M. the following morning, he had the group staked out around Rebackoff's house with orders to follow him until he picked up or took delivery of a package, at which point they were to move in and arrest him, along with the courier, if possible. Levine's only backup would be Special Agent Kevin Finnerty, who would follow him in an undercover radio car from the time he picked up Kwastel until he dropped him off again. In particular, he was to park behind Levine at the Baychester Diner and flash his lights if, and when, he heard over the radio from the group that Rebackoff had been arrested. That was all there was to it. The rest would be just a minor exercise in undercover histrionics.

As arranged, Levine picked up Kwastel at 11:30 A.M., and on the way over to the diner asked him to count the money—$34,000, the agreed price for 43,000 Canadian downers. Kwastel protested that it wasn't necessary, not after the deals they had done together, but he insisted. No matter what happened to Rebackoff, Kwastel had to know that Levine was there to do business. It also served to distract attention from the closely following Finnerty.

Around noon, just when Rebackoff would otherwise have been due to arrive, Levine saw Finnerty in his rearview mirror start to laugh. A moment later his lights blinked, and Levine allowed himself a private smile.

At twelve-fifteen, he began to sigh and consult his watch. Kwastel grinned uneasily. By twelve-thirty, Levine was drumming his fingers and making faces, and Kwastel was almost beside himself.

"That sonofabitch," he hissed. "That two-timing mother-fucker. I'll *kill* him for this."

Levine looked around with the air of a man only just managing not to run amok. "I did *ask* you," he said heavily. "We both know Barney's full of shit, but I did *ask* if this was solid."

"Yeah, you did, Mike—and what can I say? I just don't understand that scumbag, treating you like this. For a customer like you, he oughta go down on his knees and kiss your ass."

"Yeah," he agreed. "Maybe I'll have him *do* that."

Kwastel stalked off furiously to make a few phone calls and came back mystified, ready to scratch the whole deal. But as a finishing touch, Levine insisted on waiting another half hour before he finally drove him back to the Major Deegan parking lot, listening in stony silence to his apologies and promises.

So far, everything had worked perfectly. The next step was to flip Rebackoff as quickly as possible and get him back on the street that afternoon, ideally before Kwastel or anybody else even knew he had been busted. Suitably motivated, Rebackoff could be a key witness against the Californian and Canadian pill smugglers, along with their principal customers.

To soften him up, when Levine joined him in the holding cell, he allowed Rebackoff to think that he had been arrested as well, and led the dealer into a thoroughly incriminating conversation before finally identifying himself as an undercover agent. For a moment, he thought he might have overdone it. The case looked as if it was going to die then and there with Barney Rebackoff.

Gray with shock, he fell back in his chair, eyelids fluttering, hands waving feebly, dumbly imploring Levine to say it wasn't so. But Levine just read him his rights, and sensing his indifference, Rebackoff decided to recover. As the crisis passed, he showed himself a quick study, particularly when Levine explained his interest in Norman Ramis, head of the California operation.

"Jesus, Mike," he protested. "You know what you're saying?"

"What, Barney?"

"You're saying it's me or my uncle."

Levine shrugged eloquently.

"Okay." Rebackoff sighed. "Then I guess it's my uncle."

But there were still a few formalities to attend to before Levine could turn him loose. First, he had to make a statement incriminating everybody with whom he had ever had any dealings. Then he had to make a tape-recorded call to Billy Kwastel, telling him he had sold the pills to somebody else. As Levine had expected, Kwastel blew up and slammed down the phone, vowing to kill him on sight. And finally, Rebackoff had to swear to tell no one what had happened, on pain of instant rearrest and Levine's personal guarantee that he would then draw a minimum sentence of twenty-five years, without remission or parole.

With Rebackoff born again and returned to the flock, Levine now turned his attention to Robert Kuhnle (defendant 20), the Canadian courier whom the group had arrested at the same time. An unremarkable, nearsighted, thin-haired man in his mid-thirties, he was a professional gambler who dealt drugs and counterfeit money from time to time to finance his principal occupation, which was betting on trotters. A real student of the track, he would observe and clock horses in training until convinced they were ready, and then bet his shirt on them. And as jail would seriously threaten the integrity of his record-keeping, he, too, was ready to see the light. After figuring the odds, Kuhnle agreed to purge himself of sin by giving up his pill sources in Montreal, namely the Cotrone organized crime family.

Levine found this deal very acceptable, particularly as Kuhnle knew no one but Rebackoff in the New York ring, so that cutting him loose posed no risk at all to Kwastel's continuing usefulness. But it was now too late in the day to start debriefing him on so big a breakthrough, and in any case Levine needed to satisfy himself that Rebackoff had not had another change of heart. He telephoned Kwastel, who immediately told him that Barney had called.

"You know what he said, that mother-fucker? He said he sold the fucking pills to somebody else. I mean, can you *believe* that?"

"Yeah. I told you, Billy. I said—"

"Yeah, I know you did, Mike. And I want you to know I'm sorry. I shoulda listened to you. But I'll get somebody else, don't worry. I finished for good with that asshole. I'll get somebody who—"

"Yeah, yeah—never mind about that. I didn't call about Barney. I need another ounce of that James Bond shit. And I need it right now."

"You got it," he said fervently. "Go on over to Larry Sussman's house. I'll meet you there."

Rebackoff had evidently gotten the message.

Levine picked up Kwastel and Sussman, drove them to Liberty Travel, and parked outside while they went in with $2,000 of the government's money to buy a hundred grams of Donald Ackerman's cocaine.

"Listen," Levine said, when they brought it back to the car, "I really like this shit. How much is it gonna cost me if I buy weight? That's if the guy can do it."

"Wait here," Kwastel said, still eager to make amends. "I'll get you the menu."

He came back with a price list written out in Ackerman's handwriting on Liberty Travel stationery. Levine thanked him very much.

Several days of court appearances, administrative duties, debriefing Kuhnle and nighttime excursions with Garcia then intervened, restricting Levine to the undercover phone. He was now insisting that Kwastel and Sussman introduce him directly to Ackerman. When it came to laying out big money for weight, he said, he would either deal face-to-face with the guy or forget about it. For all he knew, Ackerman could be an undercover narc.

Though they laughed at his little joke, Kwastel saw his point. And no sooner had Levine confirmed arrangements for the meeting than Billy Yellowhair called, back in circulation again after his local difficulties with the New York Police Department, to offer him heroin. With more business than the group could then handle, Levine told him he had $40,000 "out front" and promised sincerely to get back to him again as soon as his cash-flow problems eased.

Donald Ackerman, a.k.a. James Bond, turned out to be a short, twitchy young hustler in horn-rimmed glasses who could hardly wait to get Levine out of his car after selling him two ounces of coke. As a buy it was okay, but it was just a necessary preliminary before taking Ackerman off *inside* Liberty Travel, with all the drugs he had on hand.

Meanwhile, the group's other cases were still piling up. Next day, at the end of another long debriefing session with Kuhnle, Levine went out undercover to assist Skippy Garcia in a buy-bust of Frank Irace and Lenny Demetrio, the two Italian heroin dealers with mob connections. It turned out to be a busy night. They arrested Frank's wife, Pat Irace, as well, and on the strength of their statements, went out again around 3:30 A.M. to pick up another defendant, Carmine Ritolo. These four had been buying their heroin from the mob.

It was nearly 10:00 A.M. when Levine and Garcia finished taking statements and processing their prisoners, and Levine had no more time to play games. With O'Neill away and the group at full stretch, the moment had come for Kwastel to work under orders. A lot less manpower would be taken up running him as a "cooperating individual" than as an unwitting informer.

Levine took a shower, changed his shirt and called Kwastel to set up the bust for that afternoon. He needed to buy all the coke that Ackerman had available, he said, and agreed without much argument to a price of $2,000 an ounce. Calling out every available agent to do them in style, Levine sent two on ahead to take up positions inside Liberty Travel, posing as prospective vacationers, and disposed the rest to cover all approaches to the corner of 67th Avenue and Queens Boulevard.

At three o'clock sharp, he drove up with Kwastel and Sussman and parked directly outside.

"Looks like he's got people in there," Sussman said. "I'll go see what he wants us to do."

"No," said Levine. "You go tell him what *I* want to do. For this kinda money, I don't do no deals on the street or in anybody's fucking car. You tell him we're here, and I wanna do business in *there*."

"He's right," Kwastel said, as Sussman hesitated. "It's safer."

"The customer's always right," Levine said absently. He had just spotted another momma's boy hanging around on the corner, trying to look inconspicuous. Remembering what had happened the first time, he had a hunch it was Ackerman's source, waiting to get paid. Or in this case, arrested.

Sussman came back smiling, and opened the door for Levine. They had a couple of time wasters inside, he said, but the stuff was ready. All they had to do was swap envelopes as soon as Don could grab a moment.

Levine graciously allowed him to lead the way inside, where they sat down at Ackerman's vacant desk and glowered at the two agent-vacationers, hoping to make them go away. But they seemed oblivious to the atmosphere, and when Levine caught Ackerman's eye, he tapped his watch meaningfully. Ackerman acknowledged this with a helpless shrug, and with an exasperated glance at his indecisive clients, left them with their brochures and went through to the back of the store. He returned with an envelope in his hand and sat down at the desk across from Levine, indicating that he should produce *his* envelope first.

Levine looked around to make sure his agents were alert for the signal, and laid it on the desk in front of him.

Bedlam.

The two vacationers bounded to their feet, guns drawn, yelling, "Federal agents. Freeze. You're under arrest." The door burst open and a squad of armed men in raid jackets jockeyed to get through.

Faces slack with shock, Kwastel, Sussman and Ackerman rose, sat and rose again, whimpering with dismay.

To set them a proper example, Levine raised his hands, looked inscrutable and allowed himself to be arrested without protest. It was not the right moment for Kwastel to find out who he was, nor for the others to realize that Kwastel had introduced an undercover agent into the circle.

Bundled outside and pushed into the back of a car, Levine had the handcuffs removed and remained out of sight until the others were driven away. He was pleased with the group's performance. The operation had gone down quickly and efficiently, and they had also taken off the kid on the corner, whose name was Donald Rosenbloom. As defendant 21 he had nothing to say at first, but he was, indeed, Ackerman's new source, replacing the DiGiovanni brothers, and already on federal probation for selling a kilo of cocaine in another case.

Late that night Levine joined Kwastel in an interview room at headquarters. Unlike Rebackoff, Kwastel was not to be drawn into any damaging conversation for he assumed at once that they had been put in together for exactly that purpose, indicating in dumb show that he thought the room was bugged. It had clearly not crossed his mind that Levine was anything other than a co-defendant. And even when Levine *told* him who he was, Kwastel resisted the truth for as long as he could.

He looked blank for several seconds. Then he smiled incredulously, shook his head and sat down with a bump. He began to look hurt. A friend had betrayed him. After that he looked frightened, as he began to realize the weight and extent of the evidence against him. This was not the one-shot coke rap he had counted on beating, having handled neither the drugs nor the money. They had more than enough to bury him for life. He started to shake, and the effort to control it made him gleam with sweat.

"Jesus, Mike," he whispered, covering his face in his hands. "You are some fucking actor. You oughta get an Oscar for that."

To pay Levine a compliment at that moment was just about the most wounding thing Kwastel could have done.

"My insides were twisting in spite of myself," Levine recalls. "But somewhere inside my head, the Producer/Director was shouting, Fuck him! You didn't put him here. He did it all on his own. If your brother had overdosed on his shit, would he have cared? Fuck him!

" 'Just doing my job, Billy,' I told him. 'You're a big boy. You knew what you were doing. And I like you. I got nothing against you.'

"His eyes were all red and glistening, but now I'm over it. From here on out, he's just another scumbag.

" 'Thing is now, Billy,' I said, 'how can we keep you out of jail?'

"Billy comes back from the dead.

" 'I mean, maybe I can fix it so you work for me,' I told him. 'Although I'll have to see results. Big cases. Big seizures. That's the only way I could swing it.'

" 'Well, shit,' he said. 'I already gave you everyone I know.' "

This time Levine was deeply gratified by the compliment. "Then here's where you widen your circle of friends, okay? And I still got a lotta cases you can help me with. Like Timothy Wells and Rhonda Taffer. Bobby Collins. The Friedmans. Derek Williams. You know, most of the people you introduced me to. So if you wanna work, there's plenty to do."

Kwastel grunted. "Do I look like a fink to you?"

"If you did, I wouldn't ask you. You'd go down the tubes for like forty years. But it's up to you. Dopers can't afford to be sensitive."

"Well, if I *did* go for this," he said cautiously, "will you do me a favor?"

"No favors. No ifs, buts or maybes. The deal is, either work for me, and I'll see the judge gets to take that into consideration when you come up for sentencing. Or *don't* work for me, and I'll see you pull the maximum on fourteen or fifteen counts of possession and conspiracy. So suit yourself. Either you do exactly what I tell you —and do it the very best you know how—or you're *gone*. Understand?"

Kwastel understood.

"Okay. Now what was the favor?"

"Well," he said, with a nervous smile, "do I have to rat on Barney Rebackoff? I mean, does he have to know? If I give you all these other people, can we maybe leave Barney till last?"

"Yeah," said Levine magnanimously. "Sure. Why not?"

Next day the Kwastel bandwagon was off and rolling again under its new auspices. As there was no conceivable way in which Levine could find time enough to exploit all these informers, he parceled them out among the other agents in his group, and left it to the Montreal office to follow through on Kuhnle's statements implicating the Cotrone family in large-scale trafficking across the Canadian border. Each of the twenty-odd cases against Kwastel's violators led off into other cases that were linked in turn with still more potential defendants, and Levine soon gave up trying to keep track of them all. In the end, there were at least fifty Kwastel-related prosecutions.

Indeed, the harder Levine worked the less time he seemed to have for his caseload. For one thing, the paperwork was always threatening to bury him, and for another, every person he arrested had to have his day (or weeks) in court. Not that Levine ever resented the time he spent testifying, for that, too, was performance, and the finishing touch to his art. As often as not, he was a better witness than the government attorney was prosecutor, and although resigned to it, he still hated to see a case he had lovingly shaped in the field come to grief in the courtroom. Several young assistant U.S. attorneys sensible enough to acknowledge their limitations and defer to his experience quickly developed reputations as good trial lawyers, but humility is not the commonest virtue of American law-school graduates, and many found him as hard to handle as his cases were easy to prosecute.

On May 5, Levine spent most of the day being interviewed by Italian examining magistrates about the statements he had taken from Claude Pastou incriminating Carlo Zippo, one of the most notorious of all international drug traffickers, who was soon to stand trial in Rome. On the 6th, Levine testified before the grand jury in Eastern District, and was interviewed at length by Canadian newspaper reporters about cocaine trafficking.

Most of the 7th he spent undercover with Garcia covering Lenny Demetrio, whom they had wired and sent out to buy heroin from the mob. On the 8th he was given a day's notice to go to England with Special Agent Dan Martin to bring back Peter Daley, one of the New York cops accused of selling French Connection heroin. Besides redeploying the group to cover his absence, Levine also delivered a lecture that afternoon on undercover tactics to the Armed Forces Police at Brooklyn Navy Yard, and after that, putting theory into practice, went out undercover again with Garcia to make another heroin buy on 106th Street.

Around 3:00 A.M. on May 9, he broke off from this case and went home to shower, change his clothes and pack before driving out to Kennedy Airport to catch a morning flight to London. Landing at around 10:00 P.M. local time, he and Martin were met by officers of the Metropolitan Police whose idea of professional courtesy was to take them on a three-day pub crawl while the legal formalities were completed, and then pour them back onto a New York flight with their prisoner, the only halfway sober member of the party.

Levine's drinking tapered off after that, and by the end of the year he had graduated into a full-fledged teetotaler, not on moral grounds, or with any proselytizing intent: he simply did not enjoy getting his head muddled anymore. "I can't think of anything I do better after taking a drink," he would say, when people tried to talk him into something stronger than diet soda.

Almost all he could remember about the London trip was the scale of his headache and the conversation he had on the flight home with Daley, who was a sick man, convinced he would die in prison.

When Martin, in no better shape than Levine, retreated to the toilet soon after takeoff, Daley leaned forward confidentially and said, "I heard you were coming, Mike, and I know you're good people. But I don't know your partner, so do me a favor. If you wanna talk, let's talk about sports, the weather—anything you want. But don't ask me about the case or the city or nothing like that because I don't wanna talk about it. Okay?"

That was fine by Levine. His attitude toward cops on the take was no different from his attitude toward anybody else who broke the law. It was not his job to pick and choose. On a personal basis, he would sooner arrest an attorney than a cop, or a doctor or a stockbroker or a politician than a cop, but he would arrest him just the same, if he had to.

He *knew* about cops, in uniform and out. He liked them, preferred their company, and shared the daily currency of their lives. He could grumble about pay and conditions with the best of them, and understood very well how a family man with kids in college or a sick wife could look around a doper's apartment as the adrenaline ran down and even up the inequities of life a little by "miscounting" the street money spilling out of the closet. He understood how easy it could be for a cop to regress from there, justifying each step to himself along the way, even to the point of smuggling French Connection heroin out of police evidence vaults and selling it back on the streets. He could even sympathize with the guy, in a way, but he would arrest him just the same.

It was his *job* to arrest him—and Levine was what he did. He had not become a cop to steal or get rich, but to catch people who broke the law. As Skippy Garcia still says, they worked well together because they both loved to fuck with the bad guys. Though Levine would come upon hundreds of millions of dollars in cash and drugs in the course of his twenty-two years as a federal agent, the idea of breaking the law himself, of diverting any part of the money to his own use, was as alien as the idea of any other kind of self-mutilation. He was no more tempted to help himself than to slash his face with a razor blade. It had little to do with *morals*. It had something to do with revenge, and a lot more to do with winning.

Not many people understood this. Liana did, but the wear and tear of being dragged along behind a compulsive competitor was more than any spirited wife could be expected to endure. His bosses, however, did *not* understand, except for the few who led from the front and felt more or less the same way.

Later on, when Levine succeeded in ranging the entire bureaucracy of the DEA against him, from the Administrator on down, his whole career was ransacked minutely over a period of several years by inspectors determined to find *something* they could use to hang him. In the end, they had to be satisfied with minor criticisms of his group's clerical work, and the charge that he sometimes played his radio too loud in the embassy in Buenos Aires when stationed there as the DEA country attaché.

He arrived back from London with Dan Martin and their prisoner late at night on May 12. Next morning he sent Billy Kwastel off on his first outing as a cooperating individual to start making a case against the Friedmans' cocaine connection, whom Kwastel had identified as Herklee Overton, defendant 22, a dangerously unpredictable black wholesaler strung out to the pitch of raging paranoia through overindulgence in his own merchandise. Following a game plan similar to the one that had worked well against Ackerman, Levine drove out to Queens with Kwastel that afternoon, bought an ounce from the Friedmans for $2,100 and ordered another pound, insisting that he meet their supplier in person for a deal of that size. The Friedmans promised to get back to him as soon as they had set it up.

On the 14th Levine took to the streets again, this time undercover with another informer, cramming in as much fieldwork as he could because the grand jury was now hearing testimony in the Ackerman case, and he could see he would soon have to drop everything to work Gilberto Otero, whom he had left on the back burner since his abortive attempt to get in cold six months earlier. Most of the 15th Levine spent with the grand jury, which duly handed up an indictment that afternoon, and after obtaining an arrest warrant for Henry Mayorga (defendant 19) he went out that evening to cover Garcia in an undercover cocaine buy on Marcie Place, in the Bronx.

On the 16th Garcia covered *him* when he arrested Mayorga and a companion, Stuart Kop, defendant 23, who admitted being involved with the group, but, as Levine had foreseen, the Otero case now took precedence over everything.

With some misgivings, Washington and New York's Regional Director John Fallon had concluded that the only practicable way of getting close to Otero, at least while René Arias remained at large, was through Albino Garro, an Argentinian journalist arrested as a co-conspirator in the operations of Maurice Skosch, a member of the Auguste Ricord brotherhood of Corsican traffickers, whose seventy-five kilos of heroin hidden in a shipment of French furniture had sparked off the case in the first place. Facing multiple charges of conspiring to smuggle large quantities of heroin and cocaine, Garro was eager to cooperate, and as he and Otero were old friends it was thought that if the two were to meet, Otero might well incriminate himself in the course of conversation, not only in connection with the seventy-five kilos, but in other cases as well.

The problem was that nobody trusted Garro, who was being held in $1 million bail. Even after his cooperation had been taken into account, he would still face a lengthy jail term, and the temptation to abscond would therefore be strong, particularly as the surveillance had to be at arm's length. Otero had been around too long to miss any suggestion of a setup, so that if the idea were to stand a chance of working, Garro had to appear free as air while in reality being closely watched.

Nobody in the New York office liked the look of the job very much, and so it naturally fell to Levine, who, as Fallon well knew, was incapable of turning down anything difficult or dangerous. Nor did it look any easier after a week of preparing Garro for the street. Levine found him to be a slippery, intelligent, educated man with a taste for high living—just the type to bolt if he saw any glimmer of a chance to escape. With May 28 penciled in for his first meeting with Otero, Garro seemed all too eager to agree to anything—to wear a hidden transmitter or recorder, and to look up any or all of his old associates with a view to corroborating statements he had already made about his drug dealings with them. By the end of the week, still trying to plan for every possible contingency, Levine found himself in command of a small army of federal agents and New York City police officers—many of whom outranked him.

On the afternoon of the 28th he drove over to the Eastern District courthouse in Brooklyn to take delivery of Garro for his first "casual" meeting with Otero at the El Quijote restaurant in the Chelsea Hotel. But before waiving the million-dollar bail condition and releasing him into Levine's custody, Judge Jacob Mishler had first to be convinced of the adequacy of his security arrangements. After questioning Levine closely, the judge seemed satisfied, but warned him, only half-jokingly, "If he gets away, Levine, I'm going to sentence *you* to do his time."

Only half-amused, Levine laughed politely.

In fact, the first phase of the operation went like clockwork. Wired with a hidden transmitter and covered by a dozen agents, Garro left his hotel exactly on time, chatted with the doorman while he waited for his limousine (driven by another agent), greeted Otero on arrival at the restaurant like a long-lost brother, and joined his party for a late and leisurely dinner in the Spanish manner, watched by Levine and Garcia at an adjoining table and half a roomful of agents eating out at the taxpayers' expense.

Played back in the early hours of the morning, the tapes of Garro's conversation with Otero and his guests proved nothing, other than that they seemed to accept his cover story. The occasion had been purely social, which was the way Levine had instructed Garro to play it. No business was discussed, but before taking his leave, Garro had proposed, again on Levine's orders, that they should meet again for a late breakfast at the Wellington, and Otero had agreed to meet him there at ten-thirty.

Still mistrustful of Garro, Levine spent the night at the hotel with his security detail, and was again in close attendance when the two met next morning. This time the tape of their conversation made it clear that while Otero was still active in the heroin business, he had nothing immediately available. Expressing disappointment, Garro, coached for days by Levine, led him on to reminisce about past deals they had done together, and Otero said enough to implicate himself in several old conspiracies with Ricord and his fellow Corsicans involving many hundreds of kilos. On parting, they arranged to meet again for dinner at the New York Hilton on June 3, when Otero thought he might have some news for him.

Pleased with the result, although not too happy with the prospect of having to cover Garro in a hotel as big and as busy as the Hilton, Levine returned his prisoner to the U.S. marshals and dismissed his army. He then took Garcia and those agents who were still awake to assist Mike Powers, supervisor of Group 32, with a complicated series of simultaneous arrests in different locations.

After that Levine crawled into bed and slept for two days.

When he returned to the office, he found that the International group had acquired a new agent named Sidney Wong, a short, stocky, cheerful Thai Chinese who spoke hardly a word of English. Slightly paranoid after recent brushes with authority, Levine went to see his division chief, Tom Taylor.

"Is this a setup?" he demanded. "I mean, is this a fucking setup? You gimme a guy who can't speak English? I can't believe the guy. How come headquarters don't know this guy don't speak English?"

"They *do* know," Taylor said calmly. "That's where he was. At headquarters. That's why they sent him to us. They want him to have street experience."

"*Street* experience?" gargled Levine. "You kidding me? The guy won't be able to open his mouth on the street. And not only that, he won't know what the fuck I'm sayin' to him."

"Hey, Levine," said Taylor. "What can I tell you? You'll think of something, okay?"

Wong, a college graduate, had worked for the CIA in Thailand and applied for citizenship after marrying an American secretary in the Bangkok embassy. He had then been taken on as a DEA agent and transferred to the U.S. to learn how enforcement worked at that end of the distribution chain before being posted back to Thailand. His wife had come with him and was also working temporarily at the New York office.

Despite his reservations Levine took to him at once, quickly learning to communicate with signs and "Me Tarzan" English. Tough as leather and skilled in the martial arts, Wong was shrewd, likable and eager to please, and the group set about training him in the finer points of American life with gusto, using the Greeko-Rican bar as his indoctrination center. With little time to spare for trainees, Levine issued strict instructions not to risk him on the streets until he had learned the ropes, and turned his attention to Garro's dinner date with Otero at the Hilton.

On the night, Levine had over a hundred men and a dozen cars deployed around the hotel, but was still depressed by the crowds on Sixth Avenue and the number of entrances and exits he had to cover. A few minutes before eight he took a deep breath and turned Garro loose on the sidewalk, urging him for the last time to press

Otero as hard as he dared for an early delivery. Garro nodded, smiled, turned toward the hotel entrance—and vanished completely in the throng.

Levine swallowed, gave him a few seconds start and then followed, looking more nonchalant than he felt. By the time he and Garcia reached the door without catching so much as a glimpse of their subject, he could feel the pressure at his temples. And when the agents outside, pretending to wait for taxis, and then the agents inside, pretending to wait for their dinner dates, all indicated that Garro had not passed that way, Levine had breathing difficulties for the first time in ten years.

Unwilling to use his portable radio in case Otero had posted lookouts, Levine left Garcia in the lobby and for the worst twenty minutes of his life systematically hunted through the street floor of the hotel. Drawing a blank, he looked in on Otero once more at the bar before raising the alarm—and saw him deep in conversation with Garro.

The tape, when he played it back, was hardly worth the nervous wear and tear. Garro had, indeed, pressed Otero to make a deal, and Otero had, in effect, said yes, but not yet. He seemed to be waiting for a shipment, but Levine was not sure he could accommodate him. Time was running short. The manpower commitment was enormous. He still mistrusted Garro's intentions. And he already had enough on tape to lock Otero up. The two had arranged to meet again for the evening of the 5th, but unless it looked then as though, with a bit more patience, they might seize some dope, Levine was ready to wrap the case up.

Next day, June 4, he and Garcia wrapped up the Friedmans, along with Herklee Overton and four ounces of cocaine. Stunned by their arrest, the Friedmans agreed to cooperate and made a statement confirming that Overton was their source, after which they made bail.

The 5th was another trying day. The Friedmans changed their minds. Panicked by the risk of reprisals, they telephoned to withdraw their statement incriminating Overton, just as Levine was marshaling his forces to cover Garro and Otero at the Havana East. Seated at a nearby table with a special surveillance radio, Levine kept control of the operation by means of a microphone taped to his forearm and a hearing aid–type earphone. In the early hours of the morning, as he alerted the agents outside to follow suspected traffickers who had stopped to chat at Otero's table, knots of puzzled waiters conferred with the maître d' about the madman in the corner who kept whispering into his sleeve.

The party finally broke up at 5:00 A.M. Levine had by then been on duty for sixteen hours, but it was hardly worth going to bed. At 10:00 A.M. the group was due on the police firing range to requalify with their handguns, and before that he had to listen to the tapes made from the miniature transmitter taped to Garro's body so that he could question him about any broken or obscure passages while the conversation was still fresh in his mind.

After agreeing in general terms to a heroin deal sometime in the future, the two had covered much the same ground as before, filling in more of the detail about Otero's involvement in past cases, so that convictions on one or more conspiracy charges now seemed reasonably certain. At one stage, they had talked at length, and almost fondly, about Claude Pastou, whom both had known well in the old days, and after handing Garro back to the marshals for the last time, Levine decided over breakfast that he would get Pastou out of jail as well, to add the finishing touch to this class reunion, before arresting Otero.

Pastou was more than willing, and after another round of legal buck-passing, Levine led his army out again for a last engagement with Otero on the 9th. Grateful for the outing, Pastou tried hard to lead Otero on, but their conversation only added to the loose ends left over from the case Levine had made already, and he now decided to close it out. He had enjoyed his biggest and most exposed command yet as a street general—another ten years would go by before he routinely took charge of even larger combined operations with the FBI and the NYPD—but he was bored with Otero.

He was also bored with the Friedmans, who were still trying to duck out of their agreement to testify against Herklee Overton. When their lawyer caught Levine on the phone after a heavy day in the field with Pastou, he was in no mood to play footsy.

"You can tell your clients," he said, "that I'm gonna ask the U.S. Attorney *not* to accept a guilty plea unless they stick to the deal they made. And he'll do it, believe me. I'm gonna make sure they go to trial, and I'm gonna make sure the judge knows they changed their story. As of right now, counselor, your clients are looking at ten to fifteen years minimum."

Next morning Levine and Mike Pavlick picked up warrants for Otero and arrested him that afternoon, but it was well into the early hours of June 11 before they ended the first phase of his interrogation, and Levine fell asleep where he sat, having worked for thirty-six hours in two days. The 12th and 13th he spent in court, testifying in various cases, and then, on Saturday, the 14th, he was summoned to the office at 9:00 A.M. for the oddest staff meeting he had ever attended.

The DEA had been under fire in the press for months, largely because Senator Henry "Scoop" Jackson had latched onto the drugs problem as an issue in his campaign for the Democratic presidential nomination. His charge that the agency was "rife with corruption" had been made so often, and answered so inadequately, that most people now seemed to accept it as gospel, much to the annoyance of its agents and supervisors, who were mostly too highly motivated or too busy or too closely policed themselves even to think of trying to get away with anything.

Inevitably, there were a few rotten apples, and inevitably in such a sensitive area of enforcement, there had to be occasional abuses of power, but for the most part, the DEA's record was very creditable. Despite all the publicity, the investigations and political pressure, there had been no arrests, no indictments and little enough in the way of hard evidence of any sort to justify such a campaign of vilification. DEA agents not only resented it personally, but had also begun to feel a potentially dangerous shift in public attitudes toward them.

Conscious of their anger, Henry Dogin, the shortest-serving Administrator in the DEA's history, flew to New York to rally his men with the morale-boosting message that no matter how misunderstood they might be by the great American public, *he* loved them just the same. It was not what they wanted to hear. Nor had morale been significantly boosted among those overworked agents who had managed to engineer a weekend off with their families, only to be dragged back to the office on a Saturday and force-fed with anodynes.

"With all due respect, Mr. Administrator," said one of them, expressing the general feeling, "we're narcs. We're street people. Alley cats and gutter fighters. Anybody hits us, they got a fight on their hands."

He sat down to a roar of approval, to which the Administrator responded with sympathy, but little else.

"I think it's unprofessional to answer these accusations," he said, summing up the view from Washington.

At this, the meeting teetered on the edge of collapse, held back from complete disorder only by the presence of John Fallon, the New York Regional Director. Amid a storm of jeers and catcalls, many agents got up and walked out, including Levine. No one could remember anything like that happening before in federal law-enforcement circles, and Dogin resigned soon after.

Although Levine shared the sense of outrage, he had no great regard for public opinion, and at this point he had no home to go to either. On Monday morning it was business as usual, and time for Sidney Wong's first outing on the street.

Skippy Garcia had arranged to buy heroin undercover in the Bronx from a West Indian street gang known to be armed and dangerous, and when Levine decided to take the whole group along to cover him, he hadn't the heart to leave Wong behind. As they watched Garcia disappear into the hallway of the tenement where the deal was set to go down, Levine looked Wong straight in the eye and said, slowly and clearly, with copious gestures, "Sidney, you go watch Skippy. Don't go in. No go in. You stand outside. You stand on stoop and watch. If Skippy in trouble, you help him. If Skippy okay, you stay outside. Understand?"

Wong nodded vehemently, and Levine let him go—not without a touch of anxiety, although he now knew the Thai was more than capable of looking after himself, and certainly looked even less like a government agent than anyone else in his ruffianly crew.

On tenterhooks, Levine watched several people go in and out of the building, each exchanging a long stare with the short, stocky Oriental on the stoop, before Garcia eventually emerged with the big, burly Jamaican dealer he had gone there to meet. Both looked suspiciously at Wong before making their farewells, the Jamaican going back inside and Garcia walking swiftly off the block with the heroin package. Shaking with laughter, he got in the car.

"What's so funny?" Levine demanded, as they drove away.

"Well, I'll tell you," said Garcia, wiping his eyes. "When I came out of there and saw Sidney on the stoop, watching us—and I mean, there's a guy who really *watches*—I couldn't resist it."

"Resist *what*, you dummy?"

"Well, see, I look him over, and out of the corner of my mouth, I say, 'Who's that?' You know, like I'm real worried and suspicious. So then the guy takes a long look at Sidney, right up close, and he says, 'Aw, don't worry 'bout *him*. He own de Chinese laundry down de street.' "

Next day the FBI came into the office to interview Billy Kwastel about Bobby Collins and Collins's employer, his source for prescription cocaine. While the agents were there, Kwastel called Collins on the undercover phone to push the deal along, but Levine was still not entirely easy with the idea of sharing his tapes, case files and informers with another agency. The FBI agents explained, however, that they needed Collins's boss as a witness in a big extortion case, and Levine promised to take no action that might compromise their investigation if they undertook to do as much for him.

The next two weeks went by in another mad blur of casework, court appearances, combined operations with Mike Powers's Group 32, teaching undercover at Albany, and the usual end-of-the-month reports and paperwork. When Levine complained again about the way administrative duties kept cutting into the working day, his division chief, Tom Taylor, told him that it went with the territory. Group supervisors were not *supposed* to spend all their time on the street. If he wanted his promotion to Grade 14 he would have to accept *all* the responsibilities that went with a supervisor's job and learn how to delegate.

Taking these strictures to heart, Levine ran the group "hands off" for several days. On July 3, Special Agent Carlos Smith bought a few grams of cocaine undercover from Carlos Mur, an Argentinian barman at La Savanna on East 57th Street, just off Lexington Avenue, and on returning to the office, reported that the guy looked good for a whole lot more. Though wary of Smith, a Vietnam veteran who had once confided that his greatest pleasure in life was kicking gooks out of helicopters, Levine told him to go ahead and set up as big a buy as he thought Mur was good for, and the group would take him off. But the Fourth of July weekend intervened, and when the deal eventually went down on the 7th, the game plan had changed from a buy-bust to surveillance. According to Smith, there was now a good chance of identifying Mur's source as well and taking them both off at another time.

Still delegating like mad, Levine took Smith at his word and showed up early to cover the meet at Yellowfingers, on the corner of 59th Street and Third Avenue, with Kevin Finnerty and Sidney Wong. The traffic that day was bumper-to-bumper and stridently bad-tempered—and on the sidewalks, much the same, what with the throngs outside the movie houses and lunchtime shopping at Bloomingdale's. Levine immediately made matters worse by double-parking in midblock, across the street from Yellowfingers, and when the horns stopped blowing, twisted around in his seat for a last-minute check of Wong's portable radio. It was of a type Levine used often on surveillance operations. Though short-range, it could be hidden in a pocket, with an earphone no bigger than a hearing aid for receiving, a microphone clipped to the underside of a lapel for transmitting, and a small push-button switch concealed in the hand for selecting one or the other.

"Okay, Sidney," he said, with an encouraging smile. "You do like I show you. Push, talk, listen. Push, talk, listen. Okay? You got that?"

"Yeah." Wong nodded emphatically. "Yeah. Sure. I got." His English had improved dramatically after a few nights with the group at the Greeko-Rican bar.

"Okay. So you watch Carlos when he come." Levine had now perfected his Wong sign language. Some of the less respectful members of the group referred to their pidgin-and-pointin' talk as Sitting Bullshit, and entertained each other mightily with imitations of the two of them ordering lunch or discussing topics of the day. "You follow Carlos when he come. Understand? He go Yellowfingers. Over there. You see? You follow, you watch. You tell us what you see. Push, talk, listen. Okay?"

"Sure, Mike. I watch Carlos. I tell."

Levine turned to Finnerty triumphantly, and in that instant they both saw Carlos Smith across the street, making his way up the block toward the restaurant.

"Okay." Levine pointed to make sure Wong had seen him, too. "There Carlos. You watch. You tell. Push, talk, listen. Okay?"

"Sure, Mike. I go quick."

Wincing, they watched him weave and sway through he traffic until swallowed up in the crowd on the opposite sidewalk. By this time, Carlos Smith had also disappeared. Levine exchanged a glance with Finnerty and shrugged philosophically.

A full minute went by, with nothing over the radio but static and the hiss of the carrier wave. Puzzled, because the restaurant was only yards from the point where Wong had reached the sidewalk, Levine reached for the microphone, gave the call sign and said, "Sidney? Sidney? Can you hear me? Come in, Sidney. Push, talk."

There was a pause, and then, over the background noise, they heard, "Where Carlos? Where Carlos?"

"Sidney," Levine said urgently, "where are you, Sidney? What's happening? Come in, Sidney."

The static was getting worse, but in a moment or two they heard again, "Where Carlos? Where Carlos?" He sounded fainter now.

"Yellowfingers," shouted Levine. "You read me? *Yell-ow-fin-gers.* Come in, Sidney. Come in. Push. Talk."

Straining for Wong's response, they eventually made out, "Where Carlos? Where Carlos?" but the signal was now very weak.

"Fifty-ninth Street," he yelled. "You read? Five-nine Street. Okay? Come in, Sidney."

He had the volume turned up to maximum. Flinching at the roar and crash of electrical interference, they finally heard, once more and very distant, "Where Carlos?" After that, there was nothing but the blizzard of static.

Levine exchanged another glance with Finnerty. With a sigh, he leaned forward to readjust the radio and hang up the microphone. Special Agent Sidney Wong was missing in action.

When Carlos Smith crossed to the car half an hour later with the ounce of cocaine he had just bought from Carlos Mur, Levine wondered if by any chance he had seen Sidney.

"Sidney?" Smith frowned. "No. Why?"

"Oh, nothing," Levine said wistfully.

They arrived back at the office around two-thirty. Nobody there had heard from Wong either. It was almost five o'clock before he phoned in. From a Bronx subway station, with trains roaring and clattering in the background. Still headed uptown, looking for Carlos.

By then, Levine had other things on his mind. He had just heard on the grapevine that the Regional Director intended to put Billy McMullen in over his head to replace John O'Neill as group supervisor.

"Oh, yeah?" he had said. "Well, it's about time. Who needs all that fucking paperwork anyway?"

Traveling flat-out as usual, he had run full tilt into an invisible wall. The surprise, and the hurt, were too much to handle. As he was not at all sure he could carry it off, he went to the men's room to be by himself for a while, to absorb the shock. The enormity of it. The stupendous injustice of it. The casual, insulting indifference it showed to his feelings, and his unquestioning, all-out commitment. They had asked for statistics, and he had measured out his life in statistics. It was too much to grasp all at once. His pride had been breached, leaving him exposed. The only thing he could think of to do was get away and repair the damage in private.

He checked out for the day and decided to ride around for a while on the motorcycle he kept in the DEA garage. Heading south, with no particular destination in mind, he called the office when he reached Virginia to say he was taking a few days' leave. He had a hundred-odd dollars in his pocket and a few credit cards. The following night, when he stopped at a motel in Georgia, he realized he was on his way to Florida, which seemed like a good idea. He was getting away from what felt like the ruins of his career as well as his family life, and appeasing his guilt about his brother, whom he had not seen since David had moved out of the house eight months earlier. After three days and nights he arrived in Miami, very late, and ran out of road somewhere in south Miami Beach.

Looking down at the water, he had to concede his problems weighed as heavily in Florida as they had in New York—perhaps more, as he seemed to have picked up a new one along the way. Nursing his wounds, and with nothing much else to think about than the mess his life was in, he had opened his mind to a doubt he knew had rooted somewhere amid the avalanche of cases but which he had not felt able to acknowledge before.

While as certain as ever that the proper place for dopers was either behind bars or in the cemetery, he was no longer quite so sure that putting them there was really the answer to the drug problem. He was beginning to wonder seriously if perhaps the whole drug enforcement effort was on the wrong track, his own included.

Too tired to think anymore, he went to look for his father.

NINE

"We *can* win. If you want to. . . ."

" Why do I *do* it?"

Levine hesitated, disinclined to get into deep water just as he was getting ready to send them back home to flush their pot down the toilet. Besides, he could see where this was headed. The guy had been laying for him all evening. There was one at every PTA meeting he spoke to, a comfortable, pipe-puffing piss-artist "intellectual." College in the late sixties. Majored in hash, magic mushroom and grass; minored in antiwar protest, burning his draft card.

"Because it's *there*. Because you *pay* me to do it." Then, in a spasm of irritation, "But mostly because I love what I do, what I am and how I live, and that's the truth. Being a narcotics agent is not something I *do*. It's what I *am*."

This chapter is based on a number of public meetings addressed by Levine and the identities of those participating in the debate have been disguised to spare them possible embarrassment.

He turned away in the slightly astonished silence, looking for another question, and caught the eye of Mr. Pipe's female equivalent on the other side of the room.

"Well, now wait a minute," she said. "You just got through telling us you can't see the light at the end of the tunnel because you can't find the tunnel. Okay. But if you're not doing any good, can you tell us why we should go *on* paying you to have a nice time?"

Levine sighed. He had seen her before, too. Single parent. Mid-thirties. Divorced at least once. Intense. Liberated. Combative pain in the ass. Only this one was not bad-looking. She had arrived late and had been eyeing him speculatively ever since.

"Because that's the game you like to play," he said. "You *need* me. Without guys like me, you'd have no one to blame but yourselves for your drugged-up kids and the stink of death on the streets. And it's okay," he went on, talking her down. He hadn't had a day off in a month and really didn't *need* this. "I know you don't want to hear that. Makes you uncomfortable. Makes you wonder about the joint in your pocketbook." He turned back to Mr. Pipe. "And the coke in the icebox."

He looked for somebody else. "I guess Prohibition didn't teach you guys *anything*," Mr. Pipe said, only pretending to be amused. "If people want a drink they're going to take a drink, and frankly, it's none of your business if they do or they don't. Just because there's a bar or a liquor store on every other block doesn't make us a nation of alcoholics. Why pay some crook with dirty fingernails for bathtub gin when you can buy the real thing from a guy who pays taxes? You've got to trust people to do what's right for *them*, otherwise we'll have guys like you sticking their noses into everything. Nothing personal, Mr. Le-

vine, but I for one don't want to live in a police state." He looked around, soliciting
support, and got some.

Levine held out a hand to restrain the chairman. "What *you* ought to learn from Prohibition," he said, "is, don't turn a problem over
to the police and then bitch about it when they
use police methods. Prohibition *could* have
worked. We just went after the wrong people,
that's all. And there *is* an answer to drug
abuse. Only you don't want to hear it."

"Sure there's an answer," said Ms. Liberated. "Legalize it."

"Legalize it?" Levine grunted, urging himself to wind this up now and go home. He'd done
his good deed for the day. Instead, he blew it.
"Look, will you tell me something? You're all
educated people. Why is it, when it comes to
drugs, people in this country have their heads
up their asses?" He puffed out his cheeks,
imagining the phone calls and letters of complaint. "Excuse me, but this really tears me
up. We can't stop people from killing themselves on the roads, so let's legalize speeding. That's what you're saying. We can't stop
people from stealing, so let's *all* do it. I
mean, what do you *want?* Do you want the stuff
packed under government supervision and sold
in candy stores? Is that it? U.S. Grade A weed?
FDA-approved cocaine? Is that what you want?
And pills, too? I mean, you could have all
kinds of pretty little pills in there. Uppers
and downers in big glass jars, right next to
the peanut brittle and jelly beans. How about
that? Because you're right. That way, you'd
sure get rid of the guys with the dirty fingernails. Only I wouldn't want *my* kids to grow up
in that kind of cesspool. And neither would
you."

"Well, I don't think Ms. Zemchuk would want
to go as far as *that,* " said the chairman, over

scattered applause. "I think she probably means that as the law against marijuana is pretty much unenforceable, we might as well legalize it and deny drug dealers an important source of income. You wouldn't agree with that?"

"No, sir, I wouldn't." He was in too deep to back off now. "If you don't start with marijuana you gotta start with cocaine and heroin, which means the damage is done. It's common sense," he insisted, over Ms. Zemchuk's protest. "If anybody here keeps grass in the house, you can bet your kids have tried it already—just like they've already worked through the liquor cabinet. It's part of growing up. And if they've tried grass what are they gonna do if their best friend shows up at school one day with some of his old man's cocaine? You wanna make book they won't take a snort? Out of curiosity? Out of peer pressure? You wanna bet they won't do coke again after that, if they get the chance?

"You wanna bet they won't do a little speed instead, if there's no coke around? Just to see what it's like. Or acid, maybe? Or a little bit of angel dust to goose up their weed? You wanna bet the day won't come, after that first harmless little joint, when they can't get out of bed without an upper or into bed at night without a downer? How the fuck do you think potheads and coke freaks and junkies get started? You wanna talk to me some more about victimless crime? The marijuana laws are only unenforceable because *you* choose to break 'em. And right there is the key to this thing."

Throwing up his hands he made himself smile. After all, what was the point? Tell 'em what they had come to hear, mingle a bit and then go.

"It's unenforceable because it's a stupid law," Ms. Zemchuk shouted, cutting across Mr.

Pipe, who had started to say, "There's an issue of principle here."

They both stopped, and Levine waited for
them to sort it out. His money was on Mr. Pipe,
who seemed to carry some weight in this group.

"The difference between a free society and a
police state," Mr. Pipe went on in a superior
tone as Ms. Zemchuk sat down, "is that freedom
includes the freedom to learn from experience. The freedom to experiment, to make mis-
takes. That's how we learn about ourselves and
who we are."

Levine nodded. He should have known. The guy
was probably a shrink.

"Drug abuse is undeniably a problem," Mr.
Pipe went on, now addressing the audience.
"We wouldn't be here this evening if we didn't
all agree about that. But so is alcoholism a
problem, even if our speaker seems to think he
could cure it by bringing back Prohibition. So
is AIDS a problem. And road safety. And firearms. And air pollution. Cigarette smoking.
Overeating. In fact, I sometimes think the human race is the most endangered species of
all."

He had evidently given this speech before,
for he paused to exact a murmur of approval.

"But how do we tackle these problems in a
free society? Not by banning alcohol and cars
and guns and tobacco and french fries and everything else that's potentially dangerous.
No, we do it by teaching moderation. By education. By making people understand the risks
they run. Maybe Agent Levine thinks he can
solve the problem of AIDS by banning sex, but I
don't think he'd find much support for *that*
proposition. Probably even less than he finds
for the marijuana laws."

He acknowledged their laughter with a
chuckle of his own and turned again to Levine.

"It's just not the American way of doing

things," he said tolerantly. "The American way is to make sure people understand what they're doing so they can make their own choices. But we're also a caring people, so we have to make sure there's help for those who choose wrong, out of ignorance or whatever. Where drugs are concerned, that means we have to have properly funded programs of support and rehabilitation. Education and counseling. That, it seems to me, is the only really *constructive* approach to the drug problem." He sat down, groping for his matches, as though there were nothing more to be said.

Scratching his chin, Levine glanced at his watch. It was a long ride back to the city. On the other hand, he hated to leave this asshole with the last word in front of two hundred people he had driven seventy miles to talk to. He nodded to the chairman, and paced up and down until he had their attention.

"I'm a cop," he said suddenly, with an expression only dopers saw usually. "I enforce the laws—I don't *make* 'em. But I'm also a citizen and a taxpayer and a parent, and I don't need any lessons in the American way of doing things. So lemme talk to you now as a concerned citizen. Not as a government agent, but as a concerned citizen who happens to know a helluva lot more about drugs than anybody else here."

He invited Mr. Pipe to challenge him, but the other conceded the claim with polite unconcern.

"All right," Levine said thinly. "Education and counseling. If you think that's the answer, you don't understand the problem. We got billions and billions of dollars worth of drugs flooding in. A hundred billion at least every year—and you know what that means? To consume that much shit? Is the whole country losing its mind? It means at least half of us have to be buying it. If I were to search all your houses tonight, how much coke would I find? How much grass?"

They shifted uneasily. Mr. Pipe seemed absorbed in his fingernails.

"Who do you think you're kidding?" Levine demanded. "You know what? I don't *have* to search because I *know* what I'd find. I'd find ten to twenty thousand dollars worth of illegal drugs. Right now. And if you multiply that by every PTA group across the country, already you got a big piece of the market. And yet here we are tonight, looking for a solution to the drug problem.

"No, wait a minute," he said, quelling Ms. Zemchuk. "Now you're gonna tell me that grass is about as dangerous as an after-dinner mint and shouldn't be *classed* as a problem. Well, all right. It's not the *real* problem. The real problem is *you*. People who wanna do drugs with a clear conscience. People who support all this bullshit about education and counseling. People who go on voting year after year for politicians who expect the DEA to police the whole world with a lousy two thousand agents, while taxpayers—like you *and* me—go on picking up the tab for more of these bullshit programs. For more psychiatrists and psychologists and therapists and social workers and all the other leeches who make a buck on the back of this fucking disease. Half the sons of bitches I lock up have been through a *dozen* programs. My own brother went through all of 'em—from Phoenix House to methadone maintenances—*and they don't work!* How come you can't see that? The more fucked-up druggies there are, the more programs we get—and that *can't* be right. If they really worked, more programs should mean *less* druggies. Or is it me that's crazy?"

He wasn't even angry anymore. Just marooned somehow on another level of experience.

"The same thing goes for education," he went on. "More should mean less, but it doesn't. Why? Well, does anybody here seriously believe that a few TV commercials and information packs are gonna weigh more with our kids than the example of their parents? More than peer pressure? More than all the phony glamour attached to the druggie world by media sleaze like *Miami Vice?* Who *are* we kidding?"

Along with most of the audience, he looked again to Mr. Pipe.

"Well, let's suppose for a moment that what you say is true, Agent Levine," Mr. Pipe said. "Where does it leave us? First, you say that conventional law enforcement isn't working, so that's not the answer. Now you're saying that demand limitation and counseling won't work either. So what's left? What are we supposed to do now?"

As a trial witness, Levine had won too many tussles in front of a jury not to sense when defending counsel had started to flounder.

"Before you do anything," Levine said, "you've got to know who your enemy *is*. If you listen to the politicians, they'll tell you it's the big international dealers and smugglers, and the governments that protect them. The guys who live on the backs of millions of half-starved Indians and peasants trying to scratch a living out of growing marijuana and coca leaves and poppies for the gringo market. Well, that's bullshit. Anybody who tells you that doesn't know what he's talking about. People who talk about going after the source or sealing off the borders—it's all bullshit.

"If you gave me a machine gun and a license to kill every major trafficker in the business—instead of spending millions of dollars trying to put 'em in jail in spite of judges who won't sentence, and U.S. attorneys more interested in their careers—if you sent me out to kill 'em all instead, you know how much difference it would make? You know how much effect that would have on the dope business?

"Nothing," he said, quickly forestalling Ms. Zemchuk. "*Nada*. You know why? Because there's too much money involved. Too much of *your* money. It's too big an operation. Is General Motors gonna go out of business if you kill the chairman of the board? The bosses of the drug world would be replaced as fast as Lyndon Johnson took over after President Kennedy was shot down in Dallas. You can't kill America by shooting its leaders, and the same thing goes for the drug empire. Sure, they're the enemy—but they're meeting a demand. Behind them is the *real* enemy. Your *worst* enemy. And that's *you*.

"Okay." He held up both hands. "Hear me out, then tell me where I'm wrong. People who do drugs carry the rottenest disease that ever hit the human race. Worse than cancer. Worse than AIDS. Don't even think about the ruined lives. Don't even try to imagine the human agony involved. Forget that drug users are selling out the country, piece by piece. Just think of the number of deaths. The ODs. The murders. The victims of drug-related accidents and crimes. The suicides. The people who slowly poison their brains and bodies and die before their time. Add up all that and you got to think of wartime casualty lists to get a handle on the scale of this disease.

"And you know what the real tragedy is?" He felt himself overheating again, and went for another walk, up and down. "The tragedy is you got the cure in your own hands. It's simple. Just stop buying the shit. That's all. If half of you do that, and the other half stop pretending this has got nothing to do with them, the disease will go away. The siege will be over. Stop buying it, and our children and our cities will be safe again. Stop buying the shit, and you'll pump billions and billions of dollars back into the economy. Stop buying it, and you'll put me out of a job. Please! You can *do* it."

He yielded to the chairman, who had been looking for a chance to intervene, but Mr. Pipe got in first.

"Well, obviously the solution to *any* problem is for people to stop doing what causes it," he said cautiously. "I'm sorry, Mr. Chairman, but that's so obvious it's hardly worth saying. If people stopped drinking we'd 'cure' alcoholism. If we all gave up sex we'd 'cure' AIDS. I'm sure we'd all be happy to put Agent Levine out of a job, but we're not going to do it by wishful thinking. All he's saying is that we must reduce the demand for drugs, and I was under the impression we were spending millions of dollars on that already. With education and counseling programs."

"Demand reduction is what it's all about," Levine agreed. "But with *teeth*." He showed his in a lethal smile. "The other day I watched Mario Cuomo, Governor of New York, talking to a bunch of black and Latin kids in the Bronx. Somebody had given him a capsule of crack, and he was waving it under their noses in front of the TV cameras. 'This'll kill you,' he says to 'em. 'It will steal your soul. This is worse than the devil.' And what did the kids say? Nothing. They just laughed. They elbowed each other and giggled.

"So then some news guy asks him, 'Well, what's the answer, Governor?' And Cuomo says, 'Demand reduction.' But the guy sticks with it. 'Well, what does that *mean,* Governor? What *is* demand reduction?' 'Well,' says Cuomo, 'we'll have to put that in the hands of the experts.' "

"Experts?" Levine clutched at his head. "He means the guys who try to make heroes out of rehabilitated druggie athletes and movie stars. He means the guys who drag their weak-minded asses out on TV to lecture kids like those he talked to in the Bronx. He means the 'experts' who make up bullshit songs and jingles and organize marches and rallies."

He returned to the edge of the stage to stare at Mr. Pipe.

"Well, I *am* an expert," he said heavily. "I've qualified dozens of times in federal court as an expert witness. That means when I testify about drugs, it's like a doctor testifying about somebody's medical condition. It means I know what I'm talking about. And God knows I ought to. I've been a federal agent for twenty-two years. I've worked undercover for most of that time, up to my armpits in drugs. Face-to-face with producers, smugglers, money men, chemists, wholesalers, couriers, commission agents, neighborhood traffickers —I mean, I *know* this scum. I live with them. I talk their language. I live with their victims. I've had drug addiction in my own family. And I'll *tell* you how to reduce demand."

He deliberately kept them waiting until all eyes were on him.

"The way the Japanese and the Chinese did it. They saw the *user* was the key. Users are the carriers. *They* are the enemy. So round them up. Isolate them because they're a danger to everybody they know. Dealers don't spread this disease. They don't have to. They let *you* do that. Once you catch it, *you'll* go looking for *them*. More than that, dealers weigh the risks against the money they make. They don't respond to fear of the law. But you people *do*. "

He looked to Mr. Pipe, and then around the audience, hoping for some kind of spark.

"We've got to make it dangerous and costly to be caught with *anything*. A shred of marijuana. A few grains of powder. A pill without a prescription. We've got to have a mandatory minimum sentence of imprisonment for possessing drugs. Period. Never mind the amount. We've also got to have a mandatory minimum sentence for committing any crime or any infraction of the law whatsoever with even a trace of drugs in your system. We test for alcohol if people are driving erratically. We've got to test for drugs if people are *behaving* erratically. If you want demand reduction, make it known that anyone caught in possession of any amount of drugs *must* do time."

Heads were being shaken, some in disagreement, but most, he thought, because they doubted that such a thing could ever happen.

"Yeah, well . . . they all laughed at Christopher Columbus, okay? Think about it. If you put Dwight Gooden and a few more guys like that away for five years, suddenly 90 percent of your athletes will stop buying the shit. Put Stacy Keach behind bars for five, suddenly 90 percent of your actors are gonna find better ways of spending their money." He paused again, singling out the likeliest users in front of him. "Put one of you straight, concerned citizens in jail for five years for possessing just one small part of the drugs I know you got out there in your homes, and I guarantee you 90 percent of the rest won't think it's worth the risk."

He held them for a moment, then let it go.

"All it takes is the will," he said, returning to his seat. "We *can* win. If you want to. . . ."

TEN

"Man, you oughta be *ashamed*. Dressed like a *priest?*"

His father was waiting for him at Arthur's Place for Steak on the 79th Street Causeway, his usual Miami hangout and unofficial place of business. Besides being the Pickle King of South Florida, Henry Levine was also a benign, part-time shylock, whose clients were mainly hookers and fiscal casualties from Hialeah racetrack.

"How did you know I was coming?"

Having greeted him after several years as though they had last met at lunch, his father shrugged and signaled the barman. "Your mother."

Levine had called her from Georgia, so she wouldn't worry about him. That led them into family talk, a large subject, because Henry had gone on to have other children and other wives, one of whom he married twice.

"Never did understand that," his son said. "You told me on the phone you'd broken the habit—you'd never get married again—and the next thing I know, you're back with the one before last."

"Well, I'll tell you." Henry leaned forward confidentially. "The first time I married her, it was so fucking bad I couldn't believe it. I had to go back and make sure."

As there was nothing in his manner to suggest he was anything but perfectly serious, Levine changed the subject and asked after his brother, who, it turned out, had just left for California to spend a few days with his half-sister. Levine was truly sorry to have missed him, but at least he now had a place to stay. His father called his brother's landlady later that night and arranged for her to give Levine the keys to David's apartment.

Three days were enough. Miami in July was not his idea of heaven, and he had to get back by the 17th to teach undercover tactics in Albany.

As a supervisor, he knew he was as good as any in the region. He had proved that. As an undercover, he was the best in government service. He had proved that, too. If his bosses failed to appreciate what he had done, then the deficiency was theirs, not his.

As for the wreck he had made of his family life, the deficiency was his, not theirs. He was ready to do anything to make amends except give up the work that had come between them. Unhappily for everybody, there was no way an undercover could divide his time, energy and concentration and expect to survive.

With the damage more or less repaired, he pointed the motorcycle toward New York and rode off to see what Providence had in mind for him this time.

On reporting back for duty, he was officially informed that when McMullen took over the International group on July 21, *he* would succeed McMullen as boss of Group 33. "Give him a street group," Regional Director John Fallon had said. "He's not smart enough for International."

Acting Group Supervisor Michael Levine took this to mean sartorially. Rarely seen around the office in anything other than his undercover street clothes, he was also long overdue at the barber's. But he was not, in any case, disposed to question the dispensations of fate *or* regional management. He was as pleased as a kid with a train set for Christmas. A street group of his own, with a supervisor's chair he was not just keeping warm for somebody else, was what he had always wanted. He had won promotion to Grade 13 on the strength of his performance in O'Neill's group. All he had to do now to confirm himself as a Grade 14 supervisor was more of the same.

And this time he had a head start, taking with him the ongoing Billy Kwastel saga, most of his other informers, and his now highly accomplished street partner, Emilio Garcia, as well as Carlos Smith and Sidney Wong. With Special Agent Bobby Joura as a backup supervisor, Tommy Dolan, Jimmy Jones and Jimmy Williams, he now had the nucleus of "The Alimony Boys," the most prolific case-making group in the history of narcotics law enforcement.

Like a marshal and his posse in the last days of the old West, they had to police a vast territory—the New York City drug scene at a time when the cocaine boom had far outstripped the manpower and resources available to cope with it. Scheming and improvising, they strove to make up for their lack of numbers by throwing everything they had into the pot, including all hope of a private life. Month in, month out, Group 33 led New York in case statistics, often making more arrests than whole divisions and sometimes whole regions. Living in the saddle, they stayed out for days on end to round up the bad guys in a last, romantic flourish before the era of the traditional lawman finally gave way to the new age of high-tech police work. And they had a *grand* time.

Levine's doubts about the long-term solution to the drug problem had not been silenced by getting a group of his own, but they were not the kind to slow him up. They were not *self*-doubts. He had long since relinquished any sense of responsibility for the circumstances around a given case, recognizing that his ability to influence the policy of the U.S. Department of Justice was as marginal as his control over the vagaries of an overloaded judicial system. As an agent and supervisor, his terms of reference were to detect violations of the drug laws and apprehend the offenders; considerations of self-respect and self-fulfillment were engaged only between those limits. What he did, he had to do well—indeed, better than anyone else. Being on the losing side had nothing to do with the way he played the game. If anything, it sharpened his competitive edge.

On the day he took charge of the Alimony Boys, Levine was called in to assist Billy McMullen and his old group in New York's first "reverse" undercover operation. In the evolution of undercover tactics, agents had, until then, invariably passed themselves off as *buyers* of illegal drugs. Now, for the first time, two officers of the French Sûreté Nationale were to play the undercover role of *sellers,* in an attempt to ensnare Charlie DiPalermo, a.k.a. Charlie Beck, a major mob heroin trafficker, and his associate, Joe "Junior" Salvato. When the two agreed to meet the Frenchmen to make a ten-kilo buy at Point Lookout, Long Island, Levine was assigned to make the arrest while the rest of his group took part in the moving surveillance that would follow the suspects as they drove out from the city.

Given the importance of the case, and since the DEA was calling the shots, they decided to make a complete photographic record of the operation, not only as evidence but as study material for training other agents in the reverse-sting technique. The Frenchmen were therefore instructed to park their car outside a vacant storefront in which Special Agent Henry Klein, a technical specialist, would set up his cameras and video equipment to cover the buy and the subsequent arrest. The plan was that Levine would hide in there with him, and when the signal was given, charge out across the sidewalk to hold DiPalermo and Salvato at shotgun point until other agents, hidden at a greater distance, arrived to complete the arrest.

On the evening of July 23 everything was set when the cavalcade turned off the Long Island Expressway. Special Agent Klein began a final check of his equipment to make sure everything was properly connected, aimed, focused and in working order, and finished just as the agents outside reported the subject car in sight.

Levine moved quietly to the door with his shotgun.

"They're rolling, they're rolling," Klein whispered hoarsely as DiPalermo's car drifted to a halt behind the Frenchmen. "The cameras are rolling."

Levine nodded, put a finger to his lips, and turned to watch for the signal that the heroin package had been exchanged for Charlie Beck's $150,000.

The moment it came, he dragged open the door, shotgun at the ready, and catapulted himself across the sidewalk. In the same instant, he heard behind him an appalling, drawn-out crash. In his excitement, Klein had kicked the tripod of one of his cameras, and in a vain attempt to stop it from falling, had knocked over all the others, wrecking the setup he had fussed with all day. Laughing like a lunatic, Levine stuck his shotgun in the faces of the two mystified mobsters, who failed to find anything even faintly amusing about it.

So did most of the passersby who now gathered around and plainly sided with Charlie Beck and Junior Salvato when they learned it was a drugs' bust. Tempers frayed, and at one point Special Agent Steve Spielsinger, a former college football star, found it necessary to remove one particularly abusive bystander bodily from the scene. Picking him up like a sack, he ran with him for about a hundred feet before they collided with a tree.

This incident, and complaints of bad language both during and after the arrest, led to the summoning of all the agents in the operation to a meeting, to have the riot act read to them by the chief of enforcement.

"Listen," he said, "some of youse fuckin' guys was usin' language out there that woulda embarrassed a fuckin' sailor. I mean, there's fuckin' taxpayers out there on the street with their fuckin' wives and kids. They don't wanna hear that kinda shit. You got fuckin' foul mouths, some of youse guys, so fuckin' watch that in the future."

They promised to do their best.

As major traffickers are even less inclined to deal with an unknown supplier than with an unknown customer, the chance of posing successfully as a high-level seller of drugs is not only rare but fraught with problems of possible entrapment. Even so, the lessons of New York's first reverse undercover exercise were not lost on the new acting supervisor of Group 33. A decade later they served him well in Operation Hun, a spectacular "sting" in which he brought down a rogues' gallery of high-flying Colombian and homegrown dealers by passing himself off as a major cocaine supplier. More recently still, in a virtual replay of the Point Lookout affair, he also severely embarrassed John Gotti, boss of the Gambino family, by snaring a bunch of his soldiers in a hotel parking lot in the course of a videotaped drug "sale."

On taking over Group 33, however, Levine found he was now expected to spend less time on the street and more in the office, making himself available to his agents for consultation, and to upper management for general administrative duties. In practice, this simply meant that he worked even longer hours than before to fit it all in—thirty-six hours straight, for instance, on the Charlie Beck case—but he did make a gesture toward lightening his caseload by bringing Garcia in undercover as his cousin to help work the Kwastel gold mine. On July 30, the three of them met Derek Williams (defendant 11) at Martell's to negotiate a deal for 300,000 Quaaludes.

But his good intentions were almost immediately frustrated by the FBI, whom Levine had been keeping informed of progress in the case against Bobby Collins (defendant 6) and his employer. As Kwastel was getting nowhere in his attempts to set up a deal for the hospital-quality cocaine Collins had promised to obtain, Levine now decided to arrest Collins for the sample he had supplied and then flip him, thereby opening the door to a much deeper penetration of his employer's business operations, including his links with the Mob and some of the biggest names in horse racing. When advised of this, the FBI had no objection.

Delegating manfully, Levine applied for a warrant and sent Bobby Joura and Carlos Smith out to Queens on August 20 to bring Collins in. When told he was under arrest, Collins said, "I was expecting you guys weeks ago," but declined to elaborate, even when Levine explained later that he faced about fifteen years' worth of conspiracy charges.

Collins's attorney had better luck. After confirming the dismal picture Levine had drawn of Collins's prospects if he refused to cooperate, he persuaded his client to make a statement to Jay Silvestro, whom Levine had assigned as case agent, and Jimmy Williams. But when they reported what Collins had said, their new group supervisor heated up to the point of combustion.

In late July a bookmaker named Joey had apparently telephoned Collins's boss and threatened to kill him. This call had been overheard by the FBI, which had a wiretap on his boss's phone. Next day two agents had come by to ask for his help in their investigations, and in the course of conversation had asked him about Bobby Collins, and if he knew what "Merck" was. What if he did? he had asked cautiously. Well, the agents replied, both he and Collins were under investigation by the Drug Enforcement Administration and could expect to be "put away" in a few weeks if he didn't cooperate.

"Collins will *swear* his boss told him that?" Levine demanded.

"He'll take a polygraph if we want him to," said Silvestro.

Levine stood up so abruptly his chair fell over.

"Wait," said Silvestro. "There's more. Collins says he's in his boss's office a couple of days later, and he hears him talking to one of these FBI agents. And the guy's bawling him out for telling Collins about the DEA investigation. 'Dammit,' he says. 'You broke your promise. You told the kid.' "

"Collins heard him say that?"

"Yes, he did. And so did another guy who shares the office. No wonder we only got a sample of that hospital shit."

To Levine, it was inconceivable that any federal officer would deliberately compromise an investigation by another agency, much less put a brother agent at risk.

"I was sick to my stomach," he recalls. "I had been part of the 'turf wars' between the old BNDD and the Bureau of Customs when agents could do their careers more good by locking up a guy in the other agency than busting the biggest doper around, but the merger had supposedly ended all that. Now here was the FBI pulling the same kind of shit, only worse. Drove me crazy. I wanted those agents indicted—and not all the warning bells in my head were going to stop me. The next morning I went for the jugular."

In a memorandum to Regional Director John Fallon and Division Chief Tom Taylor setting out the facts, he concluded, with the restraint appropriate to a newly appointed acting group supervisor, "The seriousness of the alleged disclosures surely cannot be overestimated. . . . These events occurred while a DEA investigation was being actively pursued and while a special agent was working in an undercover capacity. . . . Not only was the investigation jeopardized, but so was the life of the undercover agent."

Hitting his stride, he then took the matter up with the DEA Inspection Service, the department responsible for internal security, and sensing a lack of enthusiasm for the idea of investigating the conduct of FBI agents, called Assistant U.S. Attorney Ray Dearie, of Eastern District, with a view to framing criminal charges against the offenders and pressing for an indictment.

With the entire Justice Department now in an uproar, Levine and Silvestro were summoned to Fallon's office to discuss the case with Tom Taylor and Chief of Enforcement James Hunt, who had close ties with the FBI. After going over the evidence again Taylor and Hunt undertook to confront the offenders at a private meeting the next day, and Levine went off to lecture a citizens' group on Staten Island about the evils of drug abuse before covering Garcia on a heroin buy in Queens.

Both of the accused FBI agents denied warning Collins's boss about the DEA investigation. When Levine heard this from Taylor after the meeting, he could already sense a closing of ranks. Both the FBI and DEA were arms of the Justice Department, which had a common interest in protecting its reputation, something Levine began to perceive when the FBI assigned its internal inquiry to the supervisor of the two agents in question.

Enraged again by what looked like the beginnings of a white

wash, Levine raised another commotion, but by now the FBI had assumed full control of the inquiry into its own agents' conduct. On Taylor's instructions, he made himself available to a team of FBI inspectors who interrogated him all day as though *he* were the accused, an experience not only irritating in itself but bewildering, as he had three independent witnesses to the incident, none of whom had anything to gain by lying. Now certain a cover-up was under way, he fired off another barrage of calls and memoranda to the DEA Inspection Service and the U.S. Attorney's office.

Deliberately blind to all the hints and obstacles strewn in his path, Levine was ready to make the arrests himself, if necessary, but then John Fallon called him into his office, and in the presence of his division chief and others, told him to lay off.

"And that's an order," Fallon said sourly. "Forget it. Just drop the investigation."

Levine looked at each of them in turn. "If you say so, Mr. Fallon," he said, finding no glimmer of encouragement. "But what about Ray Dearie? If he—"

"I said, *forget* it. *I'll* call Dearie and straighten this out."

Anticipating something of the sort, Levine had taken case agent Jay Silvestro in with him as a witness, and both noted the outcome of the meeting in their diaries. As Levine saw it, a prominent businessman and several leading jockeys would now take a walk on serious drug offenses, and from that moment on a frost nipped the buds of Levine's career. Acting group supervisors bucking for promotion are not supposed to let their superiors appear in a poor light, but Levine still fancied the most important thing was to keep after people who broke the law.

It was not so much naïveté as a simple refusal to accept the facts of bureaucratic life. At higher management levels, it was more important not to upset the FBI than to pursue a felony case against two of its agents, even though in Levine's view, the lives of DEA personnel had been willfully jeopardized and a bunch of dopers had escaped indictment. Okay . . . Levine learned from that, as he learned from everything. In a crunch he was expendable. The work he did—indeed, the work of the whole agency—was apparently of less importance to those who ran it than the good opinion of their peers within the Justice Department. It was important to remember that.

Despite his reputation as a warrior Levine was a counterpuncher by nature, neither aggressive in style nor abrasive in manner (except when the situation seemed to call for it). If people were bent on confrontation he would rarely disappoint them, but on the whole he preferred to avoid clashing heads. He liked to manipulate his adversaries. He enjoyed being devious. And if his bosses had now seen fit to join the ranks of those adversaries, then he had to adjust his game accordingly.

It was clearly not enough to break your ass and bury them in statistics. With his record of achievement, first as backup, then as acting supervisor of the International group, he could see no real reason why he should not have been promoted to Grade 14 on taking over Group 33. How much more proof did they need that he could handle the job?

But he broke his ass and gave them more anyway. In the month of September hardly a working day went by without an arrest. Running around town with their informers, the Alimony Boys spent days undercover in midtown West Side hotels, cleaning out couriers, buyers and sellers. They broke up a cocaine distribution ring inside ABC Radio based on ABC's interoffice mail system. Levine and Joura bought cocaine from an attorney employed by an ecumenical council of Christians and Jews. And on the 25th they all worked themselves literally to a standstill, arresting three Colombians delivering twelve ounces of cocaine to Levine, then a black California dealer delivering a sample ounce to Bobby Joura, and finally—after processing their prisoners and attending to the paperwork—covering Tommy Dolan while he negotiated undercover for a pound of heroin.

In the same month Levine also testified in court in four different cases, addressed two public meetings, delivered a lecture at John Jay College, conferred daily with government attorneys, his superiors and fellow agents, and somehow kept up with his general administrative duties. He even found time to cultivate new informers.

Arrested on a cocaine charge, John Miller was so taken with the cool, swinging, lethal style of the Alimony Boys that he signed up to work on the spot, and was soon making quality cases. Engagingly bright and personable, he latched onto the group like a chameleon, becoming outwardly indistinguishable from his new "buddies"—except that Levine had a nagging hunch he was still dealing on the side.

Suspicion deepened into certainty one day when Miller called him from Florida, apparently just for a chat. Levine's early warning system homed in immediately. The guy's calling from Miami to find out how we're doing? Afterwards Levine made a couple of calls himself, and next day an informer in Florida sent word that Miller had boarded a plane for New York with a kilo of coke.

Levine was neither surprised nor gratified. He had simply *known*. The intuition that had so often saved his life also saved him time. He even knew what Miller would do next. Aware of how much ground the group could cover in a working day—they came and went like ghosts—Miller had made his "social" call to find out how busy they were and where they were working so that he could plot his own moves accordingly. Now he would need an update.

After sending Tommy Dolan out to La Guardia with a crew, Levine hooked up his tape recorder and settled down to do some paperwork while he waited. The flight was on time, and sure enough, minutes after the plane landed, the telephone rang and Levine set the recorder running.

"Hey, Mike," said Miller breezily, "how's with you today? How's everybody doing?"

"John?" said Levine, surprise struggling with delight. "Well, howya doin', man? What's happening? You still in Florida?"

"You bet your ass, man. Can't get enough of this Florida sunshine. I just moved on up to Palm Beach, so I figured I better check in with you. See what's happening. You know, in case there's something I can do for you down here."

"Well, that's real thoughtful of you, John, but I don't think there's much more you can do for me now. You just enjoy that sunshine while you can. Because the weather is shit up here."

"Yeah? No justice, right? Here's me working on my tan while you guys are freezing your ass off on the street. Where you working today, Mike?"

Levine smiled. "La Guardia Airport, John," he said—and right on cue, Tommy Dolan tapped on the glass of the phone booth in which Miller was sitting with his suitcase.

When they brought him in, and Dolan placed the kilo of cocaine on Levine's desk, Miller hung his head.

"Okay," he said, "why don't you just kill me. Right now. Let's get it over with."

"Well, you broke the rules, John," Levine said sadly. "No doubt about that. And I'm real disappointed. I mean, how can I go to bat for people who lie to me? Who is it?"

Miller shuffled his feet. "My cousin," he said faintly.

"Who's your cousin? What's his name?"

Miller sighed. Then he rolled his eyes and fidgeted with the papers on the desk. After that he went to look out of the window.

"I don't have all day, John."

"Marvin Zagoria," Miller said, after another silence, without looking around.

"You mean the attorney? From Atlanta?"

Zagoria was well known in DEA circles as the biggest, and richest, narcotics defense attorney in Georgia.

"Yeah. But Mike, he's *family*. I can't—I mean, if you make me try to do something, I'll blow it. He'll *know*."

Levine studied him thoughtfully. "You know the way this shit goes, John," he said, almost hoping that just for once somebody was going to stand up and put his principles first. For that he might almost have been willing to forgo the pleasure of locking up a lawyer. "It's real simple. It's *your* ass or your cousin's."

"Then I guess it's my cousin's," Miller said, hardly hesitating.

He agreed to put in a call to Zagoria, no doubt comforting himself with the thought that Atlanta's leading trial lawyer *had* to be smart enough not to convict himself on the telephone, even after Levine had laid out the conversation he wanted to hear. When satisfied Miller was word-perfect, Levine switched on the recorder, dialed Zagoria's number and handed the phone to Miller with a shrug that said there were no more favors he could do for him.

"Hey, Marv," said Miller. "It's me. John."

Silence. Zagoria cleared his throat. "I'm busy," he said. "Hang up. I'll talk to you when you get back."

"No, Marv—wait. We got a problem."

"I can't talk now. Where are you?"

"At the apartment."

"Okay. Just forget it. Hang up and come back."

"Marv, *listen*. That's the problem. We see people outside. And I don't know what to do."

For a long moment Zagoria wobbled on the edge. All he had to do to save himself was hang up. Instead, he said, "Flush it," and Levine smiled seraphically. He loved to lock up attorneys.

In October the Alimony Boys went into overdrive. The nucleus of the group—Levine, Joura, Garcia, Dolan, Jones and Williams—had spliced themselves into a team that worked almost telepathically at times, so complete was their understanding of one another's capabilities. And yet they were also intensely competitive, vying with one another in making cases, each seizing the initiative when he saw his chance and running with it, confident the others would back him with the same energy *he* would put out when it was their turn.

It was not a way of life that appealed to everybody. Around this hard core of hard men revolved the rest of Group 33, ten to a dozen agents who came and went, staying a few weeks or months before transferring out, either unwilling or unable to keep up with the killing pace Levine demanded.

On October 1, he made a start on liquidating the Kwastel collection by introducing Garcia undercover to Derek Williams (defendant 11) as a heroin buyer, so that Garcia could take over as case agent, and then sent Bobby Joura downtown for a batch of warrants for people who had sold him dope lately, including Rhonda Taffer and Timothy Wells, the pill merchants who had opened the Kwastel casebook in the Riverdale railroad yard almost exactly a year earlier. Levine intended to arrest these two himself, not least because Wells, at their first meeting, had evidently fancied his chances in a Wild Western–style showdown, but first he went on a motorcycle ride for Mike Powers and Group 32.

Powers had set up an elaborate surveillance operation, complete with a helicopter, to cover a heroin buy from a low-level organized crime figure who had insisted that Powers's undercover agent "front" him $14,000 before he went to New Jersey for the dope. It was a cold, rainy night, and Levine had already worked nearly thirty hours straight, but he agreed to take Special Agent Gerry Castillo on the back of the DEA Honda and help keep an eye on the mobster when he drove away with the government's money.

Already drenched, the two watched the envelope change hands and then followed discreetly as the target car moved off, with Castillo struggling to keep in touch with Powers and the rest of the team by portable radio. But what with the static, the noise of the motorcycle and the rain driving in their faces, he was unable to make out more than an occasional word, and it was soon obvious that they could play no part in any orchestrated pattern of surveillance, which left him to choose between keeping on top of the mobster or else dropping out of the hunt altogether, having taken a soaking for nothing.

"Fuck it," Castillo shouted in his ear. "Let him go."

Tired, hungry, cold and wet, Levine dropped back, considering this seriously, but then the target car made an unscheduled turn toward the Pulaski Skyway and picked up speed.

"It's a rip," he yelled over his shoulder, kicking down a gear and twisting the throttle wide open. "Where the hell *is* everybody?"

They had closed the gap a little by the time they reached the Skyway, but then the car began to draw away again, hitting ninety or better.

"Let him go, let him *go,*" Castillo gurgled, pounding Levine on the back as the lashing wind and rain snatched the breath from his mouth. "Fuck it. Let him go."

It was good advice. Flat out at 80 mph in a blustery sidewind, the Honda was twitching skittishly on the slippery highway, and the guy was getting away anyhow. But it was the principle of the thing. Levine decided to give it another minute—and that was just enough. As the streaky glimmer of the car's rear lights merged and lost identity in the wet blur of red and white reflections up ahead, Special Agent Richie Keckler took over, making a low pass across the highway in the DEA helicopter. Levine stayed in the hunt long enough to make sure Keckler was on the right car, and then turned for home.

Around 4:00 A.M. two men drove up to the mobster's door. They were big, heavyset, and in no mood to play games. Two minutes later, they drove away again—Special Agent John Costanza sitting beside Levine and counting through the government's bankroll to make sure it was all there.

Levine then took the weekend off, to catch up on some sleep, his laundry and the children, who seemed to have grown alarmingly in the weeks since he had last seen them. Liana was cool but gracious, and when he left the house on Sunday night, he felt as he usually did after a few hours in their company, that he had to be *crazy* to live like this.

Two nights later he crashed through the door of Timothy Wells's apartment on East 89th Street. He was again in an edgy mood, having spent most of the day with two FBI inspectors who had made it plain, without actually saying so, that the agents who had endangered his life would be allowed to retire with their records unblemished.

Wells offered no resistance, but from the safety of his handcuffs, baited Levine with boasts about how easily he could have taken him off that night in the Riverdale railroad yard.

"You could have *tried,*" Levine conceded bleakly, after finding a loaded .38 in the bedroom.

"Man, you don't know how close you came to getting blowed

away," Wells jeered. "I had a Magnum pointed straight at your gut."

Under questioning, he also mentioned that Larry Sussman (defendant 16) owned a .357 Magnum, and that he, too, had been thinking about ripping Levine off.

Within hours Taffer and Wells had made bail and were back on the street. (Wells was later rearrested and convicted on an unrelated charge of homicide.)

Now everybody had to go, before the news of their arrest scattered all his other pigeons. After a fourteen-month run, the Kwastel saga was at last set to close (except for at least another year of trials and spinoffs). Taken as a whole, it had been a model demonstration of how much could be done undercover with small resources but great resourcefulness.

Despite all the others he has handled since, Levine still sees the case as "an absolute classic in manipulation. All levels of humanity were dragged into the net, from corporation heads and top jockeys to low-life pill pushers and murderers. On Kwastel's back, I was carried through the gamut of human treachery, from family members informing on one another to law-enforcement officers 'burning' other agents' cases. I also had to deal with the full range of narcotics-enforcement situations, from rip-offs and intended homicides to links with the highest levels of organized crime in Canada and the lowest levels in California and Mexico. To my knowledge, no other unwitting informer was ever run so long or so far."

But there was no time for resting on laurels. In the middle of all this, Levine had to go to Albany to teach a two-day course at the State Police Academy, and just as he was leaving, Howard Fuchs called with news of Billy Yellowhair, who was again wanted for murder and thought to be hiding downtown with a Polish girl strung out on heroin. Promising himself to take care of this personally as soon as he returned, Levine put the case on hold for the last time. Before he had another chance to move on it, Billy Yellowhair himself was murdered.

The pace was killing in more senses than one, but Levine exulted in it. There was no time to think about anything else—about the larger significance of what he did or his shortcomings as a husband and father or the lack of official recognition for his achievements. Nothing could stand against the obsessive pursuit of every doper who crossed his path, and if his belief in Providence ever wavered, it was always restored by some new, improbable escape from disaster.

In their various ways the Alimony Boys half believed in it, too, and came to share his energy and confidence. Bobby Joura was buying speed undercover from dealers in Queens. Jay Silvestro had an undercover Quaalude case going in Brooklyn. Tommy Dolan flew out to Dallas to wrap up an undercover investigation that led to the arrest of three traffickers and the seizure of three cars, three guns and half a pound of cocaine. And on a corner of Roosevelt Avenue in Queens, Skippy Garcia and Jim Montagne helped Levine persuade the DEA to redesign its brand-new raid jacket. Of dark blue nylon, it bore a replica of a gold badge on the breast and the DEA logo on one shoulder.

An informer had agreed to buy four ounces of cocaine from a doper named Carlos, but Levine took his group to the meet instead. When Carlos failed to show up they cruised the avenue to look for him, wearing their new jackets, and as they drove past a small park, Levine saw Carlos coming through the gates with another man.

Carlos saw them in the same instant. As Levine threw himself out of the car, with Garcia and Montagne at his heels, Carlos dragged the other man in front of him as a shield and went for his gun. Measuring the distance he still had to cover across the sidewalk, Levine knew he was never going to make it, but Providence still had a use for him. Carlos's gun snagged in the waistband of his pants, and just as he wrestled it free, Levine clamped a heavy hand over it, jamming the muzzle of his own gun up Carlos's nostril.

Only then could he pay any attention to all the yelling and screaming behind him. He turned to find two bearded anticrime cops training their guns on him while the rest of the group had *their* guns aimed at *them.* Everybody was shouting at once, and it would have taken only one nervous twitch of somebody's finger to leave at least five men dead on the sidewalk.

"Jesus," one of the cops said afterwards, "that fucking jacket looks just like a gang jacket."

Levine quoted him next morning in a memo reporting the incident, and the new raid jackets were withdrawn wherever they had been issued to have the words POLICE DEA U.S. AGENT stenciled on the back in big gold capital letters.

Sailing that close to the wind, the street partnership of Levine and Garcia was nearly dissolved several times that fall. With each new escape, and each new case that subtly enlarged his experience, Levine's private conviction grew surer that he was being preserved and fine-tuned for some purpose of which he as yet had no inkling. While waiting for other things to happen, they would sometimes cruise around at night in Levine's undercover Cadillac Eldorado to see what sort of trouble they could get into, and on one such fishing expedition to the Bronx they managed to hook José Acevedo, a young Puerto Rican jewelry salesman who dealt a little coke and heroin on the side.

"Sure, I know where you can buy dope," he told them. "I'll introduce you."

And he took them to a record store, where Garcia bought an ounce of brown rock Mexican heroin from José Muriel for $2,100.

As this was the first significant Mexican case to come to the attention of the New York office, Levine told Garcia to order half a pound, and drove him up to the Bronx to take delivery, with the rest of the group tagging along to make the arrests. But when they arrived at the record store, Muriel declined to do business on the street, claiming it was too dangerous. The package was ready for them in his apartment at 413 West 130th Street, he said, where they could do business in comfort and safety.

It was a bad block on a bad street, but Levine and Garcia had little choice. It was either that or call off the buy. Grudgingly allowing their suspicions to be allayed by Muriel's assurances that they were dealing with honest businessmen, they drove over to 130th Street and entered the building with Muriel and Acevedo, acutely aware that their backup had no chance at all of getting on the block undetected.

Once inside the apartment, Levine made up his mind to take them both off as soon as he saw the dope, but Muriel was in no hurry. First, he insisted on offering them drinks, and then on seeing the money—which was just as well, because no sooner had Levine counted it out on the table than two men emerged from the closet behind him and put away their guns.

Misunderstanding his expression, Muriel apologized for taking this precaution, explaining how difficult it was to be sure of anyone these days. Levine had to agree, and as that seemed as good a cue as any, he and Garcia then drew their own guns and disarmed all four. When the group piled into the apartment in response to Levine's radio call, they seized half a pound of heroin, two kilos of mix, a quantity of cocaine and four guns. They also had to restrain

Muriel and the two closet gunmen from strangling José Acevedo, whom they loudly accused of being a stool pigeon.

After that, the Alimony Boys set a new course record by arresting thirteen people in two days—not counting these four—and still found time to requalify on the New York Police Department pistol range.

But the baggage train was catching up with them. As their earlier cases now went to trial, so their effective strength on the street was often seriously reduced by their presence in court. Somehow, a balance had to be struck between the number and quality of the cases they took on in the short term, and the weight of paperwork and court time those cases represented in the long term—and whenever Levine thought he might be getting it right, something else would come along to throw his calculations out. Two days before his thirty-sixth birthday he was called into John Fallon's office, although he could think of nothing in particular that he had done wrong recently.

"Yeah, come in, Mike," Fallon said, tossing a piece of paper across the desk. "We've got information that the Colombians have put out a contract on two of our guys."

"Yeah?" As a street agent, Levine was touchy about such things. That was not part of the game. Professional dopers and professional narcs accepted that neither would exist without the other. Among professionals, there were no hard feelings. And *no contracts.* "In my group?"

"No. Pat Shea and Andy Smith. That's all we've got." Fallon pointed at the paper, on which was written the description of two Latin males and the address of a bar on Roosevelt Avenue. "I want you to take care of it."

"Yes, *sir,"* said Levine, who took it as a compliment.

"Get hold of Detective Bobby Johnson in the Task Force," Fallon added, as Levine turned to go. "You know him?"

Levine shook his head.

"Well, Shea and Smith were working on a conspiracy case with the Gran Colombiana Lines and a bunch of Colombians out in Brooklyn and Queens. Johnson has a good stool into those people, so get together with him."

Detective Johnson had *two* informers: one of them was Oscar Toro, an unemployed salesman, married, with two children; and

Edwin Hernandez,* a professional stool, both of whom dabbled in the cocaine trade. Toro had been the first to hear rumors of a $25,000 contract to hit two federal undercover agents who had been working a narcotics case on the Brooklyn piers, and Hernandez had later confirmed his story. The principal suspects were two Colombians in Queens, known to be dealing "very large" quantities of cocaine, much of it brought ashore hidden in ships' garbage. Both men were conveniently "on vacation" in Florida.

Toro also thought that the hitmen were two of the dealers' bodyguards. Neither he nor Hernandez knew their names, or was anxious to inquire, but between them, they had come up with a rough description of the two men, and the addresses of two or three bars in Queens where they were known to hang out. One was in his mid-thirties, tall, thin, black-haired, clean-shaven, with a high, effeminate voice, and usually dressed in sneakers, denims and an army jacket. The other was about the same age but shorter, heavily built and bearded. He, too, usually wore army surplus clothes and carried an army-type bag with a shoulder strap.

That night the Alimony Boys went to war.

With Pat Shea and Andy Smith under twenty-four-hour guard in their homes, Group 33 drifted inconspicuously into Jackson Heights to stake out the El Escorial Bar at 85th Street and 37th Avenue, where the two suspected hitmen had last been seen, and to reconnoiter the battle field before launching their attack.

On his own account, Levine had come to terms readily enough with his reservations about an enforcement strategy aimed at the trafficker rather than the user. The personal risks he ran to achieve results that had no discernible effect on the scale of drug abuse were, for him, a large part of what made life worth living. He thrived on risk. Had it been lacking, he would have sought it somewhere else, for that was how he fulfilled himself. And, doubts or not, in the absence of a better strategy, he was doing what he could. In the absence of a cure for cancer, the most any surgeon could do was treat the disease case by case.

But when it came to involving the agents in his charge, Levine, as a supervisor, took almost the opposite view. He could see no merit in sacrificing anybody's life, limb, sanity, marriage, family or job in any ultimately hopeless cause, least of all in any operation in which *he* had a controlling interest. No one case, no individual

* Not his real name.

trafficker, no potential seizure, however large, could possibly be justified if the net result was likely to be as significant as lifting a bucket of water from the Mississippi River.

That was why, when he taught undercover, he was really teaching survival. That was why he organized his group's workload to minimize the risks of a job that was hazardous enough already. That was why he was usually first through the door. And that was why he was elated to find himself in Jackson Heights, untroubled by reservations of *any* kind. He had been asked, in effect, to give expression to the sense of solidarity that even the most jaded street cop felt when a brother officer was threatened.

His strategy was simple. He was going to kick ass until the Colombians got the message. Anything remotely resembling probable cause would get the full treatment. Anybody buying, anybody selling, anybody whispering on street corners or carrying a shopping bag, anybody driving too slow or too fast or cruising the block once too often or in any way acting suspiciously, and wham! With the help of the local NYPD precinct, he was going to make it impossible for any doper to deal out in the open.

When he was reasonably sure that nobody answering to the description of the hitmen was in the bar or out on the streets, Levine turned his men loose on the targets they had already picked out for themselves.

"Halt. Freeze. Up against the wall, mother-fucker. Whatchoo got there, scumbag? Where's your green card? No green card? Well, *you're* not gonna put out no more contracts on DEA agents, you sonofabitch. We're gonna kick your ass clear out of the country."

When they started the roust, the neighborhood was alive with movement, a lot of it drug-related. By midnight, the streets were almost deserted, with just the odd drunk or night worker left on the sidewalks. Group 33 had recaptured Jackson Heights.

Levine had not the least doubt that everybody would come out again as soon as he called his men off, but he had made his mark. The group had handed over about thirty Colombians to their uniformed backup—no one had really been counting—and a car from the Immigration and Naturalization Service had shuttled back and forth all evening with suspected illegal aliens. More directly to the point, no one who had witnessed any part of the operation could have been left in much doubt that the DEA disapproved strongly of anybody taking out contracts on the lives of its agents.

The following night Levine took his troops in later, around 11:30 P.M., figuring that most law-abiding citizens would be off the streets by then. As their cars moved into position, he was pleased to see it was business as usual around the hot spots they had identified the previous evening. Local dopers had evidently written off the onslaught as a one-shot token crackdown of the sort they had seen before, but during the next two hours they came to understand that the rules of the game had changed. Constitutional guarantees and due process tended to work in the long term, after lawyers had been hired and courts had delivered their judgments. In the short term, agents and police officers could lock you up, take away your money and your dope, and if your visa had expired, ship you back to Bogotá. When the roundup ended in the early hours, prisoners were still being taken to neighboring precincts for questioning, and a second car had joined the INS shuttle.

By the third night, the Colombians were beginning to learn. A few lookouts had been posted, and every so often a block would clear like magic as one of the group's cars approached. Somebody had been noting down their license tags. Some agents also encountered the first signs of resistance. Working in pairs, they had already seized a number of guns, knives and other weapons, but now that they were getting down to the hard core of the trade, the mood was changing. Suspects were slower to respond to their challenge, and less cooperative when they did.

Sensing that it was only a matter of time before a shooting incident, Levine regrouped his modest force into fewer, stronger teams with orders to crush any hint of opposition before it took hold. With their police backup mostly waiting in the wings, they were, at best, sixteen men against nobody knew how many. Probably hundreds. But there was no doubt they were getting through with their message: YOU DON'T MAKE CONTRACTS ON AMERICAN POLICE.

By the fourth evening, the Alimony Boys were a little bleary. After working cases all day, fighting a war at night had left them short of sleep and shorter of temper. The Colombians had now organized a more effective lookout system that quickly latched onto Levine's new assortment of government cars, and it was soon necessary for two or three units to work in concert if they were to cut suspects off from their boltholes. Although the catch that night was lower in total, it was higher in quality, and the trade was starting to hurt.

With the Colombians now expecting them, Levine decided on Day 5 to work only half the group each night, in alternating shifts, while the other half rested. As the first sign of their presence in the neighborhood seemed enough to clear the streets, he also decided to vary their times of arrival as much as possible, and took the neighborhood completely by surprise by showing up one afternoon, after a trial in Eastern District ended unexpectedly early. In their first sweep, they netted as many suspects as in the previous two nights.

And so it went, cat and mouse, for another week. Levine even had two cars out on Christmas Day, but he was still no closer to identifying the would-be hitmen than he had been to start with. Shea and Smith were still under guard. The two Colombians thought responsible were still in Florida. And all he knew for sure was that the Jackson Heights branch of the Colombian dope business would soon have to close for repairs.

Then, on December 29, everything changed. Oscar Toro, the informer, and his wife arrived home at 30-10 94th Street, Queens, in mid-afternoon expecting to find their two children playing with the baby-sitter, seventeen-year-old Liliana Bustamonte, who had arrived from Honduras as a live-in mother's helper just five weeks earlier. But the house seemed to be empty, and thinking perhaps they were playing a joke, Toro looked in the basement to see if they were hiding down there.

He found his daughter.

Susan Toro, aged five, had been hanged by the neck from a ceiling support with a four-foot length of gaudy nylon cord left over from wrapping the family's Christmas presents. She had been stabbed four times in the chest and abdomen. There was no sign of Oscar Toro Jr., aged ten, or of the baby-sitter.

When Levine heard the news from Johnson, he went to the men's room for a few minutes.

Conditioned, like most cops, to accept as "normal" a level of exposure to cruelty, pain and depravity unknown in any other occupation, Levine, like most cops, remained sensitive to crimes against children. The human dregs he was paid to sweep off the streets usually evoked no emotion at all, and that was their principal protection at the moment of apprehension and arrest. To a cop, an armed robber, rapist or doper might have no greater claim to consideration than a sewer rat, but unless he offered serious resistance, he generally wasn't worth the trouble of shooting. But a child killer *was.* Child killers, like cop killers, were dispensable. And this one aspired to be both.

When Levine came out of the men's room, the group was afraid to speak to him. Even Garcia. By now, they had seen him in most situations and thought they knew what to expect, but they had never seen such a cold, intent ferocity in anyone before.

No more Mr. Nice Guy. No more finesse, either. That night, around 4:00 A.M., the group hit the El Refugio bar on 90th Street and Roosevelt Avenue just as it was closing. Armed with pump-action shotguns, they crashed in like storm troopers, wearing baseball caps and raid jackets, and herded everybody up against the wall, kicking the legs out from under anyone not quick enough to please them. Pining for someone to take him on, Levine prowled through the confusion looking for anyone answering even vaguely to the hitmen's description. Johnson's other informer, Edwin Hernandez, had reported seeing the one with the effeminate voice going into the bar a few hours earlier, but he was no longer there, if he ever had been.

After handing the situation over to the police, Levine hit the El Escorial on 85th Street in the same way. It was, as he intended it to be, an intimidating show of force, and the Colombians were duly intimidated. No one resisted, though some were armed, and once again the group made sure that everybody got the message. While a threat remained on an agent's life, a worse threat would hang over theirs. Although Susan Toro's murder was a matter for the police, several of the Alimony Boys were weekend parents, like Levine. All they wanted was for some doper to get out of line.

When Levine called Immigration to report the haul of illegal aliens, the duty agent, now used to the nightly shuttle, asked if two cars could handle it.

"No," said Levine, looking out at his prisoners on the sidewalk. "Send a bus."

They were about ready to leave when he noticed four dark Hispanics drive slowly by and, at the corner, signal to a white kid who immediately went to a pay phone. That, as far as Levine was concerned, amounted to probable cause. He sent two cars to keep the Colombians under observation while he and Detective Johnson went to have a little "talk" with their friend.

His name was Michael Gray, and he was winding up a coke deal. He admitted this at once, adding that he already worked for the DEA as an informer.

It had been a long night. Using his portable, Levine ordered the surveillance team to arrest the four Colombians and returned to base as dawn was breaking with five prisoners and $16,000 in cash.

Gray had been telling the truth. He already worked for a DEA group covering Long Island, but his handling agent plainly kept him on a looser rein than Levine would have allowed. Gray had told no one about his outing that night, and had not permitted his role of informer to interfere much with his cocaine trafficking. All that now changed. Although there was nothing Levine could pin on any of them—they had sold their load for $16,000 before the group picked them up—he handed the four Colombians over to Immigration for expulsion and leaned on Gray in his usual persuasive manner.

Unaccustomed to pressure, Gray cracked like an egg. He named his Colombian suppliers and, among an assortment of customers, Nick Caturano, who played the part of Sally Rags in *The Godfather,* but whose regular job was driver to Congressman Fred Richmond. Levine liked the sound of this. He was also intrigued by Gray's suggestion that his Colombian friends knew more than they were saying about the contract on the two DEA agents and the murder of Susan Toro. Turning the screw a little tighter, he "encouraged" Gray to make a recorded call to Elsie Sanchez, his main connection, and set up a four-ounce cocaine buy. Briefed beforehand on how the conversation should go, Gray led Sanchez into admitting that "her people" were doing "crazy things." To silence an informer, they had killed his little girl and kidnapped her brother.

The deal was set for January 5. Until then, whenever two or more of the Alimony Boys found themselves with an hour or so to spend, they would show the flag in Jackson Heights, just to keep the enemy off balance and to soften him up for the night's combined operations. Incensed by the wanton killing of a child, they were no longer interested in duty rosters or time off. If it was to hit Colombian dopers, Levine could call them out at any hour, day or night.

On the 5th he split them into small teams to take off the people Gray had named in his statement, Levine himself, with three other agents, electing to go after Elsie Sanchez and her partner, Edgar Payan. The two arrived for the meet by taxi, and to his astonishment she was very obviously six or seven months pregnant. For once, surprise slowed him down. When she realized it was a trap she went for the gun in her purse, but one of the agents dumped her unceremoniously on the sidewalk, kicking a .38 caliber revolver out of her hand.

"You bitch," Levine said helplessly. A baby girl had just been brutally murdered by dopers, and here was a pregnant woman dealing dope and going for a gun. "What kind of a fucking monster are you carrying?"

He then had to break off for a couple of hours to go undercover with Bobby Joura on the Lower East Side to complete a buy-bust set up with Roberto, his orange-haired Cuban bisexual informer who lived with the female Jewish butcher. After arresting three Mexicans with a full kilo of heroin, the agents returned to the office to process their prisoners, and then picked up where they had left off with Michael Gray and the Colombians.

Around 1:30 A.M. Bobby Joura and Jay Silvestro, accompanied by Michael Gray, arrived on East 63rd Street to arrest Nick Caturano and his six-feet-six muscle man, Richard Wranick. Posing as cocaine buyers, they were not expecting trouble, but as soon as they entered Caturano's apartment and he saw Gray, he drew a Walther P38 automatic pistol, and the agents backed out again, using Gray as a shield. Emergency Services were then called in, and when Caturano was eventually delivered to the DEA offices, he was dumped on the floor in need of medical attention.

"I'm dying," he moaned, while waiting for a doctor.

"Well, hurry up, then," said the agent assigned to guard him, who was missing all the fun.

Nobody picked up that day on Gray's information proved particularly helpful, least of all the pregnant Elsie Sanchez, who was plainly counting on her condition to keep her out of serious trouble. With no new leads to go on about the contracts on Shea and Smith, Levine renewed the siege of Jackson Heights, making sure that every agent spread the word that, if necessary, he would keep it up until he depopulated the neighborhood. That night another busload of illegals went over to Immigration under guard, and holding pens again filled up in neighboring precinct houses.

On the 7th the three Mexican heroin dealers arrested in the middle of all this were duly arraigned, but in the meantime Roberto the informer had vanished. Nagged by the U.S. Attorney's office and the female Jewish butcher, Levine was forced to detach several agents to look for him while he took the rest to cover himself and Richie Fiano on what passed into legend as the Gouvatsos Case.

On the day Susan Toro was murdered, Fiano had been given a free sample of heroin by a ring of Greek and Yugoslav dealers in Queens. Now, having set up a buy, he took Levine along as his money man and drove out to the meet with two undercover cars for backup. One of them was driven by Jack Tasker,* an Irish agent whose reliance on Bushmills had started to get the better of him under the stress of continuous campaigning, and whom Levine would probably have left behind if anyone else had been available.

The plan was that Levine and Fiano would pick up one of the Greeks, who would then take them to the apartment where the heroin was stashed. After they showed him the money, he would then fetch the package and the deal would go down in their car. Finding no fault with that, Levine had instructed their backup to move in as soon as he switched on his flashers to signify that the exchange had taken place.

When Levine arrived for the rendezvous, with Fiano sitting beside him, one of the Greeks got out of a waiting car and climbed into the back of Levine's Eldorado. Uneasy at having the guy behind him, he tried to keep an eye on him in the mirror, but the Greek simply directed him to drive along Roosevelt Avenue in the direction of Flushing Meadows, and after a few minutes Levine relaxed, attributing the tension he sensed in their passenger to the usual stresses of a deal in progress.

Up ahead, a light changed against them, and he slowed, pumping the brakes to decelerate smoothly. But as they drifted to a stop, somebody smashed into the back of the car, sending them sprawling. Painfully whiplashed, Levine twisted around to see what had happened, and noticed that a gun had fallen out of the Greek's sock as he struggled to right himself, half on and half off the backseat. Fiano saw it in the same instant, and jumped out to get at him through the rear door while Levine reached over the front seat to grab for the gun.

With the Greek subdued and handcuffed, Levine turned his attention to the driver who had rammed him. He already knew from the Bushmills' fumes that it was Jack Tasker, and that Tasker had mistaken the pumping of the brake lights for the car's emergency flashers. Furious with him for screwing up the operation, not to

* Not his real name.

mention two government cars, Levine ordered Tasker to return to base and await his displeasure while he led what remained of his forces back to the rendezvous to salvage what he could of the case by picking up the other Greeks and searching their apartments.

They searched for most of the night and found nothing. There was no dope. The Greeks had suckered them into a rip-off. If Tasker had not blundered into the picture prematurely, Group 33 might well have had vacancies by morning for a replacement agent and supervisor. When Levine returned to the office, he found Tasker asleep at his desk. Bending his ear with a high-decibel character analysis, Levine simultaneously dented a filing cabinet with a "there-but-for-the-grace-of-God-goes-your-fucking-face" karate blow, and then sent him home to sleep it off.

His prisoners—Gouvatsos, Halamandaris and Blatnik—made less of an impact on the group's statistics, but they *did* refresh its vocabulary.

"Gou*vat* sos!" they would curse, at some bemused Colombian. "Don't you halamandaris *me,* you lousy blatnik."

As had happened before, with the International group, Levine had now reached lift-off speed, sustaining himself by the amount of activity he managed to pack into a day, but acutely aware, whenever the pace slackened, of the price he paid. Washed up behind his paper-strewn desk with eyelids drooping and dawn an hour away, there was a point between waking and sleeping when he could hardly avoid comparing what he had with what he had given up. He owned a comfortable home in Rockland County, but he lived in a shabby government office, with shabby government furniture, indistinguishable from all the others except for his plaques on the wall, and the fire axes, sledgehammers and crowbars heaped in one corner. He had a beautiful wife and two kids, but he lived with his group, a "family" whose loyalty and affection was real enough, but transferable. He knew that. All he had was what he did. And what he did was who he was. That was all. And that was everything.

Next morning Levine learned from Manhattan South Narcotics that there were probably contracts out on himself, Bobby Joura and Jay Silvestro as well. He was quite pleased in a way, for it suggested that his campaign in Jackson Heights had really hurt the opposition, but after a meeting later that day with Assistant U.S. Attorney Joan O'Brien, whom he had last spoken to in connection with the Ibarra case, there was some doubt as to who wanted him dead the most.

When he ordered the arrest of Nick Caturano, Levine had unwittingly cut across the path of Special Prosecutor Sterling Johnson and a police department investigation of Congressman Fred
Richmond, who was suspected of having gone beyond acceptable
limits in organizing entertainment facilities for delegates to the
forthcoming Democratic Party National Convention in New York.
Anxious to limit the potential damage that Caturano's arrest might
do his client, Richmond's attorney, Tom Bruno, agreed to represent Caturano as well and set up a conference with O'Brien to see if
the matter could be settled quickly. Richmond, he said, wished to
visit Caturano in jail, but he had advised him not to.

By now the arresting agents, Joura and Silvestro, were in some
doubt as to who had actually put out the threat on their lives, but
the Alimony Boys had acquired such a menagerie of enemies by
now that, in the absence of any hard evidence, choosing between
them served no useful purpose.

That night, just in case it *was* the Colombians, Levine mounted a
maximum effort in Jackson Heights.

Next day, Oscar Toro Jr., Susan's ten-year-old brother, was
found hanged in an abandoned post office at 46-02 Northern Boulevard, Queens. He had not been seen or heard of since his disap-
pearance at the time of his sister's murder. Dangling from another
beam, thirty feet away, was the body of the seventeen-year-old
mother's helper, Liliana Bustamonte. Before being hanged, she had
been raped repeatedly.

Levine took it hard. He had allowed himself to hope that the boy
and his baby-sitter were being held hostage somewhere to silence
Oscar Toro Sr., and that the police would find them before any
greater harm was done. Now, for the first time in his career, the
uncomplicated pleasure he had always taken in his work, and in
this assignment particularly, deserted him. The energy and commitment remained the same, but the enthusiasm hardened into
relentlessness. Begun in the spirit of a turkey shoot, the nightly
incursions into Jackson Heights now became punitive reprisals.

Over the next several days, Sterling Johnson's office confirmed
that Levine and Silvestro had been named as targets in the reported murder contract, and Levine applied for a warrant to search
Caturano's car and apartment. Besides the usual clutter of personal
effects, he found fifty pounds of marijuana in the car, some cocaine,
a badge from the Mayor's office and a parking permit for the 94th
Congress. The apartment on East 63rd Street yielded nothing ex-

cept clear indications that somebody had already removed any possibly incriminating evidence.

With an unbeatable case against Caturano, Levine conferred with Special Prosecutor Sterling Johnson to make sure Johnson extracted the maximum leverage from it in his investigation of Congressman Richmond's affairs. In return, Levine learned that Caturano's uncle, Mike Fiore, had bailed out his nephew's muscle man, Richard Wranick, but not Caturano himself. That seemed odd until it crossed Levine's mind that for as long as Caturano remained unavailable, he was providing himself with an airtight alibi.

Hardly flattered to think that somebody as dumb as Wranick might have been chosen to come after him, Levine saw no reason to take any special precautions until the following morning, when the DEA receptionist rang him in a panic from the outer office.

"Mr. Levine," she squeaked, "you better come quick. There's a guy out here says he wants to talk to you. And I mean, he's like from outer space or something. He's *huge*. And he's got this huge dog with him. So will you please hurry."

"Hey, slow down a minute," said Levine. She was sitting behind bulletproof glass after all. "Did you get his name? What does he want?"

"He wants his *things*. He says you've got his things. And he looks real mad."

It had to be Wranick. His personal possessions had been held at headquarters when he was taken downtown to the West Street Detention Center. Determined not to miss this confrontation, every agent in the group insisted on following Levine "for his own protection."

The receptionist had not exaggerated. Bundled up against the subzero cold outside, Wranick loomed larger than Boris Karloff as Frankenstein's Monster. And bucking at the end of a short leash was the biggest and worst-tempered German shepherd Levine had seen since his Air Force days.

"I want my stuff."

Wranick advanced an involuntary step toward them, bracing himself against the lunge of the shepherd, and Levine tensed.

"Okay, Richard," he sighed. "Get him out of here."

"I want my stuff."

"You'll get your stuff, Richard." Levine held his ground, watching for the slightest slackening of Wranick's grip. The dog's front paws were lashing at the air not six feet away from his face. "Just as soon as you get that dog out of here."

"Gimme my *stuff.*"

This time he deliberately took a step forward, and Levine smelled the heat of the dog's breath. Just as deliberately, he put his hand on his gun.

"I don't want to shoot him, Richard," he said mildly. "I'd much sooner shoot you than shoot him. But I *will*—unless you get him out of here."

That put the fire out. Levine knew about dog owners.

"I just came for my stuff," Wranick grumbled, dragging the dog back on its haunches. "Just gimme my stuff and I'll go."

Levine shook his head. "Get rid of your friend first," he said. "Then come back."

They stared at each other for several seconds, the dog rumbling softly and wrinkling its chops. Then Wranick abruptly turned away, unwilling to risk it, hauling the shepherd behind him.

"I just want my stuff," he muttered.

"You'll get your stuff. But if you bring that dog in here again, Richard, I'll shoot him."

Wranick glowered at them from the doorway, and dragged the dog into the hall.

"Jesus," said Joura, as Levine's shoulders slumped. "How much you think they were gonna pay him for the hit?"

Levine shrugged, a little short of breath now they had gone. "I don't know. Couple of cases of Kennel Ration?"

"No, no," Joura said. "I mean the dog."

If Wranick *had* been considering anything of the sort, he changed his mind after that, for no more was heard of a murder contract against Levine and the others. Instead, it was Skippy Garcia's turn to be threatened.

The heroin case he had made with Levine back in October, when José Acevedo, the young Puerto Rican jewelry salesman, had led them to José Muriel and his two closet gunmen, now came to trial in New York's Southern District federal courthouse in Manhattan. On January 19 no fewer than six of the Alimony Boys were present to testify, but the lead-off witness for the prosecution was Acevedo himself, who had copped a plea. When he returned to the witness room his face shone with sweat, and he could not stop trembling.

Levine looked at him curiously. "Something wrong, José?"

"Listen, you gotta protect me." He was white as chalk and almost incoherent with fear. "Muriel's brother is out there. And he says he's gonna kill me."

"*What?*" Levine put down his magazine. "You mean, he threatened you? In *court?*"

"Yeah. I'm on the stand, and he's putting his finger to his head, and his mouth is going, *'Estás muerto.'*" Acevedo was almost beside himself, doubled over and holding the pit of his stomach. "He's a pro boxer, man. A real crazy mother-fucker."

"In front of the *judge* he did this?" Levine could hardly believe it.

"I'm telling you, man," he wailed. "He's duckin' his head so the jury can't see, and when the judge looks the other way he's doin' it. The mother-fucker means business—I *know* him. You gotta protect me, man."

"Okay. What's his name?"

"Collazo. José Collazo. They got differen' names, but he's Muriel's brother."

Skippy Garcia was now on the stand, and there was nothing Levine could do for the time being. But when Garcia returned to the witness room after the court recessed at four-thirty, he, too, was white and trembling—in his case, with fury.

"I don't fucking believe it," he said. "There's a guy out there pointing his finger at his head and threatening to kill me."

"Yeah, come and point the mother-fucker out," said Levine, already heading for the door.

The hallway was thronged with attorneys, witnesses and spectators from several neighboring courtrooms, but Garcia spotted Collazo at once. He was a tall, powerfully built Latin in a light tan suit, and plainly raring for trouble. Catching sight of Garcia and Levine, he forced his way roughly through the crowd to confront them. Everything was going quiet, but he didn't give a fuck—Levine could see it in his eyes.

"Who ju mutha-fuckas pointin' at?" he demanded, dancing around in front of them with his fists up. "Ju fockin' theenk ju so fockin' bad?"

Levine surveyed him distantly. "Are you the guy that's been threatening witnesses in the courtroom?"

Collazo recoiled. "I don' need no mutha-fockin' gun, man. I fock you up weeth my han's, mutha-fucka. I'm a pro fighter."

"Don't you know that threatening witnesses is a federal crime?"

Levine asked patiently, reminding himself he was in the middle of a trial before the chief judge in the Southern District courthouse.

"Wassa matter, big man?" said Collazo contemptuously. "You a-scared I'm gonna whip ju fockin' ass in fron' of everybody?"

Levine sighed. They now had a hushed audience, but he could not appear to start anything. There were too many attorneys watching. He had to let the guy hit him first or risk going to jail. On the other hand, he couldn't allow Collazo to get away with this. He and his group had to go out on the street again. If the DEA came up looking pussy, they'd lose respect. And loss of respect on the street translated directly into injuries and loss of life.

"If you threaten witnesses," he said evenly, the resentment of recent months creeping up like mercury in a thermometer, "I'm gonna have to lock you up, understand?"

For a moment, Collazo seemed to calm down, and Garcia lost patience. He brushed past him, muttering something under his breath.

"Wha' ju say?" Collazo turned on him furiously. "Asshole?"

"I said, if it was me, I'd bust your ass right now."

"Well, ju ask for it." He dropped into his fighting stance. "Now I'm gonna killya."

Shuffling forward, Collazo shaped to aim a punch at Garcia's head, but Levine doubled him up with a round kick to the stomach. As Collazo buckled over, breath wheezing from his lungs, Levine took him by the collar and slammed his head against the floor. Collazo went into convulsions. Not sure what to make of that, Levine dashed Collazo's head against the tiles once more to quiet him down, and it was all over before the first onlooker began to scream.

Appalled by his efficiency, a number of bystanders started forward, as if to come to Collazo's aid while he was still in a condition to benefit from it, but they were instantly knocked aside or immobilized by other members of the group. As soon as Levine had him handcuffed, Joura and Jones dragged Collazo across the floor to a waiting elevator, rolled him inside like a sack of potatoes and disappeared with their prisoner. The entire episode had lasted no more than ten seconds from start to finish, and many of those contributing loudest to the pandemonium had no clear idea of what they were screaming about.

Collazo was unlucky to have crossed Levine's path at that moment. As Judge Whitman Knapp, of Knapp Commission fame, observed at Collazo's trial, if nothing else, he was clearly guilty of having picked on the wrong man at the wrong time. But Collazo had suffered no lasting damage, and to that extent he was lucky. As Levine also observed at the trial, the fists of a professional fighter could properly be considered deadly weapons, particularly when directed at somebody half Collazo's size. Levine would have been amply justified in shooting him to protect his partner, but had chosen not to.

After another heavy night in Jackson Heights, the Alimony Boys were out next day on an assortment of cases, including an undercover buy of 2,000 barbiturates by Fiano and Silvestro from a pharmacy on Union Turnpike. But by evening, the pace unexpectedly slackened, and with nearly everyone available, Levine mounted another maximum effort against the Colombians. In full raid gear, with a compelling array of weaponry and massive police support, the group carried out a four-hour sweep of the neighborhood as the bars closed, making scores of arrests for police processing and rounding up several loads of illegals and overstays for the Immigration bus.

Levine was not to know it, but it was the last major engagement of the Alimony Boys' Colombian war. The following afternoon, within minutes of the jury finding José Muriel guilty on all counts, Detective Bobby Johnson called Levine to tell him he had won. Johnson's informers had reported that the contracts on Shea and Smith had been withdrawn, and no further action was contemplated against any of the DEA agents involved in the five-week siege of Jackson Heights. The Colombians had had enough.

That night, as Shea and Smith emerged from seclusion, peace of a sort descended on Jackson Heights. Within a week the neighborhood was back to "normal," and except for Oscar Toro Sr. and his wife, the war might never have happened.

Levine was glad to see the end of it. Since the death of the children, he had mistrusted himself in his dealings with anybody possibly concerned in their murder, and it was a relief to get back to making cases, to making sure precisely who was responsible for precisely what. Although, in the Caturano case, that was still far from clear. Having cut across Sterling Johnson's investigation of Congressman Richmond's affairs, Levine now found himself caught between Johnson and Assistant U.S. Attorney Bernard Fried, who seemed bent on developing a federal case along parallel lines.

Seeing no merit in competing for the same defendants when there were so many others to choose from, Levine was prepared to work Caturano for whatever he could get out of him about narcotics, but beyond that, anything he learned was strictly somebody else's business. In any case, he didn't trust him. For reasons of his own, Caturano still declined to make bail, which was suspicious in itself. He had also offered a guilty plea on both the assault and narcotics charges, but instead of cooperating fully, was trying to outsmart everybody by spilling no more than he felt he had to. If Levine had had his way, he would have refused a deal of any sort until satisfied he had the whole story, but Fried was fascinated by Caturano's hints of high-level political and mob connections, and kept the bargaining alive.

Under pressure from Levine, Caturano gave up a fellow trafficker, but before Levine could find him, he was mysteriously tipped off and disappeared. As for the drugs found in his car, Caturano said the cocaine had come through Michael Gray from Elsie Sanchez and Edgar Payan, all of whom had been arrested, and the fifty pounds of marijuana had been stolen from three Brazilians who lived in a fifth-floor loft at 210 Fifth Avenue.

That was more interesting. Pressed for details, Caturano identified one of the rip-off men as a New York City cop whom he claimed to have seen only for an instant, although he also admitted driving the van they used for the rip-off. His description was vague enough to have fitted at least one in three of New York's finest.

When Levine went to talk to the Brazilians, they made a run for it. As he was breaking through the door, they slid down escape ropes at the back of the building, one of them burning his hands to the bone—and ran straight into the arms of Levine's agents waiting for them on the street. Although no drugs were found in the loft, one of the three turned out to be a police informer, code-named Kafka, who confirmed that *three* men—not two, as Caturano claimed—had held them up at gunpoint and stolen a load of marijuana. Where had it come from? Elsie Sanchez.

Still with nothing to show for Caturano's "cooperation," apart from somebody else's informer and two Brazilians who would be deported anyway, Levine set about disentangling himself.

"Well, if that's all he's got I'm glad it's out of my hands," he told Fried on the telephone.

"What do you mean, it's out of your hands?" Fried demanded.

"Well, I mean it's in *your* hands, right?"

"Oh. Yeah. Right."

After that, whenever Caturano's name came up, Levine was usually too busy with prosecutable cases to do much about it.

Although the DEA discouraged supervisors from working undercover and running their own informers, the New York office was still too short of Spanish-speaking agents to raise any serious objection. It was on-the-job training, Levine would say, if anybody asked. Or the only way to lead an overworked team was from the front. But the truth was the street was his natural habitat. When confined to the office, he would swivel around in his chair sometimes, hemmed in by paperwork and the tangle of phones and radio equipment, and look out the window like an animal behind bars, seeing not the skyline of midtown Manhattan, but ruined neighborhoods of unkempt tenements and shuttered storefronts, intricate with graffiti and blowing with garbage. Nineteen floors up and eighty blocks south, he could sometimes even catch a breath of ghetto air, sharp as smoke in winter, and voluptuous in summer with its musky overlay of rot and ancient cooking smells.

Any pretext would do to get back there, particularly as he and Garcia had just acquired a new stool who looked as if he could help them mount a serious attack on the Spanish Harlem heroin trade.

While undercover in the Bronx, they had taken off a couple of dealers with a few ounces of junk, and as the prisoners were bundled downstairs, one of them pulled Levine and Garcia aside.

"Listen," he said in Spanish, "let the other guys take the weight. Let me out, and I'll work for you."

In making this proposition, he used the English word "weight," which, with his heavy Spanish accent, came out closer to "hweh," so that when Levine agreed to try him out as an informer, he was automatically code-named El Hweh. Already on parole for a state narcotics violation, he was desperately eager to stay out of jail.

"Okay," he said. "Firs' I gonna geeb ju my goo' fren' Ernesto Sosa. Eef ju wan', from heem I buy an ounce, two ounce, four ounce, all ju fockeeg wan', meng. Ees goo' Mehiccan sheet. Ees pre-pack."

"Where's he get it?"

"Ha! He gonna geeb me his connection? Da's all I know, meng. Two key a week, maybe more. I theenk ees comin' from Chicago, maybe. But he no gonna say noseeng to me, meng. Ernesto ees bery careful."

"You mean he don't trust you?"

"He don' trus' nobody. E'cept maybe hees brother, José."

Levine assigned El Hweh and the Sosa case to Garcia. Volume supplies of brown heroin, prepacked in ounces, suggested a major, well-organized operation, and New York had been looking to get a handle on the Mexican trade for a long time. But El Hweh was right. Sosa was a *very* cautious man, and the case turned into a minor classic, touching every base in the DEA manual. When Garcia tried to arrange an undercover meet to make a buy himself, Sosa refused even to consider it. He would deal only with El Hweh.

Suspecting that El Hweh might be trying to make himself appear indispensable, Garcia wired him up with a Nagra recorder and sent him back to try again. And again. And again—and always with the same result. On no account would Sosa deal with anyone he didn't know.

Armed with the Nagra tapes supporting El Hweh's story, Levine sought permission to set up an informant buy. This was always a risky ploy. For one thing, its value as evidence was limited: the informer could hardly testify to the transaction without blowing his cover, thereby ending his usefulness and possibly his life. And for another, it was not completely unknown for informers to pocket a government bankroll and dematerialize. But in the present case, it seemed the only way to keep the investigation alive. To get past Sosa, they had no choice but to deal on his terms, keeping him under surveillance, and hope he would lead them to his source.

The manpower commitment was crippling. When clearance was given, Levine assigned Jones, Fiano and Williams to join Garcia in watching Sosa around the clock. And on April 8, enjoying himself hugely, El Hweh set out with $2,000 and a Nagra recorder taped to his body to buy a trial ounce of prepacked 37 percent pure Mexican brown heroin.

But it wasn't as simple as that. The Sosa brothers picked him up on the street and drove around aimlessly for half an hour to make sure they were not being followed. In fact, they *were*, by Bobby Joura and a two-car surveillance team, but the wily Ernesto still had a card to play. Though apparently satisfied they were on their own, he told his brother José to pull over and wait in the car with El Hweh while he set off on foot to collect the package. Hopelessly out of position, and under the strictest instructions not to risk the investigation by taking chances, the agents let him go.

"It ain't gonna work," Garcia complained. "The guy's paranoid. If we do that again we're gonna burn him for sure."

"Yeah." Levine thought it over. "Okay. No more moving surveillance. Let's try something else. Let's see what he does after he gets an order. Who does he call? Maybe we can get a wiretap."

"You think he's dumb enough to use his own phone?"

"Who knows? Some of these guys are too lazy to scratch their own ass. You gotta try everything."

Coached by Garcia, El Hweh called Sosa at home to compliment him on the quality of the sample ounce and to ask about prices and availability of larger quantities. Sosa said he would call him right back, and did so in less than ten minutes. Next day El Hweh had further questions for Sosa to put to his source, and again the answers came back in a matter of minutes. Paranoid or not on the street, Sosa evidently had boundless faith in the discretion of the New York Telephone Company.

With the tapes of these calls, Levine now had enough for a court order to attach a pen register to Sosa's home phone and record the numbers he called. This showed at once that each inquiry from El Hweh was immediately followed by a call from Sosa to a Brooklyn number listed to Isabel Vasquez, at 63 Suydam Street.

"Not a bad neighborhood for apartment hunting," said Levine, when Garcia reported in. "See if you can find one with a view."

Supervised by Bobby Joura, Garcia set up house with Jones, Fiano and Williams in an observation post across the street from number 63, and spent the next several days photographing everybody going in and out. Among others, they identified the three most frequent callers as Efraim Reyes, Antonio Nieves and a man known only as El Cojito. Now ready to try again, Levine scheduled a second one-ounce buy for April 30.

This time he split the group into three teams: one covering 63 Suydam Street; the second, the Sosa brothers; and the third, El Hweh (and the money). When everybody was in position, El Hweh telephoned Ernesto to place his order, and as soon as Garcia saw the pen register record Sosa's call to the Suydam Street number he raced back to the office to wire El Hweh for the buy.

As cautious as ever, the Sosas followed the same routine as before. For twenty minutes José cruised around, doubling back, speeding up, slowing down, suddenly cutting through one-way streets in the wrong direction, until finally he stopped to wait with

El Hweh in the car while Ernesto went off alone on foot to collect the package.

Content simply to stay in touch, the surveillance teams on El Hweh and the Sosas stayed well back and made no attempt to follow him on foot, relying on the Suydam Street detail to meet him coming the other way. From their observation post, Fiano, Williams and Jones trailed a totally unsuspecting Nieves and El Cojito from number 63 to the Unisex Hairdressing Salon at 93 Graham Avenue, where they were shortly joined by Ernesto Sosa.

Sosa left again almost immediately with a package, but no one followed, the agents, in their turn, relying on the other surveillance teams to pick up the trail on Sosa's return to the car. Instead, they waited for Nieves and El Cojito, who left a few minutes later and went around the corner to meet Efraim Reyes. After a brief conversation on the street, they handed him the money, and the agents followed Reyes back to 63 Suydam Street.

"All *right,*" said Levine. "Now we know more about this outfit than the people in it. Reyes is the boss, but he only knows Nieves and El Cojito. Sosa is their street man, and *he* only knows Nieves and El Cojito. And El Hweh is our friendly neighborhood connection, and he only knows the Sosas. Now we gotta get a pen register on Suydam Street. I wanna know where Reyes is getting his stuff from."

"Maybe Nieves and El Cojito take care of that, too."

"Maybe. If so, you'll have to build a circumstantial case. Correlate the calls in and out of Suydam Street before each buy. Get surveillance to place Reyes there when Sosa calls in the order. Get pictures of him taking the money from his people after the deal goes down. And don't make any dinner dates for the next six months."

Garcia snorted. "Working for you, I never get to know anybody well enough to *ask.*"

With a pen register on the Suydam Street phone as well as on Sosa's, they were now ready to tie Reyes into the conspiracy with buy number three. But El Hweh had disappeared. And as if that were not enough, the NYPD complained they were poaching. Efraim Reyes was *theirs,* said Brooklyn North Narcotics. He was one of the city's biggest heroin traffickers, doing at least a hundred kilos a year in prepacked ounces, and they already had an active investigation in progress.

"Shit," said Garcia. "Now what?"

"Now nothing," replied Levine, who was forever tripping over crossed wires. "You find El Hweh. I'll take care of the cops."

El Hweh was in trouble with his parole officer, who had threatened to send him back to jail if he went on working for the DEA. Although Garcia had obtained written permission from the head of the New York State Parole Board to use El Hweh as an informer before the investigation had even begun, apparently no one had told his parole officer. Several days of meetings and phone calls were necessary before the board finally notified Garcia that ruffled feathers had been smoothed and El Hweh was free to go back to work.

Meanwhile, Levine had established that the police were no closer to Reyes than he was. What they had were two informants on the fringe of his organization who were close enough to monitor the business he was doing but not close enough to get anyone in undercover. Against that, the DEA had an observation post overlooking his premises and a pen register logging frequent calls to numbers in Chicago, then the main distribution center for Mexican brown heroin. After kicking this around, Levine and Brooklyn North agreed to carry on as they were, keeping each other in the picture, and leave it to the Brooklyn DA and the U.S. Attorney to decide who would prosecute whom for what.

Two weeks went by before all this was straightened out, but on May 14, El Hweh set off again with his trusty Nagra to make a two-ounce buy. This was followed by four ounces on May 19, and another four ounces on June 3, when Levine went along with him undercover as the money man to meet Sosa himself. By now, El Hweh was so well in with the Reyes organization that somebody would call him whenever a new shipment came in.

At this point Garcia had all but disappeared beneath the blizzard of paperwork. As case agent, it was his responsibility to wire, brief and debrief El Hweh before and after each buy; to translate and transcribe the Nagra tapes; to collect the pen register records each day and correlate them with the surveillance notes; to relate all this to the mass of surveillance photographs; to prepare the usual case reports, and liaise continuously with the U.S. Attorney's office, the Brooklyn DA's office, the parole board and the Brooklyn North Narcotics unit. Thus preoccupied, it was some days before he realized that El Hweh had gone missing again.

He found out when Brooklyn North passed on a report from its informants that Reyes now had two kilos on hand. Surprised that

Sosa had not called, Garcia tried to get in touch with El Hweh, only to learn that, without telling anybody, the parole board had assigned him to a different parole officer. Not only that, the board had also failed to notify the new officer that his client had permission to work for the DEA, and El Hweh had been roundly forbidden even to speak to Garcia, on pain of instant removal to jail. Caught in the middle, El Hweh had simply faded into the woodwork.

This time Levine wheeled out the heavy artillery. Assistant Regional Directors Thomas Byrne and James Hunt took the matter up with the parole board, but even so, over a week was lost before El Hweh felt safe enough to surface again. He was sorry if he'd screwed things up, he said, but he couldn't go through with another buy unless the board specifically promised him he would not go to jail for it. Still another week went by before Byrne and Hunt managed to get him that assurance.

Meanwhile, Brooklyn North's informers reported that Reyes had sold all but a half-kilo of his latest load elsewhere, and when El Hweh finally returned Sosa's calls he found his customer status had slumped dramatically.

"You're full of shit," Ernesto told him. "You keep telling me you wanna buy weight, you wanna buy weight, but when I callya, you're out to lunch. So fuck you. You're not doing me no favors. I got half a kilo left, okay? That's like thirty-five thousand dollars. You want it, bring the money. You don't want it, then fuck off, and don't bother me no more. Understand?"

"Yeah, yeah. I want it, I want it," El Hweh said, as Levine nodded emphatically.

"Orright. Tomorrow. Three o'clock."

"Okay, okay," he said, again silently prompted by Levine. "You got it. Where?"

"Grand Street. Two-oh-seven Grand Street. You know where that is?"

"Yeah, yeah. I'll find it."

"Orright. It's like a garage. The Auto Body Garage. You got that? Two-oh-seven Grand."

"Yeah, I got it, I got it. I'll *be* there."

"Orright. It's your last chance. And don't be late."

"I told you. I'll *be* there."

Levine certainly hoped so. The case was now virtually watertight. With this last half-kilo buy, he planned to take everybody off, from Reyes on down, but El Hweh was a nervous wreck. Next day he was also due to report to his new parole officer for his regular monthly visit. Levine told him not to worry. Didn't he have the parole board's promise? He should go there in the morning, get it over with, and check in at the office around 1:00 P.M. so that Garcia could wire him up and do everything nice and easy. If it would make him feel better, Levine would ride along with him as the money man when he went to meet Sosa, just to make sure nothing went wrong.

It was not Sosa that El Hweh was worried about. At 1:00 P.M. the following afternoon, Levine called a briefing session for the ten agents taking part in the operation. El Hweh had not yet arrived, but that meeting was none of his business anyway. He was still missing at one-thirty, however, and as there was still no sign of him when the surveillance teams left at 2:00 P.M., Garcia drove up to the Bronx like a madman to see if, by some outside chance, he was still in his apartment.

He was. And he wasn't going *anywhere*. The parole board had again failed to advise his parole officer of the latest assurances given to Byrne and Hunt. He had sworn to throw El Hweh in jail immediately if he ever went near the DEA again.

Garcia called Levine, who called Byrne and Hunt, who called the parole board in Albany, who called El Hweh's parole officer, who reluctantly called Garcia and even more reluctantly gave El Hweh permission to take part in a "last chance" operation that was already running the best part of an hour late. It was three-thirty before Garcia, cursing and raving, half-dragged him into the office to wire him up, and close to 4:00 P.M. when Levine, the moneyman, wearing a huge black Afro wig for disguise, at last delivered him to the Auto Body Garage on Grand Street, in the Williamsburg section of Brooklyn.

Listening to the radio reports from his surveillance teams on the way over, he knew that Ernesto Sosa was still in the building with the package, which had already changed hands twice on its way there. José Sosa, Nieves, El Cojito, Reyes himself and two other members of the gang were also in the vicinity, and under observation, but growing increasingly restive in the furnace heat of a cloudless afternoon.

"You all right?"

El Hweh nodded. Trickles of sweat ran out of his hair, and his hands shook as he wiped them away, but he was ready.

"Well, you look terrible," Levine said amiably, leaning across him to open the door. "But blame it on me. Tell him I was late showing up with the money. And take a good look around in there."

Not trusting himself to speak, El Hweh half-fell out of the car and walked unsteadily across to Sosa, who had come out of the garage to meet him. Together, they went inside, Sosa waving his arms and squawking into El Hweh's ear like an angry crow. As they disappeared into the shadows, Garcia drifted by and parked a little way ahead across the street.

A few minutes later El Hweh came back alone and leaned on the open door for support. He looked at the end of his tether.

"Get in," Levine said sharply. "You see the package?"

El Hweh nodded. "The money," he muttered. "He wants the money."

"Just a minute. Where is it? The package. With Sosa?"

"Yeah."

"Anybody else in there?"

"What? Yeah. His brother. Look, I gotta get back."

"Wait. Where are they? Goddammit, where *is* the fucking package, man? In the garage? In the office? Or what?"

El Hweh waved his hands feebly, on the edge of tears. The street swarmed with not-so-friendly people. "I don't know, man. In the back there someplace. In a room. Like in a storeroom, okay? There's a whole bunch of rooms back there. A lotta doors. Now gimme the money, man, or we're gonna blow it."

"Shit."

With eleven agents, including himself, covering seven defendants in three different places, the whole operation was a crap shoot. He had neither the time nor the manpower for a room-by-room search. If he and Garcia hit the wrong spot, they would give the Sosas ample time to get rid of the evidence. Nor could Levine afford to take anybody off the other defendants. What looked like a thousand guys were out on the street, playing their radios and drinking beer or smoking dope, and they all knew what was going on. Once the signal to hit was given, the group was in trouble. The longer it took to make the arrests and secure the evidence, the less likely it would be that any of them would make it out of there.

"All right, now listen," said Levine. His head felt as if it was melting under the Afro wig, but there was no way he could sit on the block without it. "Take the money. Make him count it. Tell him I got there so late you didn't get a chance to count it yourself. Understand?"

El Hweh nodded, steadying himself with some deep breathing.

"And while he's doing that, stay close to the package. If he hears us coming, grab it yourself. I don't want 'em pitching it out of the window or nothing. Okay?"

"Okay." He even managed a smile.

Three minutes later, when Levine judged Sosa would be busy counting the flash roll, he unhooked the radio microphone and gave his call sign.

"Okay, I'm going to get out of the car now and walk over to the garage," he said. "Soon as I'm inside, you *hit.*"

It was as well they were listening. As soon as he entered the garage, he was surrounded by about twenty people. Drawing his gun, he prepared to take at least six of them with him, but then the commotion outside as the group charged, shotguns at the ready, distracted them. Seeing Garcia approach on the run, Sosa's people broke and scattered, dumping guns and drugs as they went. Levine left them to the others and ran on through to the back, where he grabbed Ernesto, the package *and* the money.

When he came out with his prisoner he found the whole block had surrendered. For the first time in his career, he and his men were outnumbered by their prisoners five to one.

"Okay, who's in charge here?" demanded the police sergeant who had responded to their call for uniformed backup. When someone pointed out Levine, he took a step back in utter disbelief. "You mean the guy in the *wig?*"

Barely five minutes after the signal to hit, Group 33 drove away through a barrage of abuse with the seven prisoners they wanted and eighteen ounces of heroin—and the first rock bounced off the roof of Levine's car.

It was another classic street case of the sort for which the Alimony Boys were famous among the enforcement agencies. Nobody had put a foot wrong procedurally (no thanks to the New York State Parole Board). Nobody had been hurt. Nobody had a chance of beating the rap, no matter what sort of hash the government made of the case in court. And the DEA office in Chicago had some interesting phone numbers to work on. It was a case that exemplified the kind of polished, resourceful, high-energy yet patient police work that his fellow professionals could only admire, and which rewarded Levine with a satisfaction that nothing else could match. After galvanizing a street group with a mediocre record into the most productive in the DEA's history, he felt justified in writing up Garcia and everybody else who had played a part in the Sosa case for an award. Including himself, because long experience told him that no one else would.

Levine at this point was touchy on the subject of official recognition. In accordance with standard procedure, the vacancy for supervisor of Group 33 had been advertised internally in November 1975, and he had formally applied for the job he was already doing. When no eligible Grade 14 agent came forward to fill the slot, Grade 13 Levine had continued in charge, but it was now well over a year since he had taken on the duties of supervisor, and he was still without his promotion. As he saw it, the DEA was taking advantage of him and saving itself a few bucks by filling a Grade 14 job with a Grade 13 agent.

On August 10 he looked up the informal grievance procedures in the agent's manual and composed a memorandum requesting that he not only receive his promotion without further delay, but also back pay for the seventeen months in which he had acted as a Grade 14. Feeling better, but anticipating no very swift response, he then forgot about it under the pressure of business. That spring and summer had been exceptionally busy even by the Alimony Boys' exceptional standards. With a small army of informers working for them, cases blossomed out of nowhere, some, like Sosa's, to occupy them, on and off, for months, others, like Rosa's, for no more than a few hours.

One morning Levine was actually in bed and asleep at 4:00 A.M. when the duty agent roused him with a message from El Hweh. A carpenter by trade, he had been hired by a trafficker he knew, José Rosa, to fit a police lock to the door of an apartment at 244 East 106th Street. While working on it through the night, he had watched Rosa and two of his guys cutting up about a pound of heroin for the street, and had finally managed to get away on the pretext of needing to buy another piece of hardware for the door. He was now on his way downtown to the office to tell Levine all about it, but there wasn't much time.

Minutes after El Hweh showed up, Levine arrived and shepherded him through to his office, where other members of the group, called out by the duty agent on Levine's instructions, were assembling in ones and twos, blearily clutching their coffee containers.

"Okay," said El Hweh, in his Gatling-gun Spanish. "Here's what I got. There's four guys up there. They all got guns. Other guys are coming and going. They got guns, too. The main man, José Rosa, he's no cherry. He got shot last year, four or five times, and already he's back on the block. That's the kind of guy he is. Last night he gets this package—a pound, maybe a pound and a half—and they're cutting it up and bagging it right now. I mean, guys are coming up there and buying it already, so you gotta move fast."

Not only that, but discreetly, for El Hweh went on to say that the apartment was a fifth-floor walk-up, and Rosa had posted lookouts on the street. A further complication was that one of his guys was asleep in the back room with a gun under his pillow. He was a fugitive who had sworn he would never be taken alive.

El Hweh drew Levine a plan of the apartment, but then he had to go. "If I'm gone too long," he said, "they're gonna put the bust down to me."

"Okay." Levine gave him an agent alert, a radio device resembling a ballpoint pen. When activated it was supposed to transmit a continuous beep signal, but as often as not, it didn't. "Put that in your pocket," he said. "If they still got some stuff when you get back, even an ounce, press the button on top. Then wait. If we don't hit in five minutes it means the fucking thing ain't working, so go to the window and show yourself. I'll get someone on the street to watch for you."

"Fine." Like most good informers, when not harried by the parole board, El Hweh really enjoyed this kind of cloak-and-dagger work. "How soon will you come?"

"Soon as I've got enough guys. Say forty-five minutes. And make sure you keep that fucking door open."

He also needed a minute to think. Assuming it was not already too late, they first had to get past the lookouts without tipping their hand. Then they had to enter the building and run up five flights, still with the element of surprise intact. Then they had to disarm whoever was in the room where they were cutting and bagging the stuff without waking the gunman in the back.

It was a tall order, and as there was no point in even trying to fill it unless some of the load was still there as evidence, Levine sent Garcia ahead to position himself on the block in case the agent alert failed to work. It was Spanish Harlem. Nobody was going to notice a little Cuban hanging around outside. After that, if the signal was go, he had to avoid raising the alarm too early or Rosa and his people would have all the time in the world to flush the stuff. On the other hand, if he raised it too late, they could have a shoot-out on their hands.

"For a while there, I couldn't see how to avoid it," Levine recalls. "I had been spared from death and injury so many times that I even wondered if Providence had deliberately brought me at last to a situation where a shoot-out was inevitable. But there *had* to be a way. In teaching undercover, I'd always maintained that shoot-outs could be avoided with the right kind of planning, cunning and downright sneakiness. Now here was the test. Somehow I had to get my guys in and out and come back with all the marbles without a shot being fired."

Shortly after 6:00 A.M. a little Cuban noticed somebody at the window of Rosa's apartment. Detaching himself from the shadows, he sauntered across the street toward the entrance to the building with his hands in his pockets. Seconds later, two Catholic priests turned the corner on foot, each carrying a shopping bag full of Bibles. Smiling and nodding at the lookouts lounging against the parked cars, they proceeded sedately along the sidewalk, pausing now and then to dispense a free Bible and the consolations of religion to anyone who looked at them twice.

Still nodding and smiling, they followed the little Cuban into the lobby of number 244. As the door closed behind them, Father Levine and Father Joura grabbed their guns and portable radios from under the remaining Bibles and, gathering up their skirts, bounded silently up the stairs. On the fourth floor, they stopped to catch their breath, very cautiously raising their heads above the stairwell to check the hallway outside Rosa's apartment. The door stood a few inches open.

Motioning Garcia to get behind them, Levine and Joura adjusted their cassocks and quietly went in. There were four men at the table, one with a gun in his waistband, and another with a gun close at hand in front of him. But the shock of being suddenly confronted by two armed "priests" paralyzed them into silence, as Levine had calculated. Even El Hweh was flabbergasted. Motioning them imperiously to back off, Levine waved Garcia around to collect their guns as Joura tiptoed across to the back room. Levine sidled after him, ready to go either way at the first sign of resistance, but the surprise was complete. Moments later Joura returned with a broad smile, towing behind him with one hand the fugitive who would never be taken alive and carrying the man's gun in the other. They were just in time. There were less than five ounces of cut heroin left on the table.

Using his portable, Levine called in their backup—five agents in three cars waiting several blocks away—and watched from the window as the lookouts scattered. Two minutes too late someone signaled up from the street with three urgent blips on the buzzer.

"Man, you oughta be *ashamed,*" Rosa said to Levine, as Garcia urged him through the door. He was scandalized. "Dressed like a *priest?*"

It was the first time the group had used its cassocks and dog collars for an actual arrest, although they had come in handy many times before on surveillance. (Levine had picked up the Bibles from the Holiday Inn on the way over. The night manager was on first-name terms with most of the Alimony Boys, who between them had probably helped as many of his guests leave the premises as the hotel doorman.) It was also the last time. The idea of agents posing as Catholic priests proved too much for the DEA management, and the group was ordered to turn in its robes.

The idea of an agent insisting on promotion had also proved too much. Six weeks after filing his informal grievance, Levine received a one-paragraph reply from the Personnel Office rejecting his complaint in terms which strongly suggested that no one had bothered to read it. Incensed by the brush-off, he now reasserted his claims by filing a *formal* grievance, again in the form laid down by the agents' manual.

Four weeks later a teletype came through from headquarters demoting him from the rank of Acting Group Supervisor and dumping him back on the street under Group Supervisor Joe Braddock, who had just returned from overseas.

ELEVEN

"... you're like a beautifully
colored but very poisonous snake."

"**Always** remember this," he told them. "Undercovers are looked on with suspicion. I don't care what agency you work for, your bosses are going to think you're a hotshot. A cowboy. No matter how good you are. No matter how professional you are. To them you're just one step above the scum you're working on. I've heard too many of them say so, in little side comments, not to believe it."

Some of the more experienced officers in the audience nodded. Levine was nearing the end of the first afternoon of a two-day seminar on undercover tactics for cops and investigators assigned to the Brooklyn District Attorney's office.

"So don't plan on building a career working undercover. It's a better way to make enemies than win awards. Everybody who knows what you do, from your supervisor on up, will mistrust you. No matter how much they may applaud you on the surface, to them you're like a beautifully colored but very poisonous snake. Me, I don't care. If you do the job for the sheer joy of doing it well, as I think *I* do, then you teach yourself not to care about such things."

It was February 24, 1977, four months since the DEA had pulled the plug on the Alimony Boys, and he *did* care. If things had looked bad then, they were now worse. His treatment at the hands of the Washington bureaucrats had inflamed his sense of grievance well beyond the bounds of prudence. Receiving no answer from headquarters to his formal complaint, and no support from John Fallon or anyone else in the region, he had committed the cardinal sin of appealing outside the DEA to the Civil Service Commission.

This had prompted another brief, unhelpful reply from Personnel and an arctic chill in the air whenever his name cropped up in management circles at West 57th Street. As he was also constantly at loggerheads with his new supervisor, Joe Braddock, from where Levine stood it looked as if eleven years of unrivaled achievement were being flushed down the DEA toilet. And as the Civil Service Commission had just ruled that it had no jurisdiction over questions of promotion, he was now seriously considering a direct approach to the DEA Administrator himself, Peter Bensinger. If that didn't work, he had been advised to file suit in federal court on the grounds of religious discrimination, but he wasn't ready for that. Not *yet*.

"So unless you're really *drawn* to undercover," he went on, "leave it to those who are. Be honest with yourself. Trust your instincts. If in doubt, don't—because nobody else gives a fuck. No case, no informer, nothing you ever do or want to do out there is worth your job or your family or your life. If something smells bad, if that little warning bell goes off in the back of your mind, *walk away*. Leave it right there. Fuck it. There's so much dope on the street you don't have to risk everything you got in the world just for *that* little bit. Get another informer. Cut another deal. Make another case.

"If you *don't*—well, figure it this way. How many here? About thirty, right? Okay. If statistics mean anything, three of you guys are gonna be in big trouble. If you work with informers or do narcotics undercover work, three of you guys are gonna lose your jobs or do time or get hurt. Those are the figures. So now it's up to you to prove 'em wrong.

"When I started out doing this I was very insecure. I felt I had to take on every goddamn thing that came along, just to prove to myself I could do it. Well, I was lucky to live through that, and it cost me my family. But I learned, and I want you to learn from me. Guys who get deeply involved in this life *must* find a way to handle it, to keep everything in its proper perspective and not put a bullet in people for getting in front of you on a theater line or cutting you off on the highway. Those that don't you read about in the papers. 'Narcs Arrested Selling Dope.' 'Narc Kills Partner in Office.' 'Narc Commits Suicide with Service Revolver.' Undercover means living on the edge, the extreme edge. At the level of optimum performance, like a surgeon. The only difference is, if a surgeon makes a mistake, the *patient* dies."

The telephone on the table in front of him started to ring, and he frowned, knowing it was for him.

"Sorry, Mike." The chief investigator scooped it up on the run. "I told 'em no calls."

Levine nodded. He even knew what it was about, but he had not expected to hear Liana's voice.

"Mike? I'm sorry. I know you're busy . . ." Her voice cracked, and for a disemboweling split second he thought it might be one of the children instead. "Mike? It's David . . ."

"Yeah?"

She struggled to get it out. "He's dead, Mike."

Yeah. It had always been going to happen. He turned his back on the room, suddenly unable to breathe.

"How?" He wanted her to say it had been an accident, or maybe a sudden illness.

"Poor David." She broke into ugly, rasping sobs, and he waited patiently. "He killed himself, Mike. He said, 'I can't stand the drugs any longer,' and he shot himself. But he did try, Mike. He did *try.*"

"What do you mean, he *said* that?" he hissed furiously. "You mean he left a note?"

"Yes." His anger had startled her out of crying.

"Does my mother know?"

"Yes. I called her."

"Okay." His head was buzzing with the overload. And he didn't want to talk to her anymore. "Okay. I'll see you later," he said. Something like that. As he hung up, he couldn't exactly remember.

"Sorry," he said, turning again to face the class. "Sorry about that."

The chief investigator reclaimed the phone, eyeing him curiously. "You okay, Mike?"

"What? Yeah. Yeah, I'm okay." He had to remember where he had stopped. There was something he had to tell these guys. Something important. "Yeah. Lemme sign off with a story that kinda sums up what I'm trying to tell you. Happened right here in New York. Stool comes in the office and tells the agent he works for that he's got a line on two guys with a load of coke—like four keys. 'Hey, that's great.' So he goes out with the stool undercover to meet these guys and set up a deal, but something is bothering him and he just can't put his finger on it. . . ."

Levine lost the thread, drifting to a stop, but pulled himself together.

"So he goes to his supervisor. 'I don't like

it,' he says. 'Could be a rip. It don't feel right to me.'

"Well, we all get feelings like that sometimes. And it's not much to set against the idea of taking off two guys with four keys of coke. So they set up the buy in the Sheraton Motor Inn. That way they can cover all the angles. Who's gonna try something in a place like that?"

Levine frowned. This had been a mistake. He should have told them it was bad news and left right away.

"So now they get a flash roll together— $160,000—and he takes it up to the room where he's meeting these guys, and he shows it to 'em. They check it out. 'Okay,' they tell him. 'Wait here. We'll come back with the dope.' Only they come back with guns. He was right. It's a rip. Boom! Boom! He's dead, and his supervisor's paralyzed for life with a bullet in his spine."

Levine sucked in a huge breath, trying to break the band around his chest.

"So listen to your instincts, right? *And know your violator.* Turned out these guys had no record for drugs—just armed robberies. A thousand people went to the funeral, and there was talk of naming a federal building after the guy. Well, fuck that. Nobody's going to name any fucking building after me. Make sure they don't name any after you."

He must have said his goodbyes and excused himself, but he had no recollection of it. His mind had seized up. The honking of cars behind him and the toll booth attendant banging on his window at the George Washington Bridge were the next things to register. He was evidently going home to Liana.

He made it onto the Palisades Parkway before an explosion of grief forced him off the road. The weight of his loss broke through the refusal to accept it with such force that it fogged his vision and punched the breath from his body. For a long time he sat and cried as though pieces were falling off him, and he was powerless to prevent it. He rested his head on the wheel, lost to reality, and waited numbly for this to pass. And in an hour or so the gust of misery blew itself out.

Aching and exhausted, he allowed himself to remember, cautiously putting things back together, piece by piece. He remembered David as a pesty kid, following him around, embarrassing him in front of his friends. He remembered having to go down regularly to Herman Ridder Junior High School P.S. 98 to get his brother's lunch money back from the Puerto Rican kids who regularly took it from him. He remembered the times when some big guy had beaten the shit out of him because he had beaten the shit out of the guy's kid brother for beating up on *his* kid brother. He remembered Alley Pond Park. He remembered the terrible night their mother had found David's works in his room, and the huge rage of frustration he had felt on being presented with a battle he could *not* fight for him.

"Are you mad at me?" David had asked, and yes, he was.

"You're *dead,*" he had shouted at him, and now he was.

Now it was over. Everything.

He looked out in disbelief at the traffic whizzing by.

Was this *it?*

Was this the moment that Providence had been steering him toward since Heywood's gun misfired against his chest?

He didn't think so.

It had to mean something. Providence hadn't set him up in this job and then kept him alive and perfected his skills and lit such a withering fire for revenge just for sport. With everything else it had stripped away to make him what he was, it could only mean another beginning. Something bigger.

David had said, "I can't stand the drugs any longer." Well, neither could he. Somebody was going to *pay* for this.

He started the car and slipped back into the traffic.